The Transition from Infancy to Language

In this important volume, Lois Bloom provides a coherent and illuminating account of her theoretical and empirical work on early lexical development. The first half of the book reviews the developments in infancy that enable the emergence of language and presents the theoretical perspective for the research described in the second half. The focus is on how affect expression, cognitive development, and social context contribute to the transition from prelinguistic expression in infancy to learning words for expressing the contents of mind.

The central thesis is that children learn language in acts of expression and inter-pretation for sharing beliefs, desires, and feelings with other persons. These intentional states underlying acts of expression are the personal, private, mental meanings for which knowledge of the conventional, public meanings of language is acquired. The details of a longitudinal study of 14 infants from age 9 months to $2\frac{1}{2}$ years are presented to show how affect expression object play, and the child's interpersonal context are integrated in the process of language development.

The Transition from Infancy to Language makes a major contribution to our knowledge of early lexical development, providing a persuasive theoretical model for researchers and students in the areas of infancy, cognition, emotion, and language.

The Transition from Infancy to Language

Acquiring the Power of Expression

LOIS BLOOM

Teachers College, Columbia University

Published by the Press Syndicate of the University of Cambridge
The Pitt Building, Trumpington Street, Cambridge CB2 1RP
40 West 20th Street, New York, NY 10011-4211, USA
10 Stamford Road, Oakleigh, Melbourne 3166, Australia

First published 1993

Printed in the United States of America

Library of Congress Cataloging-in-Publication Data

Bloom, Lois.
The transition from infancy to language : acquiring the power of expression / Lois Bloom.

p. cm.

Includes bibliographical references (p.) and index.

ISBN 0-521-44031-9

1. Children – Language. 2. Language acquisition. 3. Verbal behavior. 4. Cognition in children. I. Title.
LB1139.L3B596 1993
372.6′2 – dc20 92-47407
CIP

A catalog record for this book is available from the British Library.

ISBN 0-521-44031-9 hardback

For my mother,
whose last years gave me the strength to write this book

And for my daughter,
whose early years gave me the inspiration

Contents

Preface

This book was actually begun with the publication of the monograph *One Word at a Time* in 1973. The description of the single-word period in that monograph contained several observations of my daughter Allison's development that departed from traditional accounts in the literature at the time. Since then, the theoretical issues raised by these observations have continued to endure. The case study in *One Word at a Time* was motivated by two issues in particular. The first was that words in the single-word period have a conceptual basis, not a syntactic basis. Nothing I have read or observed since then has changed my strong conviction that the major developments in this period are conceptual rather than linguistic. The second theoretical issue was the nature of the developments in cognition that contribute to conceptual development, word learning, and the eventual emergence of syntax, at the end of the period. Many studies have since attempted to test the hypotheses I suggested, and the results of these studies have been mixed and at times controversial. One thing, however, is now clear: The second year of life is a time of major cognitive developments that contribute to learning words and the emergence of language.

The emphasis on cognitive development for early word learning in *One Word at a Time* was one of two factors that led to the chain of events that has culminated in this book. The second factor was a major omission in *One Word at a Time* and, indeed, in most accounts of the single-word period before and since: the role of affect in language development. Language emerges tentatively in the beginning of the second year at a time when infants are already very good at expressing a wide array of feeling states in their interactions with other persons. However, the relationship between affect expression and language has barely been touched on. This book, then, has to do with two aspects of development that contribute to the emergence of language and word learning in the second year, cognition and affect, in relation to a child's social connectedness to other persons.

In 1980, when questions about the relationships among cognition, affect expression, and language were taking shape in my mind, I conceived of a dream longitudinal study. The details are presented in the chapters that follow, but the broad strokes of the study deserve emphasis here. Instead of an *n* of 1 as in the case study reported in *One Word at a Time,* there were 14 children; instead of there being only one cultural context, the children were drawn from different ethnic, economic, and religious backgrounds; in addition to diaries kept by mothers at home, videotaped home visits, and standardized tests of cognition, the children were observed in a playroom where they all played with the same toys once a month from age 9 months to about 2½ years of age; instead of making a traditional transcription of the videotapes, we interfaced the video player with a computer and separated the critical variables for transcription and coding; and so forth.

The results we have reported will have to stand the test of subsequent research in the years to come. However, with respect to the original aims of the research, the study succeeded beyond my wildest expectations, for several reasons. The first reason was the enthusiasm of Tom James and the Spencer Foundation, who provided generous funding for creating the project and for the first five years of research, and Paul Chapin and the National Science Foundation, who allowed us to extend the aims of the original study to look at the social context the mothers provided for their infants' development. Support was also provided in the form of a fellowship at the Center for Advanced Study in the Behavioral Sciences in 1982; a James McKeen Cattell Sabbatical Award in Psychology in 1989; and a Research Professorship at Teachers College, Columbia University, 1991.

The second reason for the project's success was the notable crew I was able to assemble to pull it off. Richard Beckwith, Joanne Bitetti Capatides, Jeremie Hafitz, and Karin Lifter were committed to the excellence of the research from the moment each walked into 1055A Thorndike Hall and the project began, in 1981. None of what follows here would have happened without them. They were complemented by a group of dedicated assistants who helped collect and process the data, especially Virginia Brennan, Scott Browne, Wei Chang, Roxanne DeMatteo, Suzanne Gottlieb, Margaret Honey,

Cheryl Margulis, Adam Meyers, Marriette Newton-Danilo, Matthew Rispoli, Tresmaine Roubaine-Grimes, Scott Scheer, Jennifer Saldanha, Anne Spangler, Lisa Spiegel, Erin Tinker, Joy Vaughn-Brown, and Pia Wikstrom. And, finally, the project succeeded because of the loyalty of the mothers. Only a single monthly playroom session was missed in the course of the study (Charlie's family insisted on taking a month's vacation one August). We did have our trying times. One of the infants who began the study, Carlo, became depressed and was lost to us after several months when his parents separated; he was not one of the 14 infants in the studies in this book. Another infant, Reggie, kept pace with the others in his development until after his 2nd birthday, when it became clear to us that he and his parents were becoming casualties of the terrible frustrations that beset poor parents in New York City. The other children flourished, for which we were grateful.

Karin Lifter's 1982 doctoral dissertation was the original pilot study, with 3 of the children, that provided many of the important details we incorporated in the larger study reported here. The project was continuously sustained by Karin's considerable organizational skills, her unflagging energy and enthusiasm, and the insights she brought to the data analyses. In 1986, Richard Beckwith and I wrote the first draft of a manuscript, "Intentionality and Language Development," which went through several subsequent drafts and was widely circulated. For one reason or another, the manuscript was never completed to our satisfaction, and we each went on to other things. Many of the ideas and even some of the language from that paper are to be found in the pages of this book. Richard was a major influence on my thinking throughout the study, and I came to depend on his sometimes critical, often humorous, and always discerning input. He deserves much credit for what follows here.

Many others share in the credit as well. Erin Tinker came on board after the data were collected and soon assumed a major role in the activities in the lab; the thoroughness, care, and acumen she brought to the data analyses were a great gift. Peg Lahey was my conscience in pressing me to examine many of the assumptions that influenced the work; Kathleen Bloom was my major resource and sounding board for many of the statistics we used; Robert Beckwith, Karen Clark, Jim Corter, and Jane Monroe helped to develop the lag sequential analyses; and Dean Judith Berman Brandenburg provided a supporting context at Teachers College for the most recent analyses and the preparation of this book. Conversations, e-mail and otherwise, with Cathy

Best, Lila Braine, Roberta Golinkoff, Joe Jaffe, Patricia Kuhl, Joan Lucariello, Jean Mandler, Dennis Molfese, Nancy Stein, Tom Trabasso, Don Tucker, and Gerald Turkewitz were particularly helpful. Kathleen Bloom, Herbert Ginsburg, Roberta Golinkoff, Peg Lahey, Karin Lifter, and Katherine Nelson provided valuable comments on an early draft of the manuscript for this book.

Finally, and always, I thank my husband, Robert H. Bloom, for his patience, good humor, and good sense.

L.B.

Easton, Connecticut
March 21, 1993

Acknowledgments

Certain portions of these chapters have appeared elsewhere, in particular: Chapter 1: L. Bloom, Language acquisition and the power of expression. In H. Roitblatt, L. Herman, & P. Nachtigall (Eds.), *Language and communication: Comparative perspectives* (pp. 95–113). Hillsdale, NJ: Erlbaum (1993); Chapter 2: L. Bloom (1991b); Chapter 6: L. Bloom, Transcription and coding for child language research: The parts are more than the whole. In J. Edwards & M. Lampert (Eds.), *Talking data: Transcription and coding in discourse research.* Hillsdale, NJ: Erlbaum (1993), L. Bloom (1974b), and Beckwith, Bloom, Albury, Raqib, & Booth (1985); Chapter 7: L. Bloom, Beckwith, Capatides, & Hafitz (1988); Chapter 8: L. Bloom (1990), L. Bloom & Beckwith (1989), and L. Bloom & Capatides (1993); Chapter 10: Lifter & Bloom (1989); Chapter 11: L. Bloom (1991a).

PART I

Theory and Background

1

The Power of Expression

> What comes about through the development of language in the broadest sense is the coming to be of expressive power . . .
>
> (Charles Taylor)[1]

This book is about the transition from infancy to language: about how the affective lives of infants and what they know of persons, objects, and events in the world come together in the effort to acquire language. The focus is on the period that begins in the last quarter of the first year and continues through the second year of life. This is the time ordinarily referred to as the *single-word period* in language development. It is when infants begin to learn words and begin to acquire the power of expression in language.

Infants on the threshold of language are already quite successful, and have been for some time, in expressing *affect*. The importance of affect expression for regulating and communicating their internal states and relatedness to other persons has been well documented in the last two decades of research in infant communication and social and emotional development. Parents readily respond to a young infant's cries, whimpers, smiles, and chortles and depend on these signals for their caregiving and socializing practices. Since Darwin, we have assumed that these capacities for emotional expression are biologically determined. They provide signals for protecting and extending the species and help regulate physiological arousal and discharge. The 9-month-old infant has yet to learn language but is adept at deploying these capacities for expression.

By the end of the first year, infants have also discovered quite a lot about the world. As they approach the second year of life, all that they now know about persons, objects, and themselves informs their beliefs, desires, and feelings, and these cannot be expressed, much less articulated, by displays of affect alone. Other modes of expression are required, and waiting in the wings is language. Language is the preeminent mode of expression provided in a society to embody and make public what is otherwise internal and private to the individual – the beliefs, desires, and feelings we have that are our intentional states. Language makes these contents of mind public, in an expression, so that other persons can know them.[2]

The purpose of this book is to document this transition from infancy to language and to show how acquiring a vocabulary of words is connected to developments in cognition and affect expression. Children differ widely in the particulars of this period in the second year of life. They differ in when they begin to say words, how fast they acquire a vocabulary of words, and when they start combining words to form their first simple sentences. But, barring any interference, virtually all children begin to learn language in this period. At the end of the first year the infant depends largely on affect for expression; by the end of the second year the young child has acquired a vocabulary of words and may even have begun to say simple sentences.

The central thesis in this book is that the 1-year-old child's intentionality drives the acquisition of language. Our intentional states – the beliefs, desires, and feelings that we have – are themselves unobservable, but they determine how we relate to one another in everyday events. Children learn language for acts of expression in the effort to make known to others what their own thoughts and feelings are about, and for acts of interpretation in the effort to share the thoughts and feelings of other persons. Intentional states underlying acts of expression and interpretation provide the *mental meanings* for which knowledge of language – its vocabulary, semantics, syntax, and discourse procedures – is acquired.[3]

Mental meanings are constructed, as we talk and listen, from data perceived in the here and now and data recalled from the knowledge we have in memory. They have been the focus of theories of meaning and intentionality in philosophy.[4] More recently, they have been invoked in cognitive science, linguistics, and computer science as "mental models," "mental spaces," "complex mental attitudes," and the like.[5] Because such mental phenomena are hidden, language is required to make them manifest when what one individual has in mind differs from what another has in mind and needs to be shared.

A basic assumption being made here is that infants at the end of the first year of life have intentionality. All this means is that they are capable of having thoughts and feelings and that the thoughts and feelings they have in mind are *about something,* because they are directed at objects (including persons and events) in the world. Intentionality is what the representations we have in consciousness are about when we are alert and in touch with what is going on around us – what we have in mind at the moment. Attributing intentionality to infants should not be controversial; after all, we routinely attribute intentionality to a pet cat or dog. A 9-month-old is not an automaton, and neither is what the infant has in mind limited to what is immediately perceived. Just when we can begin to say an infant has intentionality is not at issue here; we are only assuming that by 9 months the human infant is an intentional being.[6] John Searle distinguished between this sense of intentionality with a capital *I* and simply intending to do something, or goal-directedness, which is intention in the ordinary sense, with a small *i.*[7] When an infant reaches for a toy, the reaching is *intended,* but the infant's *intentional state* also includes a representation of the toy, the desire to have it, feelings about having or not having it, and perhaps a plan for doing something with it.

This assumption of intentionality does not imply that 1-year-olds have a "theory of mind." We can speak of an infant's desires and beliefs without at the same time requiring that the infant have an explicit understanding of what it means to have a desire or a belief or where such things come from. Similarly, we assume an infant is attributing meaning to another person's smile or to what someone else might say without also assuming that the attribution is a deliberate one or that the infant has an understanding of why or how one makes these sorts of attributions. Sharing the contents of mind is not something that 1-year-old infants purposefully do as they set out on their language-learning careers. Instead, the motivation for sharing is in the need they have to sustain intersubjectivity with other persons and thereby locate themselves in a social world.

If intentionality drives the acquisition of language, then intersubjectivity drives the development of intentionality. Intersubjectivity comes from the appreciation infants have for "being together" with another person and depends on each attributing to the other a sense of being in touch with what they are feeling and thinking about.[8] These mutual attributions certainly happen without the infant's and probably even the adult's having a sense of where the thoughts and feelings in these situations come from. One-year-old infants do not yet have a theory of mind, but they do have a good start on acquiring a commonsense theory about the world.[9] And a large part of their nascent theorizing has to do with the other persons in their lives who care for and about them.

In sum, the mental meanings in an infant's intentional states are potentially expressible in language and are the reason why language is learned – to make them explicit and known to other persons so they can be shared. In fact, those aspects of knowledge and culture that survive from one generation to another may well be those that are most readily shared between minds. Language, obviously, is in large part responsible for determining this "sharability." And languages probably are the way they are, and children acquire language in the way they do, because of how successfully the aspects of language – its sound system, the words in its dictionary, and its procedures for generating sentences – contribute to the dynamics of sharing.[10]

This explicit focus on intentionality for a theory of language development ties language acquisition to the two aspects of mental life in the young child: cognition and emotion. However, with few exceptions, the study of language has ignored the affective life of the individual, and studies of language development have paid little attention to developments in emotion. Likewise, the study of emotional development in infants and children has ordinarily proceeded apart from the study of language and cognitive development. But we can no longer afford to separate the domains of language, emotion, and thought when we consider that speech and affect are both media of expression, and both language and affect expression have to do with the mind of the young child and its development. The intent in this book is to integrate these domains in an effort to understand the *process* of early language development in the second year of life.

The plan of the book is fairly straightforward; the first half presents the background and rationale for the longitudinal study described in the second half. To provide a context for the essential thesis of the book – that children learn language for expressing and articulating mental meanings – the rest of this chapter will compare this *expressive* perspective with an *instrumental* perspective on language and its development. The role of *representation* in a theory of language development that takes expression to be central will be taken up in Chapter 2. Mental representation is tied to developments in cognition, and studies of the burgeoning cognitive developments in late infancy that enable word learning will be reviewed in Chapter 3. The capacities for expression in early infancy before language will be described in Chapter 4, as these have been revealed in studies of social interaction and studies of the regulation and expression of emotion. This first half of the book will finish setting the stage for the second half in Chapter 5, with a review of current accounts of word learning and theories of the emergence of language in the single-word period.

Together, the first five chapters provide the background for the second half of the book and the results of a longitudinal study of 14 infants from 9 months to 2 years. The infants and the details of the research project are described in Chapter 6. Developments in the mental meanings of belief and desire – expressed by affect and speech – are described in Chapter 7; developments in affect expression are described in Chapter 8; and developments in word learning, in Chapter 9. Developments in the infants' play with objects was the window we used for exploring their developing cognition in this period of time, and these results are described in Chapter 10. The book concludes, in Chapter 11, with a synthesis of our research findings and a model of language development that emphasizes the relationship between expression and meaning. This relationship is in how personal and private mental meanings are connected to the shared and conventional meanings of language. The force of this relationship between expression and meaning is in the power children achieve for promoting their psychological and social well-being.

In contrast to this explicit focus on expression, the study of language development has traditionally proceeded in one of at least two other directions. One is in determining how children acquire knowledge of the forms and procedures for language. Studies with a focus on the language children learn are studies of the acquisition of words, semantics, syntax, or procedures for discourse, where features of utterance and context are compared in order to discover what the child knows about language. In studies of word learning, for example, the words a child says are ordinarily examined for evidence of the meaning a word has for the child and the circumstances in which the child knows to use the word. A second direction in child language studies is to determine how children acquire language as a tool for socially and strategically influencing the activities of other persons and getting things done in the world. Studies that focus on tool use and the instrumental function of language examine the pragmatics of language use in everyday contexts.

Both directions in child language research – the one having to do with the forms and content of language and the other having to do with its use – emphasize those things that are external and therefore *observable,* such as speech and social behaviors. Nevertheless, the assumption of intentionality –

that language makes the unobservable mental meanings in individual minds known to others – is implicit in much of this research, as we shall see in Chapter 5. But it is rarely made explicit. Instead, the prevailing metaphor in child language research is "tool use" with an emphasis on the external dimensions of language and its instrumental function.

THE TOOL-USE METAPHOR

The main thrust of the tool-use metaphor is that language happens between persons and that the effect of language is to influence the actions of other persons. When the focus is on the instrumental function of language, the assumption is that we use language and children learn language to get things done in the world. The emphasis in research is on pragmatics, means–end relations, and the social functions of speech.[11] Not surprisingly, therefore, Lev Vygotsky has become a central figure in contemporary language acquisition research because, in addition to considering language as the mechanism for thinking, he emphasized the communicative and organizing functions of speech and its practical importance as a tool:

> Although children's use of tools during their preverbal period is comparable to that of apes, as soon as speech and the use of signs are incorporated into any action . . . the specifically human use of tools is . . . realized, going beyond the more limited use of tools possible among the higher animals.[12]

This same sentiment regarding the instrumental function of speech for distinguishing animal and human language motivated Grace de Laguna as well:

> Speech is the great medium through which human cooperation is brought about. . . . The problem which we have before us, then, is to compare and differentiate the type of social control effected by the cries of animals with that effected by speech in human society.[13]

Contemporaries of Vygotsky and de Laguna similarly endorsed language as the defining tool of civilizations. For example, language is "the most important of the instruments of civilization . . . used to aid the process of thinking and to record . . . achievements," according to Ogden and Richards.[14] And Wittgenstein suggested that "there is no one relation of name to object, but as many as there are *uses* of sounds or scribbles which we call names."[15] The anthropologist Malinowski put forth a "situational theory of meaning," and in his "contextualist view":

Speech . . . is primarily used for the achievement of a practical result. . . . Words which cross from one actor to another do not serve primarily to communicate thought: they connect work and correlate manual and bodily movements.[16]

Fifty years later Geoffrey Sampson summarized the prevailing metaphor at that time: "Words are tools, and the 'meaning' of a tool is its use."[17]

This historical characterization of words as tools has reverberated over the years in efforts to explain early language acquisition. The development of tool use was closely tied to an appreciation of means–end relations and development of the symbolic capacity by Elizabeth Bates and her colleagues.[18] Katherine Nelson described early word learning as "*learning what words do.*"[19] The "desire to fulfil overt behavioural goals via others" was seen by Marilyn Shatz and Anne O'Reilly as one of the defining features of the conversational skills of 2-year-olds.[20] And for Jerome Bruner, the mastery of language "seems always to be instrumental to doing something with words in the real world, if only *meaning* something."[21]

When we explain the development of language in terms of "tool use" we are describing one of the things that can happen through language. Using language can influence the actions of other persons and get things done in the world. But we can influence the actions of other persons only because our words have the power to influence what they are thinking – their beliefs, feelings, and desires. A word or words can be successful as a tool only to the extent that the speaker is successful in setting up a representation in the *listener's* mind that is consistent with the representation in the *speaker's* mind.[22] Constructing these mutual representations depends upon sharing the meanings of words. In fact, I would turn Bruner's assertion around: The mastery of language seems always to be bent on meaning something, *if only* for doing something with words in the real world.

The instrumental function of language is also implied in explanations of word learning based on reference and designation. Accounts of referring typically describe observable events: When a child looks at the clock on the wall and says "ticktock," the word is being used to "make reference" to an object that is "out there." Ordinarily, characterizing a child's use of words as reference simply describes the two facts (1) the child said a word and (2) the word named something in the context. But this description bypasses the unobservable, internal dimension of language, because it omits these important facts: The child had to recall something from prior experience with the word from memory and then had to construct a mental meaning in consciousness with these objects-from-memory in relation to the objects-in-context. It is the elements in this representation in consciousness that are directed at objects in the world and that refer to those objects. "The language forms do not *refer* to such elements. If there is to be reference, it will go from the elements in mental spaces to the objects referred to."[23]

When a child looks at the clock on the wall and says "ticktock," the act of reference has a mental meaning that gives rise to the behavior we observe. The mental meaning represents and refers to the object in the world; the word the child says names the representation in the mental meaning and is its expression.

When we speak of language in terms of *designation,* we come closer to taking account of processes internal to the individual. However, the familiar "mapping problem" in child language research typically takes designation to mean that words are learned to "stand for" concepts and other sorts of knowledge that we have stored in long-term memory: a mapping between words and elements of knowledge. Such accounts also bypass the mental activity whereby elements in consciousness – mental meanings – are the objects set up and designated by words. Words point to and designate the elements in these private mental meanings and make them public, by virtue of the shared linguistic meanings vested in them. The crucial developments for language, therefore, are those that contribute to (1) the symbolic capacity, for representing elements of mental meanings in consciousness, and (2) processes of recall, for accessing words from memory to say what these representations are about.

In our zeal to explain the words of very young children, we might have been taking them too seriously by endowing their words with more linguistic status than they warrant. One-year-olds are developing concepts of objects, events, and relations. They learn words when they hear them (or see them, in the case of gesture or sign) in different circumstances in association with exemplars of their emerging concepts. Children do not so much *acquire conventional word meanings* as they develop capacities for recalling and retrieving words in circumstances that are increasingly different and removed from their original experiences with a word. Word meaning for the young child is abstracted out of the circumstances of prior use. Development in the period has to do with making the connections between what a child sees and hears and what the child already knows, and words are one part of what is learned in making these connections (see Chapter 5).

Historically, the instrumental view of language came about in *response* to the rise in behaviorism in the early part of this century, with its emphasis on observable phenomena. Indeed, Grace de Laguna called her model of language and its acquisition "social behaviorism." At the same time, the view of language as a social tool was also a *reaction* to the earlier idea of language as expression that had flourished in the previous century.

LANGUAGE AS EXPRESSION

The view that language is the expression of ideas has a long history, dating back in psychology at least to Wundt and in philosophy to Humboldt, Husserl, and Frege, among others.[24] The tool-use metaphor originated in the effort to counter this earlier notion that expression is central in language, a notion that had been articulated in particular by Wundt at the turn of the century and by Tylor, a 19th-century anthropologist:

> We must cease to measure the historical importance of emotional exclamations, of gesture signs, and of picture-writing, by their comparative insignificance in modern civilized life, but must bring ourselves to associate the articulate words of the dictionary in one group with cries and gestures and pictures, as being all of them means of manifesting outwardly the inward workings of the mind.[25]

"Language as expression" has figured in accounts of language development as far back as Saint Augustine's "recollections," in the fourth century, of how he himself had acquired language:

> And thus by constantly hearing words, . . . I collected gradually for what they stood; and having broken in my mouth to these signs, I thereby gave utterance to my will. Thus I exchanged with those about me these current signs of our wills, and so launched deeper into the stormy intercourse of human life.[26]

The most explicit statement for the study of child language and its acquisition came from Clara and William Stern: "A word is an expression of a unified content of consciousness. A sentence . . . is the expression of a unified position either taken, or about to be taken concerning a content of consciousness."[27]

The intent in this book is to revive this idea and make it explicit: Children learn language for expressing what cannot otherwise be known and shared with other persons rather than as an instrument for getting things done in the world. To be sure, words influence what other persons do, and speech is obviously and, indeed, the "one indispensable instrument for creating the ties of the moment without which unified social action is impossible."[28] And words have other effects as well, such as when they help in solving a problem or negotiating a complex set of directions. But these and other *effects* of language are subordinate to the representations words set up in a mind to create mental meanings, in an act of interpretation, and the representations in mental meanings articulated by words, in an act of expression. Social and practical effects of language depend upon what the speaker of the words wants, believes, and feels about what the hearer of the words can and will do. An expression takes the private contents of wanting, believing, and feeling and makes them available to others "as part of our activity of communicating, of being open with each other." These are things that words *do* by virtue of an expression rather than something that happens *through* them by virtue of their being tools.[29]

The centrality of expression is implicit in the tool-use metaphor, because using a tool presupposes a goal with a set of psychological attitudes about that goal. This would include, at the minimum, a representation of the goal and a belief that the goal is attainable, a desire to attain it, and feelings about the result of attaining it or not. All the functions of language originate with some representation in mind. The historical debate over which of its functions can best define language missed this essential point. One reason was that the question asked was *which one* – Which is the primary function of language, personal expression *or* interpersonal communication? – overlooking the fact that communication cannot occur without expression.[30]

To complicate things, the expressive function of speech often has the sense of conveying "emotive" or "psychological" meaning as opposed to the more explicit meaning articulated by what the words actually say. In a similar vein, utterances have been described as "expressive symptoms" when something that is said causes the hearer to *infer* some culturally or personally specific affect, attitude, or association that the words themselves do not actually say.[31] However, this is expression in only a weak sense.

Charles Taylor distinguished between this weak sense and a strong sense of expression for communication. Expression in the stronger sense involves a direct manifestation, without depending on inference. A genuine expression makes something manifest that cannot otherwise be known. And it is not only words that do this: A painting, a piece of music, a smile, a frown are expressions in different media. When pleasure is seen in a smile, or thoughts are evident in words, or sadness is experienced in a piece of music, something is made manifest in an embodiment, and an embodiment is expression in a strong sense.[32] Expressions in the weaker sense occur with inference, when we can also know the things we infer about someone or something in other ways. For example, certain signals that we give with our bodily movements or demeanor can express agitation or fatigue or the fact that we might be coming down with a cold. Reading other sorts of signals can let us infer that someone is relaxed or at peace with the world. The same is true of slips of the tongue: They are signals we use to infer something about an individual indirectly; they do not directly manifest what it is we attribute.

The difference between strong and weak expression is related to a distinction made by Sperber and Wilson between "coded communication," which is communication with language (a strong sense of expression), and "ostensive–inferential communication," which is communication without language (expression in a weaker sense). Ostensive–inferential communication is achieved by producing and interpreting such evidence as a glance, a point, a shrug, a frown – evidence that can be interpreted along with or instead of a linguistic message. But the message itself can only be displayed in coded communication, when its meaning is articulated and made explicit by language. In contrast, ostensive–inferential communication can be used on its own, without language, or it can be used with language.[33] Thus, what words name – what they actually say – articulates the message or mental meaning of a speaker in a way that makes it directly readable or interpretable by other persons. This is, in Taylor's terms, the stronger sense of expression, and he allows that other media of expression, including emotional displays, do this as well.

All the functions of language – including its instrumental, interpersonal, and problem-solving functions – absolutely depend on the power of language for expression and interpretation. This fact was recognized by Fritz Heider, the founder of attribution theory in social psychology, who proposed that the psychology of persons guides the psychology of the interpersonal.[34] Social contexts depend upon what is in the minds of the participants; beliefs, feelings, and desires of individuals must be taken into account in the effort to understand and explain coordinated social activity. Language expresses these ideas that we have about ourselves and other persons and the expectations for action and interaction that follow from them. True, persons exist by virtue of their relation to one another, but this is possible because of the power they have to take what is hidden within themselves and make it public. This is what language does.

Thus, expression is not one of the functions of language but is basic to all its functions. All the things that language can do depend on the fact that it is a medium for expressing what one has in mind. Language can succeed in influencing other persons in social contexts only to the extent that language connects the contents of individual minds. A large part of why languages began in the first place was no doubt the need in a society for individuals to have this expressive power – to make external and public to other persons what is otherwise internal and private to themselves.

Even for 1-year-olds, what they take from and contribute to an interaction has to do with what they have in mind and what they attribute to other minds. Young children know that their speech needs to be interpreted by other persons virtually from the time they begin to say words.[35] They do not ordinarily talk to inanimate objects; they may often talk to themselves and their animate surrogate toys, like dolls and teddy bears, but they do not bother to talk to refrigerators, chairs, or trees. Other *persons* interpret, care about, and respond to their messages. Children do not need to understand what it means to have a mind in order to know this. Current "theory of mind" research inquires into when and how an explicit and sophisticated knowledge of minds develops, generally crediting children with such knowledge about the beliefs of self and other at about 4 years of age.[36] But such psychological knowledge does not emerge de novo at the end of the fourth year. Just as actions serve development in other respects, children acquire increasingly sophisticated mental skills through their actions of expressing and interpreting. A concept of what it means to have a mind is acquired slowly, along with language.

What young children do need for acts of expression and interpretation is the ability to attribute to other persons something like their own feelings, beliefs, and desires *as they understand them.* This ability is intuitive and implicit rather than conceptualized and explicit – as it is as well for adults in most situations. If children engage in acts of interpretation and expression from the beginning of language, then to understand language acquisition we need to determine what these actions consist of and depend upon, and how they change with development to become increasingly informative and effective. Once we acknowledge this, the questions we ask necessarily change.

In addition to inquiring into the acquisition of language itself and how it is used, we can inquire into developments in the dynamic processes by which representations in the mental meanings underlying acts of expression and interpretation are constructed. We can also inquire into how other sorts of expression – particularly affect expression and play with objects – relate to the acquisition of language for expression. These were the motivations for the research reported in the second half of this book.

In sum, the theoretical perspective in this book departs from the commonly held view that language is acquired by children as a tool for designating objects and influencing the actions of other persons and events in the world. With language viewed as a tool, as in instrumental theories of language acquisition, the focus is on end states and the effect of a child's behaviors on the context. This focus on end states emphasizes the external dimension of language and how the child achieves a goal. The use of language as a tool should not be central to a theory of language development any more than it is to a theory of the emotions. Tool use, in general, is subordinate to the symbol-making capacity that makes it possible for us to have goals and to use tools.[37] The symbolic capacity enables us to represent entities and relations between entities in intentional states. What should be central to a theory of language acquisition, therefore, is the capacity for representing mental meanings in the acts of expression and interpretation for which children acquire language.

Three principles of language development follow from the implications of a child's intentionality in this theoretical perspective. The first is the *Principle of Relevance:* In the successful language-learning scenario, the words a child hears have relevance because their target is already part of what the child has in mind. What a child is feeling and thinking determines the relevance of the words the child hears from other persons. Clearly, children must hear many words that are not relevant to what they have in mind. However, the words that are relevant will most assuredly be the words they learn and eventually say.

The second is the *Principle of Discrepancy:* A consequence of developments in symbolic capacity is that what a child has in mind becomes increasingly discrepant from the data of perception. Children will acquire language because what they have in mind must be expressed if it is to be shared with other persons who cannot exploit clues from the context for understanding. And the third is the *Principle of Elaboration:* A consequence of learning more about the world is that contents of mind become increasingly elaborated. The more elements and relations between elements in intentional states, the more the child will need to know of the language to express and articulate what they are.

These are cognitive principles; they draw on the symbolic capacity and developments in mental representation in particular; and they are socially mediated. They will surface again in the chapters to follow as the story unfolds of how language comes together with other aspects of cognition and emotional expression in early development.

LANGUAGE, EMOTION, AND COGNITION

The power of expression comes with the ability to take something hidden within us and make it public; two modes of expression that allow us to attribute hidden mental meanings are affect and language.[38] Affect expression is in place in earliest infancy, and its forms are biologically determined. Before language, affect expresses an infant's internal states and feelings; by learning language, infants are able to say what their internal states and feelings are about. Language is the system of expression provided by society and culture, and language has to be learned. But language does not replace affect expression, as we shall see; instead, children continue to express feelings through expressions of affect as they are learning the language. The relationship between the two is an intimate one, and their integration is a part of the developmental story of language acquisition in the second year that is not ordinarily taken into account.

The affective lives of young children are typically ignored in child language research because we tend to stay within the bounds of one or another discipline. Even the study of language itself is typically fragmented, because we tend to study different aspects of language – vocabulary, syntax, semantics, pragmatics, phonology – as though they were separate domains. This is so, perhaps, because we are intimidated by language and by the enormity and complexity of the task of its acquisition. However, domains of language are not separate for the child; they are integrated from the very beginning of acquisition.[39] In studies of affect as well, we may study only one or another of the subsystems of emotion, such as facial expression or social regulation or cognitive appraisals. But we know that these subsystems necessarily cohere and develop together.

Research and theory in emotion and emotional development has increasingly recognized the role of cognition in emotional experience and expression: An emotional experience entails, at least, the appraisal and evaluation of a situation in relation to some goal.[40] But the effect of this thinking is rarely considered in studies of early cognitive development with infants and young children. In linguistics, the historical emphasis on spoken words and sentences has meant that emotion was ignored in studies of language. An exception is cross-cultural work that points to the linguistic means different societies have for the expression of feelings and attitudes.[41] When language and affect have been considered together in psychological research, the emphasis is generally on the words that name the emotions and not on the cognitive connections between speech and affect.[42]

We also tend to study language, emotion, and cognition separately because of the procedural, programmatic, and practical problems encountered in attempting to analyze collaborative influences on behavior. Innovative solutions to these problems are not easy to find. Nevertheless, even though we may study them separately, language, cognition, and emotion are fundamentally and systematically related. They could not be otherwise, as we know from the organismic and contextualist world views[43] of the giants of developmental theory: Piaget, Schneirla, Werner, and Vygotsky (not to mention more general psychological theorists like Lehrman and Lewin). Their collaboration has been recognized in research and theory in emotional development that takes an integrative perspective.[44] More recently, a related perspective has been offered in applications of "dynamic systems theory" to the study of infant development.[45]

We have made an effort in our research to explore the connections among three domains of ordinary activity – words, affect expression, and play with objects – in the development of infants in the last quarter of the first year and through the second year of life. The results of our studies are summarized in the second half of this book to show how developments in language, emotion, and cognition influence each other. The effects we found are of two kinds: large, developmental effects extending across time in the single-word period, and small, local effects in the moment-to-moment contingencies in real time as infants say words, express affect, and play with objects. Both effects require developments in (1) representation, for the construction of mental meanings, and (2) collaboration between affect and cognition, for the expression of those meanings. The relationship between representation and expression for language acquisition is the subject of the next chapter; the collaboration that develops between affect and cognition for language will be discussed in subsequent chapters.

SOME DEFINITIONS

Mental meaning is the key term used throughout this book to talk about the momentary, changing representations in consciousness that give rise to an expression and that result from an interpretion. *Mental meaning* best captures the intent of this book, and it has a symmetry with *conventional meaning* in language. Nevertheless, other terms do creep in throughout, because mental meanings are states of mind; they are intentional states; they are personal meanings; they are mental constructions and the like.

Consciousness is the wakeful state of mind for alert attention and awareness; it consists of the ordinary thinking that determines ordinary activity in ordinary, everyday events. In the sense used here, consciousness is thinking without thinking about it, or states of awareness and attention without purposeful reflection on either the act of attending or the objects of awareness. Interestingly, it is when we double up on these notions of consciousness, attention, thinking, and awareness that we enter the realm of metacognition and become aware of what we are attending to or conscious of what we are aware of or think about what we are thinking, and so forth. But this heightened sense of consciousness that figures in a theory of mind is not what is meant here. Instead, consciousness, for our purposes, is simply what we are about at any one moment in time, with representations in consciousness being the products of perception and ordinary thinking. We will return to these notions again, particularly in Chapter 2.

Affect is the essential subjective quality of "being in touch," and affect is always present in psychologically healthy individuals. It includes a subjective feeling state, a physiological state, and a motivational state that together determine an individual's adaptation to the environment. In addition to its function in organismic adaptation, affect is also communicative and socially mediating. Affect is the *unmarked* dimension of emotional experience and responsiveness.

When affect is marked, or qualified, by a cognitive appraisal that results in different patterns of expression, hedonic tone, and physiological arousal, the result is one or another of the categories of emotional experience. *Emotion* categories can be defined differently according to different theoretical perspectives. The most general categorization is based on the gradient but polar dimensions of hedonic tone: Positive and negative emotion are the marked categories, with neutral affect being the unmarked category. The more specific categorization is in terms of the discrete, so-called Darwinian, categories of joy, anger, fear, sadness, disgust, and the like that are defined by, at least, different facial expressions and cognitive appraisals. We will return to these notions again, particularly in Chapter 4.

CONCLUSIONS

Surely by the end of the first year of life the human infant is an intentional creature – having beliefs, desires, and feelings that are about something. These contents of mind are intentional states or mental meanings, and they do not require that an infant be aware of them for a "theory of mind." They are made possible by all that the 1-year-old has learned about persons, objects, and relations in the world, and they cannot be expressed by the displays of affect alone – the smiles, whines, whimpers, laughs, and cries – that served the younger infant so well. Language will have to be learned for their expression.

Language is provided by society for taking the internal, personal, private mental meanings of individuals and making them external and public in expressions, so that other persons can know them. The young infant's intentionality is the driving force for language development. And the need to sustain the self in a social world – the intersubjectivity of the infant's being with other persons – drives the development of intentionality. The social world in the first year of life is a microcosm of the world awaiting the infant in the years ahead. Expression – both language and affect – will create and maintain a place in that world for the person the infant will become. This will happen, in large part, because other persons will care about and want to share the child's contents of mind, and they will provide the language for that sharing. The use of language as a tool – its instrumental function – to influence other persons and get things done depends upon the fact that *language as a system of expression* is basic to all the functions of language in the first place.

Three principles to explain the acquisition of language follow from the intentional stance and its social context in this theoretical perspective. The Principle of Relevance is that a child will learn a word when its target is already part of what the child has in mind; the words children learn and then say are relevant when they express something of what a child's beliefs, desires, and feelings *are about.* According to the Principle of Discrepancy, the symbolic capacity makes it possible to have beliefs, desires, and feelings about things that are not apparent to others and so cannot be known by other persons unless they are made manifest in an expression. The Principle of Elaboration is that developments in cognition and knowledge about the world create mental meanings that are increasingly elaborated, with more elements and relations among elements, so that learning more of the language will be needed to articulate them. Each of these principles depends on the *representation* of mental meanings. The part played by representation in a theory of language development in which expression is basic will be taken up in the following chapter.

2

Representation and Expression

The present-day cognitivist perspective in psychology was born with Miller, Galanter, and Pribram's now classic response to behaviorism: *Plans and the Structure of Behavior.* The problem addressed in that book was the task of describing "how actions are controlled by an organism's internal representation of its universe" such that "cognitive representation" is mapped into "the appropriate *pattern* of activity."[1] Two aspects of cognitive representation were invoked: a mental plan for acting and the individual's knowledge base. In short, what determines how we act is what we know and the plans we construct for making use of what we know.

Acts of expression and interpretation require plans, just like other acts that we do. These plans include the representations in intentional states that "we set up as we talk or listen and that we structure with elements, roles, strategies, and relations."[2] Such representations are set up in the part of the mind traditionally called working memory or consciousness. They are the mental meanings that individuals express when they talk and that they construct when they interpret the speech of others. And they are the representations that give rise to feelings of emotion and their expression. The purpose of this chapter is to draw attention to these representations and to the developments that contribute to them so as to emphasize their importance for acquiring language.

COGNITIVE DEVELOPMENT AND CHILD LANGUAGE

The cognitivist perspective in child language research has had, by and large, two thrusts. One is the focus on the child's knowledge base and one or another version of the traditional child language "mapping problem": how children attach the forms of language to what they know about objects, events, and relations in the world.[3] Young infants' interactions with persons and their actions with objects in the first year of life culminate in the knowledge that brings them to the transition to language in the second year. They know something of the distinction between animate and inanimate beings and the intersubjectivity and social connectedness they can expect with other persons. They know something about objects in general: for example, that a moving object continues to exist when it moves behind another object and can no longer be seen, and that certain kinds of objects afford containment or support for other objects. And they have begun to form more specific concepts, such as concepts of cars and dogs. They know about actions and how actors and objects are affected by actions in events. The importance for language of this kind of knowledge about persons, objects, and events is by now self-evident. Most simply, children learn to talk about what they know at least something about.

Infants on the threshold of language have also begun to appreciate the causes and circumstances of their emotional states of well-being and distress. This appreciation is intimately tied to what they have learned in the first year about persons, objects, and events. At the least, they can differentiate between pleasurable and unpleasurable events and have learned to look for the one and avoid the other. And these, too, are the things they will eventually learn to talk about, in the second year.

The second cognitive focus in child language research is on development of the processes of thought that make the acquisition of knowledge possible.[4] Developmental change occurs in the forms as well as in the content of thought. Actions and feelings in the first year are very much tied to internal states and to external conditions that are perceptible. In the second year, the infant comes to think about events removed in time and space and to have feelings and to do things on the basis of these representations. Development is additive and cumulative as mental capacities increase and the infant acquires more knowledge about the world. But developmental change is also qualitative as infants come to think about things in substantively different ways and learn to act on objects as represented as well as objects as presented. The key to qualitative developmental change is the symbolic capacity for representational thought.

REPRESENTATION FOR CHILD LANGUAGE AND EMOTION

The word *representation* is used in child language research to mean several things.[5] On the one hand, the notion of representation has been central in cognitive perspectives in child language research with a focus on either the acquisition of knowledge or development of the thought processes for acquiring knowledge. We talk of the experience of objects and events in the world being represented in memory as schemas, concepts, and event knowledge. In the same way, knowledge of language is represented in memory as words and procedures for sentences that map onto what children know of objects and events. And, on the other hand, language represents aspects of objects and events when we talk about them in ordinary conversation with other persons. Two senses of *representation* have received the greatest attention in child language research. The one is that language is represented in memory, along with other knowledge, for the mapping of sound and meaning. The other is that language represents objects and events so that persons can refer to them in communicating with each other. No fewer than ten books on the single-word period in language development were published in the 1980s with a focus on the child language mapping problem in the acquisition of word meanings and on the use of words for reference.[6]

However, a different sense of representation is the focus here, one that comes from theories of intentionality in philosophy.[7] Intentional states are the representations in consciousness we construct for ordinary, everyday actions – including acts of expressing and acts of interpreting the expressions of others. These representations are ephemeral states of mind without material substances, but they can be made manifest by expressing them. Expressions are "material properties" or "embodiments," because they have substance – like a drawing, action, speech, or a display of emotion. The same representation may find different embodiments in different media; for example, speech, sign language, and printed text are embodiments of meaning in language.[8] Whatever its medium, an expression takes the internal, *personal* representation of an intentional state and makes it external and *public.*[9] Creating these representations in consciousness as we talk and listen is the critical aspect of thinking for the process of language acquisition: They are the mental meanings for language.

In the study of language acquisition, however, these representations in consciousness are rarely made explicit or taken as the object of inquiry.[10] We have paid a great deal of attention instead to the part played by what children know about the world – their knowledge base in memory – for language acquisition. This distinction between representations in consciousness and knowledge in memory corresponds to Campbell's distinction between that "domain of the organism, the contents of which are constantly changing and available to awareness . . . [and another] domain, the contents of which change only slowly [and] are not available to awareness."[11] In sum, intentionality is that aspect of mind that intervenes between what we perceive in the outer world at any one moment in time and the inner knowledge of the world we have in memory all of the time. Intentional states are the products of attending to the outer world and our ordinary thinking about it. We have these representations without necessarily being conscious of them; "even we language-using adults typically do not consciously experience our own mental representations as such; they are psychologically transparent, not noticed (or perhaps better, beneath notice)."[12]

The representations in mental meanings connect with words, sentences, and discourse in acts of expression and interpretation but do not have one-to-one correspondence with the forms and structures of language. In fact, mental meanings are constructed in other ways besides language. But when mental meanings are constructed through interpretation during discourse, the units of language act as "triggers" to set up "targets," which are the elements and relations between elements in the mental meaning.[13] In an act of expression, words are evoked to articulate these same sorts of units in a mental meaning and thereby make them manifest. But the representations in mental meanings are themselves distinct from the linguistic forms.

Representations in consciousness are as important for the experience and expression of emotion. Emotions are "about" something we have in mind, and these representations are intentional states. Although they have a material manifestation in an expression and a corresponding physiological component, emotions are states of mind rather than physical, bodily states. They come about as the result of appraising and evaluating circumstances in one or another situation in relation to a belief or to the goal and plan in a desire. A large part of emotional development, therefore, depends upon developing the cognition necessary for such appraisals and the representations that result from them. Traditional theories of the emotions since Darwin have distinguished among emotions on the basis of the facial expressions with which they are correlated, for example, the categories joy, anger, fear, sadness, and the like.[14] The more recent cognitive theories of emotion distinguish among the different emotions according to the representations in consciousness that give rise to them. Emotions very often rise and fall with the success and failure of the plans we have in mind in everyday activities of living. For example, joy is experienced with the success of a plan; anger and sadness are experienced when a goal or plan is blocked; anger and sadness differ from each other according to whether the goal is obstructed (anger) or lost (sadness).[15] In sum, intentional states include the feelings we have and the representations they are about.

Theories of intentionality in philosophy are complemented by psychological theory concerned with attention, states of awareness, and short-term memory. In psychology, the importance of early attention and states of awareness has been stressed in numerous accounts of infant cognition.[16] For example, the "quiet alert states" of the neonate and young infant are generally considered to be those moments during which the infant focuses on and attends to objects and events in the environment.[17] The objects of infant attention are the products of perception that determine what the infant learns about objects and events. Measures of attention, such as habituation, provide an index of such learning. When an infant stops attending to an old object (or event) and pays attention instead to a new and slightly different one, we can assume the infant has recognized a change and begun to appreciate the discrepancy between the two.[18]

Sometime in the first 6 months, infants begin to compare what they attend to with what they have learned from perception at an earlier time. The result is the construction of the earliest representations. And these are more than only sensorimotor representations, because they make use of a primitive system of "accessible knowledge."[19] Somewhat later, what a child is able to hold in mind in states of awareness guides such problem-solving tasks as the search for absent objects.[20] The literature is full of descriptions like these of the attentional capacities of the infant and young child and the importance of the representations that result from them. Such representations are as important for the development of language and the experience and expression of emotion as they are for cognition more generally.

Representations in intentional states are about objects in the world under psychological attitudes of belief, desire, and feeling toward them. However, in theory and research in child language, as well as in theories of the emotions, the emphasis is usually on desires that are intentions to achieve a goal or to communicate. But the intention to act and intentions to communicate are what John Searle has called only the "ordinary" sense of the term *intention*. "Intending to do something is just one kind of Intentionality along with believing, desiring, hoping, fearing, and so on."[21] The central point in the theoretical perspective in this book is that children acquire words and construct the grammar of a language in their efforts to express what the contents of their beliefs, desires, and feelings are *about*. It follows, therefore, that the developments contributing to the representations in these intentional states – for a child's mental meanings – are developments to consider in the effort to understand how language is acquired.

CONTENTS OF MIND AND LANGUAGE

What is required for learning words? At the minimum, an infant has to attend to an acoustic signal (or visual signal, in the case of sign language) along with something in the context that is relevant to what the infant has in mind. The product of this attention is, at first, a representation consisting largely if not exclusively of the data from these perceptions. However, elements in this perceptually based representation evoke some aspect of prior experience from memory to construct another representation. The elements in this new mental construction are about entities perceived in the world in relation to knowledge recalled from memory.

Early on, prior experiences recalled from memory are minimally different from the present experience that evokes them; they are episodic. For example, a child might first hear the word *ticktock* while looking at the clock on the kitchen wall. The child will remember the clock on the kitchen wall when seeing the clock in a playroom and/or hearing the word *ticktock* again. With development, the child will encode a schema in memory that includes something about the clock on the kitchen wall, the clock in the playroom, and the word *ticktock*. This schema can then be evoked in comparing objects in perception that are related but discrepant: for example, a wristwatch or a compass.

The point is that elements in a schema in memory can include a word (such as *ticktock*). Hearing the word again prompts retrieval of the original episode (the clock on the kitchen wall) or the more elaborated schema and eventually, a *concept* of clock. With the early words a child says, recalling the word will depend upon reexperiencing the episode in which it was originally heard. Many accounts of early words have stressed their episodic character. Eventually, recall will be cued by aspects of new and different episodes. The increasing discrepancy between cues for retrieval and recall and the original episode in which the word was experienced will be reflected in a child's progress from episodic to conceptually based uses of words so often described in the literature.[22]

Very young children who are just beginning to learn language depend on the *Principle of Relevance* – on hearing and using words about entities and relations they are thinking about and have feelings about that are, very often, evident in the here and now. As they learn more of the units and structures of language, physical cues from the here-and-now context become less important than the words they hear as cues for recall. And once enough of the language is learned, the data from perception can be presumed between speakers, so that words, sentences, and discourse become the primary cues for setting up represention for mental meanings. Adults surely take account of what goes on around them, but they don't ordinarily tell one another about it.

In sum, the cognitive work in learning and using words and sentences consists of forming representations in mental meanings. These representations "are not part of the language itself, or of its grammars; they are not hidden levels of *linguistic* [italics added] representation, but language does not come without them."[23] In interpreting a message, the speech we hear or signs we see provide the cues for accessing knowledge from memory in order to set up the elements and relationships between elements in a mental meaning. In acts of expression, we recruit other cues to construct a mental meaning, and language provides the forms and procedures for articulating what that representation is about. The representations in mental meanings are cognitive constructions, not linguistic constructions, but *language does not come without them.*

Consider, as an example, what is happening as you read this paragraph. What the paragraph is about has nothing whatever to do with the room you are sitting in, what you might be able to see out the window, the music that might be coming from the next room, and so forth. Nevertheless, these other things, especially now that the words you just read called your attention to them, are part of what you have in mind right now at this immediate moment as you are reading these words. Data from perception are one source of the representations we form in awareness, and perceptual data can be more or less important for constructing representations for expression and interpretation.

However, the words and sentences on the page are your only cues for attempting to understand what this paragraph is about. Within the narrow confines of the context afforded by this printed page, you are engaged in an act of construction whereby new information is assimilated to what you already know.[24] The words and their arrangements are familiar to you, familiar enough so that they can evoke things stored in memory to construct what you have in mind at this precise moment. This *representation of what the words are about* is not a picture – it is not a literal image. It is also not just the words themselves. In fact, the words and their syntactic arrangement *underdetermine* the representation you construct as you read. The words are only cues for accessing aspects of what you already know for constructing a new experience in consciousness – a configuration of elements linked by their roles and the relations between them. As you continue to read, other elements and relations will be added to the configuration. This act of construction is taking place as you read the words; it is taking place *here,* in your immediate context. The representation you are constructing is what you are attending to, what you have in mind *now.* These here-and-now contents of mind are what you understand about what is printed on this page.

Everything else you know – the record of many other experiences you have had or imagined or dreamed before this time and place – is "somewhere else" in your head. Everything else you know is irrelevant to what you have in the representations you are constructing here and now, *until* you hear the strains of a Mozart sonata or someone suggests a drink before dinner. These new events evoke other objects from memory, and your mental work shifts to constructing new representations. But the mental meaning you were constructing before these interruptions was your interpretation of the paragraphs on the page. We might expect that other persons who read this page will construct mental meanings with similar content. That is because the words and sentences on this page are part of a language that is public and shared among the community of language users. But the representations others construct will not be exactly the same as the one you have, because their own previous and personal knowledge will be different from yours.

Just as with the words on a printed page, the same sorts of things happen when we understand what someone else says. The words (or signs) cue recall of prior knowledge to construct a representation for an interpretation of what is being said. In turn, when we have a representation in mind and have reason to believe that others do not share it, we need to access the linguistic forms and procedures that will articulate something of that representation. The action of saying the words or making the signs is an expression of what we have in mind. The acquisition of language depends, therefore, on developments that contribute to the representations in mental meanings that underlie actions of interpreting and expressing messages.

Two principles follow from the proposal that changes in the representations a child constructs in mind are central to the acquisition of language. One is the *Principle of Discrepancy:* Children will acquire the public words and grammar of a language as the private contents of their mental meanings become increasingly discrepant from what can be perceived in the context. Discrepant mental meanings need to be expressed if they are to be shared with other persons. In earliest infancy, representations in states of awareness are limited, by and large, to the data of perception. What infants see is, to a large extent, what they think about. With developments in the capacity for representation, and developments in retrieval and recall, the infant comes to access data from memory that do not match the data of perception. When the representation in a child's mental meaning includes entities not perceptible to others in the context, an expression is required to make them manifest. Thus, the discrepancy between the world as it is and the world as the child expects, wants, or imagines it to be creates the demand for language, because the child can no longer exploit a shared here-and-now context for interpretation by others.

The other principle is the *Principle of Elaboration.* The consequence of learning more about the world is that representations in mental meanings become increasingly elaborated. The more elements and relations between them in these representations, the more the child will need to know of the words and structures of language to express them. Early in the single-word period, infants say one word at a time with a focus on a single entity; toward the end of this period, they begin to say successive words with a focus on a relationship between entities. The conceptual development that makes it possible for a child to hold in mind two entities, along with a relationship between them, is required before the child can begin to learn the syntax of simple sentences.[25] And 2-year-olds progress from saying simple sentences, which express a single proposition, to acquiring the syntax of complex sentences, which require a child to hold in mind two propositions and the relationship between them.[26] If the capacity to generate expressions is to keep up with such changes in mental meanings, then a child's knowledge of semantics and syntax must necessarily change. The child must acquire a language that can generate such expressions.

These principles, together with the Principle of Relevance – that the words a child learns are those that already have their target in what the child has in mind – depend on cognitive developments that make the representations in mental meanings possible.

DEVELOPMENTS FOR CONSTRUCTING MENTAL MEANINGS

Early in infancy, long before infants have had much experience with objects and events in the world – let alone experience with language – what they see, hear, and feel in the immediate present determines what they have in mind at any particular time. However, memories of prior events begin very early in life. The earliest memories are evident with what Baldwin, and Piaget after him, called "circular reactions" as the infant acts to reproduce a result that had at first happened only fortuitously with a chance movement.[27] Short-term retention of objects and events in the immediate context has been demonstrated in habituation studies with young infants. Infants "tell us" if they have seen an object before when they become bored with it and turn their attention to something new.[28] And infants as young as 8 weeks old already demonstrate primitive memories of events that happened to them a day or two before when they reencounter the original event in a new experience.[29]

Thus, the cues very young infants use to construct representations in consciousness are initially reencounters with the same or similar episodes evoked from memory. Following the Principle of Discrepancy, development occurs in the ability to recall aspects of prior events using cues that are farther and farther removed from the original encounter with the event. Children eventually come to be able to think about, and talk about, objects outside the episodes in which they were originally experienced.[30] With development, episodes recalled from memory become increasingly discrepant from the perceptual cues that evoked them until, ultimately, speech and signs provide cues for recall in the absence of other perceptual data.

Infants begin to have pairings of words with events (objects, actions) in memory at least as young as 12–14 months.[31] When the word is heard again or the event is seen again, either the word or the event (or both) cues recall of the original word–event pair to set up a mental meaning in an interpretation. The representation in this mental meaning, then, is the joint product of the contextual cue and the word–event pair accessed from memory. The important point here is that if the child then says the word, that word is an *expression* of this representation.

The early gestures and words of infants depend upon such cued recall: waving "byebye" when someone leaves the room; looking up at a clock on the wall of the playroom and saying "ticktock"; climbing off the chair and saying "down"; and so on. In instances like these, the child has to have recalled something not there in the context, such as, for instance, someone leaving at another time and waving "byebye"; the clock on the kitchen wall and the word *ticktock*. In sum, the child's gesture or word is an expression of a mental meaning constructed out of data recalled from memory with the benefit of cues from the context. Development occurs in the sorts of cues the child uses for retrieval and recall to construct these representations – beginning with reencounters with the *same* cues (the clock on the kitchen wall cues recall of the same clock at a previous time), progressing to *similar* cues (the clock in the playroom cues recall of the clock on the kitchen wall), and eventually taking in *linguistic* cues ("Where's the clock?" or "What time is it?").

Infants are soon able to generate their own cues for accessing items from memory. For example, a child might see a pile of blocks on the floor and then go to the toybox for a doll to ride a train. Seeing the pile of blocks (a perceptual cue) evoked a plan to build a train, and the representation of a train in that plan evoked a likely passenger. Infants come to be able to anticipate events that are not present in the context, to discover new means to an end, or to construct representations with novel contents never actually experienced before, as in dreams or pretend play. Ultimately, the speech the child hears (or signs the child sees) will, in the absence of more literal cues from the context, be a source for constructing the representations in mental meanings for acts of interpretation and expression. Just as the words printed on this page are the only cues you have to what is expressed here, so too will the words the child hears or the signs that others make become the cues used for setting up representations in the interpretation of messages.

What developments contribute to the representations in mental meanings – for both words and emotion? At the least – and leaving aside for the moment developments in conceptual structure (taken up in Chapter 3) – we have to consider the consequences of developmental changes in (1) capacity, (2) notation systems, and (3) pathways into and out of the knowledge base in memory. These aspects of mental activity contribute to the resources the infant uses for all sorts of thinking and problem solving. They have received a good amount of attention in psychological theory and research with somewhat older children, particularly in neo-Piagetian accounts of cognitive development cast in terms of "information processing" and cognitive "resource models."[32] However, their importance for language development has not generally been acknowledged.[33]

One implication of the Principle of Elaboration is that the *capacity* for representation in mental meanings changes in the first several years of life, when many of the basics of language are acquired. The use of language can be diagnostic of the elaboration of mental meanings and changes in capacity. Examples were given earlier of progress from representations with a focus on a single element (saying a single word) to representing more than one element with a relation between them (saying successive single words and, eventually, simple sentences) to mental meanings that represent the propositions underlying two simple sentences and a semantic relationship between them (complex sentences). The ability to construct such increasingly complex mental meanings in plans for expression depends on the capacity of working memory.[34] The Principle of Discrepancy also assumes an increase in what can be represented in mental meanings and implies greater capacity. When mental meanings are discrepant, something more is represented than just what can be perceived. However, capacity is essentially limited, and this means that, for greater efficiency, developments are required as well in the notation system used for representation.

The *notation system* adults use for representations in consciousness is the subject of debate and speculation.[35] In fact, the study of development during the period in which language is acquired might shed light on whether the required notation systems are componential (a system of symbols and procedures for assembling them) or holistic (propositional or imagistic). At the least, we might expect that the ways mental content is encoded would differ before and after language is acquired. Before language, representations are more likely to be literal and holistic, tied as they are to the data of perception. With developments in conceptual categories, such literal representations become less parsimonious as the need increases for accessing more complex concepts and the networks of relations between them. Once language begins, lexical items and syntactic arrangements can point to elements and relations between them in mental meanings, leading to a more componential notation system. However, language will not be acquired in the first place unless a child possesses a notation system for representing mental meanings in consciousness and the procedures for connecting mental meanings to the units of language. Aside from invoking development of the symbolic capacity, we know very little about how notation systems develop. They obviously cannot be learned from the environment but must develop in connection with the acquisition of conceptual and linguistic categories.

In addition to developments in capacity and notational systems that make mental meanings possible, we also need to consider the path to and from the knowledge base. Setting up elements and the relations between them in a mental meaning requires that data from perception and memory be integrated. This ability to use perceptual data for accessing elements of memory is a developmental task. In addition to acquiring more knowledge about the world in memory, infants also develop in their ability to use more and different cues for retrieval and recall to access knowledge.

All these developments relate to how infants and young children are able to get information from the stimulus world around them and what they do with sensory information so as to make it usable for acting and for learning. Such cognitive activity depends on developments that contribute to the efficiency of the brain for handling data in working memory.[36] Still other aspects of cognitive development concerned with what an infant learns about persons, objects, and events in the world are needed as well. The result is that infants emerge at the end of the first year and begin to make the transition to language because of who they are and what they know.

CONCLUSIONS

If the study of language development is the study of capacities for acts of expression and interpretation, as is claimed here, then a theory of language development needs to address these capacities and the representations in the plans that they entail. To this end, we are in need of what Miller, Galanter, and Pribram called a "re-enactment" – for simulating the process of language development – in addition to our descriptions of the product that is acquired:

> Description is of course important. Even more, it is *essential* to science that we have accurate descriptions available. But there is another ingredient required, one that we

seem to forget and rediscover in every generation of psychologists, at least since Brentano's Act first competed with Wundt's Content. Life is more than a thing, an object, a substance that exists. It is also a process that is enacted. We have a choice in our approach to it. We can choose to describe it, or we can choose to re-enact it.[37]

We have many descriptions of children's language and changes in child language from one time to another. But language acquisition is a process that is enacted each time a child learns the system of expression available in a culture or society. If we are to reenact or model the *process,* we need a plan that closely resembles the child's. This plan will include the representations in intentional states underlying the acts of expression and interpretation for which language is learned. We have to understand, at least, the representations in mental meanings that a child is capable of creating, the data the child uses for these representations, and how mental meanings connect with the conventional meanings in the linguistic forms and structures provided by the language. In Chapter 3, the cognitive developments in infancy that help make that happen are reviewed in some detail. The child's plan will also include the social context in which language is embedded, and developments in infant expression and social connectedness are taken up in Chapter 4.

3

The Emergent Infant

The fundamental question in development is how a child comes to understand reality so as to be able to deal effectively in a world of persons, objects, and events. Language is a part of that reality, and this chapter is about the developing cognitive abilities in infancy that bring the infant to the threshold of language at the end of the first year. The emphasis here is on how an infant comes to know about the physical world – a world of objects. How infants learn about persons and a world of social connectedness will be taken up when we turn to development of the expressive infant, in Chapter 4.

Over the years, two important influences on my thinking about cognitive development in infancy have been Jean Piaget and J. J. Gibson. I am aware that their respective theories are not often juxtaposed in this way; in fact, the followers of each have more often used the other's theory as a starting point of disagreement. For example,

> Piaget has taught many psychologists to think of the development of the constancies [e.g., size, shape, color] as a *process of intellectual construction* [italics added]. . . . [But] since stimulation occurs over time, as well as over space, and has temporal as well as spatial structure, invariants are present in the stimulus transformations over time . . . [and] it is *pickup of these invariants that permits perception* [italics added] of the permanent properties of things.[1]

Gibson saw development in terms of learning to *perceive* the invariant properties of things. Piaget saw development as qualitative change in a child's *theories about* the properties. However, I have always been impressed with what is intuitively right about each and with what I see as a fundamental compatibility between them. Gibson was concerned with "the education of . . . attention to the subtleties of invariant stimulus information."[2] Piaget was concerned with the process of that education and changes in the developing mind of the infant that enabled it. Gibson's theory, then, is a theory of *perception*. Piaget's is a theory of *adaptation* and how children learn to use perception in their theories of objects and space for acting in the world.[3]

The major task of infancy is to become aware that the myriad sights and sounds that the baby sees and hears have a certain regularity and order. To that end, babies begin very early to attend to moving objects and salient noises. Gradually they begin to build memories of their perceptions, and these provide the background against which they attend to new objects that move and noises that appear. Eventually, they begin to discover that their bodies move and do things. Infants develop the capacities for learning language as they learn to see, hear, and do.

If we had to deal with and make discriminations among all the possible visual and auditory input from the environment at once, we would need too large a brain. Fortunately, our capacity for attention allows us to select certain aspects of experience and inhibit others.[4] Attention lets us give most of our cognitive resources to a manageable part of the input at any particular time. Over the generations, the organization of the nervous system has evolved so as to make certain stimuli in the environment more salient than others. Virtually from birth, infants attend selectively and orient to stimuli having pattern and movement. Infant attention guides cognitive development for the acquisition of knowledge, and the two are mutually informative: At the same time that attention determines what children learn from the environment, the accumulation of knowledge in memory influences and directs what they attend to.

In addition, infants enter a world in which persons, objects, and the kinds of things that ordinarily happen to persons and objects are essentially orderly and consistent. Events are neither random nor arbitrary. The nervous systems of even the simplest organisms are geared to detect and recognize the invariant and consistent aspects of events. Because events are essentially orderly and consistent, they are eventually predictable. A major achievement in development is for infants to learn to predict both the actions afforded by the properties of persons and objects and the consequences of those actions. This discrimination depends upon such factors as relevance, salience, and frequency: The more experience infants have, the more their attention is drawn to the consistencies around them.

Just how we represent information about regularities in the environment in memory is still an unanswered question and is a subject of intense research and theoretical activity in concepts and concept development. Questions of categorization and concept development have everything to do with language development, because conceptual structure provides the basis for acquiring word meanings and the semantic structure of language. However, much of this work has to do with children at least 4 years old, who already know language, with conceptual categories already embedded in the divergent and culturally relevant theories they have about the world.[5] Other work has been directed at the period of infancy, before language, with revisions to the classic positions regarding the relationship between concepts and infant thought.[6] Researchers are only beginning to ask the questions that would bridge the developments between these two points of time, and these are the questions that are particularly relevant for early word learning.

However, we do have a convergence in the literature from early child language and adult linguistic theory that bears on conceptual development in infancy. Many of the meanings of children's early sentences, at about age 2, have to do with movement and changes in location resulting from movement; movement and location have been invoked as well in explaining the conceptual basis for adult language.[7] Similarly, developing concepts of objects and relations between objects contribute to both word learning and the semantic organization of the adult lexicon. The foundation for the semantic structure of language, then, is in the theories of objects, movement, and location that begin to be formed in the first year of life. Categorization is pertinent to language development, in addition, because learning the forms of language depends on detecting other kinds of regularities that are specifically *linguistic:* regularities in the sounds, words, and sentences of the language children hear. Before they get to linguistic categories, however, two factors influence what infants learn about the world: movement and change.

MOVEMENT AND CHANGE

Certain things in the environment do not change.[8] The baby's crib, the room the crib is in, the house with the room with the crib – all provide relatively static backgrounds for perceiving change. Although these static backgrounds do not themselves change, infants are continually moved with respect to their backgrounds. They are picked up and put down, rocked, and carried about. In this way their own orientation changes in relation to the background. With these movements in space, they begin to form memories of the spatial context, but the objects in the context may not yet be perceived as independent from one another.

At the same time, objects also move and change in relation to the baby. Most obviously, persons come into and out of view, and their movements affect what the baby sees, hears, and feels. Other objects, in addition to persons, also have a dynamic quality: for example, feeding bottles and blankets. A blanket appears when the baby is put down to rest, and then it disappears when the baby is taken up for feeding and playing. The blanket is one of the first objects that the baby can feel and smell, and, moreover, its movements are integrated with the baby's own twisting, turning, trying to rise up, and so forth. The baby's crib is a static space that provides a background for salient objects that move. Moving objects are gradually discriminated in this way from their contexts and from one another.[9]

So children become aware of particular objects and their typical locations very early – before they begin to know any language at all. And when they begin to say words, their earliest words express something about objects that move.[10] Both conceptual categories and eventual linguistic categories build on an infant's nascent theories about objects, motion, space, and causality, and these theories originate in the early experiences that come about with movement and change in location.

This development culminates in what Piaget considered the principal achievement of cognitive development in infancy – when infants can think about and act on the basis of the representations of objects in a mental plan and are no longer limited to acting directly on the objects themselves. It is a gradual development in the first two years, beginning in the first few months of life. It is the development underlying the principles of Discrepancy and Elaboration for language, introduced in Chapter 2, as the mental meanings in an infant's beliefs, desires, and feelings come to include elements both remembered and anticipated.

A major result of infants' appreciation of the consequences of movement and change is the development of a theory of objects. Two sorts of knowledge make up a theory of objects. One is knowing about what is true for objects as a general class, or general object knowledge. The other is knowing what is true for individual categories of different kinds of objects, or object concepts. Each of these will be taken up in turn.

GENERAL OBJECT KNOWLEDGE

Just what an infant's theory of objects is and how it develops have been sources of disagreement and confusion. Two major perspectives are reviewed here. Both assume that the world is a systematic, relatively well-ordered place and that the infant has to come to understand how and why that is so. Both assume that movement and invariance in the face of change are important contributors to an infant's theories. Where they differ is in how they have conceptualized development and its function.

The first is the traditional Piagetian account of object permanence, which is the infant's appreciation of an object's continued existence in space and time even when it cannot be seen and acted upon. This is a theory about objects in general, and it develops in the course of the first year and a half of life in intimate connection with an infant's other developing theories about the world – theories of space, time, and causality in particular. For Piaget, this process of development is one of active construction, and its function is for the young child's *adaptation* to the world through action.

The second perspective is the more recent account of the physical knowledge which very young infants have about objects that guides their perception. This physical knowledge, too, is about objects in general as they are perceived in space and time. For Eleanor Gibson, the process is one of learning to pick up the invariant properties in the environment. More recently, Elizabeth Spelke described the process as an "enrichment" of the physical knowledge with which infants start out in life. In this view, the process involved is a more passive one, and its function is *perception*.

The traditional Piagetian account of object permanence is the one that has had the greatest influence on efforts to understand the developmental relationship between language and thought in infancy, as we shall see in Chapters 5 and 10. Both the hypotheses about the relationship and efforts to test them have centered on the descriptions Piaget provided of the steps in an infant's progress toward learning to search for hidden objects.

Traditional Object Permanence

In the early months of life, infants act as though an object that is out of sight is also out of mind: When an object is hidden from view, they do not look for it.[11] But sometime toward the end of the first six months they begin to understand that a whole object exists when they can see only a part of it, and they will try to retrieve the object by removing the cover that is partially concealing it. A baby still will not search for an object that has been completely hidden or follow a ball that rolls under a chair. But if part of the object can still be seen, the baby will go after it. At this point, we can infer that the baby sees the exposed part of the object as an indication that the whole object is there and can act to recover the part that is missing from view. Seeing part of the object is a cue for the baby to remember the whole object.

Piaget made these observations originally with his own children, but the behaviors he described have since been observed with many children and tested experimentally. Many studies have been done in the effort to determine just what the baby thinks happens when an object disappears from view and whether infants act as though they *know* the object continues to exist or act on some other basis. In one such study, T. G. R. Bower observed infants' reactions to objects that vanished behind a screen. He showed how infants would follow the path of a moving object with their eyes as the object disappeared. He also measured acceleration of heart rate as an indicator of either anticipation or surprise when the object reappeared from behind the screen. The conclusion from a series of such experiments was that infants as young as 2 to 4 months of age can track a moving object and anticipate its reappearance.[12]

However, even after the object had stopped moving and did not reappear from behind the screen, the infants in these experiments continued to move their heads as though they were still following the path of the moving object. Did this mean that they believed that an object that travels behind a screen and disappears is the same object as the one that reappears, or a different object? To answer this question, Bower replaced the object after it moved behind the screen with an entirely different object and observed that infants followed the path of movement even when it was a different object that appeared from behind the screen. However, though infants did not seem to notice or care that the object was changed, they did become disturbed when the path in which it moved changed. *Movement,* then, was the critical factor: either the movement of the object or the path of movement or the infant's head movement while following the object. Other features of the objects themselves were probably not taken into account by these 2- to 4-month-old infants. Holly Ruff has since shown how the effects of the motion of objects and the motion involved in the infant's own activity are critical to the development of object perception.[13]

After the first six to eight months, infants are able to find an object that has been entirely covered by a cloth or hidden behind an obstacle such as a pillow. Knowing to look for an object after watching it disappear requires an appreciation of the relationship between the object and the place where it was last seen. This object–place relationship is a strong one, and infants make a curious mistake. Even though they see the object moved again to a second place, they continue to look for it at the place where they first saw it disappear. Infants may be bound by their perception of the original place of hiding, or they may be guided by the success they experienced when the object was found originally at the first hiding place. However, failing to find the object at the original place of hiding, an infant will learn to look for the object in the place where it was hidden last (with a new appreciation that objects can be located in different places).[14]

After the first year, babies no longer make the mistake of searching for an object in the first place they saw it hidden or where they had just found it. As long as they see where an object disappears, they can search for it at that place. However, imagine that the infant sees an object disappear under one obstacle and then the object is moved to a second hiding place but this time without the infant's seeing it moved. Infants will look for the object under the first obstacle and, failing to find it, will not think to search for it under the second obstacle. In fact, they will often act as though it is lost. Piaget described this as a failure to take account of "invisible displacements." Although such tasks border on trickery, the fact is that eventually, by the middle of the second year or shortly after, most children are able to succeed in recovering objects after several of these invisible displacements. Even though they have not seen the object hidden or otherwise disappear in successive places, they will know to search for it and will persist in searching in different places.

When children are able to search for objects that are hidden, we know they can think about absent objects. This ability to think about absent objects and to act on the basis of those representations depends on the development of the symbolic capacity and, for Piaget, marks the culmination of development in the first 2 years. The infant's thinking "goes beyond the perceptual field, anticipating relations which are to be percieved subsequently and reconstructing those which have been perceived previously."[15] By the end of the second year, memory for an object's location in large-scale natural environments is well developed and provides the basis for the continued development of spatial memories in the preschool years and well into childhood.[16]

Infants' theories about objects, space, time, and causality evolve together throughout the period of infancy. Progress in one theory is integrated with progress in the others, and progress at one time is integral to progress at subsequent times. This means at least two things. One is that appreciation of the permanence of objects – that they exist in space and time – is constructed over time and is not something that "happens" at some point in the second year. Cognitive development consists of slow and progressive changes in how and what infants think about objects in relation to each other and in relation to themselves. For Piaget, a developmental achievement does not "arise as a new power, superimposed all of a sudden on completely prepared previous mechanisms, but is only the expression of these same mechanisms" at increasingly higher levels of adaptation.[17] This essential feature of Piagetian theory (and of constructivism more generally) is often overlooked, or at least not always well understood, perhaps because of the emphasis given by Piaget to stage-dependent descriptions of development and the false assumption that stages are discrete.

The second point is a corollary of the first point: Developments along the way are constitutive of object permanence. Each piece of understanding reached by the infant contributes to but does not itself consist of the full ability to think about objects removed in space and time and to mentally act on representations of objects in their absence. This is the sense of object knowledge that we, as adults, take for granted in a profound sense in our everyday lives. The fact that this object theory is basic to the thinking of 2-year-olds but not to the thinking of younger infants is the developmental discontinuity that distinguishes between them. Alison Gopnik pointed out that "asking whether or not the six-month-old has a concept of object-permanence in the same sense that the 18-month-old does is like asking whether or not the alchemist and the chemist have the same concept of gold, or whether Newton had the same concept of space as Einstein."[18]

Developments in the first year, then, along the way toward object permanence are part of its development and contribute to it but are not by themselves its ultimate achievement.[19] This fact has been overlooked in two very different lines of research. One is in efforts to measure the achievement of object permanence for comparison with developments in other domains, such as language (as discussed in Chapter 10). The other is in efforts to demonstrate that infants in the first half year of life have more sophisticated physical knowledge for a theory of objects than Piaget's theory would have us believe.

Early Physical Knowledge

In an elegant series of studies, Elizabeth Spelke and Renée Baillargeon have demonstrated that infants as young as 3 to 6 months old perceive an object as "cohesive" and "bounded" even when it moves behind another object.[20] Given a choice of looking at two different displays, an infant will prefer looking at one that is different or not consistent with one seen before. Using such preferential looking as an index of an infant's expectations, Spelke and Baillargeon have shown that infants behave in ways that indicate an understanding of an object's integrity even when part of the object cannot be seen or the object is hidden.

For example, in one such study, 4-month-olds watched as a rod moved behind a screen in such a way that both ends of the rod could still be seen at either side of the screen.[21] After they habituated to this first display and lost interest in it, they were shown two new displays, side by side. One showed only the two ends of the rod moving together, which is what they had actually seen of the rod at the two sides of the screen when the rod was moving behind it. The other display showed the whole, intact rod, which is what had presumably continued to exist as it moved behind the screen. The infants looked longer at the display with only the two ends of the rod moving together, meaning that they were more interested in it because they perceived it to be different from the original condition, to which they had habituated.

The fact that infants did not prefer looking at the whole rod was interpreted to mean that they perceived it to be the same object they had seen before – that when the rod moved behind the screen originally, they knew it was a continuous object even though all they could see of it was the two ends. From this experiment and a number of like experiments that carefully varied and controlled the properties of the objects and the direction of movement, Spelke concluded that object knowledge consists of "an early developing theory of the physical world . . . [that is] central" and already in place at the beginning of life rather than "constructed" over time, as Piagetian theory would have it.[22]

Subsequently, Spelke and her colleagues devised a series of experiments focusing on infants' sensitivity to the physical constraints on moving objects: continuity, solidity, gravity, and inertia.

> For these studies we have devised an invisible displacement task similar to that of Piaget ([1937] 1954). . . . Infants are shown an object that moves out of view behind a screen. Then the screen is raised, revealing the object at rest in either of two positions. One resting position is consistent with all physical constraints on object motion; the other

resting position is inconsistent with one or more constraints. . . . This method meets all of Piaget's requirements for revealing true physical knowledge. . . . [In particular,] it presents a situation that can only be understood by [the infant's] representing a hidden object and inferring its hidden motion. . . . This task can serve to investigate development of physical knowledge in infants too young to engage in object search.[23]

In one experiment, for example, a ball was dropped behind a screen, and infants were subsequently shown two different outcomes. In one, the ball came to rest on a shelf above the floor of the display, a condition in which two constraints were honored – the continuity of the ball moving behind the screen and the solidity of the surface of the shelf in the path of the falling ball. In the second outcome, the ball was shown resting on the floor of the display under the shelf, a condition that violated the solidity constraint. If infants appreciate that a falling object continues to move when it can no longer be seen and also that one object cannot move through another solid object, they should look longer at the second and surprising outcome, which they did.

The interpretation given to this result is that infants as young as $2\frac{1}{2}$ months are able to "represent the continued existence and the continued motion of the hidden object . . . [and] are sensitive to the relevant constraints on object motion."[24] However, whereas very young infants showed understanding of the two constraints of continuity and solidity, it was not until 6 months that infants began to show a tentative appreciation for the constraints of gravity and inertia. These results, taken together, led Spelke and her colleagues to conclude that there is "considerable invariance over cognitive development" and that the physical knowledge that is central to how adults view the world is present very early in infancy. But although appreciation of continuity and solidity "may derive from universal, early-developing capacities," knowledge of gravity and inertia depends on more experience with objects.

In all these experiments, infants demonstrated these abilities with respect to objects that *move.* In earlier demonstrations of young infants' behaviors with respect to objects, Bower had emphasized the role played by movement in the ability of 3-month-old infants to follow the path of an object that disappeared and then reappeared from behind a screen. He had concluded that an infant's tracking behaviors in following a moving object conferred a "temporary identity" on the whole object.[25] These demonstrations and the interpretation by Bower in effect confirmed Piaget's description of the beginnings of "practical object permanence" in the period of the first "acquired adaptations," between 1 and 4 months. However, in Piaget's terms, it is the infant's "action" that confers a "momentary conservation" on the object.[26]

Infant perception of the integrity of an object as it moves in space is central to the development that contributes to full object permanence, but it does not consist of that development. A theory of objects clearly begins very early in infancy, and experiments have shown its beginnings in perceptions of objects that move in relation to a physical field. They have surely shown that Piaget was wrong in claiming that an infant needs to create the movement by acting; the child can learn about objects from perceiving their movement. They have not, however, demonstrated an appreciation of the continued existence of the object independent of its motion or the places through and to which it moves.

Although the original interpretations (or perhaps overinterpretations) of infant behaviors in the preferential looking studies claimed evidence of object permanence much earlier in development than Piaget's theory would allow, recent interpretations are more in line with his original theory. In particular, Spelke has attributed infant abilities in apprehending objects to "an early developing *theory* of the physical world" and has suggested that development consists of "*theory enrichment*" rather than theory construction.[27] Whether and how processes of enrichment differ from processes of construction remain to be determined. For Piaget, "there are indeed complex structures or 'configurations' in the infant's sensori-motor intelligence, but far from being static and non-historical, they constitute 'schemata' which grow out of one another by means of successive differentiations and integrations. . . . [This is the reality] of genetic development and the process of construction that characterizes it."[28]

In sum, the expectations young infants have about moving objects are impressive. Piaget, however, may not have been surprised by the data. These early abilities in *perception* are very different from the eventual ability to "think about" absent objects and act on the basis of that representation – the hallmark of true object permanence. Perception is critical for this development, to be sure, but it was not Piaget's major concern. For him, the function of a theory of objects was the child's adaptation in interaction with the environment – adaptation requiring the active use of perceptual data, to be sure, and much else besides.

In a recent review, Graeme Halford reminds us that "it was because of the logical connection between object permanence and understanding of movements in space that Piaget investigated them in conjunction. . . . Concepts of the object, space, causality, and time were all considered together" in his infant books, most notably in *The Construction of Reality in the Child.*[29] Cognitive development is not reducible to change in separate and independent dimensions of thought. Instead, it is a systematic advance involving logically interrelated categories of thought. Advance in the one domain logically entails advance in the other. The development of object permanence is one of several developments that result in the construction of objective space and the child's theory about the world. "To do Piaget's theory justice, the development of thinking in the infant should be seen as the application of qualitatively different forms of thinking to the same content area (such as the movement or location of objects). This content area will always be a domain that has to be handled, at any point in life, but the *way* that it is handled will change developmentally."[30]

Behaviors like watching a moving object, looking for hidden objects, and grouping objects together are things a child can do with many different sorts of objects. Babies learn to watch, search for, and find things as different from one another as bouncing balls, nursing bottles, and kittens. This is, in part, why many aspects of development are universal across cultures.[31] The achievement of object permanence is one aspect of general object knowledge; still other aspects of a general theory of objects pertain to their locations relative to each other – objects can be placed alongside, inside, or on top of one another. Infants come to behave in similar ways with many kinds of different objects according to such expectations. But how they approach different objects and what they expect from their perceptions of and actions on particular objects depends as well on how they differentiate among objects and form object concepts.

PARTICULAR OBJECT KNOWLEDGE: OBJECT CONCEPTS

Certain objects and events recur with comforting frequency. A parent's face, a nursing bottle, a favorite blanket are a few of the most immediate objects that are experienced again and again. How does the baby come to know that an object is the same object when it reappears? And how does the baby come to know that an object that looks just like another is in fact a different object? The ability to evaluate the relationships among recurrent events is critical for processes of recognition and identification and for the eventual discovery of such regularities.[32] Two achievements in discovering the regularities in the environment are, first, the realization that an event – for example, the mother's face or a favorite blanket – is the same event when it recurs. The second is the realization that certain events are of the same kind – that they are equivalent and form a class. The propensity for categorization is assumed to be biologically determined and to begin to operate virtually at birth. But it nevertheless remains for experience and development to fill in the details of the categories.

Infants' categorizations before language consist of object concepts – information about the perceptual and functional features of different objects – and relational concepts – information about the ways in which different objects go together thematically. Knowing about objects and how objects go together begins in earliest infancy. When the baby sees an object again and again, information about its physical appearance is extracted to form a mental schema that will allow the object to be recognized as the same object when it is seen again, or another object to be recognized as an equivalent one. This "figurative knowledge" about the perceptual features of objects is distinguished from the "operative knowledge" of patterns of activity through which infants form mental schemes for acting with objects according to their functions.[33] The two are interdependent: Object schemas include functional as well as figurative data, whereas relational schemes for acting take the figurative properties of objects into account.

The baby starts out experiencing particular instances of a favorite blanket, a pet cat, a nursing bottle, or a Daddy.[34] Babies may remember information about individual objects in such a way that there are many Daddys, with each reappearance being another instance of a Daddy. More likely, however, the singular instances in their environments (mother, father, favorite blanket, bottle, pet cat) are a stronger influence on infants to believe at first that there is only one bottle or only one cat. Early on, then, certain objects like Mommy, Daddy, the pet cat, a favorite blanket, and the like are instances of classes with only one member, in the same way that the Empire State Building and the Queen of England are each a class with only one member. Eventually the infant learns that objects can be related to other instances of like objects to form categories according to the perceptual and functional features they share. Particular objects, such as Daddy or the pet cat, are also objects from different categories, persons and cats, each of which has many members. These categories of basic objects are, in turn, embraced in a superordinate category of animals or animate beings.

This kind of object knowledge is represented in concepts and networks of concepts in relation to each other in memory. Such terms as *concept, schema,* and *image* all imply the idea of "a central tendency analogous to a composite photograph."[35] Edward Sapir spoke of an object concept as an "average" of one's experiences with exemplars, and Piaget spoke of "summary images."[36] Knowing about an object, then, entails the summary mental record of the experiences a child has had with the perceptual and functional characteristics of like objects. Children's earliest categories are usually taken to be "basic-level" concepts of objects such as cats, trucks, and cookies in which instances within a concept are maximally similar to each other and dissimilar to instances in other categories. This level is more "basic" than the superordinate category level (for example, animals, vehicles, or foods) because members of a superordinate category (vehicles) are more dissimilar to each other than are members of the basic level (cars).[37]

Children's early categories may be most often for basic-level objects, but they also appreciate distinctions captured by superordinate and contextual groupings.[38] Infants at 16 months of age studied by Jean Mandler and her colleagues differentiated between basic-level categories when they came from different superordinate categories (e.g., dogs vs. cars) but not from the same superordinate class (e.g., dogs vs. horses). She suggested that at least some of the earliest categories may be more diffuse and global, such as the classification captured by the distinction between animate and inanimate things, than bounded by strictly perceptual and functional distinctions between objects. Although children may respond categorically to the class of animals, unless they also distinguish its subclasses of dogs and horses they have most likely represented a global category rather than a superordinate one.[39]

Roger Brown had pointed out that the principles of category formation may be similar for both adults and children, but the categories they form can be different, because children know far less about the physical, cultural, and social worlds in which objects play a part. They also pay attention to different attributes and functions of objects.[40] In line with this, Carolyn Mervis distinguished between child basic-level and adult basic-level categories: A round candle is a candle to an adult but can be a ball to the child.[41]

The structure of a category is highly dependent on the relationships within it as well as its connections to other categories in accordance with an individual's knowledge about the world. Douglas Medin and his colleagues suggested that similarity among exemplars is insufficient to explain the richness of conceptual structure and proposed that conceptual coherence depends on both the internal structure of a conceptual domain and how a concept relates to the rest of an individual's knowledge base. Concepts, then, are not the same for all individuals but are embedded in the naive theories people have about the world (such as their understanding of animacy, biology, reproduction, ingestion, locomotion, and the like)[42] as well as the large epistemological theories of objects, space, time, and causality that govern more local theories.

Whether and how things are considered to be similar for concept development can be highly dependent on a child's emerging theories and causal beliefs, and this has implications for word learning. Children of different ages (and in different cultural contexts, for that matter) may have the same "intuitive sense" about a concept (*uncle,* for example). But they may very well understand the concept and use the word for it in different ways because of how they construe the biological and psychological causal connections in their beliefs about kinship. Concepts consist of both a network of associative relations and sets of explanatory/causal beliefs. "The notion of concepts as being embedded in networks of associations and beliefs makes it clear that there is no simple one-to-one mapping between lexical items and corresponding items in concept structure."[43] Words are learned from the complicated interplay between their associations in circumstances of use and how a child's developing theories about the world influence the child's experiencing those circumstances.

Still other things enter into the complex relationship between words and concepts, such as the extent and ease with which they can be shared among persons and their informativeness. At the level of a society or culture, the extent to which concepts survive historically depends on how easily they can be explained and communicated, or their "sharability."[44] Conversely, the words that survive in a language are those that work best for expressing what a concept is about. And one reason why categories of basic-level objects are basic and survive in a culture is because they are most informative in allowing the maximum number of inferences and predicting individual instances.[45]

In sum, infants acquire a theory about objects in general that includes an understanding of what they have abstracted from their experiences with many different sorts of objects, such as the facts that objects generally appear in certain places, can be moved, disappear, and appear in other places. Objects are located relative to one another, and a large number of objects afford containment or support for the locations of other objects. Specific object concepts depend upon detecting the perceptual and functional regularities among instances of like objects, and this occurs in the mental context of other things a child may believe about the world. Both kinds of knowing – about the behaviors of objects in general and distinctions among particular objects – are acquired in the context of everyday events. Events in which children act and observe the effects of their own and others' acting on and with objects contribute as well to their developing theories of space, time, and causality. This means that a child also acquires concepts of *relationships* between objects and between persons and objects in the context of learning about particular objects and categories of like objects.

RELATIONAL CONCEPTS

The considerable literature on categorization and concept formation has been concerned, by and large, with concepts of objects. However, the objective world is a world of *affordances* based on the relationships in which objects belong and into which they can enter.[46] When children use words like *up, more,* and *gone,* we can infer that they know something about the relational concepts for such words.[47] But children show us, in many ways, that they know something about the ways persons relate to objects and objects relate to each other long before they use the words that express such relationships. Their earliest relational concepts are not learned through language. We know something about children's relational concepts, and we have some information about the kinds of activity between infants and their contexts in the first two years that contribute to an appreciation of how things go together thematically for the formation of relational concepts.

Children learn about relationships between objects by observing the effects of movement and actions done by themselves and other persons. In addition to such general effects of movement as disappearance, reappearance, relocation, containment, and support, more specific movements have more specific effects. When objects move, the movement has a source – frequently a person who acts to cause the movement – and an effect – either on the object itself or on another object. Objects that move include balls, bottles, cats, Mommy, Daddy, and so forth, and objects that typically do not move include sofas, bathtubs, refrigerators, and the like. Certain movements the child makes produce specific effects, such as rolling over, splashing, eating, and throwing. Still other movements by other persons have specific effects on the child, such as stroking, rocking, and swinging. Infants learn to detect and recognize the regularities among a movement, its origin, and its effect, just as they learn to detect the perceptual and functional consistencies among objects. Thus, concepts and relationships between things and between persons and things are embedded in an infant's emerging theories of objects, space, time, and causality – the epistemological theories that Piaget delineated for studying the development of thinking in infancy.

This essentially constructivist account of how the infant thinks about the physical and social world is the subject of some debate. For example, Alan Leslie and others have characterized the "mental architecture" of infant cognition differently, crediting infants with a very early knowledge of the physical world that is innately determined. In their view, infant cognition consists of a "variety of specific mechanisms" with an overall design that is the starting point for development rather than its outcome. Again using data from preferential looking studies, Leslie concluded that 6-month-olds understand causality when they perceive contingency between the submovements in an event (for example, when one moving object collides with and launches the movement of a second object).[48] Other research has also demonstrated infant attention to causal connections in simple events and the relative contribution to such effects from animate and inanimate objects.[49] However, other data have suggested that the perception of causal connections between two objects is developmental and the result of a "gradual stepwise construction . . . from 7 to 10 months of age."[50]

For Piaget, the essence of infant causality was in the relation between actions and their physical effects, both of which can be perceived. For example, the baby pulls a string and watches a toy move. These causal connections typically consist of perceptible means–end and consequence relations, and early causality is limited to the data of perception, to what is evident in the context. Later the baby is able to reconstruct a cause in the presence of an effect and, inversely, given an object, can foresee the effect of an action on the object. Eventually, children are capable of mentally representing a causal connection that is not given directly in the context.[51] The recent infancy research using preferential looking has provided evidence that infants have an appreciation of the causal connections between the movements of inanimate objects independent of their own actions and earlier than Piaget had believed. However, these appreciations are tied to the perception of moving objects. It remains to be shown whether infants can anticipate a consequence given a causal event or appreciate causal connections in a static array.

The relational concepts that result from the effects of movement, location, and causality begin to develop before language and contribute to providing the content of language as it develops in the early childhood years. They include such concepts as nonexistence, disappearance, and reappearance, which contribute to learning particular words (*gone* and *more,* for instance).[52] Other concepts, for instance, containment, support, agency, effectance, and the like[53] embrace a multitude of particular thematic relations between objects: pouring milk into and out of cups, putting hats on heads, eating with a spoon, sitting on a chair, and so forth. These thematic relations are, in turn, part of the everyday events with persons and objects that contribute to a child's knowledge base and eventually to the semantics of sentences.

CONCLUSIONS

The human infant is born to perceive, to interact, and to learn and is its own shaping force in development. Certain basic cognitive capacities that will eventually serve speech and language are already in place at birth, and others will evolve as the result of experience in the first year. The result is the emergence of an infant in the second year of life who is ready to begin to meet the conventional requirements of language – ready for the first words. This chapter has been concerned with learning about the objective world and developments in the infant's knowledge base that contribute to the representation of mental meanings that are potentially expressible in language. An infant's developing theories about the world and concepts in memory provide data for the construction of mental meanings for all of a child's intentional actions, including actions with language. We will return to the cognition required for language in Chapter 10, with the results of our studies of object play, which provided a window on the cognitive development of the children we studied in the period of early word learning in the second year.

The emergent infant is also an expressive infant. Cognitive developments bring the infant to the threshold of language only in conjunction with other developments in expression and social connectedness. We turn now to the social developments and developments in expression in the first year that occur at the same time as the infant is learning about objects, events, and relations in the world.

4

The Expressive Infant

In the first few hours of life, a human infant can tell the difference between its own mother's voice and a strange female voice.[1] An infant as young as 1 month old can hear the difference between categories of speech sounds, such as the difference between /p/ and /b/.[2] And from the moment of birth, infants display affect signals that their caregivers interpret as meaningful. We know, then, that certain basic capacities serving communication and language are already in place at the beginning of life. By the time language begins, in the second year, and the rudiments of speech sounds have only just begun to appear, the development of affect expression is well under way. Smiles, giggles, laughs, frowns, whines, and cries appear effortless and automatic at a time when emerging words are fragile, tentative, and inconsistent. The purpose of this chapter is to show how developments in expression and the social life of infants in the first year of life bring an infant to this threshold of language.

Two aspects of expression in infancy are particularly relevant for understanding the transition to language. The first is the *nature of the expression* itself: what it looks like, what it sounds like, and what it means. The second is the development of the *infant as a profoundly social being,* virtually from the beginning of life. The two major divisions in this chapter will deal with developments in expression and in the social life of the infant, respectively.[3]

THE NATURE OF INFANT EXPRESSION

In *The World of the Newborn,* Daphne and Charles Maurer tell us that

> a newborn baby may feel comfortable or uncomfortable at times, but . . . is born without emotions as we know them; . . . does not feel happy or sad; and . . . feels very

little pleasure or pain. Yet looking at a baby, it is difficult to believe this. When a baby cries, he looks miserable, and when he smiles, he glows.[4]

Two things about infant affect expressions are particularly noteworthy. One is the simple fact that they are so close to our own adult expressions. This, more than anything else, contributes to our identification with the baby as human. But, second, a baby's smiles and cries allow us to attribute something else to the baby, something more than just the smile or cry itself. We can attribute glowing or miserable, delight or distress, happy or angry. In short, the external and public expression we are seeing allows us to attribute something internal and private that the baby is feeling. And it is this attribution that we respond to when we respond to the baby.

The study of human emotions as we know it today began in the 19th century when Charles Darwin proposed several "principles of emotion." One of these principles was that strong excitement leads to an uncontrollable, involuntary desire for *movement* of some kind due to the need for "liberation" of "nerve force." A second principle was that certain of these movements are *expressive* actions if they regularly accompany "a certain frame of mind."[5] Such actions could be a movement of any part of the body: for example, shrugging the shoulders, hair standing on end, a dog wagging its tail, and the like. Because expressions are the external and public manifestations of something internal and private, an expression is a "license to attribute"[6] something more to the individual than just what is observed. For Darwin, affective expressions were a license to attribute such basic and discrete categories of emotion as anger, disgust, joy.

According to Darwin, the constellations of expressive movements that signal the different discrete emotions are the result of complex events in evolutionary history. An example is the "oblique eyebrows" and "knit brow" characteristic of the expression of grief. The expression of grief originated in something like the following evolutionary chain of events. When an infant screams because of hunger or pain, the circulation is affected, causing the eyes to become gorged with blood and the muscles around the eyes to contract strongly for protection (see Fig. 4.1, from Darwin). With the benefit of "advancing years and culture," the "habit of screaming" was repressed, but the muscles around the eyes still tend to contract whenever even slight distress is felt. Over the course of many generations, this action of the eye muscles became fixed, so that it became inherited. It is accompanied, however, by a

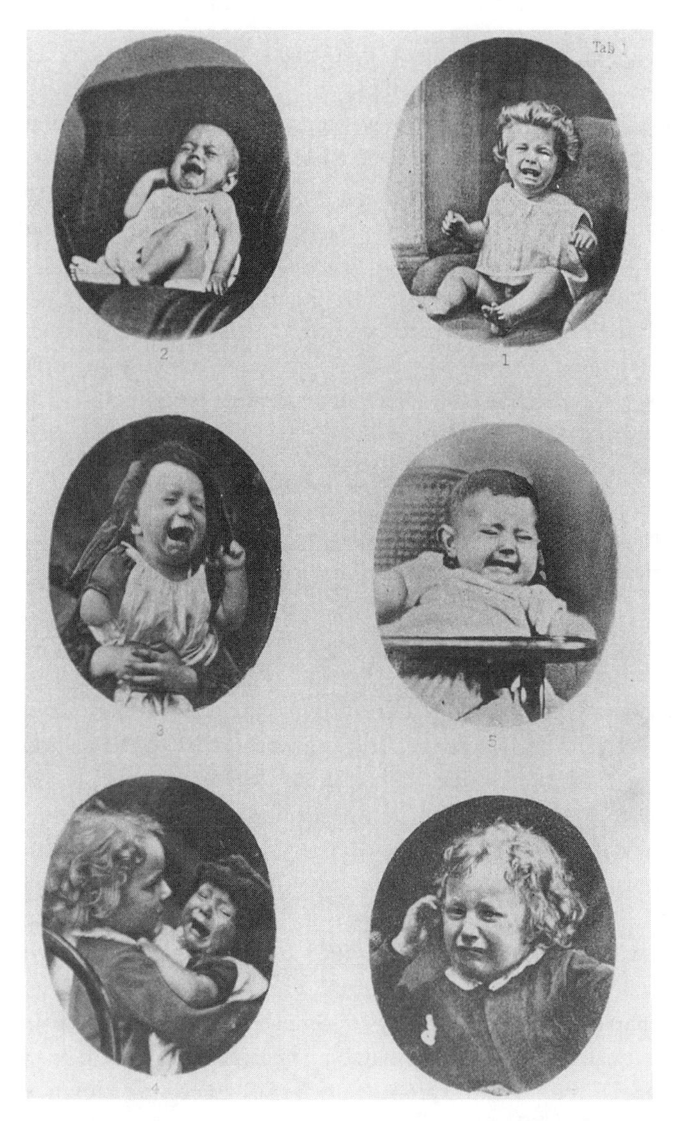

4.1 The effect on eye and brow movements of expressions of hunger and pain by infants and young children. (Darwin, 1892/1913, p. 178)

corresponding involuntary tendency to check these contractions: Darwin's principle of "antithesis," the habit of performing movements under opposing impulses. These opposing movements consist, in this case, of a contraction of the frontal muscles that produces the wrinkling of the forehead known as *knit brow* (see Fig. 4.2, from Darwin). Such slight movements as these in the adult expression of grief are the last remnants of the more primitive and more strongly marked facial movements of the screaming infant. But they are "as full of significance."[7]

For Darwin, and for researchers who have continued in this tradition of research into the "differential emotions," the expression is strongly identified with the emotion.[8] Since the expression is innate, the assumption has been that the emotions themselves are innate. Contemporary researchers have developed empirical systems for categorizing groupings of facial movements in order to capture these expressions and identify the emotions. One widely used system for coding discrete emotions from facial expressions is the "Maximally Discriminative Facial Movements," or MAX, coding system developed by Carroll Izard. The faces in Figure 4.3 are MAX examples of neutral expression (top) and expressions of pain and sadness, showing knit brow (bottom).[9]

An assumption in differential emotions theory is that the *experience* of the emotion (its feeling component) may be influenced by "patterned feedback" from the facial musculature. This means that the expression itself can contribute to the generation and regulation of the feeling state. With development, children learn to moderate these expressions in response to both socialization pressures and cultural norms. As a consequence, the expression is suppressed or "miniaturized." This suppression of the emotion with age is not, however, accompanied by a corresponding decrease in emotional feeling. Older children and adults who have the capacity for representation and mental imagery can simply imagine making a sad face, and this image can lead to feelings of sadness and depression. This means that the miniaturized and fleeting expression on the face can continue to provide the necessary feedback for the experience of the specific emotion that is expressed even though overt and public aspects of the expression are dampened because they may be socially unacceptable. Older children and adults do not have less emotional feeling than infants; rather, they express their emotions under constraints that are reponsive to social rules and cultural expectations.[10]

Two contributions in particular from differential emotions theory have

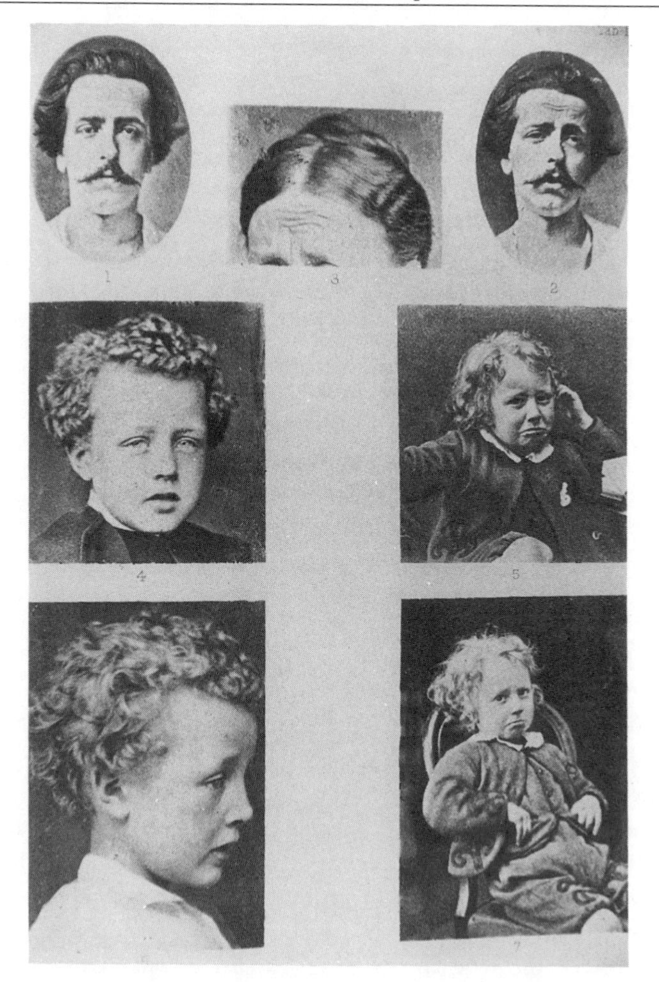

4.2 The "oblique eyebrows" and "knit brow" characteristic of expressions of grief. (Darwin, 1892/1913, p. 179)

strongly influenced research and theory in infant emotional development. One is the emphasis on the discrete emotions and their identification in infant expressions. The same core of differentiated affect, tied to particular relationships between events and goals, has been presumed to continue throughout the lifespan.[11] For example, with joy, a goal is achieved; with anger, a goal is obstructed; with sadness, a goal is lost.[12] The content of an individual's goals and obstructions to those goals in everyday life events change with

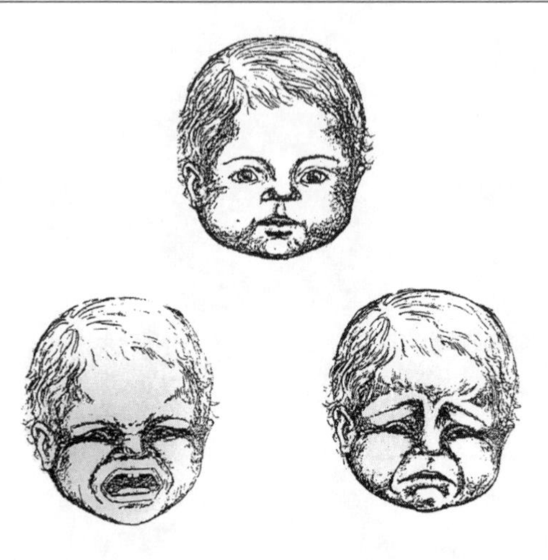

4.3 Neutral expression compared with knit brow in expression of pain (left) and sadness (right). (Izard, 1979a)

development – the goal of an infant might be to grasp a spoon; the goal of an adolescent might be to make a varsity team; the goal of an adult might be a job promotion; and so forth. But the discrete emotions – tied to different expressions and defined by the *relationships* between goals and events – do not change.

The second contribution is the emphasis on emotion as the "primary motivational system" that *regulates* human behavior throughout the lifespan. The "psychologically constructive functions" of emotions and the regulative function of emotional experience have now been widely embraced from several different theoretical perspectives. These are not necessarily tied to the discrete emotions or to differential emotions theory.[13] For example, the organizing and regulating function of emotion has been a major influence on theory and research in the attachment literature, including the work of Margaret Mahler and many others.[14] And Piaget described the relationship between affectivity and intelligence as a "functional" one: Affectivity plays "the role of an energy source on which the functioning but not the structures of intelligence . . . depend[,] . . . like gasoline, which activates the motor of an automobile but does not modify its structure."[15] A related development is the reciprocal regulation of affectivity and its expression.[16] The relationships between affect and other aspects of development are mutual,[17] and the influence that affect and language have on each other was one result of the studies discussed in Chapter 8.

Developments in Affect Expression

Darwin's suggestion that the expressive actions identified with the emotions are inherited and innate, and not learned from experience, called into question the role played by learning. The response came in the form of some rather startling experiments in the newly minted field of behaviorist psychology. In 1917, John Watson presented newborn and older infants with a variety of aversive stimili and situations and observed their "behavior responses" to determine which were innate and which were the result of conditioning events in the environment. Three emotions emerged in these studies as basic because they were elicited very early in life: love, fear, and rage. The other emotions were pronounced "learned" as a result of environmental conditioning. Reading about the experiments performed to demonstrate such learning, in those years before the rights of human subjects were taken into account, is an emotional experience in itself.[18]

The first warm light on the study of development of emotional expression in infancy was shed by Katharine Bridges in 1932. She studied the emotional expressions of 62 infants, from less than 1 month to over 24 months old, in the wards of the Montreal Foundling and Baby Hospital: "After observing the behavior of babies *under one month* of age, the writer felt more than ever convinced that the infant does not start life with 3 fully matured pattern reactions, such as have been mentioned by the behaviorists and named fear, rage, and love." She suggested, instead, that the emotions appear developmentally and are differentiated out of the originally "vague and undifferentiated emotion of excitement" that she observed before 1 month of age. The first two to be differentiated were "distress and delight" at 3 months. The emotions fear, disgust, and anger were differentiated from distress by 6 months, and elation and affection were differentiated from delight by 12 months.[19]

The problems with Bridges' research are obvious: the fact that the infants she studied were institutionalized "foundlings" and the necessarily subjective nature of her observations. Nevertheless, her observational research is noteworthy, first, because it was an alternative to the radical research of Watson. But more important, her proposal that emotions are differentiated out of the positive and negative affects of "distress" and "delight" anticipated an important contemporary question: whether early affective development consists of developments in categories of discrete emotions or developments in gradient properties, such as positive and negative emotional tone.[20]

Many studies have replicated Bridges' observations of differentiated distress and pleasure in the first 3 months of life. However, mothers do attribute discrete emotions to their infants in these early months. In cross-sectional and longitudinal studies, Robert Emde and his colleagues documented mothers' attibutions of the emotions interest, enjoyment, surprise, fear, anger, and distress to their babies. All the mothers in both studies identified interest and enjoyment by 3 months of age, and at least 65% of the mothers reported all the other emotions by 3 months as well.[21] Emotions have also been reliably identified in older infants, beginning at the end of the first year. These studies have typically used the attachment paradigm to rate infants' emotional responses in a well-defined situation in which the infant is observed during episodes of play, separation, and reunion with the mother, with and without a stranger present in the room. At least the emotions of fear, anger, sadness, and undifferentiated distress have been reported, along with interest and pleasure, and these are generally specific to the episodes of play, separation, and reunion in the attachment paradigm.[22]

In a recent longitudinal study of discrete emotional expressions in infancy, Carol Malatesta and her colleagues observed 58 infants in face-to-face interaction with their mothers in a laboratory playroom. They identified discrete categories of emotion expression in 14.58%, 13.07%, and 17.33% of the seconds that were coded in a 5-min episode of play at 2½, 5, and 7½ months, respectively, using Izard's MAX coding scheme.[23] They did not report the infants' expressions in the remaining 85% of the seconds in the episodes; these were presumably expressions of neutral affect. In addition to the emotions joy, interest, anger, sadness, and surprise, three other expressions were also identified in the Malatesta study: the knit brow (counted as a negative emotion), compressed lips, and lip biting. The three most frequent expressions of emotion, in order of frequency at each age, were knit brow, joy, interest at 2½ months; joy, knit brow, interest at 5 months; joy, interest, knit brow at 7½ months.

The MAX facial coding scheme used in this study is essentially *interpretive*, because it is tied to the categories of the discrete emotions. In contrast, the Facial Action Coding Scheme (FACS) developed by Ekman and Friesen and adapted for infants' faces by Harriet Oster is *descriptive,* because it identifies the minimal actions of the muscles of the face pretheoretically. Coding units are not categories of emotions. Instead, the mechanics of the actions of the facial muscles are captured by a set of neutral, anatomically defined elementary units. These include dynamic cues of direction of movement and changes in the appearance of facial features and contours. The obvious advantage of such a descriptive system is that it allows for alternative interpretations.[24]

Using the FACS coding system, Oster identified an interesting temporal relationship between brow knitting and smiling by two infant girls in the period from 3 to 11 weeks of age. The infants' smiles were frequently preceded by knit brow, and if the brows were knit before a smile, "they nearly always relaxed when the smile began and remained neutral throughout the smile." In interpreting these findings, Oster argued against the assumption that the knit brow always signifies negative affect (as Darwin had initially proposed and Malatesta et al. presumed). The knit brow observed immediately before smiling showed no signs of distress and did not resemble immediate precursors to crying or fussiness. Instead, Oster suggested that brow knitting and smiling reflect two distinct "states of mind" or psychological processes in the infant: "Brow knitting may reflect a special form of attention" that precedes a positive appraisal reflected in smiling.[25]

In this account, Oster provided a *process*-oriented interpretation of affective expression in infants. Affect displays can reflect specifically *cognitive* activity as well as underlying emotional feeling states. We can see this with adults in ordinary conversation and other everyday events. A particular emotional expression such as a knit brow or even a frown when one is trying to understand what someone else is saying has nothing to do with sadness or grief, for example. It is like shifting one's eyes away from the listener when thinking of a word while speaking.[26] Processes of attention and cognition were attributed to the emotions category of interest by Izard; however, Robert Wozniak questioned whether interest is even properly considered an emotion.[27] He pointed out that interest is fundamentally different from the other emotions. For example, interest is frequently sustained over time rather than transient; appears to have a different neurophysiological substrate; is under voluntary control; and is not tied to specifically adaptive actions or, indeed, necessarily tied to any action at all.

In sum, particular affect expressions (such as knit brow or expressions of interest) may or may not be expressions of emotion. Even when the baby *looks* angry or sad and caregivers and researchers reliably identify expressions of joy, anger, sadness, fear, and disgust, we can question whether these have the same meaning for the infant as they have for adults.[28] In fact, Michael Lewis and his colleagues suggested that infants' early facial expressions are actually at odds with their internal states. Citing the occurrence of the endogenous smile and early facial expressions of such emotions as contempt, they suggested that facial expressions may be relatively unrelated to internal states in the early months, because the infant is patently unable to experience the cognitive and social requirements for the analogous emotions as they are experienced by adults. Others have also questioned whether very young infants have the necessary cognitive skills for appraisal of the relations between goals and events.[29] The extent to which expressions correspond to internal states probably varies with the different emotions and their intensity. By about 6 months of age, however, emotional states are sufficiently differentiated and more accurately reflected in their corresponding expressions.[30]

An analogy in infant vocal behavior is instructive. Infants often *sound as if* they are asking a question or making a statement or an exclamation when they babble. Moreover, adult judges can reliably identify discrete question, exclamation, and statement contours in infants' babbling. Although these differences in intonation may have meaning for the baby, we know that young infants do not have an appreciation of the pragmatic and discourse constraints that govern acts of asking questions or making statements.[31] Infant affect expressions are no doubt *emotional* from the beginning, but the question is what the quality of the infant's emotional expression *means.*

Many researchers have questioned the extent to which affect is differentiated into discrete emotions at all, either for adults or for infants.[32] The more general dimensions of positive and negative affect may be more "basic," because they are more psychologically real for infants than discrete emotions. For this reason, many researchers have followed the path that Bridges originally illuminated and looked at developments in emotional expression as a process of differentiation, beginning with expressions of positive (pleasure) and negative (distress) affect.[33] Others have looked at the development of particular emotional behaviors, such as smiling, laughter, and crying.[34]

There is more to the baby's smile than happiness. Changes in facial expressions of 8-month-old infants, particularly smiles, occur at times of obvious shifts in attention.[35] And babies are more apt to smile when they have an audience: Smiling by 10 months of age indicates positive emotion, but positive feelings do not necessarily result in a smile unless someone is there to see it.[36] Clearly, infant facial expressions such as the two we have discussed, knit brow and smiling, have social and cognitive meanings as well as emotional meaning.

Arthur Jersild pointed out that "emotion is involved in the whole business of living"; takes many different forms; and involves a complex coordination of feeling, perception or awareness, impulse to action, and visceral and muscular activities. Further,

> the term emotion . . . covers conditions of both a "positive" and "negative" character, conditions in which the organism may be described as being eager, zestful, jubilant, and *moving toward,* as well as conditions in which it is disturbed, distressed, and *moving against* or *away.*[37]

The positive–negative polarity and other gradient dimensions of affect are central in the development of emotional expression. In fact, in the study of differentiated emotions in infancy by Malatesta and her colleagues, the main effects reported in their monograph were with aggregate categories of the positive and negative emotions and not with the individual emotion categories themselves.[38]

An important feature of expression in infancy is the prevalence of neutral affect. In the period from 9 to 21 months, the infants whom we studied were expressing neutral affect approximately 84% of the time (see Chapter 8). This is consistent with studies of somewhat older preschool children and younger infants as well, in whom emotional signals are typically separated by relatively long periods of neutral expression.[39] Neutral affect expression has its antecedents in the "quiet alert states" during which neonates and young infants attend to visual and auditory stimuli. These quiet alert states are generally considered to be the moments during which infants are perceiving and learning from objects and events in their environments.[40] Just as quiet alert states support the cognitive activity of the younger infant, neutral affect supports the cognition required by the older infant for the transition to language, as we shall see in Chapter 8.

Developments in Vocal Expression

Developments in prelinguistic vocalizations have been studied from two perspectives that are relevant to our concerns in this book. One is the study of vocalization associated with affective expression in the effort to determine whether different patterns of vocalization mean different things because they are associated with different feeling states. Other researchers have looked at the phonetic features in vocalization that anticipate the sounds of speech, describing the shape and form of the baby's vocalization. However, they have not been concerned with possible meaning or what the baby may be expressing, as have still other studies of the context of infant vocalizing (to be discussed subsequently).

The affective vocalizing of adults is less reliably associated with the particular feeling states and categories of the discrete emotions than are their facial expressions, for a variety of reasons.[41] We needn't be surprised, then, that studies that set out to catalog the features of vocal affect associated with the different emotions in infants' expressions have met with little success. Instead, infant vocal behaviors have been more successfully discriminated on the basis of their positive and negative hedonic tone.[42] Part of the reason may be that young infants perceive the vocal and facial features of other persons' emotional expression holistically, rather than componentially. For example, 5-month-old infants were more successful in discriminating happy, angry, and sad vocal expressions in a habituation task when given the facial expression as an added cue.[43]

As long ago as 1936, M. M. Lewis underscored the importance of affective tone in the speech infants hear: "From the outset, heard adult speech comes to the child steeped in affective quality. In the first month it soothes him; a month later it makes him smile."[44] One highly salient feature of adults' speech to babies is its melody, or intonational quality, and infants respond to speech based on intonation long before they respond to the words. An infant will actually respond in the same way to messages that have different words and meaning if the intonation contour is the same. "Conversations" with babies sound like conversation because infants are particularly sensitive to patterns of pitch contour (intonation) from an early age.[45] Ann Fernald pointed out that the message in the melody of adult speech to infants is a pragmatic one – prohibitions, affection, impatience, and the like – rather than informational. Moreover, the different melody contours for these pragmatic messages are essentially the same in talk babies hear from speakers of such widely different languages as Japanese, German, Italian, and English,[46] and infants hearing them respond similarly, even though much else about the sound patterns in these languages is very different.

Infants show development in how they respond to the vocalizations of others in the first year of life. Again, some of the most prescient observations are from the early work of M. M. Lewis, here citing a study by Charlotte Bühler in German. Infants begin to respond with positive affect at 2 months; at 3 months, they begin to match their own positive and negative responding to friendly and angry tones in the speech they hear; and at 6 months, they begin to respond with neutral expression to voices with either friendly or angry tones. Neutral affect expression increases until 10 months, at which time it is joined by a renewal of positive responding. This developmental sequence – in particular, the appearance and increase in neutral responding and "the *new* [italics added] positive responses" toward the end of the year – was attributed to new forms of "understanding."[47]

Lewis also reported a complementary sequence in the first year in the frequency with which infants vocalize in responding to the speech of others. Vocal responding is particularly high at 3–4 months but then decreases dramatically as infants begin to pay increasing attention to the speech they hear. Again, at about 10 months of age, infants increase in their own vocalizing in response to others' speech.[48] This sequence was confirmed in a study by Kiki Roe of 28 male infants from similar backgrounds. She reported a U-shaped curve with a decrease in "neutral talking" (vocal responding other than fussing, crying, or laughter) to a low point at 9 months before an increase again between 11 and 15 months. However, infants who were more or less developmentally precocious (according to the Gesell schedules) differed in when they showed the early peak in vocal responding; only the more precocious boys showed the peak Lewis had described at 3 months.[49]

Infant vocalizations accompany their own affect expressions more often than not; this is obviously true for crying and laughter. From birth, the newborn's cry begins to develop in complex ways as a function of physiological changes that take place in the vocal tract and developments in the capacity for articulatory–acoustic connections.[50] Different patterns of cry have been identified that correspond to different internal states. A baby's cry is typically prolonged and waxes and wanes, but discomfort cries, for example, are made up of short series of cry bursts. Virtually from birth, caregivers can attribute something of the baby's feelings and physiological states on the basis of the shape of the cry.[51] And vocalizations, especially cooing, regularly occur along with infant smiling by the third month of life.[52] The development of smiling and laughter from that point on is continually informed by the integrated cognitive and affective development of the infant and young child.[53] And the integration of the expressive behaviors of infants – affect expression, vocalizing, gaze, and hand movements – is influenced as well by other developments in their more general motor abilities.[54]

However, far more information about infant vocalization has come from phonological studies looking for the precursors of the sounds of speech and from more socially oriented studies looking for the origins of conversational exchange and intersubjectivity in the turn-taking patterns of infants and caregivers.

Origins of the Sounds of Speech

In English, the word *car* "stands for" the object car, and rising intonation signals a question, whereas falling intonation signals a statement. These are entirely arbitrary facts about the English language. In fact, other languages, notably Chinese, make different uses of intonation, just as they make use of different sound combinations for words that mean car. Connections like these between form and meaning evolve gradually in a language over time, because the members of a speech community need to agree upon them; they are conventional. But whereas the relation between sound and meaning is arbitrary and conventional, the forms of language themselves are not arbitrary. Instead, the forms of language are articulated and acoustic (in the case of spoken language) and manual and visual (in the case of sign language) because humans are remarkably facile at making and perceiving vocal sounds and hand gestures. The vocal mechanism and the ear transmit and receive sound, and the hands and the eyes transmit and receive gestures, because these are the most flexible parts of the human anatomy. Thus, we make use of the tongue, lips, ear, eyes, and hands for language because they are most easily adapted for the very rapid movements required for perceiving and producing speech and gesture.

We know from studies of infant perception and production of speech sounds and hand gestures that the nonarbitrary behaviors serving speech and sign languages are already available in early infancy before language. However, infants need to learn how these essentially nonarbitrary resources – the movements and sounds they make – can be used to serve the arbitrary sound-meaning (or gesture-meaning) connections of language. This is the case for the sounds and hand movements produced in infant babbling, the intonation contours of the baby's vocalizations, and the perception of speech sounds. With each, a certain degree of facility is present from a startlingly early age as infants show us they know something about the forms of language. Yet these same behaviors, or behaviors derived from them, do not begin to become functional and integrated with meaning content and the pragmatics of language use until much later, in the second year.[55]

A crying baby is already beginning to learn speech sounds, because the cries and other noises the baby makes during feeding and breathing evolve eventually into the complex sounds of speech:

> Most, if not all, of the articulatory features of speech are present in the earliest sounds of infants in a remarkably well-organized form. For example, the feature stop, produced at the glottis, initiates many cry segments and the feature bilabial place of articulation is present in the brief clicks of sucking. . . . These [articulatory] gestures, and the pattern of auditory and spectral features resulting from them, are not organized in a manner resembling speech. The features do not form bundles but simple and quite limited associations with one another in primitive segment types.[56]

With increasing neurophysiological and articulatory–acoustic maturation, subsequent development consists of organizing elements from these earliest sounds into the qualitatively different patterns of the sounds of speech.

The units of speech production consist of syllables, which are larger vocal-articulatory gestures than single phonemes. Their development depends upon maturation of the anatomy required for speech and maturation of the sensorimotor connections between audition and production systems.[57] Infant vocalizing can begin to assume the contours of syllables as early as 3 months of age, when infants are engaged in reciprocal and contingent verbal turntaking with an adult. These findings mean that 3-month-olds are able to adjust what they themselves "say" to the syllabic quality of what they hear an adult say. But this happens only when the adult vocalizes just after the baby does, so that some representation of the infant's own vocalizing presumably remains in attention.[58] The subcortical sensorimotor connections in such primitive articulatory "matching" afford a growing sensitivity to verbal input and an appreciation of the likenesses between the sounds the baby hears and the sounds the baby can make.

The beginning of the articulatory capabilities for actual words comes with the onset of babbling, sometime between 6 and 9 months, when infants develop the muscle control needed for coordinating a consonantlike sound with a vowel sound. In babbling, the baby's vocalizing has a clear syllabic form, consisting of a series of consonant–vowel combinations. Each of these syllables in a string of babbling may be the same, so that the babbling is reduplicated: for example, "dadadada," "nananana," "yayayaya." The consonants may be stops (like /d/), nasals (like /n/), or glides (like /y/). Adults now find it easier to imitate the baby, because both the timing of syllables and the sounds themselves increasingly resemble the rhythm and sounds of adult speech. A more mature form of babbling – called "nonreduplicated," "variegated," or "jargon" – sounds even more like conventional speech and had generally been thought to begin somewhat later.[59] Variegated babbling consists of strings of different syllables with combinations of different consonants and vowels that sound more and more like efforts to say words. However, recent research has established that although babbling increases over time in general, and multisyllabic babbling becomes more frequent in particular, both reduplicated and nonreduplicated patterns occur from the beginning of babbling at around 6–7 months of age.[60]

Deaf infants of deaf parents who use sign language also babble in the same age range, using manual movements that have the same consistent phonetic and syllabic patterning as is observed in hearing children's vocal babbling. These regularities in infant babbling across modalities led to the conclusion that "similarities in the time course, structure, and use of manual and vocal babbling suggest that there is a unitary language capacity that underlies human signed and spoken language acquisition."[61] Although the vocal modality is obviously central for speech, it is not privileged for the development of language. One wonders if development of manual babbling in deaf infants can be traced to the early hand positions and movements described in very young infants,[62] in the same way that vocal babbling has been traced to hearing infants' early cry, comfort, and feeding sounds.

Traditionally, the babbling of infants was thought to be unrelated to the sounds of speech.[63] However, this is not the case; babbling "exhibits many of the same preferences for certain kinds of phonetic elements and sequences" found in later meaningful speech.[64] The consensus now is that early words grow out of a small number of core sounds that the infant has favored in babbling. Moreover, the sounds that infants babble before speech help to determine the words they do or do not acquire subsequently. Babbling does not cease when words appear but provides the phonological context out of which the young language-learning child continues to extract the sounds for early words.[65] The pioneering work on early phonology by Charles Ferguson and his colleagues made clear that the contrastive unit in the child's first *linguistic* productions is the *word* and not the units of sound.[66]

Words in a language could have evolved to begin with according to whether or not they were within the learning capabilities of the young language-learning child. Early vocabularies are dominated by words that are among the most frequent and shortest words in the language. The fact that the sounds infants babble are the same sounds they use in their first words and, indeed, in the first several years of word learning may be due to two related things. First, frequent words in the language – the words that children also learn earliest – no doubt contain the most frequent sound patterns in the language. And second, the sound patterns that are most frequent may be those that are most consistent with the capacities of the developing acoustic–articulatory system. Words in a language that are relatively infrequent, longer, and learned later may also be words that contain the sounds that are underrepresented in early vocabularies (the fricatives, affricates, and liquids). We might expect that the "good enough" (to borrow from D. W. Winnicott) language tutor probably uses those words that are both consistent with infants' sound-making capacity and relevant to what infants attend to and therefore learn about in the environment.

In sum, both results – (1) that early words share the sound patterns of babbling and (2) that phonological selectivity influences which words children learn – are probably a function of the words in the language. And, in turn, the length and frequency of words in the language are probably responsive to the production capacities and constraints on the young language-learning child – including their capacities for speech perception.

Infant Speech Perception

Contemporary research in infant speech perception began in the early 1970s with a study by Peter Eimas and his colleagues that was startling when it first appeared but has since become a classic.[67] Infants as young as 1 month old were responsive to speech sounds and could discriminate between speech sounds. Moreover, they were perceiving speech sounds "categorically," in the same way as adults do – hearing the differences between two sound categories (/p/ and /b/) more reliably than the differences within a category ([p] and [p~]). The findings from this original study were subsequently replicated with other speech sounds, with infants from different language communities, and with other orienting responses. We now know, for example, that newborns are able to detect differences between vowel sounds when the measure of attention (orienting response) is heart rate deceleration.[68]

The basic conclusion has endured: Infants perceive the sounds of speech in much the same way as adults do, even though they have had relatively little exposure to speech and virtually no experience in producing these sounds themselves.[69] However, these constraints are not specifically linguistic; the infant's ability to perceive speech sounds is mediated by a general psychoacoustic mechanism. Not only human adults and infants but also other mammals – chinchillas, for example – perceive the sounds of speech categorically.[70] And categorical perception is not limited to the sounds of speech. If other mammals perceive speech sounds categorically, and sounds other than speech sounds are also perceived categorically, then categorical perception must be due in large part to the mammalian psychoacoustic mechanism.[71] The infant data tell us that the processing system must be operative shortly after birth, providing a form of perception that surely facilitates the acquisition of speech.[72]

The capacity for categorical perception is most probably a part of the innate biological makeup of the infant. In fact, the infant of any species comes into the world with "innate direction" to learn. In studying the acquisition of bird song by the white-crowned sparrow, Peter Marler observed an early stage of "subsong" that he compared to infant babbling. The white-crowned sparrow must hear the mature song in order to learn it, but the song must be conspecific – that is, the song of the bird's own species – and the bird must be exposed to the song during a "critical period" of infancy. Bird song develops, with these constraints, with reference to an "auditory template." The template directs the infant bird's attention in the direction of the criterial features of the conspecific song, but the infant must have the necessary exposure to the song in order to fill in the details. Both bird song and speech will develop in a process whereby infants (bird or human) match auditory signals they hear from others to their own "auditory templates." In this way, learning is not left to chance but "takes place within a set of constraints which seem designed to ensure that the learning bird's [and human infant's] attention shall be focused on a set of sounds that is biologically relevant." But the infant remains perceptually plastic so as to be modifiable as a result of perceptual experience.[73]

All the research demonstrating infant abilities to perceive speech sounds categorically has used synthetic, computer-generated speech stimuli. A great deal needs to happen, both maturationally and developmentally, for infants to be able to use the phonetic information from the actual speech they hear.[74] An infant 1 or 2 months old is a very wonderful but in many respects a very immature organism. Relatively little attention has been given to the *development* of speech perception in infancy. We do know that infants have come a long way by 6 months of age and have categorical perception for natural sound categories in real speech by that time. They know that a particular consonant is the same consonant when they hear it paired with different vowels and spoken by different male and female speakers.[75]

However, we still have the problem of connecting these early perceptions to the eventual production of speech sounds, and this perception–production connection has only barely been touched on in studies of speech perception and sound production in infancy. How are the categories of early infant speech perception related to the sounds in infants' own vocalization at the same time and to the speech sounds needed for words at a later time? For adults, articulatory movements and the auditory sounds of speech are integrated in a highly flexible system. Even in infancy, the individual sounds of speech are perceived intermodally, which means that the perception of speech is sensitive to recruitment from cues in the visual, tactile, and motor modalities. By 4–5 months, hearing infants respond preferentially to a speech sound with exploratory looking and rudimentary articulatory behaviors.[76] Perceptual and productive abilities are ultimately joined in an infant's discovery of how sound and meaning come together in words, but in ways we do not yet understand.[77]

In sum, neuromotor maturation in the first year has made it possible for the baby to organize and then reorganize elements from cries, coos, gurgles, and grunts into the tentative sounds and syllables of early speech. To learn a word is to learn a phonological shape, to be sure. But learning a word means many things besides that bear on cognitive, social, cultural, and linguistic matters. Cognitively, to learn a word is to learn how to express a mental meaning, something the infant has in mind that is directed to objects, events, and relations in the world. Socially, learning a word is learning how persons in a society make public what is otherwise private and internal to themselves so as to influence the thoughts, feelings, and actions of one another. Culturally, to learn a word is to learn something of the values that have evolved in a society for creating and sharing a world view.

Putting sound and meaning together isn't easy for infants. Fortunately, however, they don't have to do it alone. The important fact that infants *want to* make the sounds of speech and say words comes from the success of other persons who have nurtured the baby's mind as well as the baby's body and provided a context in which speech is personally and socially meaningful.

THE SOCIAL INFANT

An anonymous contributor to *New Yorker* magazine offered the following experience on suddenly becoming a father:

> Thirty minutes after her birth, my daughter was already taking my measure. She lay in my lap, startlingly alert, scanning me as I scanned her, our gazes moving about each other's bodies, limbs, faces, eyes – repeatedly returning to the eyes, returning and then locking. The same thing happened, I soon noticed, as she lay cradled in my wife's embrace, this locking of gaze into gaze. And it was only gradually that the wondrous mystery of that exchange began to impress me – for not even an hour ago my daughter's eyes had been sheathed in undifferentiated obscurity, and now what seemed most to capture their attention? Other sets of *eyes.* (Not noses, mouths, lights – *eyes!*) How could this be? Of all the possible objects of regard, what is so naturally compelling about two dark pools of returned attention? I could already imagine the scientific explanations.[78]

Scientific explanations indeed! We have seen a host of scientific studies, motivated by very similar observations in largely western cultures, and the data and conclusions are consistent: Social awareness begins virtually at birth to influence shared understanding between infant and parent, and this sharing begins by gazing into one another's eyes. In fact, when the eyes of an adult talking to a 3-month-old baby are hidden behind opaque glasses, the baby is much less likely to vocalize.[79] The "compelling" experience of eyes and mutual gaze between parent and infant is dramatically underscored in Selma Fraiberg's poignant description of the effects of blindness on early exchanges between parents and infants.[80]

The second factor contributing to the mutual social awareness between babies and adults is the timing of their interaction. The mutual and shifting gaze between parent and infant was originally described by Catherine Bateson as "proto-conversation."[81] The timing itself cannot be separated from the entire "social package" in which it is embedded – the rich array of visual, auditory, and kinesthetic information in a social display. This means that sensitivity to timing involves sensitivity to affective and cognitive information in the interaction as well. But regardless of its content or modality, the timing in an exchange says something about the relatedness between two partners.[82] The basic synchrony in the patterns of infant and parent alternately gazing at one another and looking away is actually a statistical analog of the rhythms of adult conversation.[83] Often parents and infants also vocalize in unison as they gaze at one another, and this mutual and simultaneous gazing and vocalizing create "quite special moments" between them.[84]

We have known for a long time now that an infant's vocalizing can be modified by a responding adult in a social situation. When an infant vocalizes and an adult vocalizes in turn, then the infant will be likely to vocalize again.[85] Moreover, this effect happens only when the response to the infant is a human voice; the same result is not obtained when other noises, like a bell ringing, are presented in response to the infant's vocalizing.[86] The original behaviorist interpretation of these results was that the adult's role was a reinforcing one: Babies vocalized more because their behavior was conditioned by the adult. However, we now know from the work of Kathleen Bloom that this is fundamentally incorrect. She compared 3-month-old infants vocalizing under conditions in which adults responded to them either contingently or noncontingently and found that the amount of infant vocalizing was the same in both conditions. She pointed out that the earlier operant conditioning interpretation failed to take account of infants as fundamentally social creatures. Vocalization with a socially responsive adult, whether contingent or random, *elicits* social responding from the baby. What changes in the two conditions is the patterning of infant vocalization. Infants who experience contingent responding are more likely to pause after the response, so that their interactions assume a basic property of turn taking.[87]

Thus, the sounds of infancy are functionally differentiated on the basis of social cues and other aspects of the context, even in the first few months of life.[88] Differences in the amount as well as the quality of infant vocalizing have been observed as a function of where the baby is – whether on the floor, in a tub, or on a lap, and whether an adult or a familiar object like a favorite blanket or a nursing bottle is around.[89] The rise–fall intonation contour of the baby's vocalizing, which increases in frequency in the first year, is more frequent when infants vocalize in "conversing" with their mothers than when they are alone, and more frequent when they vocalize in the presence of silent toys they can see and touch (stuffed animals, for instance) than with toys that also make noise (like rattles and keys).[90] Such sensitivity to context has been described as the beginnings of the relation between sound and meaning in language.[91]

However, these patterns of looking and vocalizing are not universal. Looking and vocalizing are two behaviors that are available to all infants from the beginning, and in western cultures mothers and fathers readily join in, creating the exchanges in which infants and adults look at each other and vocalize together or vocalize in alternation. But in nonwestern cultures, such as in New Guinea and Samoa, these patterns are rare.[92] In fact, gazing into the baby's eyes is often a taboo. Instead, infants are held by their mothers so that they face outward – away from them and toward other persons in the conscious effort by mothers to socialize their infants with other persons from a very early age. For example, Bambi Schieffelin observed Kaluli mothers in Papua New Guinea holding their babies up, facing outward to other persons, and vocalizing in a high-pitched voice to make believe that it was the baby who was "talking."[93] The fact that babies in nonwestern cultures acquire language at about the same time and rate would indicate that the early face-to-face interactions, with mutual gaze and vocalizing, observed in western cultures are not necessary for language. However, these patterns of gaze and vocalizing do indicate that the basic capacities for synchronized interactions in communication are in place virtually at birth, however differently caregivers in different cultures tap into them.

The threads of continuity from early prelinguistic communication to later communication with language can be found in different aspects of infants' social interactions.[94] One of the prevailing themes in this research has been the sharing of meaning between baby and caregiver – the "intersubjectivity" that develops between them.[95] This shared understanding between caregiver and baby in the first year of life has to do most often with infants' subjective feeling states. Parents adapt to and respond to the expressions and responses of their infants, and the infants, in turn, assimilate this subjectivity into their own patterns of communication. Intersubjectivity is expressed in different ways and makes use of different behaviors, but its hallmark is turn taking, as in the context of breast feeding and other social activities that entail synchronized looking, vocalizing, playing, and so forth.[96]

The development of shared understanding builds upon such joint activity between baby and caregiver. In turn, joint activity builds upon the baby's capacity to attend to both the caregiver and the activity: for example, to an object that both are playing with.[97] Very young infants attend almost exclusively to persons and not to objects until about 5 months of age, when their interest begins to shift to objects. Until about 10 months of age, the baby seems not to be able to attend to both a person and an object at the same time. This kind of joint attention – when the baby can attend to person and object together, looking to one and then to the other – has been described as "secondary intersubjectivity" and is a substantial achievement in the development of communication. When the baby glances from an object to caregiver and then back to the object again, the glance is interpreted by the caregiver as communicative.[98] Eventually, caregiver and baby are able to integrate more and more of their different behaviors – vocalization, gaze, and body movements – in "coactional" sequences. They move from an interactive context with shared affective meaning to a context for expressing meaning in speech. In doing so, they indicate their shared understanding in mutual attention to an object or event through their joint adjustments in posture, gaze, and head orientation toward one another.[99]

These interactions and fine adjustments in an infant's social interactions have been attributed to the infant's biological capacities for displaying primitive meanings, or to the mother's ability to recognize and attribute meaning to the infant's behaviors, or to some combination of the two.[100] In one view, the shared understandings between infant and caregiver originate in the meanings and interpretations that caregivers attribute to the baby's facial expressions, gestures, and vocalizations. The baby's early actions are interpreted and the baby is treated as a participant in the interaction from the start. In this view, it is the *caregiver* who creates intentions for, and shared understandings with, the infant.[101] An alternative view is that infants are born with capacities to act in different ways and mothers know how to respond to these. By 2 months of age, infants have the beginnings of an organized emotional system and are able to express their distress when caregiving behaviors are inconsistent with the expectations they have. In this view, it is the basic capacities of the *baby* that lead to and determine shared understanding.[102]

The subjective world of the infant is a deeply social one from the beginning; the infant is born to interact. This view of infancy, however, departs from traditional psychodynamic theories. When applied to development, psychoanalytic theories essentially work backwards from a pathology in older children and adults in order to understand what has gone wrong.[103] For example, Margaret Mahler's desire to understand such clinical conditions as childhood autism and overdependency led her to propose that such clinical phenomena exist, in some preliminary form, as a part of normal infant development. In her theory, all infants experience a normal period of autism, in which the infant is self-centered and "egg-like." This is followed by a period of normal symbiosis, in which the infant cannot distinguish self from other, before a phase of separation of self from other and individuation develops. These successive phases represent a restructuring of the infant id and ego.[104] According to Stern, the object-relations theorists (Melanie Klein and D. W. Winnicott, for example) focused on the infant's experience of self and other only as secondary to ego development. In contrast, he suggested that the nature of the infant's experience and sequences of development in infancy point to the development of a sense of self "not encumbered with or confused with issues of development of the ego or id."[105]

Others have also implicated the infant self in efforts to explain development. For example, development of the ability to experience basic, primary emotions has been linked to the beginning of self-awareness at the end of the first year. Younger infants are evidently in some sort of emotional state when they cry or laugh, but without self-awareness these emotional states do not count as emotional *experience.*[106] Specific developmental landmarks in attachment, cognition, and language have similarly been tied to the development of self in the first and second years.[107] However, Robert Emde emphasized the "self as process rather than as fixed attainment" in development and described the infant self as in a continuous state of becoming, from the very start of life.[108]

In D. Stern's theory, a sense of self is the primary organizing principle in development, but it is centered on a *sense of self and other* from the beginning; the infant is always differentiated from others and always part of a relationship. There is no autism, no symbiosis, no period of undifferentiation. From the beginning, the infant has a sense of "self being with other" in many different forms. He described a succession of emergences of new senses of self in the first 2 years. These do not replace one another; rather, each emerges in its time and continues to develop throughout life. Two organizing perspectives about the self and other have emerged by the time an infant reaches the second year. One is self and other sharing world knowledge gained through the personal experiences they have shared. The other is the ability to "objectify" this knowledge with the words of language that convey meanings for sharing and negotiations. This marks the emergence of the *verbal self.* Once the infant can create and share meanings, the possibilities for "interpersonal happenings" are "almost limitless."[109]

However, the question of what infants are expressing with their affect displays and vocalizations is not ordinarily asked, except in the assumption that affect displays express an infant's feeling states or the basic emotions. The development between affect expression and saying words receives little if any comment in the literature. However, we shall see in the second half of this book that children are learning to talk about those things they have feelings about. But the two forms of expression, affect and speech, do not come together easily when infants begin to say words. This is because expression through speech and expression of emotion both require cognitive effort and compete for the essentially limited resources of the young language-learning child. That is the developmental story in the second half of this book: the collaboration that develops among cognition, affect expression, and saying words in the period of transition from infancy to language.

CONCLUSIONS

Infant abilities and social contexts develop together in the first year. Infants show us in many ways that they are biologically prepared for expression; virtually from birth, they have capacities that serve emotional expression and expression through speech or manual signs for language. An infant's cry in the first hours of life is an expression of discomfort and dismay and at the same time contains the rudiments out of which the sounds of speech will develop. The ability to hear that categories of speech sounds are different, the tendency to gaze into another pair of eyes, the inclination to smile, and many other behaviors as well are there to begin with, awaiting the caring, comforting, and coaction of responsive and responsible other persons. Accounts of subsequent development in the first year differ greatly in whether they place an emphasis on social or biological influences, but all agree that both are crucial.[110] Hearing speech and seeing gestures, human infants cannot help exploiting their basic capacities to acquire the conventional forms of a language – if interpersonal and cognitive developments happening at the same time give them something to say and a reason to say it.

In these last two chapters, we have seen how developments in an infant's basic capacities in the first year anticipate the form, content, and use of language. Although they are originally separate capacities, they will begin to come together at the end of the first year in the effort to acquire words.[111] We turn now to an account of word learning in the second year that will finish setting the stage for the longitudinal study that is described in the second half of this book.

5

The Transition to Language

First words have been the subject of serious attention for more than 200 years, ever since a few scientists and other parents began to keep diaries of their babies' words in the 18th century.[1] We still study the classic diaries; researcher-parents continue to keep diaries; and researchers even train parents in how to keep diaries so they may study the early words of larger numbers of children. More objective observations of infants under controlled conditions also yield information about how children acquire a vocabulary of words in their second year. And now diary and observational studies are supplemented by experimental studies in which researchers teach words to 1- and 2-year-olds.

Two hundred years later, what do we know about First Words and the development of early vocabularies? Certain landmarks in the literature can point the way in answering that question. The summary chapters by Dorothea McCarthy in 1946 and 1954 are a good place to start. They provide a wealth of material from studies that had accumulated at each time. The study *Infant Speech* published by M. M. Lewis in 1936 is a source of many theoretical and empirical observations of early language that continue to reverberate in research today. The diary study that stands out for both the breadth of its coverage and the depth of its insights is in the four volumes published by Werner Leopold between 1939 and 1949. The contemporary scene began in 1973 with the publication of three studies, by myself, Eve Clark, and Katherine Nelson,[2] and flourished in the 1980s with the publication of at least 10 books on children's single-word speech.[3]

To begin an answer to the question "What do we know?" we can paint a fairly consistent picture with certain broad strokes that most researchers would agree on, at least those who have studied the emergence of language in western cultures. Just about every account of early language in the recent literature echoes a summary offered by Evelyn Dewey in 1935:

> The literature is in general agreement that the first sounds of the newborn infant are the overt elements from which speech develops, that vocalizations are used as a means of communication before words proper are used; that comprehension appears before the use of words; that the normal child has a repertoire of a very few words by one year of age, that development is slow in the first months of the second year, but that toward the end of that year a great increase in the speed of progress appears; . . . that [use of words] for specific meanings is a developmental process; . . . that the first words have the force of a phrase or sentence, and combinations of words do not begin for some time.[4]

Few would disagree with these "facts," and they seem to be repeated every time we write about the emergence of language. So what have we added that is new in the more than 50 years since? We can answer this question by taking apart Dewey's description. For example, we can pursue the subsequent literature on infant vocalizations and the emergence of speech sounds to see how "the first sounds of the newborn infant are the overt elements from which speech develops."[5] Or we can look at the literature that has accumulated to show how "vocalizations are used as a means of communication before words proper are used,"[6] and so forth.

Several pieces of Dewey's description are especially pertinent to the research in this book: that "development is slow in the first months of the second year," that "toward the end of that year a great increase in the speed of progress appears," and that the use of words "for specific meanings is a developmental process." First Words begin at about the first birthday, give or take a few months. First Words are tentative, imprecise, and fragile, and new words are acquired slowly in the several months after words begin to appear. Sometime toward the end of the second year, things pick up, and children begin to learn more and more different words, learn words more rapidly, and use their words more easily and readily. The words infants learn in the second year are guided by the perceptual attributes of the objects and actions they name, as Eve Clark pointed out. They are also learned in the context of actions and the functions of the objects they name, as Katherine Nelson pointed out. And, as I pointed out in *One Word at a Time,* development from the tentative and fragile First Words in the beginning of the period, to a Vocabulary Spurt and the emergence of multiword speech at the end of the period, depends on learning about objects and events *in general* and acquiring concepts of *particular* objects, events, and relations.

Studies of lexical development in the second year have since appealed to at least five theoretical perspectives in efforts to explain early word learning. One is the *social–pragmatic* focus that emphasizes the personal and instrumental functions of words as tools. Another is the focus on *reference* and the criteria for a word's use: both extensional criteria (the circumstances of context in which a word is applied) and intensional criteria (the conditions the child knows for applying a word). A third theoretical perspective emphasizes certain principles or *constraints* that guide word learning. The fourth theoretical focus is on the *cognitive* developments that contribute to lexical development and a fifth is the role of *affect* in the transition from prelinguistic vocalizations to conventional words.

The research in the second half of this book was motivated by the last two perspectives – the acquisition of words in relation to developments in cognition and affect expression. The purpose of this chapter is to finish laying the groundwork for the following chapters by reviewing what we already knew about the single-word period in development before we did that research.

In order to define the transition from infancy to language, we identified two achievements. One was a child's First Words, and the second was a sharp increase in number of words, a Vocabulary Spurt – or "great increase in the speed of progress," as Evelyn Dewey put it – toward the end of the second year. The consensus from most descriptions of early word learning is that these two achievements mark the beginning and end of the single-word period in development. However, they are not sharply defined boundaries with clear contours.[7] At the beginning of word learning, infants grope to control phonetic and acoustic cues as they seek to grasp the connections between what they hear and what they see and know. At some point a child is heard to say words that are somehow recognizable even though they may be incomplete, indistinct, and imprecise in meaning. Words are few and far between for a while, but the child eventually begins saying more different words and using these words more readily and more frequently. Soon after a spurt in vocabulary, many children tentatively begin to combine words for their first simple sentences.

What are the developments that contribute to these two achievements, First Words and a Vocabulary Spurt? Why does the child begin to say words in the first place, and what has to happen for the child to begin to learn and to use words more readily? These are the questions we addressed. This chapter provides an interpretation of existing accounts of word learning by children in the second year and explanations offered for First Words, the Vocabulary Spurt, and developments between the two.

EXPLAINING FIRST WORDS

The following discussion presumes that First Words have both relevance and a consistent form that make them recognizable by parents and interested others as conventional words in the language. Endowing an infant's vocalization with the status of *word* is a more serious business for the researcher than it is for the parent. Parents are allowed to overattribute, and in fact they and their infants may well enjoy and benefit from such attributions. But the researcher has the responsibility of transforming an infant's so-called words into *data* for one sort of analysis or another in order to obtain *evidence* for one or another conclusion, and so the importance of the criteria used cannot be minimized.[8] Such criteria draw on several aspects of an infant's vocal behavior, including its phonetic form, consistency, frequency, and relevance (or meaningfulness) to something going on in the situation. The two criteria most often recruited together are a phonetic shape and an aspect of relevance that share some resemblance to a conventional word in the language. Before this time, many children use forms that may be more or less phonetically consistent and "endowed with meaning" but do not have conventional shape and/or relevance.[9] Werner Leopold categorized such words as "non-standard" or "unconventional"; Michael Halliday called such forms "proto-language"; and John Dore called them "indexical expressions."

This discussion also presumes that similar developments underlie acquisition of both spoken and signed words by hearing and deaf children, respectively. In studies of the acquisition of signed words, some mothers of young deaf infants have reported conventional signs at a very early age, much earlier than is typically reported for words spoken by hearing children.[10] However, many of the hand movements that all young infants make have a counterpart in later gesture and mature sign languages, which raises the question of overinterpretation on the part of deaf parents asked to look for the occurrence of signs. In studies that used more controlled observations, differences in onset of spoken and signed words have been nil or negligible,[11] and children learning sign language do not show an age advantage for later aspects of language acquisition.[12] "Speech" is emphasized here and and in what follows, because our research was with hearing children.

Infants experience words (or signs) as one part of a complex event. When the child hears a word (and perhaps a larger speech unit like a phrase or sentence), the word is entered in memory along with other perceptual and personal data about its circumstances of use. The fundamental importance of this kind of associative learning has long been recognized in language studies: "For both the 1-year-old and the adult, the relationship between the word 'shoe' and the object it refers to is learned by association."[13] The data for these associations consist of the perceptual and functional contingencies experienced with the word. These can include an action, by the child or someone else, as well as an object in the context. The speech unit, then, is one element of an episode with other elements that include persons, objects, and actions and relationships. Virtually all developmental accounts of children's first words have noted the strong association between word and object, word and action, or word and event.[14]

The spoken word or phrase is not at first dissociable from the episode of its first encounter and enters into what in *One Word at a Time* I called a "word–image representation" in memory (similar to Schlesinger's "referent pairing" as the basis for learning early words).[15] These compounds of utterance and episode enter the memory system as a virtual fusion of form and content. Because of their linked storage, recalling the word is interdependent with recalling other aspects of the episode. Thus, when some aspect of the same or a similar episode reappears, these reencounters serve as perceptual cues for recalling the word/episode compound from memory. In sum, early words are strongly context-bound because the representation of the word in memory includes something of the circumstances of its experience. Saying the word is dependent upon reencounters with the same or similar circumstances.

The eliciting cues and conditions for recalling these early words are responsive to the child's own agenda and are not easily manipulated by others. Witness the frustration of parents when they try to show off their child's talk. For example, the coaxing "Gia, what does the butcher give you? The butcher, what does he give you when you visit him? Come on, you know, what does the butcher give you?" draws a blank in Gia's living room. But as soon as she enters the butcher shop Gia can say the word *bologna*. The perceptual cues in such reencounters are required for recalling a word in a word/episode compound; they will make it more likely that the child will use the word, because word and episode are stored together.

The child's capacity for recall and retrieval determines just how percepts and the elements accessed from memory fit together. Early words occur in the context of a close match between perceived and recalled content, as when a child looks at a clock and says "ticktock," holds out a cup and says "cup," or points to a stove and says "hot." These expressions of presentational, self-evident content are similar to the ostensive episodes in which children experience many words and their circumstances of use. The importance of ostensive naming has always figured in descriptions of early language learning, beginning with Saint Augustine's account in the fourth century of his own history of language acquisition:

> Passing hence from infancy, . . . I was no longer a speechless infant, but a speaking boy. . . . It was not that my elders taught me words . . . in any set method. . . . When they named any thing, and as they spoke turned towards it, I saw and remembered that they called what they would point out, by the name they uttered. And that they meant this thing and no other, was plain from the motion of their body, the natural language, as it were, of all nations, expressed by the countenance, glances of the eye, gestures of the limbs, and tones of the voice, indicating the affections of the mind, as it pursues, possesses, rejects, or shuns.[16]

The problem with ostensive naming as a general language-learning mechanism is that it would seem to apply only to learning the names for concrete objects. However, Richard Beckwith has shown how "naming ceremonies" in a child's early experience of language can extend to learning such "abstract" terms as emotion words and even the argument structure of verbs for syntax.[17] All ostensive learning depends upon the fact that the speaker and the listener have the same thing in mind. Thus, a child might form ostensive associations when seeing someone cry and hearing the word *sad.* Moreover, ostensive communication extends far beyond the paradigm case in child language of "pointing out." Sperber and Wilson underscored the pervasiveness of ostensive–inferential communicating through a glance, a shrug, a frown – much as Augustine described. What they called "coded communication," with language, does not occur without it.[18] For infants, ostensive–inferential communicaton is available long before language and is the context in which coded communication is acquired.

Constraints and Principles for Word Learning

An objection raised to the notion that children learn words in ostensive contexts is that a new, unknown word could potentially mean many things in the situation in which it is heard. How is it that a child ever knows that a word is a word in the first place, with a meaning that has something to do with a particular object? The single object that has played the lead-in role in attempts to answer this question is a fuzzy white rabbit. Added to the legendary rabbits of the world – including but not limited to such kinds of rabbits as have been given to us by Albrecht Dürer, John Updike, Harvey, and Beatrix Potter – we have the rabbit (also called "Gavagai") of the philosopher Willard van Orman Quine. This particularly linguistic rabbit was conceived by Quine for the purpose of discussing the problems inherent in efforts at translation from one language to another where there is not a "shared culture." This is the problem of

> *radical* translation, i.e., translation of the language of a hitherto untouched people. . . . The utterances first and most surely translated in such a case are ones keyed to present events that are conspicuous to the linguist and his informant. A rabbit scurries by, the native says "Gavagai," and the linguist notes down the sentence "Rabbit" (or "Lo, a rabbit").[19]

With the child cast once again as a "little linguist" (or "little anthropologist") and caregivers as the child's language informants, the dilemma is posed: How is the child to know that "rabbit" means the whole object and not some part of it (like an ear) or a quality (like fuzzy or white) or the action (like scurrying) of the rabbit? Quine's translation problem was a complex one, but the essential point is that the available data overdetermine the meaning of the word.[20] So many things present themselves to the young child when someone names an object that many have wondered how it is that the next time a rabbit scurries by, and maybe even a brown one at that, the child calls it a rabbit. How could the child have known what the word meant?

The answer has come in a recent spate of studies directed at the acquisition of word meanings, with the conclusion that from the beginning children are guided in their efforts to learn words by certain *principles of word learning.*[21] Different sorts of principles have been suggested, some quite general and some more specific. Some are pragmatic, others more linguistically driven, and some the product of still other aspects of cognitive and social development. The literature that has accrued contains many experimental accounts to prove or disprove one or another set of principles. Fortunately, there is no need to review that literature here, because others have ably done so.[22] However, two general aspects of this work deserve comment, because they appear to be undergoing important theoretical shifts. These are the issue of innateness and the fact that most lexical principles are directed at names for objects.

Among the earliest formulations of principles for word learning, the prevailing theme was that they took the form of biases or constraints that are biologically specified and therefore innate. Either the principles themselves or the ontological categories on which word meanings are based have been attributed to inborn cognitive and/or linguistic constraints that guide language learning "from the beginning." This view was, tacitly at least, a continuation of the innatist argument from syntactic theory – notably, Chomsky's observation that a child acquires the rules of a grammar despite the fact that rules are nowhere given in the input the child receives; certain grammatical principles, therefore, must be a part of an individual's biological endowment. However, for grammar, the argument for innateness is based on the notion of "poverty of the stimulus," or the fact that children do not experience in their everyday interactions what it is they must learn. In contrast, the problem for word learning is altogether different. Here a child is supposedly presented with too much information in the situation and needs to be guided in narrowing the range of options in order to know what is important for the meaning of a word. Principles for word learning have been invoked to provide that guidance.[23]

A strong challenge to assumptions about word-learning principles came from Katherine Nelson. She pointed out that children receive a great deal of guidance and support for word learning from a variety of sources. Chief among these are their own propensity to categorize objects and events, and helpful adults, who not only label objects and events but provide a whole lot more information about them besides:

> The typical way children acquire words in their first language is almost completely the reverse of the Quinean paradigm. Children do not try to guess what it is that the adult intends to refer to; rather, they have certain conceptions of those aspects of the world they find interesting and, in successful cases of word acquisition, it is the adult [at least in western middle-class societies] who guesses what the child is focused on and then supplies an appropriate word.[24]

This is, essentially, the Principle of Relevance. In the typical word-learning situation, infant and adult exploit their mutual signals of ostensive–inferential communication to share a focus of attention and the most likely candidate for what a word means. A child might well want to know the name of that part of the rabbit called "ear," and adults might well be naming a part or other feature (like calling it "white" or "fuzzy" or "cute" or "cuddly"). But the chances are that the intentional states of both child and adult will have been expressed ostensively, so that the target of translation is conspicuous. Words are learned when they are relevant to what a child has in mind: "Relevance is the single property that makes information worth processing and determines the particular assumptions an individual is most likely to construct and process."[25] Certainly children hear a good deal of talk that is not relevant to what they have in mind, but words that *are* relevant will be the words they learn.

The Principle of Relevance narrows the range of possible meanings any particular utterance could have and is one implication of a child's intentionality. Fauconnier put it this way with regard to sentences:

> The speaker-listener does not consider all the interpretations of a sentence and then discard the inappropriate ones. He sets up a space configuration [a mental meaning] starting from the configuration already available at that point in the discourse. There will of course be choices and strategies, but the potential of a sentence, given a previous configuration, is always far less than its general potential for all possible configurations. (*A brick could theoretically occupy any position in a wall, but at any stage of the actual building process, there is only one place for it to go* [italics added].)[26]

Thus, in the successful language-learning scenario, the word a child hears has relevance when its target is already part of what the child has in mind. Like Fauconnier's brick, the word could *theoretically* mean any of a number of things. But in enough situations in which the child hears it the options are already greatly diminished, and the word, like the brick, finds its target.

More recent claims have been decidedly muted with respect to innateness, with a growing consensus that principles are a product of development at the same time as they contribute to the process and guide word learning. This means that principles themselves have a developmental history; they are not static. They appear sequentially in time and can also change over time.[27] Correspondingly, principles for word learning have also been attributed to more general learning strategies rather than being specifically linguistic.[28]

The second point is that the prevailing emphasis in the literature so far is on how children learn names for objects. As a consequence, the constraints on learning words that have been offered are typically *object*-specific.[29] There are several reasons why. For one, object names are presumed to be the largest class of words in the language and in many early vocabularies as well. For another, they are relatively easy to study experimentally. However, we also know that children are learning different kinds of words – not just object names – and for some 1-year-olds, more than half the words they know are not object names.[30] This fact has begun to sink in, and more recent theorizing has attempted to stretch the principles so they are more generally applicable to whatever words a child needs to learn, including words that name actions and relations between objects.[31] For example, Ellen Markman has pointed out that her taxonomic constraint (the assumption that a word, like *cat,* names things of like kind, or only things that are cats) could apply to words that name categories other than objects, such as properties, substances, actions, and events. For example, a child would be expected to use the word *soft* for nonrigid substances only, whatever material an object is made of.[32]

Nevertheless, thus far in the literature, the principles that have been offered to explain early word learning have been largely object-specific, and the experiments to demonstrate the principles have to do with learning object names. Some of the most influential of these have come from the work of Markman and her colleagues in which they have explored the categories children form and the influence of words that label those categories.[33] They began with the common observation that very young children are extremely sensitive to the ways in which things from different categories typically go together. Young children appreciate the thematic relationships between such pairs of otherwise different objects as a dog and a leash, a shoe and a foot, a bird and a nest, and so forth. The principal evidence for such thematic relations has come from how children sort objects in experimental tasks. So, for example, given the three objects a dog, a cat, and a leash and asked which two go together, young children show a strong "thematic bias" in typically choosing the dog and the leash. The importance of thematic relations for the event representations in young children's memories has been stressed in several accounts of infant cognition.[34] And the study Karin Lifter and I did of how children learn to construct thematic relations in their play exploited the appreciations children acquire of how different objects go together.[35]

What is the role of language in how children judge things that go together? That was the question pursued by Markman and her colleagues. The two main tasks they presented to children were these. First, a child was shown pictures of two objects from the same taxonomic category (dog), such as a German shepherd and a poodle, along with a picture of some dog food as a thematically related object. In the first – "no word" – condition, one of the dogs was indicated, and the child was asked for "another one that is the same as this." Children typically chose the other dog only about half the time, which was not different from chance responding, and this was interpreted to mean that they retained the thematic bias (in choosing the dog food instead).

However, the situation changed when the child was given a novel label for one of the objects. When told that one of the dogs is a "sud" and asked to "find another *sud*," children typically chose the other dog. These and a succession of related findings were attributed to a "taxonomic constraint": "When children think they are learning a new word, they look for categorical relationships between objects and suppress the tendency to look for thematic relations." The problem is thereby simplified, because the taxonomic constraint limits "the number and kinds of hypotheses that children need to consider."[36] In other words, when children hear a new word, they believe that the word names an object and does not name any one of a large number of things that could be related to it.

I have chosen this one among a number of such principles attributed to young children's word learning because it has received so much attention in the literature.[37] In assuming that a child is biased to believe words are names for categories of objects, Markman asked: "Given that . . . thematic, eventlike organizations are a natural way of construing the world, why should languages force a taxonomic or categorical structure rather than capturing this thematic bias? Why don't we have single words for a boy and his bike, a baby and his bottle, a spider and its web?"[38]

In fact, however, languages do provide richly for naming thematic relations, and they do so with verbs and prepositions primarily. These syntactic categories occur with nouns to express thematic relations in sentences and begin to make their appearance in child speech toward the end of the second year. They also occur among single-word utterances – for example, the ubiquitous *up* and *down* in many early vocabularies. The important point is that an object can appear in many such thematic relationships: Consider all the possibilities for *boy* in addition to riding a bike: the boy eating a sandwich, climbing a tree, up in a tree, in bed, and so forth. Given well-known frequency and salience effects for the names of objects in the sentences children hear, it should not be surprising that they are picked out for learning. Verbs and prepositions are not so easily picked out.

Nevertheless, infants do indeed learn such words as *more, up, there,* and *gone,* which name relationships, and these relational words are among some 1-year-old children's most frequent words.[39] And, as we shall see in Chapter 9, they were the kinds of words that predominated in the vocabularies of the children we studied (see also discussion of the importance of relational concepts for word learning in Chapters 3 and 10). According to Markman, in order to learn relational words and verbs, a child would have to "override" the taxonomic and "whole-object" constraints.[40] However, associating *gone* with the disappearance of milk or *more* with the recurrence of milk in a glass is more likely the result of the same processes as contribute to associating *milk* with the liquid that disappears and reappears and gets poured, drunk, spilled, and the like. These would include, at least, frequency and salience effects in the input, focal awareness in intentional states, and a child's developing concepts in the knowledge base – things that contribute to the Principle of Relevance.

Another frequently invoked principle comes from the observation that if a word for an object is already known, a child is not likely to use another word to name it (as in an overextension). Words, then, are extended on the basis of contrasts between things.[41] Children are thought to act with the guiding principle that two different words ought to mean two different things; Markman named this the Mutual Exclusivity Principle, and Eve Clark called it the Principle of Contrast.[42] The two are not the same, as Markman points out: "Mutual exclusivity is one kind of contrast, but many terms that contrast in meaning are not mutually exclusive." For example, *dog* and *animal* are not mutually exclusive, but their meanings contrast, because the two words do not mean the same thing.[43]

However, the simpler explanation of the resistance children show to accepting a new name for an object that already has a name is the strength of the connections between word and object in memory. If an object already has a name to go by, then seeing the object would be likely to cue recall of that name – blocking the new name for the same object – and press the child to look around for something else that does not already have a name. Learning words is an associative task, and children give strong evidence that they are very good at making and remembering word associations. Perhaps the best example is "fast mapping." In the original fast-mapping experiment, children were asked by a teacher to "bring me the chromium tray, not the blue one," where *chromium* named olive green (a novel color) and was the default choice, since the children already knew the color blue.[44] Half the children remembered the novel word *chromium* a week later, which means they continued to associate the new word with the new color olive green – even though they had heard it only one time. Thus, reencountering something of the same or similar circumstances cued recall of the word originally experienced in those circumstances.

Markman's Taxonomic and Whole Object constraints were assumptions about the cognitive categories that figure in language learning. However, Mutual Exclusivity and Contrast, along with Clark's Conventionality Principle, differ in that they are essentially linguistic. (Clark called contrast and conventionality "general pragmatic principles" for word learning.)[45] They are linguistic assumptions because they come from the very definition of what languages are and what they do. First, if two things are different, then different words will ordinarily be required to talk about them *in relation to each other.* And if we need to talk about two equivalent things, two pencils for instance, then we will use other words to mark the differences between them and talk about the short pencil or the yellow pencil or the sharp one. Languages provide contrast in ways like these because of the abundance of similarity and potential ambiguity in the world. Second, unless folks agree on the ways in which words are assigned to meanings, which is what conventionality is, meaning cannot be shared among them. The Contrast and Conventionality principles apply in word learning simply because it is a language that is being learned; as principles for guiding language learning, they are, therefore, essentially circular. Rather than guiding acquisition, they describe the result of what it is that is being acquired; children acquire these two principles (at least) by virtue of their learning a language.

Another point is whether or not principles are dogmatic and meant to apply to all object names a child hears and is expected to learn. Those that are presented dogmatically have run into the most trouble in the form of being disconfirmed or being incapable of being disconfirmed or being too general or too specific, and so on. Roberta Golinkoff and her colleagues opted for a more parochial approach with "strategic principles [that] provide one of many possible routes into the word learning game." For example, the strategic assumption that a new word labels an object from an unnamed category is "analogous to a heuristic in problem-solving." It represents a child's first effort at a solution when encountering a word. Other solutions are also possible.[46]

Finally, are lexical principles truly explanatory or only descriptive of what children do (after the fact)? In our zeal to make sense of early word learning, we may have generated more theoretical machinery than is necessary. At the same time, several important things were left out of the questions asked to begin with and the principles that have been offered to answer the questions. Chief among these is the powerful part played by infants' attentional and discriminative capacities; the equally powerful part played by the environmental effects of salience and frequency; the healthy respect infants gain for the boundedness and salience of moving objects (as we saw in Chapter 3); the importance of relational concepts as well as object categories for infant cognition; the sensitivity and attributions of any "good enough" language tutor; the induction of the child into the culture, virtually from birth; and so forth. Quine's original translation problem was posed as a dilemma in the extreme case where there are *no* "hints available from interpreters,"[47] which is hardly the case for a young child. By the time language learning begins, *the culture the child is born into is no longer that of an "untouched people."* Child and native speaker have already spent a year or more getting in touch, and, as we saw in Chapter 4 especially, they are very adept at reading each other's ostensive signals. These are the capacities that come together to guide early word learning.

Underextensions and Overextensions

Because early words depend on recalling something from the circumstances of prior use, they can have personal and idiosyncratic extensions – what Susan Braunwald called "situated meanings"[48] – rather than conventional meanings as an adult would understand them.[49] A classic example is from the diary notes of Charles Darwin: A child said "qua-qua" to refer to both a duck and water after having first heard the word spoken when a duck was swimming. Heinz Werner in citing this example suggested that the child had not differentiated between the duck and the water on hearing the word originally, and so both were stored together with the word.[50] In hundreds of examples like this one in the literature, the tendency has been to take the child very seriously and to assume that the extensions of the word's use are an indication of what the child believes the word means.[51] Two kinds of idiosyncratic extensions have been identified as characteristic of early word learning: underextension and overextension.

In cases of *underextension,* a word is used in only one of several circumstances in which it has been experienced. A frequently cited example is the word *car* from *One Word at a Time:* Allison first said "car" only when she was sitting on a window ledge looking at cars on the street below; she never said "car" when she was riding in a car, playing with cars, looking at a car in a picture book, or even seeing cars as she walked along the street.[52] In the case of underextension, the association between a word and what is either the original or most frequent circumstance of its prior use is a strong one because of the relevance it had for the child originally. Thus, relevance in the original circumstances of use was responsible for the associative strength of the word's connections, temporarily blocking access to the word in different circumstances. Other experiences of cars did not cue recall of *car,* because the original experience of the word was so strongly associated with the context of looking at cars moving on the street below the window.

Such highly restricted use of early words has been observed repeatedly in studies of other children.[53] In a study of four children's first 10 words by Barrett and his colleagues, 22 of these first 40 words were "context-bound" in this way. To determine the role of input in these children's underextensions, their mothers' use of the same words was examined. The mothers of these children used only 6 of the 40 words in an "invariant manner," and for most of the words a mother's most frequent use of a word closely resembled her infant's use of that same word.[54] However, the direction of influence is uncertain, since mothers are influenced in their naming practices by their children's behaviors.[55]

The second kind of idiosyncratic extension is in the child's complexive use of words "on the basis of either or both figurative and functional features of the contexts in which they are perceived."[56] A number of complexive uses of words in which successive instances share at least one feature with a "central or 'nuclear' instance" were described by Bowerman in her daughters' speech. For example, Eva first said the word *moon* while looking at the moon and then subsequently extended *moon* when looking at a half grapefruit, a lemon slice, the circular chrome dial on the dishwasher, a crescent-shaped piece of yellow paper, pictures of yellow and green vegetables (squash and peas), and so forth. The central instance was most often the "*first* referent for which the word was used" and the one most frequently modeled in parent speech (presumably the moon in this example).[57] Such complexive overextensions are often reported in children's speech early on, but they appear throughout the single-word period.[58]

According to Bowerman and others, the idiosyncratic uses of words all relate to the meaning a word has for the child. However, these uses may not be instances of meaning so much as they are instances of recalling the relevant prior circumstances of use: for example, recalling the moon when seeing a half grapefruit. A reencounter with a perceptual and/or functional feature consistent with the original circumstances of use serves as a cue for accessing the original object or event from memory and the word associated with it. In each instance of *moon,* for example, Eva said "moon" because the object (grapefruit half, lemon slice, and so forth) served as a cue for both the word *moon* and the real moon she had seen when she first heard the word. I doubt she believed that all these different objects had the same name any more than she believed the grapefruit half and lemon slice were each a moon. In fact, this contention is consistent with the principles of Contrast and Mutual Exclusivity, offered by Eve Clark and Ellen Markman respectively, which are built on the assumption that children expect different objects to have different names. The explanation, however, works less well for later examples. For instance, the last entry in the list of overextensions of *moon* is a hangnail. Some 8 months after the original episode of *moon,* Eva said "my moon is off" after pulling off a hangnail, and Bowerman described this as a "routine usage" (1978, p. 266). The early instances are more moonlike than the later ones, and it is not as clear by this time that what she recalled to mind was in fact the original moon episode.

Unfortunately, we cannot evaluate the alternative interpretations without knowing about the input; Bowerman might have played the game and persisted in calling a hangnail a moon herself. One problem with the diary data Bowerman collected is that we have no record of the input her children received. We do not know, for example, if they were ever corrected for their "mistakes," which were the focus of their mother's diary study. Did Bowerman supply a better term in these instances? One would hope so. The overextensions she reported for the word *snow* lasted for a period of only 7 days, as opposed to the 8 months during which *moon* was overextended. "Snow" was first said when Christy Bowerman was playing with snow and was then extended to a white tail of a horse, a white part of a boat, a white bed pad, and milk spilled on the floor. Perhaps the relatively fast recovery from the overextension of *snow* was due to someone's supplying Christy with the word *white.*

The suggestion that overextension is really cued recall of the original circumstances of use does not require that all the child's uses of words are idiosyncratic. We know that in many, if not most, instances another object from the same category of objects cues recall, and the child extension overlaps with adult extension. One possibility is that children's extensions are determined by the relative frequency with which they encounter different exemplars from a category. Many complexive overextensions seem to occur with objects that are unique or encountered relatively infrequently (like the moon and snow, respectively). Overlapping (partially "correct") extension seems to occur with more common, basic-level objects. As long ago as 1897 James Sully pointed out that "children are driven by the slenderness of their verbal resources to 'extend' the names they learn."[59] I suggested in *One Word at a Time* that many overextensions occur in situations where the child has not yet acquired a better word to use, like seeing a horse in a field and calling it a dog. "It is almost as if the child were reasoning, 'I know about dogs, that thing is not a dog, I don't know what to call it, but it is like a dog!'"[60]

In sum, if such under- and overextension really consists only of cued recall, we have been taking children's so-called reference with early words too seriously. In the example from Darwin, seeing the water cued recall of the duck (Werner did suggest that the two were stored together in memory), just as Eva's seeing a half lemon slice cued recall of the moon. To cite one of the most familiar instances in the literature, the child who says "Daddy" on seeing a man who is not Daddy could have recalled the real Daddy to mind. Saying "Daddy" would then be an expression of a mental meaning with a representation of the child's Daddy. The child was not calling the stranger "Daddy." Neither did the child really believe that *Daddy* is a name to use for all large male persons in jeans or a business suit. Similarly, when hearing the telephone ring cues recall of Daddy's voice on the phone, the child saying "Daddy" is not naming the telephone a *Daddy*. Seeing another man or hearing the telephone ring cued recall of the real Daddy in a mental meaning for the child's expression.

Nonetheless, such events are important, although for a reason different from the one ordinarily offered: that they indicate the meaning the word has for the child. In most of these situations, a "good enough" language tutor (mother, father, big brother, caregiver) will provide an alternative for the child: for example, "That's a *window*," "That's a *hangnail*," "That's a *man*," or "Daddy's on the *telephone*." In this way, the child has another word-object pair to store away waiting to be called up in future encounters with the same or similar objects and events.

DEVELOPMENT FROM FIRST WORDS TO VOCABULARY SPURT

The most frequent description of development in the single-word period ordinarily invokes the notion of decontextualization to explain how children come to use their words in more diverse contexts.[61] Development from First Words to a Vocabulary Spurt corresponds to Piaget's classic description of development from sensorimotor to symbolic representation. Piaget made the distinction between indices or signals that are a *part of the thing expressed,* on the one hand, and personal and individualized symbols and social signs, that make their appearance in speech, on the other hand.[62] The study by Elizabeth Bates and her colleagues, *The Emergence of Symbols,* built on this distinction and documented its development.

Many studies have now converged on the broad strokes of development from First Words to Vocabulary Spurt. Children begin by associating a word with an episode; words become associated with more or less generalized concepts of objects and events; and, at the end of the period, words become associated with one another. Development proceeds, then, from episodic associations to conceptual associations to the beginning of a semantic (linguistic) system.[63]

The details of this development have been worked out differently by different investigators, but the fundamental architecture of the period is basically the same in most accounts: from episodes to concepts to a semantic system for word meaning. The point is that development in the period is largely conceptual, and the acquisition of true word meanings probably doesn't begin until near the end of the single-word period, at which time it is marked by a vocabulary spurt. The sequence is empirically as well as logically invariant. However, manifestations of development could be influenced by individual differences in the maturation of acoustic–articulatory connections for actually saying words. Some children might not be ready to say words at the time they begin to form word–episode associations in memory, and their first words could come later in the period, after words are associated with better defined concepts. However, it is important to keep in mind that attaching a word to a concept does not wait for the concept to be fully defined. Concepts have their beginnings in earliest infancy, as we saw in Chapter 4. Words emerge in the second year as concepts continue to evolve, and each influences development of the other.[64]

Two things no doubt contribute to freeing words from the earliest experiences with which they were stored initially. For one thing, the same word is heard in different circumstances, and for another, more different words are heard in the same or similar circumstances. Both kinds of experience contribute to loosening the original compound so that word and episode become less closely bound. At the same time, children form concepts of objects by abstracting regularities from events, as described by Nelson, for example, or form prototypic representations based on their experiences with holistic, contextualized exemplars, as described by Kuczaj.[65] Their words come to be associated with these more generalized conceptual representations rather than with specific instances.[66] This development – the abstraction of words from the utterance–episode compounds in which they were stored – results in associating words with new episodes and with other words. Of course certain words will remain closely connected to particular experiences, as, for instance, hearing a certain sonata invariably cues recall of the word *Mozart*. The association of word and episode is now a complex, however, inasmuch as the elements are separable in a way that the elements in the early compounds were not.

The changes that occur with development from *episode* to *concepts* to *semantics* are in the cues a child can use for recalling a word from memory. With the earliest words – which are fragile, tenuous, and often characterized by underextension – recall depends upon reencounters with the episode with which the word was originally associated, or one just like it. With the formation of concepts, different instances and even entirely new instances of an object, event, or relation can cue recall. This happens even as a concept is being learned. A classic example, the word *fafa* (flower), observed originally by M. M. Lewis in his son's development, was described by Roger Brown as follows:

Somehow the recurrent word *flowers* . . . serves to attract relevant experiences, to sum them over time into a conception governing the use of the word. . . . The second named instance of flowers, at the age of sixteen months and thirteen days, is the same as the first. Both are yellow jonquils growing in a bowl and so recognition requires only that the child have the conception of an enduring object. At this point *flowers* is the name of an "identity category." With the next instance the reference becomes an equivalence category. The flowers are of a new species and a different color but still in a bowl. At age 17:24 an immense abstraction is called for. The flowers are pictures in a book, lacking odor, texture and tridimensionality. . . . At the end of the record [at

22:26] . . . he is correctly labeling embroidered flowers and sugar flowers on a biscuit.[67]

Once a number of words have been acquired in this way, words themselves can be cues for recall, both taxonomically for objects, events, or relations within the same category, and thematically for objects, events, or relations from different categories, as happens when children say successive single-word utterances.[68] Only when words begin to cue recall of other words can we speak of the child's acquisition of word meanings and the beginning of the development of *semantics.* This development is crucial, because semantics is specifically a *linguistic* system, having to do with arbitrary and conventional units and the formal and functional relations among them.

The result in the child's speech is typically an increase in both the number of words and the frequency of use of individual words – a vocabulary spurt sometime toward the end of the second year. The notion of decontextualization describes this development but does not explain it. Explanation can rather be found in developments in the child's knowledge and in the kinds of cues that the child can use for ways into and out of that knowledge base stored in memory. It is not that the child's words occur with less dependence on the context (or relevant "action schemas" and the like); context is always, and necessarily, a factor in language use. Instead, developments occur in the different cues in the context the child can use for retrieving and saying words.

Early words depend for their retrieval and recall on perceptible objects and well-known actions and events. Younger children understand more words than they say and can even be taught to recognize novel labels for novel objects[69] because the cues they are given in an experimental comprehension task are episodic and perceptible. In effect, they perform a "fast mapping" that allows them to recognize the novel word relatively easily by recalling the episodic cue with which it was associated on presentation. Fast mapping in comprehension tasks has generally been used to explain the relative ease with which children seem to acquire new word meanings,[70] but it is, in effect, a demonstration of cued recall. Words are recognized when recall depends on accessing the episode on which a word was originally mapped. Hearing a word is a very narrow cue for accessing the relevant episode experienced with it (and taken to be its "meaning").

But when it is the word that needs to be recalled, as in a production task, the object or event that is given in the context is a less discriminating cue, because it may be associated with other words in memory as well.[71] Even a novel word in such tasks, however salient it may be, is necessarily embedded in a context with other words when it is presented. As a result, words are more difficult to recall. For example, fast mapping is more difficult to demonstrate for saying words,[72] and it is also notoriously difficult to teach 1-year-old children to say new words.[73]

The relevant developments in the single-word period, leading to the vocabulary spurt, are in the cues children can use for accessing the words they have stored in memory. These cues become less episodic and increasingly farther removed from the original experience of the word, and can include other words as well. The ability to use more diverse cues for recall depends on several things. One is developments in knowledge, particularly development in conceptual representations of objects, events and relations. Another is development of the symbolic capacity – for representing perceptual data in relation to information recalled from memory in intentional states.

This distinction – between knowledge, which is represented in memory and is timeless, and the time-bound representations in intentional states – was the starting point for the theoretical perspective in our research.[74] Robin Campbell made essentially the same distinction, in different terms, and wrote of that domain of thought (intentionality) in which "*ad hoc* links [are] established between perception, information, and action."[75] Similarly, the cognitive activity for intentional states is captured in Fauconnier's mental spaces, Jonhson-Laird's mental models, and the like. The developments that contribute to representations in intentional states are tied to development of the symbolic capacity (and are essentially Piagetian in that regard). These representations, in turn, feed and are responsible for acquiring knowledge about objects and events. Two results of this process, in the case of word learning, are establishing the "relationship between word and world" and establishing "a relationship between words."[76] Developments in both word-to-world and word-to-word relationships lead to the vocabulary spurt and the culmination of the single-word period in development.

EXPLAINING THE VOCABULARY SPURT

A vocabulary spurt in early language learning has been reported in the development of individual children at least since the classic diary study of

Clara and William Stern.[77] It is a sharp increase in the number of new words toward the last half of the second year and, as such, is a discontinuity in development. The important question is whether this quantitative discontinuity actually corresponds to qualitative changes in development.[78] Several qualitative developments have been offered as candidate explanations, and these are, alternatively, *cognitive, pragmatic,* or *linguistic.* Ultimately the truth will be found in an amalgam of these three.

Cognitive Explanations

The original suggestion, in *One Word at a Time,* was that one could not know the name for an object unless one also knew about objects: that they exist, are acted upon, and relate to one another and to themselves in more or less consistent ways. Similarly, one cannot know that different objects have different names unless one also knows that the objects themselves are different. Developments in both general object knowledge (i.e., object permanence) and concepts of particular objects and events contribute to the sharp increase in learning words that is the vocabulary spurt. Katherine Nelson has attributed the vocabulary spurt to a shift in the basis of object naming from "perceptual paradigms or contextualized situations" to "concepts of objects and actions" in the second half of the second year.[79] These issues are the focus of Chapter 10, and the relevant literature has been reviewed elsewhere.[80] For the purpose of this chapter, I will only point to a few studies that have underscored the importance of developments in cognition for achieving a vocabulary spurt.

A vocabulary spurt is itself only one of several developments that have been cited as evidence of major cognitive changes at the end of the second year.[81] The evidence from a number of sources points to qualitative differences in an infant's capacity for thought that are responsible for the quantitative change captured by a vocabulary spurt. Both developments in object permanence and developments in the ability to sort objects into categories (necessary for forming concepts) have been shown to be related to a vocabulary spurt.[82] The developmental relationship between word learning and object concepts was demonstrated in Joan Lucariello's study of concept formation and word learning by beginner and advanced infant speakers.[83]

The relatively late appearance in the single-word period of "action" or "event" words, which are verbs in the adult language, has been noted repeatedly in studies of English-speaking children.[84] In contrast, children learning Japanese and Korean learn verbs earlier in the period, at least earlier than is typical for children learning English. However, in a study of linguistic and cognitive development by Korean children in the single-word period, the meanings of their early verbs were similar to the meanings of the relational words identified in early English vocabularies: for example, words for disappearance, success, and failure.[85] This finding underscores the fact that characterizing early vocabularies in terms of their linguistic counterparts in adult parts of speech (e.g., verbs) can be misleading. The concepts contributing to constructing the mental meanings expressed by a child's words are more informative of what a child is learning.

Pragmatic Explanations

One of the clearest findings in the infant communication literature is the fact that infants engage in turn-taking sequences from a very early age. Before they begin to say words, they can already participate in the "rhythms of dialogue."[86] Several investigators have stressed developments in discourse interaction and communicative function in the single-word period without necessarily addressing explanation of the vocabulary spurt directly. Two of the most influential of these appeared in back-to-back articles in the pages of the *Journal of Child Language* in 1975. In the first of these, Jerome Bruner set forth his theory of the importance to the infant of "joint experience and joint action" with caregivers for developments "from sense to sound."[87] The second article was John Dore's account of how words and grammar are acquired in the context of the child's "communicative intentions," which he suggested are "language universals."[88] For both Bruner and Dore, social interaction in general and dialogic exchanges in particular are the major force for learning words in the single-word period.[89] The communicative functions of single-word speech have been described in several accounts. In reviewing these studies, Patrick Griffiths found that directives and expressives (which "express a psychological state about the propositional content") were reported from the beginning of the period but that assertions did not appear until the end[90] (presumably in connection with a vocabulary spurt, although that achievement is typically not the focus of pragmatic explanations).

Linguistic Explanations

This is the most traditional explanation of a vocabulary spurt because it is also the oldest, having been offered originally by Clara and William Stern in 1907. A "decisive turn takes place . . . in the development of speech with the *awakening of a faint consciousness of the meaning of speech and the will to achieve it.*"[91] In his 1924 book, W. Stern compared this "moment of discovery" with the vivid description by Anne Mansfield Sullivan of Helen Keller's sudden insight "that everything has a name."[92]

Two versions of the insight are in Helen Keller's autobiography. Her own version was published originally in 1902 when she was 22 years old:

> Earlier in the day we had a tussle over the words "m-u-g" and "w-a-t-e-r." Miss Sullivan had tried to impress it upon me that "m-u-g" is *mug* and "w-a-t-e-r" is *water*, but I persisted in confounding the two. [Later that day] We walked down the path to the well-house. . . . Someone was drawing water and my teacher placed my hand under the spout. As the cool stream gushed over one hand she spelled into the other the word *water*, first slowly then rapidly. I stood still, my whole attention fixed upon the motions of her fingers . . . and somehow the mystery of language was revealed to me. I knew then that "w-a-t-e-r" meant the wonderful cool something that was flowing over my hand. . . . There were barriers still, it is true, but barriers that could in time be swept away. (Keller, 1905, pp. 22–24)

We cannot know, of course, how much Helen's own account, 16 years after the experience, was influenced by having others in the intervening years tell her about the event. But we do have Anne Sullivan's account.

In Sullivan's version, written at the time the event occurred, the initial confusion was between "mug" and "milk."[93] In a letter just 3 weeks after she arrived to teach Helen (who was then 6 years, 8 months old), she reported:

> Helen has learned several nouns [imitations of finger spelling in her hand] this week. "M-u-g" and "m-i-l-k" have given her more trouble than other words. When she spells "milk," she points to the mug, and when she spells "mug," she makes the sign for pouring or drinking, which shows she has confused the words. She has no idea yet that everything has a name.[94]

Two weeks later she wrote:

> In a previous letter I think I wrote you that "mug" and "milk" had given Helen more trouble than all the rest. She confused the nouns with the verb "drink." She didn't

know the word for "drink," but went through the pantomime of drinking whenever she spelled "mug" or "milk." This morning, while she was washing, she wanted to know the name for "water." When she wants to know the name of anything, she points to it and pats my hand. I spelled "w-a-t-e-r" and . . . it occurred to me that with the help of this new word I might succeed in straightening out the "mug–milk" difficulty. We went out to the pump-house, and I made Helen hold her mug under the spout while I pumped. As the cold water gushed forth, filling the mug, I spelled "w-a-t-e-r" in Helen's free hand. The word coming so close upon the sensation of cold water rushing over her hand seemed to startle her. She dropped the mug and stood as one transfixed. A new light came into her face. She spelled "water" several times. . . . In a few hours she had added thirty new words to her vocabulary. Here are some of them: *Door, open, shut, give, go, come* and a great many more.[95]

The attribution of a vocabulary spurt in children's single-word speech to the insight that things have names has been made repeatedly over the years.[96] My purpose in citing Helen Keller's experience at length here is to show how the observations we make today often ring true when we encounter them in other contexts. In the truly astounding accomplishment wrought by Anne Sullivan (and one has to read the original *Story of My Life,* particularly the "supplemental account," to appreciate it) we see examples of overextension through the confusion of early associations (mug, milk, and drink), early gestural naming,[97] and the sharp increase in new words (many of them verbs and other relational terms) after the initial realization of the crucial relationships between words and between words and things.

But the change that is heralded by a vocabulary spurt is hardly a complete breakthrough; children give evidence of struggling to use their new-found abilities with words. For example, overextensions tend to be more frequent,[98] and children have been shown to be more variable and inconsistent in their accuracy when asked to point to pictures of words they already "know," apparently confusing them with other but contextually relevant words.[99] With the ability to use more different cues for recall, the likelihood of confusability evidently increases.

So far I have suggested that early words and the relevance they had for a child in their circumstances of prior use are simply stored associations (word–image pairings) and dependent on cued recall for their use. Now I am suggesting that the vocabulary spurt occurs when other *words* become cues for recall and the child begins to appreciate the relations between words. Anne Sullivan made purposeful use of this possibility ("it occurred to me that with the help of this new word I might succeed in straightening out the 'mug-milk' difficulty"). This appreciation of the relations words have to one another has two manifestations. One is in the observation that children begin to learn words for different objects in a superordinate category, like *dog* and *horse,* and even the superordinate terms themselves, like *animal.* Words can now cue other words taxonomically for forming word classes. This is the beginning of semantic categories and, I would add, the true beginning of the acquisition of word meanings. The second observation is that for many children, multiword speech begins shortly after a vocabulary spurt. Here the implication is that words cue other words thematically for combining words in simple phrases.

This explanation of the vocabulary spurt is consistent with connectionist theory and a spreading activation model of the early lexicon.[100] The input to a connectionist model would begin with the child's stored associations of words with the original circumstances of prior use (similar to Schlesinger's "referent pairings"; Bowerman's "prototypical referent"; the "event representations" of Barrett and Nelson; or what I called "word–image representations" in *One Word at a Time;* and so forth). These associations are the bases for primitive lexical nodes. The vocabulary spurt occurs when the child begins to *build relations between these nodes* for organizing the mental lexicon. This organization of words into a primitive semantic system has wide ramifications for the rest of the course of language development, both lexical and syntactic. It has its counterpart in phonological development as well; for example, Richard Schwartz suggested that the organization of the sound system begins when children have acquired approximately 50 different words.[101] We cannot talk about either a semantic system or the child's organization of words until this time; words that appear early in the period are not organized relative to one another.[102]

A question is sometimes raised about whether all children do indeed show a vocabulary spurt. Children's vocabularies grow slowly at first, and all children learning language normally have to begin showing an increase in the number of words they learn from month to month. Based on vocabulary studies in the literature, George Miller commented on the ability of preschool children to "soak up words." By the time they reach the preschool years, the number of new words children are apt to learn in any given day is impressive. Susan Carey estimated that an average child has learned 14,000 new words, or an average of 9 new words a day, by age 6. Miller estimated that before the age of 18 the average child has learned 13 new words a day.[103]

But the question is whether acquisition of vocabulary always shows the sort of quantitative discontinuity toward the end of the second year that is represented in a sharp increase in the number of new words. Just as children differ in when they begin to learn words and how fast they acquire a vocabulary of words, they differ as well in the slope of the increase in new words represented by a vocabulary spurt, as we shall see in Chapter 9. The comparison interval reported could make a difference; monthly intervals might be more likely to show a sharp increase than weekly intervals. Another issue is whether one plots a cumulative vocabulary (with all the words – both old and new – a child knows) or only the new words from one month to the next. A vocabulary spurt will more readily be seen in a monthly plot of only the new words but may still be apparent in a weekly vocabulary count. For example, Esther Dromi presented the numbers of words her daughter learned each week between 10 and 17 months. The criteria we used for the vocabulary spurt in this study (in Chapter 7) – an average of 3 new words per week, or at least 12 new words from one month to the next, after at least 20 words have already been learned – appear to have been met at 14 months. At 13 months, 11 days this child had about 30 words, and at 14 months, 9 days she had about 52 words, a gain of 22 new words.[104]

Smooth, continuous growth curves in vocabulary acquisition have sometimes been reported in studies that used parent report data obtained through diaries and checklists to assess production and identify a vocabulary spurt.[105] The possibility exists that this is a result of mothers' rather than children's behaviors. Just as children differ in onset and rate of development, mothers differ in their observing and reporting skills. One problem with using parents' diaries and/or checklist inventories is the extent to which parents differ in their perceptions, persistence, and accuracy in reporting. Good and poor parent reporters may have children who do and do not show a vocabulary spurt, respectively. In addition to inherent differences among mothers, gender of child and birth order may also contribute to individual differences among mothers in their reporting accuracy.

The use of parent report instruments has been justified by citing the high correlation between the number of words recorded in a laboratory playroom and the results of mothers' reports found by Bates and her colleagues.[106] In addition, validity of a standardized vocabulary checklist for parents' reports was reported based upon correlations with the Bayley Scales of Infant Development and other measures of children's vocabulary and syntactic abilities.[107] According to these studies, parents are reliable reporters of some of the basic facts of their children's language. The fact remains, however, that in any individual study using parent reports of vocabulary growth we have neither inter- nor intrarater reliability.

THE INTENTIONALITY PERSPECTIVE

The explicit position taken here is that understanding language development requires attention to on-line processes in which a child's acts of expressing and interpreting are determined by the representations in intentional states that are their beliefs, desires, and feelings. Although this perspective is rarely made explicit, it is implicit in much work in the field. We conclude this chapter by citing some examples from the child language literature that demonstrate how what a child has in mind influences how and what the child learns about the language.

Studies of infants and mothers have revealed again and again that communication between them occurs in contexts of "joint attention."[108] Infants' early gestures in these contexts (pointing in particular) have been interpreted as "orienting" responses, indications of attention to something in the context, and communicative acts.[109] However, the importance of attentional processes for language development – *from the child's point of view* – is rarely the focus. Instead, the emphasis in studies of joint attention is typically on the part played by the *adult,* who does or does not take the child's attentional focus into account in the interaction. Mothers in such interactions have been shown to differ in the timing of their response to their infants' vocalizations and also in their tendency to name the object that their infants are attending to. Both factors influence subsequent vocabulary size, and differences among mothers are reflected in differences among their children.[110] Children evidently learn more words when their mothers respond promptly to their vocalizations and also say something about the objects of the infant's attention. Similarly, an optimum occasion for learning words is provided when caregivers fail to understand an infant's expression and "negotiate" the form of the message in subsequent exchanges.[111] When this happens, infants are presented with the forms that can more successfully articulate what they have in mind.

The labels mothers provide their children indicate how they take a child's perspective into account in their interactions. Children's initial concepts of objects reflect a child basic-object level (e.g., a round candle is a ball) rather than the adult level (candle). Accordingly, the extensions of children's early words are not identical to those of the adult, and this is independent of mothers' labeling instances of these concepts. For example, a mother may initially call a round candle a candle. However, rather than continuing to label according to the adult basic level, mothers take their cues from their children's actions (e.g., the child rolling the candle) or expressions (the child saying "ball") and use words that are consistent with the basic-object categories the child has in mind.[112]

The meanings of children's relational words (for example, *there* and *more*) in the single-word period are directed at the plans they have in mind, as Alison Gopnik pointed out. In particular, they use such words to express something about their goals in relation to their actions and to aspects of the context. For example, *there* expresses the success of a plan; *no* and *gone* express failure to attain a goal; *more* expresses recurrence of a plan; and so forth.[113] In a series of experiments with older (4-year-old) children, Hamburger and Crain took explicit account of the computational demands attributable to underlying plans in sentence processing. They found that certain phrases varied in difficulty for children as a function of their relative cognitive demands rather than their syntactic complexity.[114]

Finally, a key component in learnability theory is the child's hearing and making use of sentences in the input. In any learnability theory, input sentences are required for the acquisition of latent principles of grammar assumed to be a part of the child's endowment. The structures of syntax cannot be realized, that is, acquired in a grammar, unless the child ascertains their relevance to something in the input. However, this process of matching an input sentence to a grammatical principle would have to include a mental meaning set up by hearing the sentence and, where available, elements from the perceived situation that the sentence is about.[115]

The research in the second half of this book was very much concerned with underlying and on-line processes for learning words and saying those words in increasingly different circumstances. The focus was on the representations we can attribute to the beliefs, desires, and feelings that are a child's intentional states and on the cognitive work of constructing those representations and expressing them. Developments in language depend upon changes in what the child can hold in mind and the *sources* for these contents of mind. The cognitive developments in infancy that enable these developments for language were the subject of Chapter 3. The social and expressive developments in infancy that enable development of language for expression were the subject of Chapter 4. We now turn to the longitudinal study in which we documented how these developments continued in the second year.

CONCLUSIONS

The earliest words are tied in memory to the relevance of the original circumstances of prior use in which they were heard. They depend for their recognition and recall upon encounters with the same or highly similar circumstances. Later words are attached to more clearly defined concepts of objects and events that have been abstracted out of those original episodes and the subsequent episodes in which the child continues to hear words. And once enough words are stored in memory, words themselves become the cues for learning and recall.

Thus, the quantitative change captured by the Vocabulary Spurt is also a qualitative developmental change as a child proceeds from an episodic basis to a conceptual basis to a linguistic basis for word learning. The thread of continuity that ties together these bases for word learning is the representation of mental meanings in intentional states and the 1-year-old's efforts to make these known to other persons. But these have generally not been the focus of attention in the literature so far. What changes with development are the resources that a child can bring to bear on the process whereby the representations in mental meanings are formed. Changes occur both in knowledge, with acquisition of concepts and procedures for acting, and in the symbolic capacity, for constructing intentional states that are increasingly elaborated and discrepant from the data of perception.

Lexical principles that have been proposed for children's word learning are, so far, more descriptive of the results of the process than they are explanatory. To the extent that principles are object-specific, they cannot account for the fact that children learn many words that are not names for things. More general principles for word learning that are not tied to learning object names are required. The candidate principles offered in this book are the principles of Relevance, Discrepancy, and Elaboration.

The rest of this book is an account of the development of a group of infants from the last quarter of their first year to the end of the second year. The children and the details of how we studied their development are described in the next chapter. The remaining chapters are taken up with what we learned about their affect expression, play with objects, and word learning and how these intersected with one another in this crucial year of language acquisition.

PART II

From 9 Months to 2 Years

6

Translation from Theory to Method

Since 1968 I have taught a course called "Early Language Development" at Teachers College, Columbia University. The subject matter has changed over the years, but one prevailing theme has not. The theme is what I call the *accountability of evidence* in child language research.[1] We need to hold whatever evidence we obtain accountable to the conclusions we draw. Talk is cheap: Young children are talking all the time, and it is easy enough to write down or record what they say. The ultimate value children's talk may have as data and evidence depends upon the methods we use to process the talk and the interpretations we give it. The value of talk as data depends upon the methods we use. The value of data as evidence depends upon the interpretations we make. Both theory and method inform one another in the transformation *Talk* ⇒ *data* ⇒ *evidence,* and both change over time with advances in technology, in what we learn about language and its acquisition, and in what we learn about children and their development.

The research reported here began with several basic theoretical and methodological assumptions. The first theoretical assumption was that infants learn language in their endeavor to express and articulate some aspect of a mental meaning – some representation of the way the world appears to be or the way they want the world to be in their beliefs, desires, or feelings. A second theoretical assumption was that developments in cognition make it possible for the infant to have such mental meanings and to learn the language to express them. And finally, as infants are working to articulate the objects of their beliefs, desires, and feelings, they are already quite adept at expression through affect, and have been for some time, since before language began. We were concerned, then, with how developments in affect expression and cognition come together with emerging language in the second year.

The first methodological assumption that guided the translation from theory to method was noncontroversial: the assumption that beliefs, desires, and feelings come about as infants interact with the social and physical world. Accordingly, we set out to observe young infants in the social context of interacting with their mothers and in the physical context of play with objects. The second assumption was only somewhat more controversial: that infants' play with objects could serve as a window on what they know about objects for inferring something about developments in cognition. And the third assumption was, perhaps, more controversial: that infant affect expression could be captured in a continuous record of changes in the valence and intensity of expressed affect rather than in expressions coded according to the discrete emotions.

The principal data we collected were monthly hour-long video-recorded observations in our laboratory playroom, beginning at 9 months of age and continuing until after the development of simple sentences. In addition, the infants and mothers had come to the playroom for a get-acquainted visit before the visits for data collection began. The furnishings in the playroom consisted of a child-size table with two chairs; a plastic slide with a crawl-through space under its incline; and an infant changing table. A group of toys was on the floor when the infant and mother came into the playroom, and other groups of toys were brought in every 8 min according to a schedule. After the first half hour, a snack consisting of juice and cookies for the baby and coffee for the mother was introduced instead of another group of toys. The schedule of toys was resumed after the snack, and by the end of the session toys from six presentations were on the floor.

The virtue in the design of the data collection was that the context was the same over time for all the child–mother pairs; they all had the same toys available to them for play, in the same sequence and in the same context throughout the study. Systematic *change* over time, in the infants and in their interactions with their mothers, could therefore be attributed with some confidence to their development. And *differences* among the children and mothers could be attributed to inherent differences among them and how they interacted with each other. The shortcomings in the design were obvious: Only a single social context and one kind of physical context were sampled. Accordingly, although we are comfortable with the consistency in the procedures for data collection among the children and over time, we recognize the limitations in our ability to generalize from our playroom observations to all the contexts in our infants' lives.

In fact, however, we collected several kinds of data from the infants we studied. We also visited them at home every month until they were 15 months old and every other month thereafter. These sessions were also video recorded and provided reassurance that the interactions sampled in the playroom were typical and consistent with what might have happened at home. We instructed the mothers to keep diaries of the words their infants appeared to understand and the words they said at home in the 1-month interval between play sessions; the diaries were reviewed during periodic telephone calls to the mothers each month. In addition to the infants' spontaneous, naturally occurring affect expression, play with objects, and speech, we elicited other behaviors through standardized tasks. These included a series of word-comprehension tasks, a block building task, and the scale for the Development of Visual Pursuit and the Permanence of Objects from the sensorimotor scales developed by Uzgiris and Hunt.[2] The procedures for these different aspects of data collection will be described when we discuss the results from our studies in the chapters to follow. The first purpose of this chapter is to describe the children and the toys they played with in the playroom. The second purpose is to present the rationale we developed and the procedures we used for computer-assisted data processing.

THE CHILDREN

In the 1960s, several longitudinal studies were undertaken by independent investigators, in different parts of the country, with the same purpose: to determine the syntax of children's first sentences. Of the landmark studies in this period, only Roger Brown introduced some sociocultural variation among the subjects he studied: Two were children of college-educated parents, one of whom was black, and the third was the daughter of white working-class parents. The children studied by Wick Miller and Susan Ervin-Tripp at Berkeley and by Martin Braine in Washington, D.C., were white, and their parents were college educated.[3] The subjects in my own longitudinal study, begun in the mid 1960s, were white first-born children of college-educated parents living in university communities in New York City.[4] By virtue of the criteria for subject selection in these studies, therefore, the account of child language they offered was ethnographically relevant to a particular population at the time.

Since then, children from other populations have been studied. Children learning altogether different languages are both different and similar to children learning English, depending upon the languages studied in general and the aspect of language studied in particular.[5] However, the semantics and syntax of the sentences from 2-year-old children learning American English in different ethnic and economic populations were similar to those of the white middle-class children studied in the 1960s (in the studies by Ira Blake and Ida Stockman of black working-class children and the study by Peggy Miller of white working-class children in particular).[6] Perhaps even more important, no differences were found in the linguistic abilities of black low-income and white middle-income 5-year-old children engaging in neighborhood dialogs in a study by Lynne Feagans and Ron Haskins. The structure of these children's dialogs; the quantity, complexity, and functions of the language they used; and such things as the concreteness and animacy of topics did not differ.[7] Together, these results support our decision to study subjects from different ethnic and economic backgrounds so that we might enhance the generalizability of the findings. Nevertheless, we are well aware of the literature on poverty, which has consistently pointed to language as being particularly vulnerable in the development of poor children.[8] And we are also conscious of the importance of cultural context for language development and the rich diversity in socialization experiences among children from different cultural groups. We will return to this point in Chapter 8.

We cast a wide net in the metropolitan New York area in our search for subjects. We sent a letter to all pediatricians in the five boroughs of New York City asking them to post an announcement of the study or otherwise tell their patients about it. We also posted notices soliciting subjects on bulletin boards in housing projects, community centers, well-baby clinics, neighborhood laundromats, supermarkets, banks, and the like. As a result, our children came to us from the Upper West Side of Manhattan, Harlem, Bedford-Stuyvesant in Brooklyn, Queens, Long Island, and northern New Jersey. We reimbursed the mothers for taxicab fares to and from Teachers College. Those families who fell below the poverty level were given a modest remuneration each month and a United States savings bond when the study ended. At the end of the study, we gave all the children a photo album with a collection of candid pictures we had taken each month in the playroom and a "Teachers College Diploma" as a certificate of our appreciation for participating in the study.

Our subjects were 14 infants – 7 girls and 7 boys – from different ethnic, economic, and religious backgrounds. Of these, 12 participated in all the studies we report here; 2 were not included in the studies of affect expression, which began at 9 months, because we first saw them after the age of 9 months (but before they began to say words, one at 11 months and the other at 12). None of them had experienced birth complications, and all gave every indication that they were developing normally.

The ethnicity of our children is as follows: 10 are Caucasians; 2 are African-American; 1 is mixed African-American and Puerto Rican Hispanic; and 1 is mixed Caucasian, Dominican Hispanic, and Native American. The 4 children of color were among the 12 subjects who participated in all the studies. As for incomes, 4 families earned less than $10,000 a year; 3 earned between $10,000 and $30,000 a year; and 7 earned more than $30,000. (The threshold of poverty in the United States in 1981, when the study began, was an income of $9,287 a year for a family of four, and the median income for 1981 was $22,390.)[9] We were confidant we had tapped a wide range of the general population in metropolitan New York in 1981.[10] The factors of ethnicity and poverty were compounded in our population, since our 4 infants of color were also from our poorest families and receiving public assistance. However, race and poverty are very often coextensive in urban communities like New York,[11] and these children added to the representativeness of the sample of children we studied. As we shall see, the ethnic and economic differences among the infants did not, in fact, differentiate among them in the results we are reporting in the remaining chapters.

We imposed three restrictions in selecting subjects. For obvious reasons, English had to be the only language spoken with regularity in the home, except for family names and occasional words (for example, "agua"). But in addition, to assure that the infants had only adult language models and that their mothers had similar opportunities for experience with infants, all the children were first-born, and their mothers were their primary caregivers throughout the period of the study. This last restriction is one that is becoming increasingly difficult to impose and may soon be obsolete. With more and more women working outside the home, the question of who is actually doing the caregiving and, as a consequence, providing the input for language learning is a serious one for studies of language development and language socialization.[12] As the study progressed, some mothers did begin working on a part-time basis out of the home, either as students or in free-lance work of one kind or another. The mothers ranged in age from 17 to 34 years at the time the study began, and their mean age was 27.6 years.

Each infant–mother pair was the responsibility of one pair of investigators who worked as a team in collecting the data throughout the period of the study, both in the playroom and in the home visits. The subjects and investigators were matched for ethnicity, and because they saw each other twice a month and spoke on the telephone fairly often, they were familiar with each other and at ease during the observation sessions.

We used two measures of general maturation: age of walking and block building (stacking 1-in. cubes to form a tower). On both measures, the children developed within normal limits.[13] The mean age of walking (two independent steps unaided) was 12.6 months, and the range was from 10 to 14 months. The block building task was administered at home every 3 months. Of the 11 children who were presented with the task, none succeeded in building a tower of six blocks without direct help at 18 months; 7 succeeded at 21 months and the 4 others succeeded subsequently.[14] The important finding was that both progress in walking and the ability to stack the 1-in. cubes were unrelated to any other developments in language, affect expression, or play with objects, as will be shown in the later chapters. We have interpreted these results to mean that the developmental interactions we observed among language, affect expression, and object play were a function of fundamental underlying cognitive processes and not simply attributable to maturation.

To give the reader some feeling for who our subjects and their parents were, brief portraits of a few of them are presented here.[15] These were written while the data were being collected by the investigator team who knew the family well. Together they capture some of the differences in personality and circumstances represented in the group. The children and their parents are called by pseudonyms in these vignettes and elsewhere in the book.

Diana

Diana's crib was one of the few pieces of furniture – along with a sofa, two chairs, and a small coffee table with a lamp – in the living room of the apartment she and her mother, Dena, shared with her grandmother and her mother's two younger siblings. The walls were bare except for a picture of Jesus; a Bible sat on the table; the apartment was neat and clean; there were few toys. Dena, who is African-American, was 17 years old when Diana was born. Diana's father, Ricardo, is Puerto Rican Hispanic, 23 years old when she was born, and lived with his mother and siblings in another apartment building in the same neighborhood on the east side of Manhattan's Upper West Side (below 110th Street). The neighborhood was considered safe and consisted of high-rise apartment "projects," brownstone row houses, schools, churches, and bodegas, with a lively mix of English, Spanish, and Yiddish spoken in the apartment-house lobby and on the street. Dena and Ricardo were unemployed and took much of the responsibility for their younger siblings, since neither of their mothers was well; the families depended on public assistance. Diana and her mother saw Ricardo about twice a week. Diana's extended family included her godmother, great-aunt, and great-grandmother in addition to her aunt and uncle who lived with her. Her mother, grandmother, and godmother provided primary caregiving, and her aunt and uncle read to her and played with her, mostly contact games and romping. She was very much the center of their attention.

At the start of the study, Dena was shy and reluctant to play with Diana on the playroom floor. Diana, for her part, approached the toys and took the lead in trying to interest her mother in playing: showing and extending the toys to her, usually to no avail. Dena was just as shy at home and seemed to assume that it was the responsibility of her brother and sister to play with her daughter while she attended to feeding, dressing, and bathing her. Nevertheless, by the end of the study 18 months later, Dena was more outgoing and was playing with Diana in the playroom. Her life had also changed in important ways. She had enrolled in a course in forensic medicine, determined to establish a career for herself; she had met another man, and they were making plans to marry.

Greta

Greta's room doubled as the living room in the family apartment in Queens. The rocker and stuffed chairs surrounded her crib; her changing table, toy cabinet, and shelves filled with stuffed animals, baby dolls, and picture books shared wall space with the stereo system and magazine rack. Little teddy bears were suspended from the ceiling; numerous Sesame Street characters cluttered unpredictable places about the room; and a large teddy bear poster hung on the wall. The room was Greta's. Her parents, Irene and Phil, were casual about housekeeping; the rooms were cluttered and lived-in, and Irene was not afraid of Greta's making a mess; in fact, she seemed to enjoy it. Irene was 25 and Phil was 24 years old when Greta was born; both had graduated from college, and Irene had worked before Greta's birth. Phil worked in the publishing sales industry by day and on a novel he was writing at the typewriter on the kitchen table by night.

Greta frequently took bottle breaks during the playroom and home sessions: She would lie on her back and produce a few fussing sounds, and Irene would say, "I know what you want; how 'bout this, a bottle, a bottle; are you a little thirsty?" Greta would drink her bottle and watch her mother, who sometimes sang to her during these breaks; they were moments of quiet contentment. These periods of calm and quiet were separated by periods of constant activity; Greta moved easily about the playroom, first crawling and eventually walking, cruising from one end of the room to the other, from the slide to the table to the door, touching each and then moving on. Early on, her interest in the toys was brief: She would finger the beads, then the truck, and then the baby doll and seemed more interested in cruising. As she grew older and started talking, she would ask for her "naenae," her bottle, which was always the familiar, constant object among the confusion of toys in the playroom. Her favorite toy was the baby doll; her mother would pretend to cry and say, "Greta, the baby's crying," and Greta, picking up the baby and putting it on her shoulder, would "make nice," saying "ah ah."

Jessica

Jessica's arrival in the world was carefully orchestrated, down to the music she heard when she was brought home after birth to her parents' two-bedroom co-op apartment in Washington Heights: It was Copeland's *Appalachian Spring.* She and her parents, Cindy and Pete, lived in an early 1920s luxury apartment building left behind by a privileged class who had retreated, one imagines, before the safety lights and theft-proof benches were installed in the park across the street, just north of the George Washington Bridge in Manhattan. Her parents met as undergraduates at a university known for its political activism at the time. Both went on to take master's degrees at Columbia University; he worked in journalism, and she was a counselor at a sheltered workshop for retarded adults.

Despite the careful decisions that were made for her, Jessica was consciously treated as her own person and responded by typically acting that way. What some might call willfulness was in Jessica a strong sense of self that was as appealing as it was reassuring. This sense of self was particularly evident when we tried to put demands on her: During object permanence testing, for example, she typically crawled (and eventually walked) away. Cindy herself put few demands on her daughter, and the movement between them always flowed with Jessica. Cindy would follow her lead, making suggestions or arranging things only to the extent necessary for her safety. As Jessica moved from one activity to the next, Cindy moved with her. The result was a great deal of exploration by Jessica and interaction between them that was always in sync.

After spending a year at home after Jessica was born, Cindy returned to work, taking her along to her office at the sheltered workshop. Cindy became pregnant again toward the end of Jessica's second year and, 8 months pregnant, cheerfully continued bringing her 2-year-old to our playroom.

Robert

The white comforter in Robert's crib had been hand quilted with boldly colored cars by his mother, Renira, a working artist whose paintings hung on the walls of their spacious two-bedroom apartment in Forest Hills, Queens. Robert's room was sunny, with shelves and cabinets neatly filled with toys and a large collection of picture books. His father, David, has an MBA degree and commuted daily by subway to the financial district in lower Manhattan; he was 32 years old when Robert was born. His mother has a BA degree and painted at home; she was 27 years old when he was born. Two cats, Delicious and Tipper, were the other members of the family, and Robert's name for Delicious, "Didi," was one of his early words. His grandparents lived within walking distance, and he heard some Yiddish words from them. Renira had relatives living in Spain, and the family spent three weeks there when he was a year old; both parents occasionally used Spanish words with Robert. David and Renira evidently enjoyed parenting, and David was one of the few fathers who took a particular interest in the research project; he accompanied Renira and Robert on their first visit to the playroom and attended subsequent sessions from time to time.

One of Renira's most frequent nicknames for Robert was "Wildman," which didn't so much reflect his actual behavior as it did his mother's evident pleasure in his strapping appearance and active personality. Once he learned to walk, he didn't so much toddle as launch himself around the playroom. Renira also described him as "easygoing," and all who knew him agreed; he was characteristically good-tempered, and his resistance to one or another activity was more likely to be a simple "no" than a physical or loud protest. Before Robert could walk or talk, he delighted in the simple repetitive games and routines that his mother set up for him: giving and taking a pillowcase, putting on and taking off an oversized hat, and the like. They played actively and adventurously with the toys in the playroom.

THE TOYS

The toys, the configurations in which they were presented, and the schedule we used to bring them into the playroom are described in Table 6.1. We had two concerns in mind when we selected these toys for the children to play with. Because we were interested in developments in play, we provided equal opportunities for manipulative and for enactment play. For example, the set of plastic nesting cups was a manipulative toy, and the bendable family figures were enactment toys.

Because we were also concerned that gender-stereotyped toys might have different appeal to boys and girls, we also provided equal opportunities for the children to play with traditional girl toys (e.g., the baby doll), boy toys (e.g., the dump truck), and neutral toys (e.g., the nesting boxes). Our wisdom in controlling for this variable has since been confirmed in experimental play research reporting that children show greater involvement with same-sex stereotyped toys.[16] Furthermore, other research has shown that type of toy can influence the language children hear while playing. When children play with dolls, their mothers are more likely to ask questions, and when children play with trucks, mothers are more likely to produce imperatives.[17] This last finding is particularly important, because earlier research had already shown that the relative frequency with which mothers use these different sentence types correlates with rate of language development. High frequency of questions has been shown to correlate positively with language growth, whereas high frequency of imperatives is negatively correlated with language growth.[18] These findings, taken together, suggest that if girls either have more girl toys at home or favor girl toys when they play, they will hear more of the sentence types correlated with faster language growth.

Because of these intriguing findings and because the toys in our study were balanced in a way that allowed the children approximately equal opportunities

Table 6.1. *Schedule of toy presentation*

Group 1	Bendable family figures (Mommy, Daddy, Baby); wooden peg people placed in holes in the seesaw; wooden nesting/stacking boxes (nested); plastic child-size slide; inclined wooden roadway/ridge (connected) with small truck beside it; two-part slide (base and ramp connected) with 4 discs beside it
Group 2	Plastic dump truck; bendable farm animals (horse, cow, calf, pig); wooden beads and the string, separate, in a box
Group 3	Toy silverware in a tray; wooden lockbox with 4 closed, empty compartments; soft stuffed lamb; baby doll (black or white, depending on the child's ethnicity)
Snack	
Group 4	Wooden hammer/ball/frame set (assembled); wooden train pieces (unconnected); plastic nesting cups with lids (nested); plastic nesting boxes (nested)
Group 5	Cardboard box with cover; pillowcase; bendable family figures (boy, girl); bendable farm animals (colt, sheep, bull); toy silverware pieces
Group 6	Large plastic bowl; plastic chunky nuts and bolt (unassembled); wooden fruit puzzle (assembled)

Note: The Group 1 toys were on the floor in front of the camera at the beginning of the session when child and mother entered the playroom. The 5 other groups of toys were brought into the playroom at 8-min intervals thereafter, in group order 2 through 6.
Source: Lifter & Bloom (1989)

to play with different toy types, Scott Scheer and Richard Beckwith did a post hoc analysis of the effect of toy type on their mothers' speech to them.[19] The main objective of the study was to observe a child's selection of toy type and the sentence type the mother used when she talked to her child. Mothers' speech was coded as questions, declaratives, or imperatives. The potential referents of mothers' speech were the enactment toys balanced for traditional gender stereotype (e.g., dolls [for girls], trucks [for boys], animals [neutral]); the manipulative toys (e.g., nesting boxes); the other objects in the playroom (e.g., the chairs and table); and no object (when they talked about something else).

The prinicipal finding was that type of toy was the single reliable predictor of the sentence types mothers used. The mothers used many more sentence types when their children played with the enactment toys and the manipulative toys than when they talked about other objects or no objects. Among the enactment toys, girl toys elicited significantly more sentence types than boy toys or neutral toys. Mothers asked more questions with the girl toys and gave fewer imperatives with the neutral toys; no differences in sentence type occurred with the boy toys. Finally, play with the manipulative toys elicited more sentence types than any other situation. These results mean that when we controlled for the types of toys the children played with, we also provided a measure of control over the types of sentences they heard their mothers use.

Mothers of girl and boy infants did not talk differently to their children: They used the same pattern of sentence types and similar numbers of sentences about the different categories of toys; there were no gender-specific subject effects. In yet another analysis of how the mothers responded to their infants' emotional expressions, we found no difference between mothers of girls and mothers of boys in their talk about the causes and circumstances of the children's emotional experiences.[20]

In sum, the children's gender did not influence the kinds of sentences their mothers used, but the toys they played with did. Types of toys children play with (based on personal choice or parents' selection) may ultimately influence development through a child's interactions with parents and others during play. We do not know whether play with the different toys influenced what the children themselves said with their own words and simple sentences; that study is still waiting to be done. We were satisfied, however, that whatever effects the toys had on their own or their mothers' talk, the effects were the same for all of them.

DATA AND EVIDENCE

People have been writing down what infants and young children say for at least the last 200 years. Two parallel lines of development in this time have influenced how we transcribe the data of children's language for understanding how language is acquired. One of these developments has been conceptual: The different questions researchers ask influence the sorts of data that are collected. At the same time, electronic innovations provide increasingly more sophisticated equipment to supplement (but not replace) pencils and paper. The purpose of the rest of this chapter is to (1) discuss the conceptual and procedural developments that influence contemporary observational research in child language and (2) describe the rationale and procedures for the computer-assisted transcription and coding we developed for this study of the emergence of language in relation to developments in affect expression and cognition.

Observing and Preserving the Data of Child Language

Conceptual and procedural influences on methods of research are not independent of one another. The old adage "when the only tool you have is a hammer, everything looks like a nail" applies to the behavioral as well as the practical sciences. The tools we have available determine the way in which we approach a task and also determine the sorts of tasks we consider feasible.[21] At the same time, the questions we ask and the tasks we address have driven us to pursue alternative methods and means.

Four main themes provided a background and rationale for the procedures we developed for data transcription and coding. These began with the pervasive attention to only the spoken word in the history of child language research. The second was the subsequent recognition of the importance of phenomena hidden within and between individuals for understanding both the nature of language and its development in young children. The third theme pertained to the issue of the selectivity that emerges whenever complex events are studied. And the fourth was a perspective on data transcription and coding that evolved from these other themes to take advantage of the sophisticated tools available from parallel developments in electronics, notably the video recorder and the microprocessor. This was the separation-of-covariables approach to computer-assisted transcription that we used in our studies.

The Spoken Word

For a very long time the study of child language was restricted to the spoken word. The earliest research was the diary study in which parent biographers made the heroic effort to catch and write down all the sounds and words they heard their infants and young children say. With the rise of behaviorism in the 1930s, a reaction to these diary studies set in; the issues raised were, by and large, issues of sample size and observer bias rather than the kinds of data they reported. Controls over data collection were introduced in the effort to add experimental "rigor" to the enterprise. The goal became one of determining "norms" of development for children in general rather than descriptions of the development of individual children. The result was a large number of studies that investigated language development by counting particular aspects of the speech of relatively large numbers of children. The typical procedure was to collect a corpus of 50 or 100 utterances from children who differed in age, sex, sibling status, social and economic background, and the like. The features of these utterances were then counted: for example, the number of different sounds and the number of different words; or the number of nouns, verbs, and adjectives; or the length of sentences and whether they were complete or incomplete, simple, compound, or complex; and so forth.[22]

These studies were successful in that they provided the "developmental milestones" that are still widely used in pediatricians' offices, day-care settings, well-baby clinics, and the like. Moreover, we learned certain "facts" about speech in the first five years of life that endure and are still referred to in contemporary research. However, in the 1950s, Roger Brown began a program of research in which he pointed out that the really important questions about language acquisition have to do with developments in the *knowledge* children have that produce the changes in what they say.[23] That knowledge consists of rules, procedures, or principles of language.

Linguists, at least in this century, had always operated on the assumption that language was rule governed. But the galvanizing influence from linguistics on the search for the child's knowledge of rules for sentences came from the theory of generative transformational grammar introduced by Noam Chomsky.[24] The presumption was that children learn a grammar when they acquire language, and the grammar they learn is a transformational one. The search for child grammar in the studies that followed sought evidence of grammatical rules from the regularities in early two-word speech.[25] The lasting insight in these studies was that the early word combinations of children are indeed systematic. However, the resulting "grammars" were only descriptions of the regularities in frequency and word order in children's speech. Even though the goal of research had been to uncover the child's underlying rules of grammar, the data that were used in the endeavor still consisted of only the spoken word.

Hidden Phenomena

A linguistic fact assumes significance in relation to its "element of experience . . . content or 'meaning.'"[26] The meanings children express in their efforts to learn language determine what they acquire of the grammar of the language. These meanings have to do with what the young child has learned and is learning about objects, events, and relations in the world. If children acquire meaning from events in the context, then the context ought to be a preeminent source of information about the meanings children express. The suggestion was made, therefore, that we attend to and use information from the context of children's utterances in our efforts to learn how and what children are learning about language. This meant going beyond the spoken word and inquiring into the underlying meaning of the words as inferred from what children *talk about.*[27] The suggestion was taken up by Roger Brown, who coined the term "rich interpretation" for what became the dominant method for pursuing the meanings hidden in early speech.[28]

Rich interpretation is not without its detractors among those who feel that what is hidden in the child is not evidence for the language-acquisition enterprise. Nevertheless, children provide us with a variety of signals that let us know what they are thinking and feeling, and they express in language what they think and feel. We make use of these kinds of signals quite readily and easily in our everyday interactions, with adults as well as with children. Indeed, not only the meaning of an individual utterance but also developments in pragmatics and the unfolding of discourse can be studied by attention to "language in context."[29] Moreover, the contexts of language acquisition include not only the immediate circumstances that surround acts of expression and interpretation but, indeed, the cultural world view of the individuals in a society.[30]

In sum, contemporary research that takes a developmental perspective is conducted with the fundamental assumption that language is acquired in connection with other developments and events in the life of the young language-learning child. Children acquire the sounds, words, structures, and discourse procedures of a language embedded in a context of other cognitive, social, and affective developments. We now recognize the importance of paying attention to a great deal else besides the spoken word in our efforts to understand language development. This recognition has paid off in that we know much more than ever before about the language-learning process.

However, we have also had to deal with important conceptual issues concerning our methods for deciding what we use as evidence and how.

Selectivity

Individuals observe and interpret what children do every day, by necessity, in order to interact with them, and they rarely think about it. But as researchers we have to establish a certain distance from what children do so that we *can* think about it, describe it, and attempt to explain it. One reasonable goal might be to approach the task without regard to any expectations that we might have. This was the admonition of Claude Lévi-Strauss: "On the observational level, the main – one could say the only – rule is that all facts would be carefully observed and described, without allowing any theoretical preconception to decide whether some are more important than others."[31]

However, our preconceptions cannot help creating and influencing our expectations, as many people, including the ethologist Colin Beer, have since pointed out:

> For both logical and practical reasons, there can be no such thing as pure observation [because] one's ideas evolve with one's research, reading and thinking. . . . Trying to put oneself at sufficient distance for clear vision is like trying to leap over one's shadow. . . . [Accordingly, we have to] start out with selection of one out of an infinite number of possible descriptive strategies, in accordance with whatever one's wits and experience offer as the best bet.[32]

We are, then, as researchers the products of our own intellectual histories, and these cannot help influencing our view of evidence. Such selectivity, on the whole, is not only to be expected but is even to be encouraged, as Elinor Ochs pointed out. How else is our current and future work to benefit from what we already know about children, language, and the acquisition process? However, the researcher needs to be aware of the filtering process and take such inherent selectivity into explicit account. Moreover, "the problems of selective observation are not eliminated with the use of recording equipment. They are simply delayed until the moment at which the researcher sits down to transcribe the material from the audio or videotape."[33]

As soon as we make a recording, we have begun a process of data reduction and have introduced selectivity into the data. Whether recorded by hand or by audio or video electronics, something is necessarily left out of the record. The microphone and the camera, much less the eye, the ear, and the hand, can never preserve the detail, nuance, and complex circumstances of events. Transcription reduces mechanically recorded data even more drastically and provides a serious constraint on the available information. Quite simply, copying the richness of tone and detail that can be preserved on tape, as reduced as it is from the original event, is an impossible task. The process of transcription, then, provides the real moment of truth for the observer.

In sum, transcription presents two problems. The first is the set of biases and distortions that creep in because of the necessarily selective view of the observer. The second is the massive data reduction that results from the sheer physical limitations of mechanical devices that make the record to preserve the data and of the persons who do the transcribing. The system of transcription we developed was created in an effort to minimize these problems.

DESCRIPTION AND INTERPRETATION

In effect, a rich interpretation depends on lean transcription. Not only is attempting to capture everything on a recording a hopeless task, but too much detail in a transcript produces clutter and distraction.[34] Further, the transcription must necessarily aim to represent a description of events rather than an interpretation.[35] Admittedly, where description ends and interpretation begins is probably not definable. Indeed, one might well say that any description is by nature a form of interpretation. The point is to aim at preserving the data in such a way as to allow for different analyses and different resulting interpretations. The following example is trivial, but only on its surface:

> A child picks up a small block, says "more," puts it on top of another block, smiles, and looks at her mother. Her mother smiles back.

This event might be interpreted in various ways. At the minimum, we might want to say something like "initiates activity," "builds a tower," "expresses recurrence," or "expresses pleasure" to capture what happened. However, these or any other evaluations of the event must come from what we have preserved in our transcript *after the fact*. If all we recorded in the transcript was something like "initiates activity" or "expresses recurrence" other interpretations would not be possible from the transcript. For example, the timing of the child's smile, in relation to saying the word *more* and her action with the blocks is highly relevant to several theoretical concerns. The smile could be interpreted, again at a minimum, as an act of social referencing or, alternatively, a smile of recognition or accomplishment. The fact that the baby did not smile before or at the same time as she said "more" is relevant to understanding the way the two systems of expression, affect and speech, come together in the single-word period. However, if one transcribes a piece of behavior only according to its meaning, its function, or its effect, then information about the event is lost that might contribute to an additional interpretation or an alternative interpretation and, perhaps, a better interpretation.

With the advent of audiotape recorders, research was confined to the spoken word, and we worried about the accuracy with which we represented what was said in a transcription. For example, we had to decide whether to transcribe orthographically or phonetically, and if phonetically, how broad or narrow a phonetic transcription. When we began to include information from the context in the transcription so that we could interpret something about meaning, we took notes at the time of recording and then tried to fill in the contextual details surrounding what was said at the time of transcription. The introduction of the video recorder seemed, at first, to solve all our problems. We could use the video data instead of taking notes or trying to remember events and circumstances in the context. The first video transcriptions were, in effect, modeled after our audio transcriptions and differed only in the detail added.[36]

However, a video record presents other sorts of problems. The amount of detail preserved on videotape is enormous, even though the information present in the original event is necessarily reduced in the sense described above. This detail can be overwhelming to the researcher trying to decide what to include and what to leave out of the transcription. In the effort to preserve a description in the transcript rather than an interpretation, we could easily be engulfed by the details. The level of detail preserved on video can also be seductive in leading the transcriber down one or another garden path. The effect of watching a small scrap of an interaction over and over again is to reveal some incredibly fine details. The result is often a severe narrowing of focus and excessive attention to details that may turn out to be, in the final analysis, irrelevant.

In this research, we did not attempt a full transcription of all relevant behaviors and accompanying contexts, which has been the standard operating procedure with audio and video data. Instead, we have pulled the audio and video record apart – exploded it, so to speak – and separated out the variables of interest according to one or another research question. The advantage of having the video record is that it is impervious to these operations. This was pointed out as long ago as 1935 by Arnold Gesell, who pioneered in using film to study infant development:

> The behavior record becomes as pliant to dissection as a piece of tissue. Any phase or strand of behavior may be exposed to view. If the view is an intricate one it may be repeated numerous times without in any way damaging the original record. Here the dissection of behavior forms has a striking advantage over anatomical dissection. Bodily tissue suffers from the scalpel, but the integrity and conformation of behavior cannot be destroyed by repeated observation. A behavior form can be dissected over and over again in increasing detail without loss of form.[37]

More than 50 years ago, Gesell anticipated the way in which we have exploited the technology available to us today. We can separate the variables for examination to study the relationships between them in many different ways without sacrificing the integrity of the original record.

If we return to the episode above, we can see what this means. We were concerned in our research with developments in cognition and affect expression in the transition from infancy to language. The relevant variables in the research so far have included child speech, mother speech, the situation accompanying mother speech, child affect expression, mother response to child affect expression, child object play, child object search, and so forth. Certain of the questions we asked centered on object play as a window on developments in cognition, and on affect expression in relation to the emergence of expression through speech. With such data as in the example above, we separated the covariables in independent passes through the video record and transcribed or coded (1) child speech ("more"), (2) child affect expression (a smile with Level 1 intensity), (3) mother response to child affect expression (a smile with Level 2 intensity), (4) child object play (putting one block on another), and so forth. Independent coders were assigned to transcribe or code one variable at a time. One person would transcribe only child speech; another would code only child affect expression; and so on. The beauty of the system is that we can go on to code or transcribe however many variables we might need, bound only by the conceptual issues that we pursue (and the vagaries of available funding).

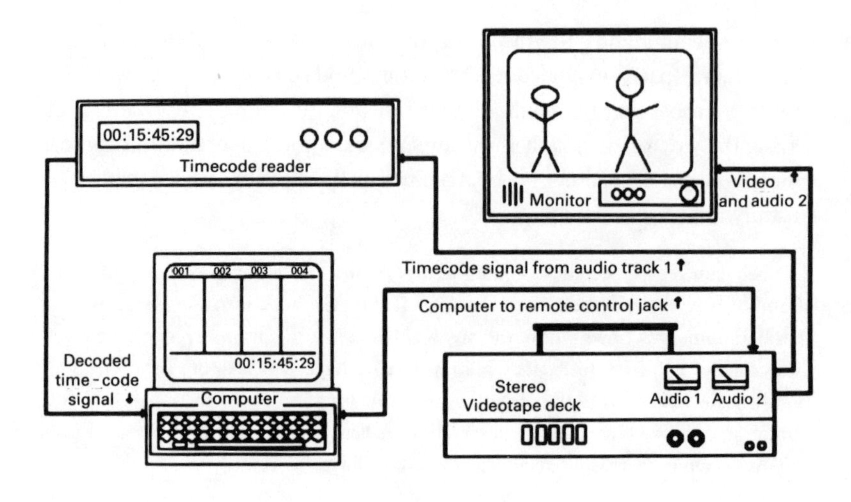

6.1 Computer-interfaced transcription/coding system. (Beckwith, Bloom, Albury, Raqib, & Booth, 1985)

A Plan for Computer-Assisted Transcription

Because the variables in the stream of activity do, in fact, covary, we had to have a way of putting them back together again.[38] This is the distinctive feature of the system. The system we devised used state-of-the-art (ca. 1981) equipment, schematized in Figure 6.1. Similar hardware is either commercially available or reproducible in some way. At the time of the original observation, the audio signal from the interaction was recorded on one sound track of the stereo videotape while a computer-readable timecode was being recorded on the other. Videotape runs at 30 frames per sec, and the timecode generator (SMPTE FOR-A) lays down a unique discrete audio signal for each frame, that is, 30 times every sec. At the time of playback, the video deck (Sony stereo Betamax) was interfaced with a microprocessor (Apple II Plus) via a timecode reader. This entailed a simple multiplexing circuit made to connect the 32-bit timecode readers with the 8-bit Apples.

The Apple controlled the video deck: turning it on, moving it forward or backward, slowing or speeding the playback, freezing the frame, and so on.

More important, the Apple could also read the timecode, giving it the ability to find any particular frame in the recorded observation.

A person sitting at the Apple keyboard would watch the video monitor and decide when a behavior occurred that was relevant to the variable being coded. The coder used the keyboard to stop the playback and then decided on which frame the behavior began and/or ended. This was done by telling the computer to move the videotape forward or backward a specified number of frames until the desired frame was targeted. When the onset or offset frame was found, the coder entered an edit mode and typed in the data. Data could be entered as a string of up to 255 characters and could include anything that can be typed. The four columns on the computer monitor in Figure 6.1 (here labeled 001, 002, and so forth) represent any 4 of the 135 separately coded variables that the system is capable of handling. At the time of transcription, the researcher could call up any 3 variables in relation to coding a 4th variable. For instance, in coding the intentionality underlying the children's words, the coder asked the computer to locate words in one column, the mother's speech to the child in another column, and play behaviors in a third column. The intentionality code (Chapters 7 and 9) was then entered in the fourth column.

Once entered, the data were stored in files ordered sequentially according to timecode. An example of a data file is presented in Figure 6.2. Each line in the file represents one record. Each record has three fields. The first field is a hexadecimal number (2 columns) that identifies the particular variable coded (child speech is 01, mother speech is 02, and so forth). The second field in the record is a hexadecimal number (6 columns) that represents the frame count for hour, min, sec, frame. The third field consists of text of variable length (up to 255 characters). This text may be transcription of speech or any one of a number of codes that we have devised for representing the different data variables. The coded data can be manipulated to (1) generate a hard-copy transcript for traditional sorts of descriptive analyses and (2) perform a variety of quantitative analyses for statistical treatments.

Generating a Transcript

Since the data were stored electronically, they were amenable to manipulation before output. Thus, transcripts could be set up in any number of ways with different combinations of the separate coding passes. Moreover, because the computer can read the timecode and every coding decision is associated with a

```
01 CHILD SPEECH
02 MOTHER SPEECH
05 CHILD PLAY
14 CHILD AFFECT
19 CHILD SPEECH INTENTIONAL STATE
1A CHILD AFFECT INTENTIONAL STATE
32 MOTHER SENTENCE/SITUATION
05 0052E5 CO-MS-IM-GE-NA
19 005325 d:a<go(bff in (slide-in))>d/n
01 005325 in/
01 005337
02 005340 In?/
14 005342 N
02 00534E
32 00535A [GO](ENTITY = cff)(CAUSE = child)(SRCE = NIL)(PATH = NIL)(DEST = slide-in)
02 00535A You can put the boy in./
05 00536B
02 00537C
32 00539F [GO](ENTITY = bff)(CAUSE = child)(SRCE = NIL)(PATH = NIL)(DEST = slide-in)
02 00539F Boy in./
02 0053B6
05 0053FF CO-MR-IM-GE-NA
19 005407 d:a<go(fff in (slide-in))>a/n
01 005407 in/
01 005419
32 00541D [GO](ENTITY = fff)(CAUSE = child)(SRCE = NIL)(PATH = NIL)(DEST = slide-in)
02 00541D Put the man in./
02 00543D
19 005483 d:a<go(fff in (slide-in))>d/n
01 005483 in/
01 005498
32 0054A5 [GO](ENTITY = child)(CAUSE = child)(SRCE = NIL)(PATH = NIL)(DEST = mff)
02 0054A5 Go get the, yeah, go get the girl./
01 0054AC /ə/
01 0054B9
05 0054C0
1A 0054CA d:a<go(fff in (slide-in))>b/y
14 0054CA +1
02 0054D9
32 0054DD [GO](ENTITY = mff&fff&cff)(CAUSE = child)(SRCE = NIL)(PATH = NIL)(DEST =
slide-in)
02 0054DD Put them all in./
02 0054F4
```

6.2 Example of a data file with seven variables.

time of onset and/or offset, the separate codes could be merged sequentially. The merging produced an integrated record, with the relevant behaviors in each of the variables lined up according to the original temporal relations among them. An example of such a computer-generated transcript is presented in Figure 6.3 using data from the file in Figure 6.2; the total elapsed time in this example was 15 sec, 13 frames. The codes represented in the data displayed in the two figures are explained briefly in Table 6.2.

HILD 'EECH	CHILD SPEECH INTENTIONAL STATE	CHILD AFFECT	CHILD AFFECT INTENTIONAL STATE	CHILD PLAY	MOTHER SPEECH	MOTHER SENTENCE/SITUATION
				00:11:47:11 CO-MS-IM-GE-NA		
:49:15	00:11:49:15 d:a<go(bff in (slide-in))>d/n					
:50:03						
					00:11:50:12 In?/	
		00:11:50:14 N				
					00:11:50:26	
					00:11:51:08 You can put the boy in./	00:11:51:08 [GO] (ENTITY = cff) (CAUSE = child) (SRCE = NIL) (PATH = NIL) (DEST = slide-in)
				00:11:51:25		
					00:11:52:12	
					00:11:53:17 Boy in./	00:11:53:17 [GO] (ENTITY = cff) (CAUSE = child) (SRCE = NIL) (PATH = NIL) (DEST = slide-in)
					00:11:54:10	
				00:11:56:23 CO-MR-IM-GE-NA		
:57:01	00:11:57:01 d:a<go(fff in (slide-in))>a/n					
:57:19						
					00:11:57:23 Put the man in./	00:11:57:23 [GO] (ENTITY = fff) (CAUSE = child) (SRCE = NIL) (PATH = NIL) (DEST = slide-in)
					00:11:58:25	
2:01:05	00:12:01:05 d:a<go(fff in (slide-in))>d/n					
2:01:26						
					00:12:02:09 Go get the, yeah, go get the girl./	00:12:02:09 [GO] (ENTITY = child) (CAUSE = child) (SRCE = NIL) (PATH = NIL) (DEST = mff)
2:02:16						
2:02:29						
				00:12:03:06		
		00:12:03:16 +1	00:12:03:16 d:a<go(fff in (slide-in))>b/y			
					00:12:04:01	
					00:12:04:05 Put them all in./	00:12:04:05 [GO] (ENTITY = mff &fff &cff) (CAUSE = child) (SRCE = NIL) (PATH = NIL) (DEST = slide-in)
					00:12:04:28	

6.3 Transcription generated from the data file in Fig. 6.2.

This example of a transcript reproduces the seven separate columns containing (1) transcription of child speech, (2) the code for the intentional state attributed to child speech, (3) mother speech, (4) the situation code for mothers' sentences, (5) child object play, (6) child affect, and (7) the code for the intentional state attributed to child affect. The entries in the columns are associated with times of onset and offset. The seven columns are integrated with one another sequentially according to the timecode. This restored the temporal relations that existed among all the variables at the time the behaviors actually occurred.

A transcript such as this one can be used in much the same way as a traditional transcription. We can examine the unfolding of events in regard to

Table 6.2. *Explanation of codes for examples from data file and transcription*

---

19 Child speech intentional state

19 005325 d:a⟨go(bff in (slide-in))⟩d/n

A child desire (d:) that is achieved (a) to put the boy family figure (bff) into (in) the interior space of the slide (slide-in); said during the action (d) and not directed (n) to the mother

05 Child play

05 0052E5 CO-MS-IM-GE-NA

A construction (CO), related to something the mother had said (MS), that was an imposed (IM) general (GE) relation; (NA) = further coding not applicable

14 Child affect

14 005342 N

Neutral affect expression; only onset times coded because affect expression was coded as a continuous variable (onset of an expression = offset of the preceding expression)

14 Child affect

14 0054CA + 1

Affect expression with positive valence (+) and low-level intensity (1)

1A Child affect intentional state

1A 0054CA d:a⟨go(fff in (slide-in))⟩b/y

A child desire (d:) that is achieved (a) to put the father family figure (fff) into (in) the interior space of the slide (slide-in); the action happened before (b) the expression of emotion, which was directed (yes [y]) to the mother

32 Mother sentence/situation

32 0054DD [GO](ENTITY = mff&fff&cff)(CAUSE = child)(SRCE = NIL)(PATH = NIL)(DEST = slide-in)

The child (CAUSE) moving ([GO]) the mother, father, and child family figures (ENTITY = mff&fff&cff) to the interior of the slide (DEST = slide-in), (SRCE) = source; (PATH) = path; (NIL) = not applicable

---

Source: L. Bloom (1993).

one or another research question, perform descriptive analyses, generate new hypotheses, and so forth. In addition, since the data are electronically stored, the computer can perform many of the data analyses we need.

Quantitative Analyses to Assess Qualitative Domains

The coded data were transferred from the Apples to an IBM-PC and stored in a standard form – delimited ASCII – that allowed access from any number of different programs we developed for converting and manipulating the data. Most simply, the data points coded within a variable could be counted for relative frequencies and contingent probabilities. We know, for example, as a result of several such analyses (reported in the following chapters), how frequently our subjects expressed positive and negative affect; the relative time spent in positive and negative affect expression; and the average duration of individual expressions. We also know how the children's ages at certain language milestones correlated with these measures of affect expression and corresponded to developments in object play. We have looked at the relative frequency of expression of different kinds of mental meanings (derived from the intentionality coding) expressed by affect and words. In still other studies of how the mothers in our sample influenced their children's development, we looked at the mothers' words and sentences and other behaviors around their children's speech, affect expression, and play with objects.

In addition, we looked at the timing of one behavior relative to another – for example, affect expression in relation to speech – and instances of these expressive behaviors in relation to object play. Thus, we were able to show how affect, which had been in place since early infancy, and speech, which was just emerging, came together in the single-word period in relation to each other and in the relation of both to play with objects.[39]

To be sure, very many qualitative phenomena will always resist such quantitative treatment. This is to be expected whenever we delve into the domain of human expression. Nevertheless, in our efforts to understand how young children acquire the power of expression, we must of necessity make the relevant phenomena accessible for study. This means recording the phenomena so as to preserve them in the first place, and transforming the recording for the analyses that we do. Our plan for computer-assisted transcription made use of the technology currently available in order to respond to problems of selectivity in transcription that have been around for a very long time.

Closing the Gap

This chapter has continued the dialog concerning the *accountability of evidence in child language research.*[40] The problems of selectivity in transcription will always be with us. However, we believe we succeeded in making at least modest progress toward closing the gap between an act of expression and the record we make of it in our efforts to understand it.

On the face of it, separating the covariables contained in an act of expression in order to attend to only one variable at a time would seem to be indeed a radical reduction of the data. However, separation of covariables is not the same as isolating the variables, because we necessarily attend to whatever surrounds the target variable in making coding decisions regarding it. Furthermore, separating a variable for the purpose of coding or transcription assures us that we have preserved the integrity of that particular variable beyond what would be possible if we tried attending to many or even several aspects of behavior at the same time. The effect of narrowing the focus in this way was to enlarge our view of the target variable, enabling us to see it more clearly and consider it more carefully. In addition, transcription problems having to do with training and reliability were far more manageable than they would otherwise have been. But most important, *we can always add variables.* Our transcript is never limited by whatever questions or concerns motivated the research at one particular time or another. Thus, separation of covariables reduces the data only to enlarge our view of the evidence.

Two other factors contributed to our confidence that we were avoiding at least some of the susceptibility to investigator bias inherent in observational research. The use of coders and transcribers who were uninformed about the research questions and hypotheses in our studies reduced the tendency to interpret rather than describe in the decisions made during transcription. Another factor was the delicate balance in confidence we have between persons and machines for making decisions regarding timing in events. Persons make the original decisions regarding onset and/or offset of a particular piece of the action. But machines are far more adept than persons at putting the pieces of the action back together again.

CONCLUSIONS

We began this chapter with the simple transformation: *talk* ⇒ *data* ⇒ *evidence* and pointed out that both theory and method inform each other in the transformation. The value of talk as data depends on the methods we use to describe it – by recording, transcribing, and coding the talk and whatever else is relevant to it. In turn, data become valuable as evidence according to how successful we are in describing the talk for the interpretations we make of it.

The system for coding and transcription we used is an example of how conceptual developments in the field and developments in technology came together in the most recent two decades of child language research. Studying language in context and studying the development of language in the context of other developments in the child's life require that we preserve far more than just the spoken word in the record we make of the data we collect. Nonindustrial video recording became available at just about the time that context was introduced into the study of child language, in the late 1960s. A video record confronts us with an overwhelming amount of information, even recognizing how much is lost in the inevitable reduction of data that occurs through recording. The resulting problems of selectivity have begun to seem more manageable with the development of personal computers in the last 10 years. We can only wonder how the ways in which we study children's language may change in the 21st century as a result of what we learn from our present research and the developments in technology to come.

We turn now to the different interpretations we made of the different sorts of data we collected – observations of the children's speech, affect expressions, and play with objects, and their mothers' actions in regard to these.

7
Developments in Expression

This chapter begins by showing how we defined the two expressive behaviors we observed, affect and words, with the coding categories for affect expression and the criteria for achievements in word learning we used. The frequencies of words and emotional expressions at the beginning and end of the period are the first result reported here to show that emotional expression does not decrease as words are acquired. Following this is a description of certain aspects of the mental meanings attributed to the intentional states underlying the children's emotional expression and words.[1]

AFFECT AND WORDS IN THE SINGLE-WORD PERIOD

Affect Expression

Expressions of affect carry both categorical and gradient information. Categorical information is the discrete emotion that is expressed, such as anger, fear, joy, or sadness. Gradient properties include qualitative descriptive features of an expression, such as its intensity and valence. Intensity is the relative fullness of a display and can vary from a barely perceptible frown to a raging cry, or from the slightest of smiles to hysterical laughter. Valence is the hedonic tone or value of an expression, such as a positive tone in joy and pleasure and a negative tone in sadness, anger, and fear. Neutral affect is the presence of hedonic tone without either positive or negative valence. Neutral affect is not a lack of affect, because affect is always present. And it is not to be confused with the so-called flat affect sometimes seen in certain instances of pathology. Neutral affect is the expression accompanying states of quiet, wakeful attention or awareness – a baseline level of affective engagement.

Gradient and categorical information in an affect display are complementary rather than mutually exclusive. In fact, there is a long tradition in the study of emotion in which the gradient dimensions of pleasantness and arousal have been used to define categories of emotions and the relations among them.[2] Obviously, the positive emotions include joy and happiness; the negative emotions include anger, sadness, and fear; and neutral affect has been associated, at least in part, with the discrete emotion of interest.

We had no empirical or theoretical reason to expect that categories of the discrete emotions would contribute to understanding how children learn words. For this reason, we opted to code infants' affect displays at the level of description, using gradient information of valence and intensity. The gradient properties of affect expression are theoretically neutral with respect to a theory of emotion as well as a theory of language. Thus, we took a pretheoretical stance in the coding scheme we developed for the children's affect expressions, knowing that identifying and labeling expressions of the discrete emotions are always options at another time or in other contexts.[3]

With the basic assumption that affect is always present, we coded the children's affect expressions continuously in the stream of their activities in the playroom. An affect expression was defined as any observable change in the valence and/or intensity of the child's facial expression, body tension or posture, and/or affective vocalizations (whining, laughing, and the like). The result of the coding categories and the decision rules for applying them was a continuous record of affect expressions and the duration of affect expression from one change in expression to another.

Every change in expressed affect was identified and entered into the computer with the time of onset; the offset time of the expression was the onset time of the next change in affect expression. The average margin of error among coders for coding affect onset time (after extensive training) was remarkably small: only 16 video frames, or approximately $\frac{1}{2}$ sec. This was somewhat greater than the margin of error in onset and offset times for speech, because of the fact that several kinds of continuous cues were used to code affect (facial expression, body tension, affective vocalization). The margin of error was within 2 video frames (or $\frac{1}{15}$ sec) for word onset time and within 5 video frames (or $\frac{1}{6}$ sec) for word offset.

Affect expressions were coded for their *valence,* whether neutral, negative, positive, mixed, or equivocal hedonic tone. A neutral expression was defined as the face being in a resting or baseline position, without movement, as

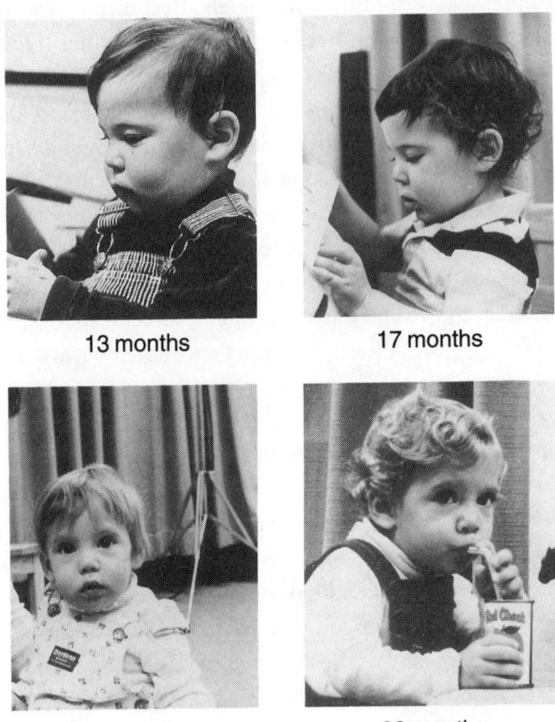

7.1 Examples of neutral affect expression. (L. Bloom, Beckwith, Capatides, & Hafitz, 1988)

described by Paul Ekman and his colleagues, and without body tension or affective vocalization.[4] The photos in Figure 7.1 are examples of neutral affect expression from two of the children in our study, Clark and Shirley, both at two ages (Shirley at 11 and 22 months; Clark at 13 and 17 months). The photographs in Figure 7.2 are examples of mixed affect expression, which included elements of both positive and negative valence. Equivocal affect was neither positive, negative, nor neutral, as happened with expressions of surprise or excitement, as in the photos in Figure 7.3.

The photos in Figures 7.4 and 7.5 are examples of positive and negative expressions, respectively, each at three levels of *intensity* indicating the fullness of a display. The photos in Figure 7.4 are examples of the three positive

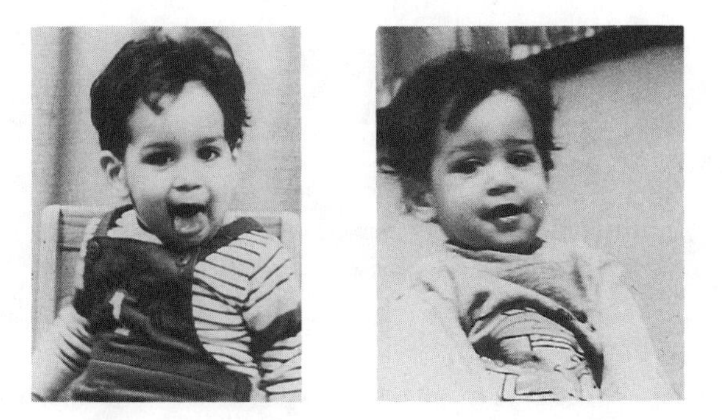

7.2 Examples of mixed affect expression. (L. Bloom, Beckwith, Capatides, & Hafitz, 1988)

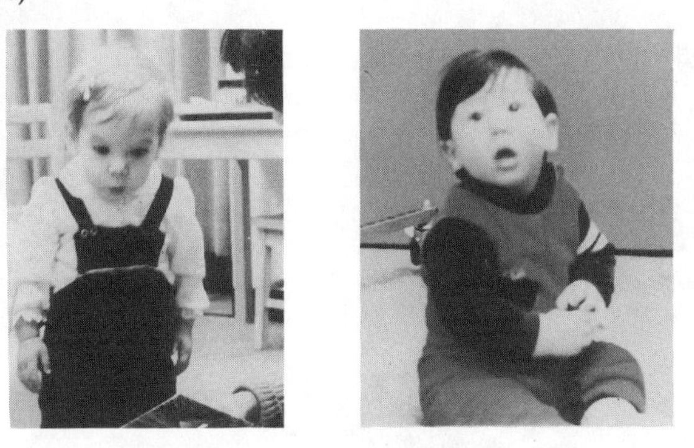

7.3 Examples of equivocal affect expression. (L. Bloom, Beckwith, Capatides, & Hafitz, 1988)

categories +1, +2, +3, and the photos in Figure 7.5 are examples of the negative categories −1, −2, and −3. In sum, using gradient properties to describe the quality of expressed affect yielded three levels of intensity (1, 2, and 3) and five qualities of valence (neutral, negative, positive, mixed, and equivocal). The coding categories consisted of a combination of two values, one for valence and one for intensity, with a descriptive code for affective vocalizations (wn= whine, lf = laugh, and so forth).

The examples in these figures are from the still photographs we took each month. They were not taken originally to use for the purpose of showing examples of affect expressions but rather for the album of monthly photos we presented to the mothers as a way of thanking them at the end of the study.

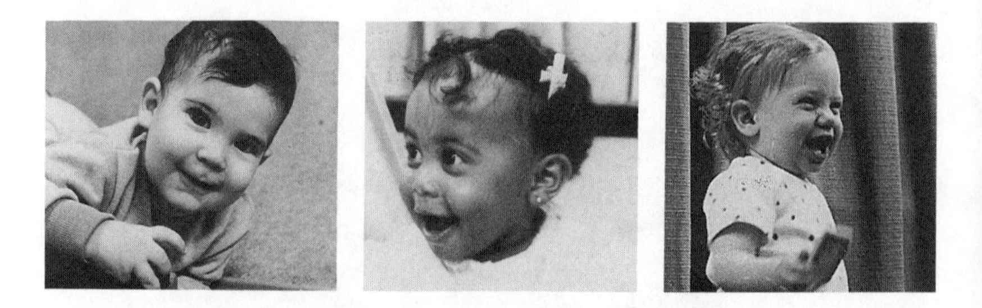

7.4 Examples of positive emotional expression at three levels of intensity. (L. Bloom, Beckwith, Capatides, & Hafitz, 1988)

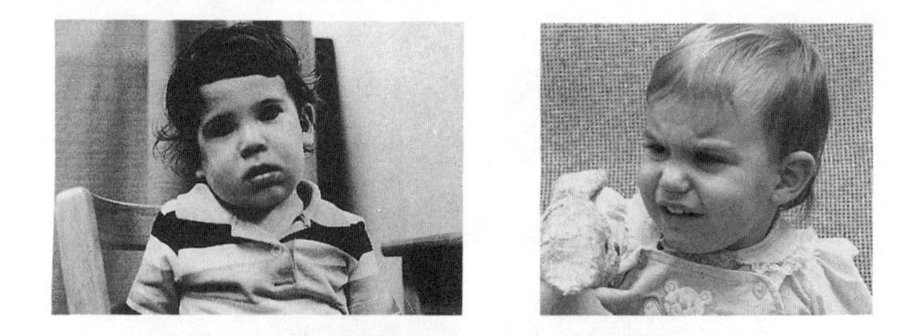

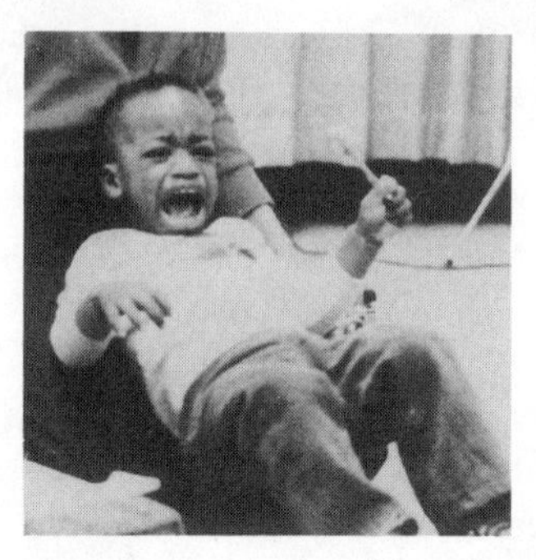

7.5 Examples of negative emotional expression at three levels of intensity. (L. Bloom, Beckwith, Capatides, & Hafitz, 1988)

These still photos do not reveal the richness of cues available for coding from the dynamic displays on the video screen.

Sometimes a momentary vocalization or facial movement could not be assigned to one of these coding categories. These ambiguous cases were relatively infrequent; for example, an average of 12 ambiguous expressions occurred in a half hour when the infants were 9 months old. Interestingly, ambiguous expressions were most frequent (an average of 20 instances) during the session in which the infants first began to say words in the playroom, when they were about 14 months on average. In addition, the children were sometimes moving away from the camera or the face was not visible for coding, and there were no other cues from body tension or affective vocalization. All instances of these intervals of "backturn" and ambiguous expression were coded for onset time so that coding affect in the stream of the child's activity was not interrupted. Together these episodes of ambiguous affect expression and backturn amounted to an average of from 4 to 6 min of the 30 min we coded for each session; they were not included in any of the data analyses.[5]

The continuous record of changes in expressed affect and duration of each expression was coded in the computer. This made it possible to count expressions with different valence and levels of intensity to determine how frequently the individual children expressed affect overall, how frequently they expressed positive and negative affect, how frequently an expression shifted from one level of intensity to another (for example, from +1 to +2 or from −2 to −1), and the like. Because every coding decision was associated with the time of onset, we were also able to count the number of video frames to determine the average duration and total time of the different kinds of expressions. And finally, because the other variables we coded – including speech, play, mothers' speech, and so forth – were also associated with times of onset and offset, we could merge the coded records to restore their original sequence and the temporal relationships among them. This made it possible to analyze dynamic relationships among variables at one time and across time.

The results of our studies of these aspects of affect expression will unfold in the remainder of this chapter and in the chapters to follow. However, a picture can be painted here in broad strokes of the quality of the infants' affect expressions in the playroom sessions in which we observed them. Recall that the children played with their mothers and groups of toys introduced on a schedule in the course of an hour. Affect expression was coded for only the first half hour of a session, and during this time the children and their mothers had a snack. Sometimes the mothers changed a diaper or offered a bottle. It was, essentially, a relaxed time. (What standardized testing we did took place during the home visits or after the play session.)

Two features of the general profile of the children's affect expressions were noteworthy. One was the prevalence of neutral affect: The children spent most of their time in neutral affect expression. At first we thought this result might have come from the fact that they were attending to the toys for much of the time.[6] However, we have been struck with how often this same result has appeared in other studies of young children's affect expression, often in very different circumstances.[7] Very young children apparently do not express positive and negative affect with great frequency: in fact, only about 16% of the time on average (with important individual differences, as we shall see). The second feature of these sessions was that the nonneutral affect they expressed was mostly positive affect; they were enjoying themselves in the playroom, and the quality of their expressed affect reflected this. Both results might well have been different if we had visited the children in their homes at different times of the day. For instance, we might have seen much more nonneutral expression, and especially more negative expression, had we visited the children at bedtime.[8]

The value of our playroom sessions was in the consistency they provided for all the children and for each child over time. Because the children were less likely to be influenced by the effects of different contexts, we had greater confidence that systematic changes in the expression of affect and in the expression of affect in relation to saying words and playing with objects could be attributed to developmental process. The major results of our studies consisted of such systematic relationships among affect expression, speech, and play during this early period in language development.

Achievements in Word Learning

One of the few "facts" about language acquisition that everyone agrees on is that children vary widely in age of onset and rate of progress. Certain milestones are well established. Most children begin to say words at around their first birthday, give or take a few months; begin to combine words sometime toward the end of the second year; and acquire the basics of simple and complex sentences before they are 3 years old. Within these "norms," however, we find a great deal of "normal" variation, so that age alone is not a dependable criterion for predicting language development. For this reason, and in order to discount differences among them that might have resulted from differences in their language abilities, we equated the children on the basis of achievements in language for many of the analyses.[9]

The three language achievements we identified were First Words (FW), a Vocabulary Spurt (VS), and the onset of sentences, Multiword Speech (MW). First Words was the first occurrence of at least one conventional word used at two different times in a playroom session – having both a phonetic form consistent with a word in the language and relevance to something in the context or between mother and child. Mothers of several of the children had been reporting in their diaries that their children were beginning to say words at home before they were saying words in the playroom (3 months before, on average). Thus, the session we labeled First Words was not literally the very first time a child might have said a word. However, saying words outside the support of the home context is an achievement in itself, and once the children said their first words in the playroom, they continued to do so from then on. Individual mothers varied in the consistency with which they reported words at home, but the criteria for first words in the playroom were the same for all the children.

The acquisition of new words was tracked from one month to the next in the playroom. We considered that a child showed a vocabulary spurt when the number of new words in a session (1) showed an increase equivalent to at least 3 new words per week or 12 new words from one month to the next (2) after the child had already learned at least 20 different words. Mean age for the 14 children at the time of First Words was 13.8 (13 months, 26 days), and they said an average of 4.7 different words (range = 2 to 12 words). At the time of the Vocabulary Spurt, their mean age was 19.2 (19 months, 7 days), and they had said an average of 51 different words (range = 34 to 75 words). The average increase in new words from one month to the next, beginning at First Words and continuing through the month after the Vocabulary Spurt, is shown in Figure 7.6. The criteria we used – 3 new words a week after having learned 20 different words – revealed a vocabulary spurt for all the children.[10] Children's vocabularies grow slowly at first, but the rate of increase in new words inevitably accelerates. Using our criteria, all children would eventually have to show a vocabulary spurt.

The third of the achievements in language we identified for comparison with other aspects of development was the beginning of sentences or Multiword Speech. The MW achievement was identified as the first month in which the child's average length of utterance reached 1.5 words. Again, this

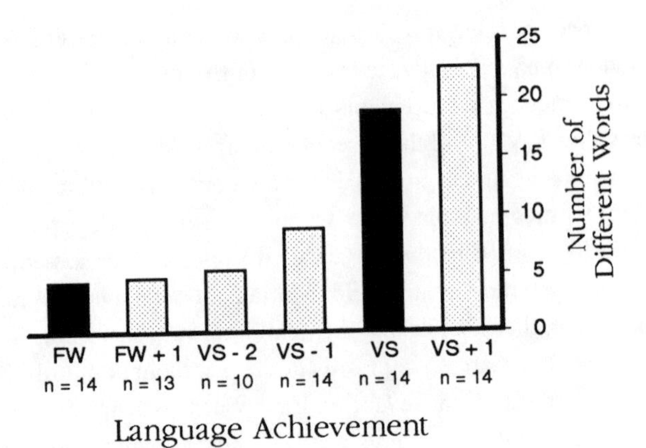

7.6 Average monthly increase in new words, from First Words to 1 month after Vocabulary Spurt, with 3 months representing the interval between achievements.

was strictly a quantitative measure; different linguistic factors can contribute to increase in utterance length with different children.[11] However, few would disagree that the ability to combine words for phrases and simple sentences is a major qualitative development and effectively signals the end of the single-word period. The mean age at each of the three language achievements – FW, VS, and MW – is shown along with the range in the children's ages in Figure 7.7.

Most of the results we shall be talking about in this and the remaining chapters pertain to developments between FW and VS. These two milestones effectively defined the *transition to language:* FW was the beginning of the single-word period and marked the tentative *emergence* of words; VS occurred toward the end of the period and marked the *achievement* of word learning and a basic working vocabulary.[12]

Frequency of Words and Emotional Expressions

At the most basic level, we looked, quite simply, at just how often the children said words and how often they expressed emotion (positive, negative, mixed, or equivocal affect) at FW and VS. The frequencies of words and emotional expressions are presented in Figure 7.8; these are total numbers of tokens at FW and VS for the group of 14 children as a whole.

As expected, emotional expressions were far more frequent than words at

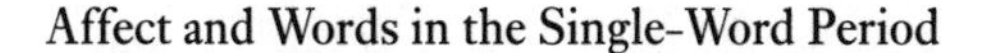

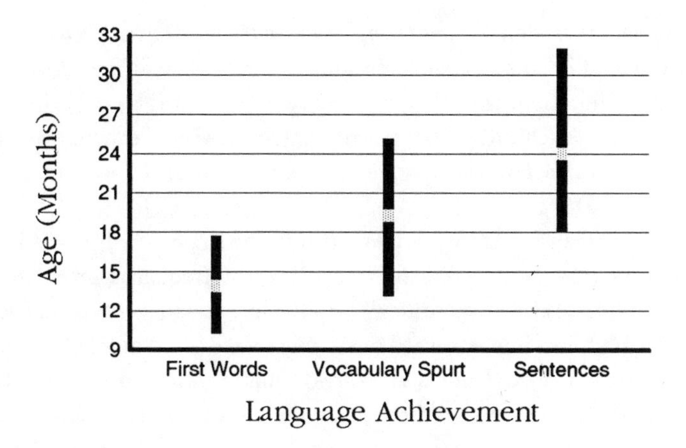

7.7 Mean and range in age at the three language achievements.

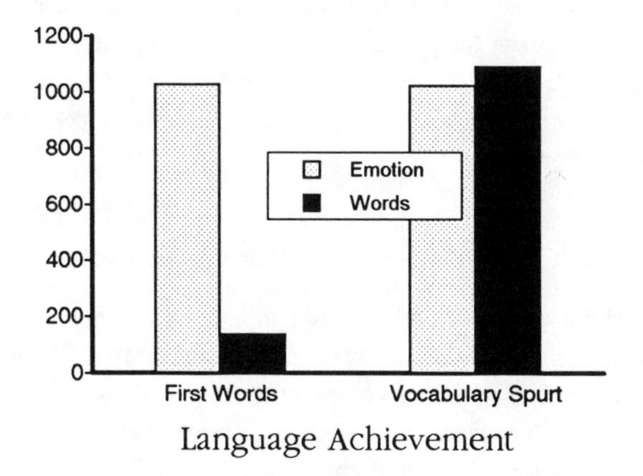

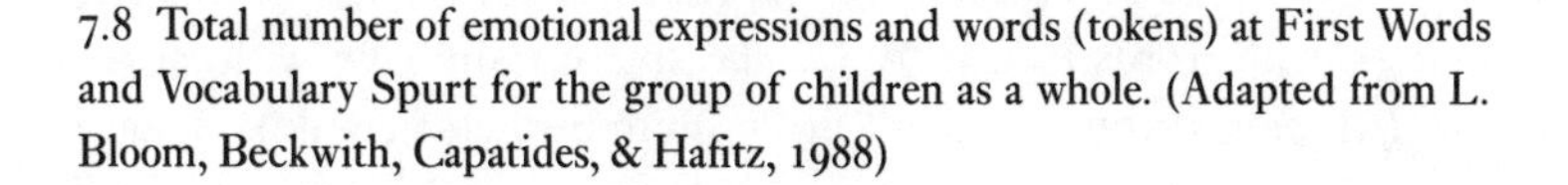
7.8 Total number of emotional expressions and words (tokens) at First Words and Vocabulary Spurt for the group of children as a whole. (Adapted from L. Bloom, Beckwith, Capatides, & Hafitz, 1988)

FW. At VS, words were eight times more frequent than they had been at FW. This was neither surprising nor interesting, because an increase in number of words was the criterion we used for identifying the vocabulary spurt. However, although words increased, the frequency of emotional expressions remained essentially the same from FW to VS. This means that the frequency of emotional expression did not change *between the two language achievements* for the group of infants as a whole. In addition, individual differences among the infants in how frequently they expressed emotion were also stable between the two language achievements; the correlation between frequency of emotional expression at FW and frequency of expression at VS was significant (Pearson $r = .636, p < .025$).

The first conclusion is that development in the single-word period is not simply an increase in overall expressivity, because frequency of emotional expression did not also increase along with the increase in words from FW to VS. Although the children learned to say more words, and linguistic expression increased, they did not also express emotion more frequently. But, equally important, expression through speech did not replace affect expression, because emotional expression did not decrease from FW to VS. Saying words was not something these children learned to do *instead of* expressing affect. They continued to express their feelings in emotion displays, as they were learning language for expressing and articulating what their thoughts and feelings were *about*. This was the focus of the following study of intentionality, in which we attributed mental meanings to the children's words and emotional expressions.

ATTRIBUTIONS OF MENTAL MEANING

We were interested in words, affect, and play as modes of expression and the mental meanings we could reasonably attribute to these behaviors. An expression is an embodiment of a mental meaning, and children can express something of the same mental meaning (for example, making a toy train) with different embodiments. A child might connect two objects in an action (like putting two railroad cars together) or express their connection with a gesture (pointing), with words (saying "train" or "make train"), or with an affect display (whining if the cars don't fit or smiling when they do). Because a child's talk is typically about events that others in the context can also appreciate, attributing meaning is essentially straightforward. Indeed, communication between young children and their caregivers depends on it.

We attributed meaning to the children's emotional expressions in the tradition of rich interpretation in studies of early language. We know that feeling states are accompanied by particular behaviors like crying and smiling, and these allow us to say something more than just that an infant is crying or smiling. At the least, the cry or smile tells us that the baby is experiencing some emotional state. But, more than that, something must have caused the emotion; some event underlying the feeling state is the object of the emotion or what the emotion is about.[13] If the object of an emotion caused the emotion, then it must also have caused its expression. We can therefore attribute the object of the emotion to the expression of the emotion. As with children's speech, we can often determine what caused the emotion by observing the context of affect displays. The things a child's emotions are about are frequently part of the context, so that we are licensed to attribute thinking about those things to the child. Objects and events in the context are often part of a child's goals and mental plans to achieve those goals, and emotions are expressed in connection with the success and failure of goals and plans.[14] When we see someone act in a particular way, we are licensed to attribute to that person the desire to act in that way. If the person's action ceases after the action leads to some effect, we are licensed to attribute to that person the plan to achieve that effect.[15] These sorts of attributions are not mysterious; parents make them routinely in their everyday caregiving practices. Infants count on their doing so and soon learn to do the same.

Coding the full content and structure of intentional states would be an unreasonable task – that is, we could never verify all the units, with their roles and the relations among them, in a child's mental meaning at any one point in time. But we could make attributions of what a child's beliefs and desires were about, which is what caregivers do routinely. When a baby whimpers, they might attribute hunger or discomfort or an inability to reach a toy. We made the same sorts of attributions of what children were thinking about when they displayed an emotion or said a word. In coding these attributions, we used the kinds of cues that caregivers use – what the child says, what the child does, what has been said or what is subsequently said, what is observable in the context, and what we know of the child from past experience. Moreover, we could do what a caregiver could not do. We used our videotapes to watch and listen to the moments that surrounded an expression, over and over, and we could look ahead as well as backwards for relevant cues.

In sum, several modes of expression are available to the young child, and we are licensed to make attributions on the basis of each of them. To make these attributions, we need only acknowledge and make explicit the practice of making attributions based on *language as expression* and then expand the practice to other forms of expression. This is what we did with infants' affect expressions and early words (described in what follows here and in Chapter 9) and play with objects (Chapter 10).

Beliefs and Desires

Although the relative frequency of emotional expressions and words was interesting, we were more interested in what these expressions were about. We began with the basic assumption that words and emotion displays were expressions of beliefs and desires. Belief and desire are the most fundamental of the psychological attitudes in intentional states.[16] Expressions based on belief or desire were also relatively easy to distinguish and therefore to code in the data. The decision was whether infants expressed a desire with a goal to change the world or expressed a belief in the way the world appeared to them. This was invariably a straightforward decision, and reliability was extremely high (at least 90% agreement between pairs of coders). The result was the relative frequencies of attributions of belief and desire to words and emotional expressions at First Words and Vocabulary Spurt.[17]

Desires were expressed more frequently than beliefs, by emotional expression and by words. Just as the frequency of emotional expression did not change from FW to VS, the 2 : 1 ratio of desires to beliefs expressed by emotional expression did not change from FW to VS. The ratio for words was similar at VS, 1.8 : 1. However, desires were attributed to words more often at VS than at FW; the ratio of desires to beliefs attributed to words at FW was 1.3 : 1. Words, then, tended to express desires relatively less often than affect expressions, particularly at FW. Thus, when words first appeared, they were less likely than affect expressions (or words at a later time) to be used for achieving goals or changing the world to fit the child's view of it.

Beliefs and Desires about Self and Other

The question in this analysis was whether desires and beliefs were about the children themselves or about their mothers – doing, going, or having something. Desires were most often about the *child's* actions rather than desires for their mothers to do something, at both FW and VS. The ratios for emotional expressions were somewhat higher than for words. The self : other ratio in desires attributed to emotional expressions was 5.7 : 1 at FW and 5 : 1

at VS. The ratio for words was 4 : 1 at both times. Thus, the children were expressing desires concerning primarily their own actions in regard to their own purposes and goals. Even though they expressed desires more often than beliefs, their expressions of desire were not used primarily as tools for manipulating actions by other persons.

A different picture emerged with respect to the expression of beliefs. In contrast to their expressions of desire, the children's beliefs were primarily about their mothers and their mothers' actions. For example, Charlie looked up at his mother, who was watching what he was doing, and smiled at her, or Vivian watched her mother rolling the truck down the slide and said "down." The overall ratio of beliefs about the mother to beliefs about the self (attributed to both words and emotional expression) was 8 : 1 at FW and 3 : 1 at VS. Thus, the children's expression of beliefs had to do most often with something in the world that included their mothers. But with development from FW to VW, the ratio decreased as the children expressed beliefs that concerned something about themselves relatively more often.

However, expressions of beliefs about the mother were attributed relatively more often to the children's emotional expressions; the ratios were 12 : 1 at FW and 6 : 1 at VS. The ratio of beliefs about the mother to beliefs about the child expressed by words was 2 : 1 at both times. This was in contrast to the ratios for affect and word expression of desires, which were similar for both kinds of expression and in the other direction, with *self : other* ratios of about 5 : 1 for affect and 4 : 1 for words at both FW and VS. In sum, beliefs were more often about other persons than about the self, for both kinds of expression, but emotional expressions were more likely than words to express beliefs about another person (the mother primarily).

The high ratio of *other : self* beliefs expressed affectively takes on added meaning when we consider the relative frequencies of beliefs and desires attributed to the children's emotional expressions and words. The children expressed emotion far more frequently than they said words at FW, so it was not surprising that affect expressed the greater proportion of all the categories of belief and desire at FW. These proportions are presented in Table 7.1; overall, words expressed an average of only 14% of the attributions at FW but an average of 55% of the attributions at VS.

With one exception, words at VS expressed the greater proportion of every category of propositions except one. The exception was expressions of beliefs

Table 7.1. *Attributions of children's beliefs and desires about self and other* (N = *14)*

	Belief		Desire	
	About other	About self	About other	About self
First Words	*n = 386*	*n = 50*	*n = 174*	*n = 948*
Emotion	347 (0.90)	29 (0.57)	144 (0.83)	825 (0.87)
Words	39 (0.10)	21 (0.43)	30 (0.17)	123 (0.13)
Vocabulary Spurt	*n = 459*	*n = 152*	*n = 478*	*n = 2,117*
Emotion	257 (0.56)	46 (0.30)	186 (0.39)	953 (0.45)
Words	202 (0.44)	106 (0.70)	292 (0.61)	1,164 (0.55)

Source: Adapted from L. Bloom, Beckwith, Capatides, & Hafitz (1988).

that included another person; these continued to be expressed by emotionally toned affect relatively more often than by words at VS. This result underscores the *social* function of emotional expression. Smiling, for example, in addition to signaling the experience of positive emotion, is socially motivated from an early age. Infants smile more when their mothers are with them than when they play alone with toys or with a peer, and they are also more apt to smile during play with objects when their mothers are attending to them than when they are not.[18]

In sum, the children whom we studied expressed desires more often than beliefs – with both emotional expressions and words – but expressed beliefs relatively more often when words first appeared, at FW. By the time they reached a vocabulary spurt, desires were expressed essentially twice as frequently overall. Most of the desires they expressed were about themselves and their own actions rather than about those of other persons, with both emotional expressions and words. However, most of the beliefs they expressed were about other persons, primarily their mothers, who were with them in our playroom. Beliefs about another person, moreover, were relatively more likely to be expressed with affect at both FW and VS; the only category of attributions at VS in which the majority of expressions continued to be emotional expressions were those beliefs that concerned something about the mother or another person.

CONCLUSIONS

Words did not replace emotional expressions as the children acquired a vocabulary in the second year. The frequency of emotional expressions – and the profile of mental meanings attributed to them – were quite stable between the two language achievements. Although words increased from FW to VS, the frequency of emotional expressions did not increase. This stability in frequency of emotional expression was complemented by stability in the 2 : 1 ratio of desires to beliefs, the higher ratio of self to other persons attributed as the actors in desires, and the higher ratio of other persons to self attributed to beliefs. The stability in these findings is evidence that the children began their language learning with a system of emotional expression that was already well defined and well established. Words did not replace affect expression but emerged as a new system for expressing mental meanings – with names of persons, objects, actions, and relations – as affect continued to express a child's feelings about these things.

In addition, beliefs about another person were more likely to be expressed affectively than with words at both times and were reminiscent of descriptions of "social referencing" in exchanges between infants and caregivers.[19] Whereas words came to assume most of the responsibility for expressing mental meanings at the vocabulary spurt, the children continued to express beliefs about other persons and their actions toward them primarily through expression of emotionally toned affect. This finding underscores the conclusion in other studies that affect displays, in addition to expressing emotion, are socially motivated from a very early age.

Two versions of the transition from infant affect communication to the emergence of language have ascribed different functions to affect expression before and after speech appears. In one version, affect is described as the "content" of communication in infancy but becomes the "context" when speech appears. In another version of the transition, affect is the "topic" of communication in infancy, but once speech begins words name the topic and affect functions as the "comment" on that topic.[20] Both these views imply that the function of emotional expression changes in this period. However, the function of affect expression does not change. Children continue to express how they feel about their beliefs and desires affectively, whereas words are learned to express what these are about. And, finally, the finding that desires were about something the child wanted to do more often than what they wanted another person to do meant they were not learning words primarily to influence other persons to do things.

In the next chapter we look more closely at developments in affect expression to see the influence that learning to say words and expressing affect had on each other. The details of the words these children learned and how they used words for expression in progressing from FW to VS are taken up in Chapter 9, where still other aspects of the mental meanings expressed by the children's words are described.

8

Developments in Affect Expression

Certainly by 9 months of age, infants appreciate what is happening around them, and these appreciations influence affective expression. Both valence (whether they smile or frown, laugh or cry) and intensity (whether they smile or laugh, frown or cry) depend upon how they evaluate what is going on around them in relation to what they have in mind. We may disagree about the kind of thinking that contributes to these appraisals for the experience and expression of emotion. But no one believes that the 9-month-old's emotional expressions are mindless, least of all the infant's caregivers who care about and respond to expressions of emotion as communicative events. At the same time, 9-month-old infants are beginning to pay attention to words they hear and to think about the connections between those words and what they feel and see and do. We have asked how the cognition for attending to words, learning new words, and saying words is related to the cognition needed for the experience and expression of emotion, and how the responses of a caregiver to a child's emotional expressions provide information about the causes and circumstances of emotional experience.

We have already seen, in Chapter 7, that the frequency of emotional expression and certain aspects of the mental meanings we attributed to the children's emotional expressions did not change between the two language achievements FW and VS for the group of infants as a whole. Nevertheless, the emergence of language did interact with developments in these children's affect expression in the period in which we studied them. Both local effects and large effects were observed. Local effects occurred in the moment-to-moment contingencies between actually saying a word and expressing emotion. Large effects were seen in developmental trends in affect expression during the second year and in the relationship between affect expression and language achievements. This chapter is about the local and large effects in the mutual influence between affect expression and language, and how the mothers in our study responded to their infants' emotional expressions in this period of early word learning.

COGNITION, AFFECT, AND LANGUAGE

Several perspectives on emotion research and theory, beginning at least with Magda Arnold in 1960, have attempted to explain emotion in cognitive terms.[1] The results of this research with adults and older children, especially in the last decade, have shown how emotion and cognition influence each other. On the one hand, we know that how an individual appraises the situation in relation to goals and plans can lead to experiencing different emotions; these factors help to define the discrete categories of emotions as well as ways of coping.[2] For example, anger and sadness differ according to whether the focus of an appraisal is on the cause of a blocked goal (which ordinarily leads to anger) or on its consequence (which ordinarily leads to sadness). On the other hand, different emotional states and moods can either enhance or inhibit such cognitive activity as recall from memory and problem solving.[3] People tend to perform tasks better when they are feeling good than when they are feeling bad, and the kinds of material they recall can also be influenced by the mood they are in. However, the relationship between emotion and language, which is itself a part of cognition, has barely been touched on in this research (except to inquire into how words that name the emotions are learned and used).

Consider, first, what might be required to express emotional feeling. At the minimum, we can identify three things. Something of what the feeling is about has to have been noticed and attended to, whether it originates outside the self or from within. This object of the emotion has to consist, at least at some level of understanding, of an evaluation of circumstances in relation to an aspect of a mental plan, usually a goal.[4] In addition, there is the feeling itself: the visceral and autonomic changes that are the "felt emotion."[5] And finally there is the display that we see. The order in which we talk about these three things may well be theoretically motivated: whether one considers the cognition or the feeling or the expression to be primary.[6] However, regardless of their relative primacy, all three require some sort of effort; even the display entails motor movements and their control. The experience and expression of emotion may appear to be automatic and effortless, but they are not.

Now consider what might be required to learn a new word. Again, at the minimum, we can identify three things. First, the infant has to notice and attend to an acoustic event (or hand movement for learning a sign) and to something that is relevant in the context. Second, the infant has to draw some sort of connection between the two, if only to associate the two things because they happened together. And, more often than not, these things will also be relevant to how the infant feels about them: for example, hearing "milk" as milk is poured into the glass, or hearing "uhoh" when the glass is knocked over, or "more" when the glass is refilled. And third, this association between word and event has to be stored in memory as an episode that is more or less related to past experiences of hearing those words and seeing milk being poured, spilled, drunk; glasses and other objects being knocked over; and all sorts of things that recur again and again. These things all require mental effort: to attend to the word in the first place, to associate it with something else that is going on – including how the infant feels about it – and to encode and store the association in memory.

Finally, consider what is required for saying a word or making a sign. The infant has to construct a mental meaning out of what is perceived and what is recalled from past experience. The infant has to recall the word or sign from memory. And the word or sign needs to be executed. Again, all three require cognitive effort: to attend and reflect on the relationship between data from perception and data from the knowledge base in memory, to recall the word, and to execute the motor movements for saying the word or making the sign.

How do these things fit together? How do an infant's feelings and the cognitive requirements for expressing emotion, learning words, and saying words relate to one another in this period of word learning in the second year? The essential answer to this question is that cognitive effort is required for the experience and expression of emotion and for learning and using words, and these efforts compete for the essentially limited cognitive resources of the 1-year-old child. The developmental relationship between emotion and language, therefore, falls out of the need for cooperation among competing processes in deploying the resources that each requires.

The rest of this chapter is concerned with developments in affect expression in the second year in relation to the emergence of language. We will begin with a bit of history and recount efforts in the recent and not so recent literature to explain the relationship between affect expression and the origins of language. Then, in describing the results of our research, we will begin with an account of what we have called the local effects that happen in real time when children are both expressing positive or negative affect and saying a word. Then we will describe the larger developmental effects we have observed in two ways. First, the results of correlations between measures of affect expression and age at the time of the language achievements FW, VS, and MW are presented to show that they are related. Second, in the effort to show *how* they are related, developmental trends in affect expression will be described with the children equated for age rather than language achievement. These developmental trends encompass the 1-year period that began before the appearance of words and ended after the mean age of the vocabulary spurt: from 9 to 21 months of age. Third, we will discuss the developments in these children's affect expression in terms of the influence that the emergence of language might have had on individual temperament. The chapter concludes with an account of how the mothers of the children we studied provided information about the meaning of emotion when they responded to the children's emotional expressions.

AFFECT EXPRESSION AND THE EMERGENCE OF LANGUAGE

Intuitively, one might expect emotional expression to somehow guide the emergence of language and early word learning. First, the simple fact is that affect expression begins virtually at birth and is well under way by the time words begin a year or more later.[7] One-year-olds who are just beginning to learn words have been expressing feelings of one kind or another since earliest infancy. And in addition, much of the form and content of social interaction and communication between infants and their caregivers in the first year of life depends upon this affective expression.[8] Thus, not only is communication through affect expression already in place in late infancy, it is obviously far superior to language for communicating even after words begin to appear. Both developmental precedence and communication effectiveness, therefore, have made it seem that word learning ought somehow to build upon affect expression.

Several theories of language have indeed appealed to the expression of feelings and emotions for the origins of words. These are both phylogenetic theories to explain the origin of language in the species and ontogenetic theories to explain the origin of language in children. One of the most influential among the classic phylogenetic theories of language was offered by Condillac in the 18th century. He proposed that the conventional signs of speech originated when the involuntary vocal gestures that accompanied "the passions of joy, of fear, or of grief" were deliberately repeated for the benefit of other persons in the absence of their eliciting conditions.[9] The sounds of emotion presumably began to assume the status of words when they were produced voluntarily with the intention to communicate something to another person about an absent state of affairs.

Echoes of such theories can be found in contemporary ontogenetic accounts that trace the origins of meaning in communication to affective exchanges between infants and their caregivers in the first year.[10] Without question, infants come to appreciate the "meaningfulness" of these exchanges, and they form the core of intersubjectivity. Coming from two very different perspectives, the psychological and the linguistic, respectively, Daniel Stern and Michael Halliday have eloquently described how prelinguistic infants "learn how to mean."[11] In a very real sense of the word, *meaning* means mutual understanding, and such understanding need not require words for expression. But the issue here is the emergence of language for the expression of meaning, and so we need to be concerned with how words are learned for expressing meaning.

Two conflicting sets of possibilities presented themselves when we asked how affect expression might be related to early words. On the one hand, infants ought to be learning to say words that would let them talk about the things that their feelings are about – that would be predicted by the Principle of Relevance. These need not be the words that actually name the different feeling states – words like *happy* or *mad* – because the infant's pleasure or displeasure is already apparent in the emotion display. Instead, they should be learning the words that let them express what they are feeling pleasure and displeasure about – words like *more*, *uhoh*, *Dada*, and *choochoo* – which is what we found (Chapter 9). In addition, because affective expression is already functioning for communication, infants might be expected to attempt saying words to articulate these shared meanings in the moments when they are expressing their feelings. Older children and adults can certainly convey something of their feelings as they talk (although the empirical research is still relatively scant).[12] For one or both of these reasons, then, saying words and expressing emotion ought to cluster together in time.

On the other hand, the assumption that words emerge out of emotional expression seems too simplistic when we consider what is required for expressing emotion and learning to say words. If emotion and language both require cognitive resources – and these compete for the limited resources of the young language-learning child – then we ought to see accommodation and compensation effects in the behaviors of saying words and expressing emotion. Furthermore, these effects may be most apparent in the early period of language learning, before the processes of lexical recall and motor movements for speech become more automatic. These were the issues addressed in the several studies described in what follows here. The first study documented the local effects that occurred in the moment-to-moment contingencies between saying words and expressing emotion; the next three studies revealed the larger developmental effects that occurred over time.

The children in these studies were the same as those for whom development of expressions in affect and speech from FW to VS was described in Chapter 7, with two exceptions. We began data collection at 9 months of age with 12 of the 14 infants. These 12 are the subjects included in the analyses reported in this chapter, because we were interested in how affect expression in the last quarter of the first year developed in relation to later developments in learning words. Accordingly, the 2 infants who were 11 and 12 months old when we first saw them were not included in the following analyses. The subjects for these studies were 6 girls and 6 boys, 4 of whom, 1 girl and 3 boys, were the children of color.

Talking and Feeling

If emotional experience and expression took up "cognitive space," and saying words required cognitive effort, then the children might be more likely to say words when they expressed neutral affect than when they expressed emotionally toned affect. We tested this hypothesis in several ways.[13] The first analysis was based simply on a *frequency* measure: how often a word was said at the same time affect was expressed. The relative frequency of overlapping word and affect expression – neutral affect expression and the different intensity levels of positive and negative emotion – is shown in Figure 8.1 at

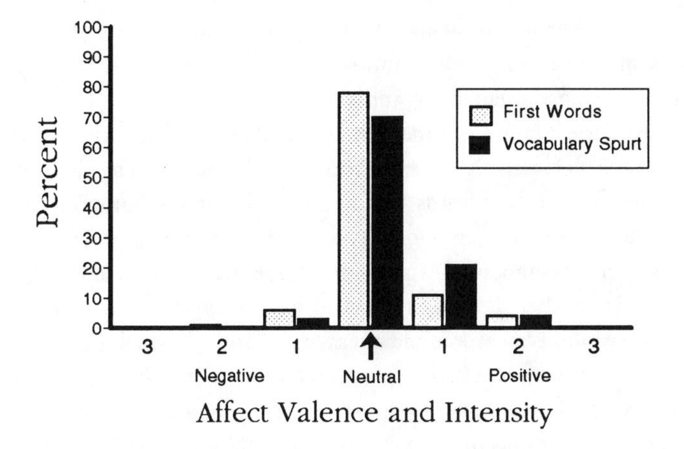

8.1 Overlapping speech and affect expression. (L. Bloom & Beckwith, 1989)

FW and VS. The infants said most of their words while they were expressing neutral affect. When they did say words and express emotion at the same time, that emotion was more likely to be at a low level of intensity (+1 or −1). At VS, given the overall frequency of emotional expression with different levels of intensity, significantly more words were said with Level 1 intensity and fewer words with Levels 2 and 3 than expected. Thus, these children were not inclined to be speaking when they were expressing emotion with heightened intensity (+2 and +3 or −2 and −3). (Here, and elsewhere, only results that reached levels of statistical reliability, with p = .05 or less, are reported; the details of the procedures and analyses can be found in the original reports.)

However, one could argue that words were said with neutral affect because the children were expressing neutral affect most of the time. To test this possibility, we determined the actual *time* spent saying words and expressing affect by counting the number of video frames (1 sec = 30 frames) for time spent saying words with neutral and emotional expression, and time spent in neutral and emotional expression without saying words.

Time spent expressing neutral affect was used to predict the amount of time the children might be expected to say words with neutral affect by chance. At FW, this was, in fact, the result: The time they spent in saying words with neutral affect was not different from what one might expect, given the amount of time spent expressing neutral affect overall. The ratio of neutral affect to emotional expression was roughly 6 : 1 for time spent speaking as well as for time spent not speaking. We took this result to mean that the two systems of expression, speech and emotion, were essentially independent when these infants began to say words at FW.

However, the amount of time that emotional expression overlapped with saying words increased significantly between FW and VS. The children were still saying most of their words with neutral affect at VS, but more time was spent saying words with emotionally toned affect than was predicted by the amount of time in emotional expression. The result is presented in Figure 8.2 as the ratios at VS of time in neutral expression to time in emotional expression while saying words and not saying words. We concluded from these results that the two systems of expression had come together by the time the children reached the vocabulary spurt. However, their integration happened with certain constraints on both the valence of the emotional expression and the words the children said with emotion.

The integration of emotional expression and words at VS was due to the occurrence of words with primarily positive emotional expression, which is what we had expected based on assumptions in the literature about how the cognitive requirements for positive and negative emotion differ. The positive and negative emotions differ with respect to both the direction and the outcome of the evaluation of a situation relative to an individual's goals and behavior. Positive emotion is associated with the success of ongoing behavior, whereas negative emotion is ordinarily associated with the interruption of behavior. With the positive emotions, a goal has been achieved, and no new cognitive activity may be required. In the case of the negative emotions, the result of evaluation often points to constructing a new plan to remove an obstacle to a goal or creating a new goal.[14] More cognitive work, then, is apt to occur with experience and expression of negative emotions, because the mental meanings expressed are more elaborated than the mental meanings of positive emotion. For this reason, we compared the time spent saying words with positive and negative emotional expression.

If the children expressed emotion at the same time as they also said a word, the emotion they expressed was significantly more likely to be positive than negative. This result is presented in Figure 8.3 as a ratio of time (number of video frames) spent in positive affect expression to time in negative affect expression, both while saying words and not saying words. These results mean that saying words and expressing emotion came together at VS with a

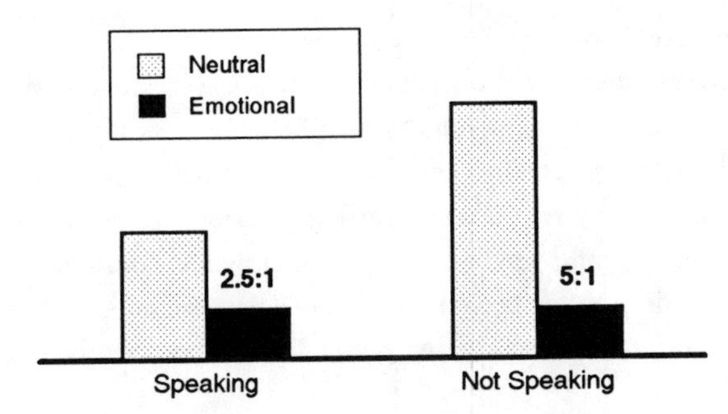

8.2 Ratio of time spent in neutral to time spent in emotional expression while speaking and not speaking, at Vocabulary Spurt. (L. Bloom & Beckwith, 1989)

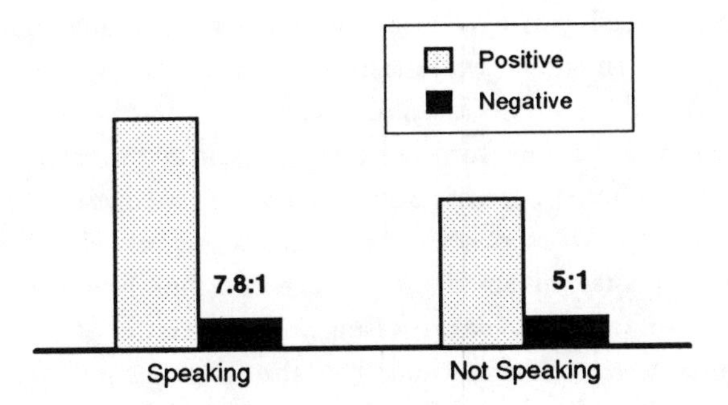

8.3 Ratio of time spent in positive to time spent in negative emotional expression while speaking and not speaking, at Vocabulary Spurt. (L. Bloom & Beckwith, 1989)

constraint on affect valence as well as intensity. The children were not likely to say words when they were also expressing negative affect. Moreover, as will be seen in Chapter 9, there was also a constraint on the words they said with emotional expression. They were among a child's most frequent words and/or those learned relatively early – presumably, the words the children knew best.

Finally, we looked at the immediate effects between a word and emotional expression in the moments surrounding the word. These effects were in the relationship, in real time, between saying a word and expressing emotion as revealed in a form of lag sequential analyses.[15] Given that a child said a word, what was the likelihood that the child also expressed emotion at the same time and in the 10 sec intervals before and the 10 sec intervals after saying the word? If the two sorts of expression, emotion and words, were unrelated, then the result would be an essentially random interaction between expressing affect and saying words; the rate of emotional expression before and after words should not differ from baseline levels of expressing emotion overall. Nor should the children differ between FW and VS in the rates with which they expressed emotion before and after words. In fact, both kinds of differences were found.

The result is presented in Figure 8.4 for all the words said by the 12 children combined, both at FW and VS.[16] The vertical line in the figure represents the occurrence of words, as the target events, with 10 1-sec lags before and 10 1-sec lags after. The intersecting horizontal line represents the baseline level of emotional expression averaged for the 12 children. The results at FW and VS are the mean differences from this baseline, standardized as *z* scores, at the time words were actually said and in each of the 1-sec lags before and after the words. Scores above the baseline level mean that emotion was expressed more often than expected; scores below the baseline mean that expression of emotion was below baseline levels and that the children were more likely to be expressing *neutral* affect.

If the children were learning to talk about the things that their feelings were about, which the Principle of Relevance would predict, then words and emotionally toned affect expression should tend to occur close together in time. This is what we found: The expression of emotion clustered around the words. First, emotional expression was most likely to occur around words and peaked immediately after words. We interpreted this contingency between emotional expression and saying words to mean that the children were indeed talking about those things their feelings were about. However, with rare exceptions, the words the children said were not the names of the emotions: labels such as *happy*, *mad*, or *sad* for telling others just what emotions they were feeling (see Chapter 9). Other research in the literature that has reported emotion words in early vocabularies has been based on mothers' reporting whether their children ever said such words at all. We looked instead at what the children and their mothers actually did say in the moments when a child was expressing emotion. Even in those moments when the children were actually expressing emotion, they did not use words to tell others *what* it was they were feeling. They didn't have to; a child's feelings are evident in the

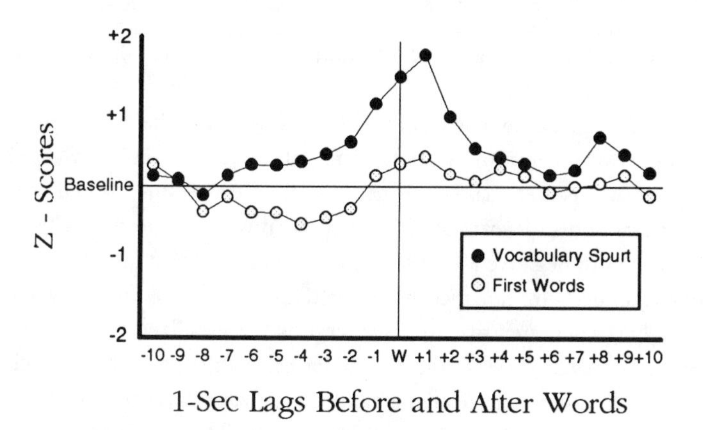

8.4 Profile of emotional expression around words at First Words and Vocabulary Spurt. (L. Bloom & Beckwith, 1989)

affect display itself. Instead, the children said words like *Mama, cookie, more, cow, up, no,* and *whee* that named the persons, objects, and other circumstances that were the causes and consequences of their feelings.

Evidence of an influence from cognition on the integration of language and emotional expression was inferred from the expression of *neutral* affect. At First Words, emotional expression was least frequent and below baseline in the 2 to 8 sec before words, and the children tended to be expressing primarily neutral affect. The time just before a word is the time a child uses for constructing a mental meaning and the other cognitive work that recalling and saying a word entails. Consequently, to conserve resources, the mental activity required for the experience and expression of emotion was essentially preempted. This was one kind of evidence for inferring that processes for language and emotion cooperate in sharing resources for a child's expressive behaviors.

The importance of neutral affect for saying words was particularly great when words were just beginning. The difference between FW and VS was consistent with the results of earlier analyses of the overlap of time spent in speech and in emotional expression: Development occurred between FW and VS in the ability to say words and at the same time express emotionally toned affect. By the time of the vocabulary spurt, the children had integrated the two forms of expression, although with certain constraints: Words were more likely to be said with positive than with negative emotion and with low levels of intensity, and the words said with emotion tended to be the words the children knew best (Chapter 9).

These results are not consistent with the suggestion that words emerge in the context of feelings of "anxiety" and "affective conflict."[17] Most of the children's words were said with neutral affect expression. When they did express emotion and words at the same time, it was with positive affect more often than with negative affect. Others have observed that infants are able to integrate smiles with nonspeech vocalizations by the time they are 8 months old and have suggested that words emerge as the socialized forms of infants' affective vocalizations.[18] However, nonlexical vocalizing before speech and saying words once language begins cannot be equated in terms of their relative cognitive cost to the young language-learning child. The ability to produce speech with emotional intonation is the result of development and is not innate, as has been suggested.[19] Although the forms of emotional expression may be innately determined, integrating these forms with speech is a developmental process.

The competition for cognitive resources we have invoked to explain our results may well have a neuropsychological basis related to what Marcel Kinsbourne called a "lateral gradient of attention." When cognitive processing requires skills that are specialized for the different cerebral hemispheres, the result is competition for "relative degree of activation" of the two hemispheres.[20] Emotional expression and language involve different regions of the brain. The emotions involve both subcortical and cortical regions, and emotional expression and monitoring emotional arousal have predominantly right hemisphere specialization.[21] Most aspects of language, as is well known, are associated primarily with left hemisphere activity. However, sentence intonation and prosody have been attributed to right hemisphere function, as have the prosodic aspects of speech that are expressive of emotional feeling.[22]

Evidence from infants suggests that cerebral asymmetries such as these are present in early infancy before the emergence of language, and may be predetermined rather than developmental.[23] Integration of the processing activities in the two hemispheres and allocation of attentional capacities are mediated to a large degree by the corpus callosum. However, the corpus callosum is particularly slow to mature, and this fact has been cited to explain the relative lack of early hemispheric integration in other developmental domains.[24] The question of integrating the results of separate processing by the two hemispheres of the brain was raised by Donald Tucker, who suggested that "lateralized contributions to communication . . . may develop before the child has the capacity to coordinate them." Saying words with emotionally toned valence may be particularly difficult when language begins.[25]

However, the effects we observed are probably not limited to the earliest stages of language learning. Older children and even adults may well experience the same competition for cognitive resources between the two systems of expression at times when the experience of emotion is particularly heightened and/or the content of speech is particularly abstract, complex, or obscure. So far we have seen how the on-line cognition required for the experience and expression of emotion interacted with saying words. We turn now to studies that revealed several of the larger developmental effects between learning words and emotional expression.

Affect Expression and Language Achievement

On the one hand, if language development somehow built upon the developmental precedence of affect for communication, then one might expect children who express emotionally toned affect more frequently would learn words earlier and more easily. On the other hand, if saying words is associated with the expression of neutral affect, and early words preempt emotional expression, as we found, then *learning* words may also be associated with the expression of neutral affect. In fact, earlier age of language achievement was highly associated with the expression of neutral affect.

For this next analysis,[26] we returned to the individual differences among our children with respect to the ages at which they reached the language achievements FW, VS, and MW (shown in Fig. 7.7). Differences among them had been entirely expected, since children who are developing language quite normally are known to vary greatly in onset and rate of progress.[27] We know some of the reasons for this typical variation. For one, firstborns, more often than laterborns, ordinarily hear speech that is directed to them and to what they are attending to, and they also tend to learn language earlier and somewhat faster.[28] Knowing this, we set out in advance to study only firstborn children. For another, many conflicting claims have been made over the years concerning differences between girls and boys in their language development, and for this reason we dutifully selected equal numbers of girls and boys for our research. In fact, gender differences may have accounted in part for onset in word learning but not for differences in rate of language development. The girls in our study did say their first words earlier than the boys, but girls and boys did not differ in age when they reached the vocabulary spurt or began to say sentences, at MW.[29] However, gender differences notwithstanding, we found that age of language achievement was correlated with aspects of these infants' emotional expression.

Simply looking at how frequently the children expressed emotion at FW and VS in relation to how old they were when they reached the three language achievements yielded the results shown in Table 8.1.[30] These correlations were all in the positive direction; the more frequently the infants expressed emotion – including changes in valence and shifts in intensity without a change in valence – the older they were at the time of the language achievement. The same relationship between frequency of emotional expression and onset and rate of language acquisition has been reported in other studies.[31] In addition, frequency of emotional expression did not predict the number of words (either the number of different words or the total number of utterance tokens) at FW and VS. Thus, high emotionality was associated with later age at language achievements and did not predict either the number of words that the children learned (types) or their frequency of speech (tokens).

The corollary was the percentage of time the children spent in neutral affect expression. This was obviously not independent of how frequently they expressed emotion but provided a measure based on time in addition to simple frequency. These correlations, in Table 8.2, between time in neutral affect expression and age at language achievements were all in the negative direction. Thus, the more time these infants spent in neutral affect expression at FW and VS, the younger they were at FW and VS. Moreover, the time they spent in neutral affect expression at VS predicted their age at MW.

Together, these results mean that frequent emotional expression did not facilitate early word learning. Instead, early word learning was associated with the expression of neutral affect, as was saying words. Neutral affect expression is presumably an optimal state for the sort of attention that both learning and saying words require. We will return to this point.

Finally, gender had no effect on either frequency of emotional expression or number of words; girls and boys did not differ in frequency of emotional expression at FW or VS. Nor did they differ in either the number of words they had learned (word types) or in the total number of words they used

Table 8.1. *Frequency of emotional expression and age at language achievement (N = 12) (Pearson r)*

Frequency of emotional expression	Age at FW	Age at VS	Age at MW
At FW	.658	.593	(.476)
At VS	.662	.684	.668

$p < .05$ except for value in parentheses.
Source: L. Bloom & Captides (1987a).

Table 8.2. *Time spent in neutral affect expression and age at language achievement (N = 12) (Pearson r)*

Time spent in neutral expression	Age at FW	Age at VS	Age at MW
At FW	−.697	−.578	(−.538)
At VS	(−.522)	−.828	−.711

$p < .05$ except for values in parentheses.
Source: L. Bloom & Captides (1987a).

(tokens) at FW and VS. However, the differences among these infants in their language development were clearly associated with differences among them in emotionality.

In addition to gender, the infants also differed in ethnicity and economic background; 4 were poor children of color. We did not know of any studies of emotionality that used race as a variable, so we had no basis on which to generate expectations concerning the relationship between emotionality and ethnicity in our population. But the literature on poverty has pointed to language as being particularly vulnerable in the development of poor children.[32] We might have expected, therefore, that our poor infants, who were also our children of color, would be among the later language learners. The distributions in Figures 8.5 and 8.6 for FW and VS, respectively, make clear that they were not. The infants of color appear throughout the distributions.

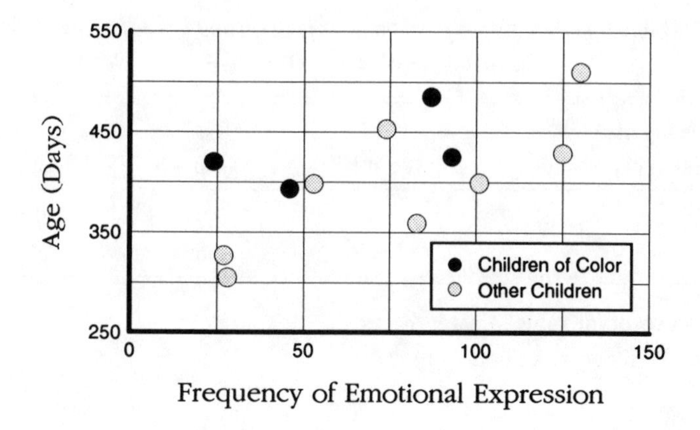

8.5 Distribution of children according to frequency of emotional expression and age at First Words.

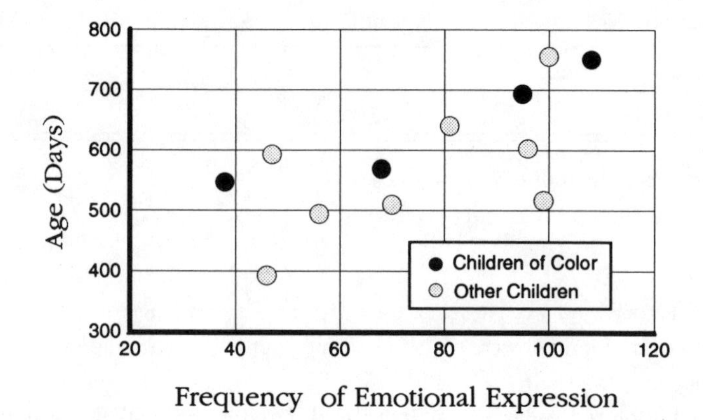

8.6 Distribution of children according to frequency of emotional expression and age at Vocabulary Spurt.

We actually tested this conclusion by repeating the correlation analyses between frequency of emotional expression and age of language achievement with only the Caucasian infants in our sample; with an *n* of 8, we did not expect significant results.[33] In fact, as can be seen in Table 8.3, all the correlations remained extremely high (compare Table 8.1). These results

Table 8.3. *Frequency of emotional expression and age of language achievement for white children only (N = 8) (Pearson r)*

Frequency of emotional expression	Age at FW	Age at VS	Age at MW
At FW	.804	.671	(.527)
At VS	.670	(.606)	(.532)

$p < .05$ except for values in parentheses.

mean that the association between emotionality and age of language achievement was attributable to something other than the ethnic mix in our subject population.

We also had to consider the possibility that these findings could have been related to developments in affect expression in this period of time. We already knew that the group of infants as a whole did not change in their frequency of emotional expression between the two language achievements FW and VS. The number of expressions was essentially the same, and frequency at FW was correlated with frequency at VS. However, given the differences among the children in their ages at FW and VS, they might still have increased in how frequently they expressed emotion over the course of the second year. Some children moved from FW to VS in as little as 1 or 2 months, and others took as long as 8 months after FW to reach VS. If emotional expression increases in the second year in general, then the infants whose achievements in language came later in the year would also (coincidentally) have been the children who expressed emotion more frequently. More time spent in neutral expression might have been inadvertently associated with earlier age of language achievement and frequency of emotional expression inadvertently associated with later age of language achievement. The next set of analyses addressed this question.

Developmental Trends in Affect Expression

Robert McCall has persistently reminded us that correlational analyses of individual differences across variables are only part of a developmental story, because they are "potentially independent of developmental function." Thus, individuals within a group may differ from one another and maintain their differences over time while the group as a whole or naturally occurring subgroups change across time. Even though the performance of an individual child remains stable relative to others in the group, change in the group itself or in subgroups would indicate dynamic developmental process. Analyses of individual differences (their rank order relative to one another) and analyses of developmental function (the average performance of groups of individuals over time) contribute different sorts of information to our understanding of development. Studying both individual differences and developmental trends is required.[34]

So far we have described the infants' affect expression at the two language achievements FW and VS. In order to look for developmental trends in this period, we also equated them for age and coded affect at the same ages for all of them for a period of 1 year – beginning before their first words at 9 months, and at 4-month intervals thereafter, at 13, 17, and 21 months.[35]

Given how the infants differed from one another in their affect expression in relation to language development, and given the stability of this difference, they could have differed in developmental trends in affect expression as well. If one suspects that all the children in a group might not show the same development, then the mean of the group as a whole is not appropriate for describing development over time. Because affect expression was highly related to age at language achievement, we had to consider the possibility that children who differed in age at language achievement might also differ in development of affect expression. Thus, in addition to the relation of affect expression to age at language achievement at a given point in time, differences in age at language achievement might predict different courses of affect development over several points in time.

For determining developmental trends, therefore, we divided the infants into two groups, earlier and later word learners, based upon their ages at the time of the first language achievement, first words (FW). The mean age at FW was 408 days (range = 305–510 days); 6 infants below the mean and 6 infants above the mean formed the subgroups of earlier and later word learners (EWL, LWL), respectively. The mean ages of the two subgroups at FW, VS, and MW are presented in Figure 8.7 in relation to the mean for the group of 12 infants. As can be seen, the subgroup means did not differ substantially from the group mean; our later word learners were not children whose language development was delayed or otherwise at risk.

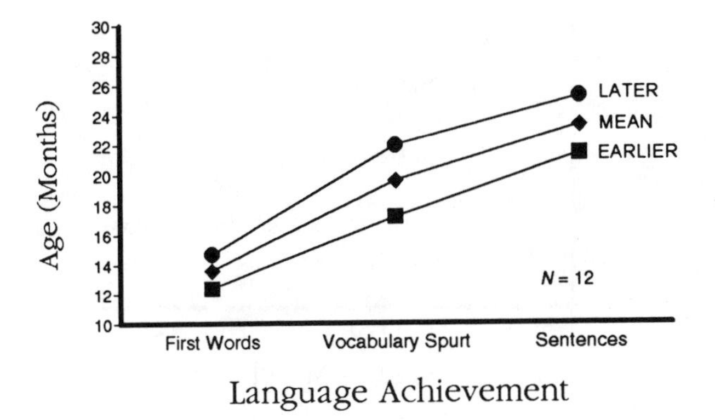

8.7 Mean age of language achievement for the group and for subgroups of earlier ($n=6$) and later ($n=6$) word learners. (L. Bloom, Beckwith, & Capatides, 1988)

Those infants in the two subgroups who fell closest to the mean age of language achievement could actually have been similar and overlapped in affect expression, since language achievement was correlated with affect expression. This likelihood of overlap meant that splitting the group in half this way was the most conservative test of differences in developmental trends. If our two groups of earlier and later language learners still differed in affect development over time, we could be confident that language achievement was related to affect expression.[36]

Developments in affect expression from 9 to 21 months were evaluated with three sorts of measures. These were frequency of emotional expression, both frequency overall and frequency for positive and negative emotion separately; average duration of emotional expressions; and time spent in positive, negative, and neutral affect expression.

Frequency of Emotional Expression. The first result is presented in Figure 8.8. The two groups of infants were not different at 9 months, but earlier and later word learners did indeed differ developmentally over time in the frequency with which they expressed emotion. Those infants who began to say words relatively early (EWL) did not change in how frequently they expressed emotion. In contrast, the infants who did not begin to say words between 9 and 13 months of age (LWL) increased in their frequency of emotional

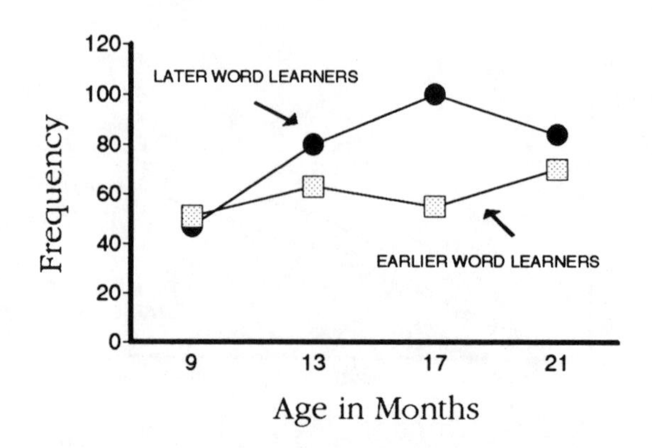

8.8 Mean frequency of emotional expression by earlier and later word learners. (L. Bloom, Beckwith, & Capatides, 1988)

expression instead. Moreover, these later word learners subsequently *decreased* in frequency of expression from 17 to 21 months, which was the period that encompassed their transition from FW to VS.

An increase in the frequency of emotional expression in the period beginning at 9 months of age was reported in a study by Adamson and Bakeman.[37] In the present study, before we took subgroups into account, the group of 12 infants as a whole also showed an increase in emotional expression from 9 to 21 months. However, this increase in emotional expression was due to the later word learners; they increased in emotional expression instead of saying words early and accounted for the overall increase with age for the group as a whole. The infants who began to say words relatively early did not change in the frequency with which they expressed emotion throughout the single-word period and into their transition to multiword speech.

The valence of most emotional expression was positive, 79% on average, and most of the positive expressions were of +1 intensity: 66%, 68%, 71%, and 77% of the positive expressions at 9, 13, 17, and 21 months, respectively. The developmental trends for frequency of all positive expressions for the two subgroups are presented in Figure 8.9. Again, the later word learners, but not the earlier word learners, increased in frequency of positive expressions in the period between 9 and 17 months and decreased between 17 and 21 months; the two subgroups were significantly different at 13 months and at 17 months.

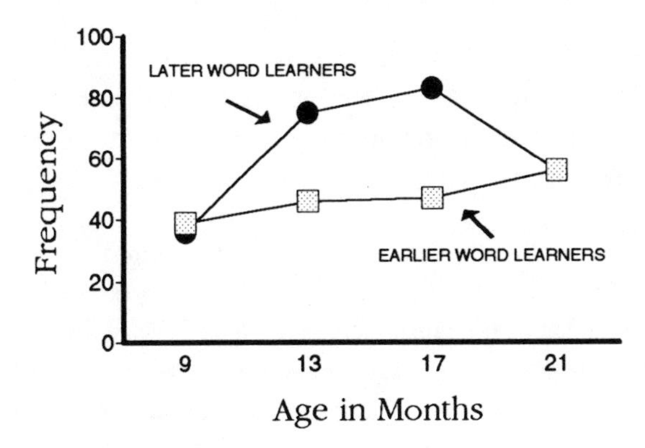

8.9 Mean frequency of positive emotional expression by earlier and later word learners. (L. Bloom, Beckwith, & Capatides, 1988)

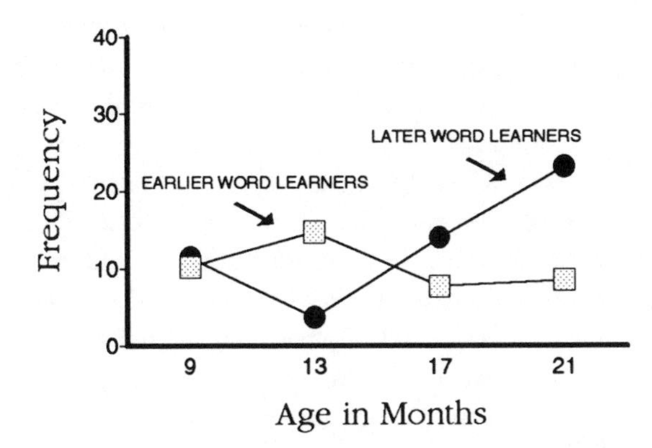

8.10 Mean frequency of negative emotional expression by earlier and later word learners. (L. Bloom, Beckwith, & Capatides, 1988)

Negative affect expression was relatively infrequent, and most expressions of negative affect were of −1 intensity: 73%, 75%, 81%, and 67% of the negative expressions at 9, 13, 17, and 21 months, respectively. The developmental trends for frequency of negative expressions were different for the two subgroups of infants, and this result is presented in Figure 8.10. The earlier word learners expressed negative affect more frequently at 13 months – the age that coincided with their achievement of FW. The later word learners increased in frequency of negative expressions between 13 and 21 months. These results suggested that certain of the language achievements were associated with an increase in frequency of negative expression: FW for the earlier word learners and the transition from FW to VS (between 17 and 21 months) for the later word learners.

Average Duration of Expression. The length of an emotional expression was the time from its onset until the onset of the next expression (since affect expression was coded continuously). Overall, for all 12 infants at all four ages, the average length of an emotional expression was 2.98 sec. Positive expressions (M = 3.34 sec) were somewhat longer than negative expressions (M= 2.63 sec), but the difference was not significant. Changes did not occur in the length of positive expressions over time, and the two groups of infants did not differ in the length of their positive expressions.

However, developments in the average length of negative expressions (Fig. 8.11) complemented, in part, the developments in frequency of negative expressions. For the earlier word learners, length of negative expressions increased between 13 and 17 months, the same period in which we saw a decrease in frequency of negative expressions. For the later word learners, the length of negative expressions decreased from 9 to 17 months, whereas the frequency of negative expressions had shown an increase from 13 to 21 months. Thus, either frequency or average duration of negative expressions increased at some point in this period of word learning, suggesting an association between expressions of negative emotion and language change. One possibility is that negative affect might be associated with perturbations accompanying developmental change just previous to a breakthrough in learning. Another is that negative affect might reflect effort in saying particular words before they become more automatic.

Amount of Time in Affect Expression. However, the infants spent very little time expressing negative emotion: only 2 to 3% at each age on average, and time spent in negative expression did not change with age. The two subgroups did differ at 13 months, and it was the earlier word learners who spent more time expressing negative affect (3%) at 13 months than the later word learners (1%).

In contrast, the group of infants as a whole was in positive affect on average 13% of the time: from 10% of the time at 9 months to 15% at 17 months. The

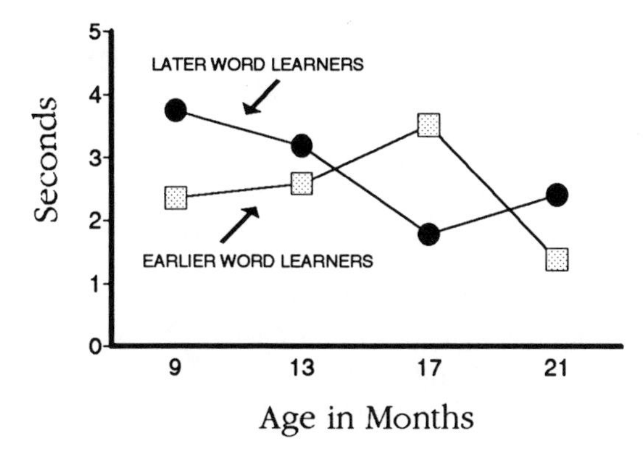

8.11 Average length of negative emotional expression by earlier and later word learners. (L. Bloom, Beckwith, & Capatides, 1988)

time the children spent expressing positive emotion was not, of course, independent of the frequency of positive expressions. Both measures indicated different developmental trends for earlier and later word learners, with the later word learners increasing and then decreasing in the percentage of time they spent in positive affect expression while the earlier word learners were not changing. The two subgroups differed in time spent in positive emotion at 13 months and at 17 months. The increases in both frequency of positive expression and the percentage of time spent in positive expression were related to each other but independent of the average length of a positive expression, which did not change over time.

As has already been said, the infants were expressing neutral affect most of the time – on average, 84% of the time at 9, 13, 17, and 21 months – and comparable results from other studies were cited previously. Time in neutral affect did not change from 9 to 21 months for either of the subgroups. However, the earlier word learners spent more time in neutral affect expression than the later word learners at 13 months and at 17 months. Thus, the infants who started to say words relatively early spent more time in neutral expression at the ages that encompassed their developments in language.

The two subgroups of infants did not differ on any of these measures when they were 9 months old, before they began to say words, as could be seen in the figures. However, all of them increased in their expressivity, some learning to say words relatively early and others increasing instead in frequency of emotional expression in general and in the frequency and time spent in positive emotion in particular. This result was not influenced by gender; at each age from 9 to 21 months, the boys and girls in our study did not differ on any of the measures.

Mutual Influence of Affect and Language

The consequence of studying both individual differences and developmental trends was to reveal mutual effects in the interaction between developments in language learning and affect expression. The first effect was in the interaction between *neutral* affect expression and language. Neutral expressions could best be described as expressions of alert attention similar to the periods of "quiet alert states" or "alert and focused" states described in early infancy. Quiet alert states support the cognitive activity of the first few months of life, and measures of attention in infants in the second half of the first year have been shown to predict later developmental outcome.[38]

A major shift in infants' attentional capacities at the end of the second year was described by Jerome Kagan. He suggested that "1-year-olds show more sustained attention because they are better able to retrieve the past and hold representations of the past and present in active memory for a longer period of time."[39] Similarly, we have suggested that learning words requires that infants attend to an acoustic signal and some aspect of the context and compare these contents of mind with prior experience recalled from memory. More time in neutral affect expression would enhance an infant's attention for the cognitive activity required for early language achievements in the second year. The neutral affect expressions of the infants we studied included expression of the emotions category of "interest."[40] Interest has been considered the important emotion for processes of attention and cognition in differential emotions theory.[41]

The corollary of the interaction between achievements in language and neutral affect expression is the interaction between developments in language learning and nonneutral, emotional expressions. However, positive and negative expressions did not interact in the same way with language learning. The second effect of the interaction between developments in language learning and affect expression was in the increase in frequency or average duration of negative expressions at one time or another for different children in this period of word learning. Negative emotion was associated with the effort involved in saying early words, particularly at times of developmental change and before the use of words becomes more automatic. The third effect was in the interaction between positive emotional expression and word learning. Infants who increased in positive expression and spent more time expressing positive emotion were somewhat later in beginning to say words and slower in building a vocabulary.

Although our interpretation of all these effects points to a developmental process in the interaction between language learning and affect expression, the attribution of causality is by no means straightforward. Infants may increase in the frequency with which they express emotion in their efforts at expressivity because they are not yet ready to begin learning words for some other reason. Another alternative to the *process* explanation we favor for explaining the pattern of results that emerged in these several studies is that differences in patterns of emotionality are attributable to differences in underlying *temperament*. Infants who spend more time in neutral affect expression and express emotion less frequently may also be infants who are predisposed to learn language earlier, and, conversely, infants who are particularly expressive emotionally may be temperamentally predisposed to learning language somewhat later. However, we shall see, as we turn now to the last analysis of affect expression and language learning, that these infants' emotionality might have been influenced instead by their language learning.

Language Development and Temperament

Like language, personality is an aspect of human development in which we expect variation and individual differences. Individual differences in adult personality are presumed to originate with differences in temperament in infancy and early childhood, and one factor often encountered in theories of temperament is emotionality.[42] Variations in what is usually referred to as emotionality or mood are included in most temperament questionnaires and research based on parent interviews or observations in controlled experimental situations. Emotionality is ordinarily described in terms of positive and negative valence and includes such parameters as latency, intensity, and duration of emotional response – essentially the same measures we used in our longitudinal studies of spontaneous, continuous affect expression in naturalistic interactions. The results of these studies, then, yielded developmental profiles of emotionality for these children that ought to be relevant to questions of temperament.

In order to explore whether the profiles of emotionality that emerged were a function of temperament, we turned to a construct that is typically evoked in studies of temperament: stability over time. Continuity of a behavior variable over time is ordinarily taken to mean that it derives from something endogenous and part of the constitutional makeup of the individual. Several theories of temperament point to stability of traits as an important component. Others, however, have suggested that some behaviors that are not stable over time may nevertheless be part of the personality structure of the child. The factor of stability may itself, within the realm of emotionality, be a measure of individual difference and a dimension of temperament in its own right.[43]

So far we have found that individual differences in age of language achievement were correlated with differences among the infants in their expression of affect at the time of the language achievements FW and VS. These individual differences were, in turn, related to differences among the infants in their developmental trends in affect expression over time from 9 to 21 months. In this next analysis, we looked for patterns of stability over time by correlating frequency of emotional expression at 9, 13, 17, and 21 months.[44]

The earlier word learners in our study were, in general, more stable in their profiles of emotionality than were the later word learners. The most striking differences between the subgroups was in how stable they were in the amount of time they spent in positive affect, and these results are presented in Tables 8.4 and 8.5 for earlier and later word learners, respectively. For the earlier word learners, all the correlations for time spent in positive affect expression at 9, 13, 17, and 21 months were significant. In contrast, stability was observed for the later word learners only between 17 and 21 months.

One possible interpretation of these findings is that differences in emotionality are differences in underlying temperament and that it is temperament that influences the course of language development. A temperament profile with more time in neutral affect expression and stable and less frequent emotional expression over time may predispose infants to learn language earlier. Such a temperament profile would facilitate the processes necessary for early language learning, because neutral affect expression allows the states of attention needed to construct the mental meanings for learning words. In contrast, the evaluative stance underlying an emotion and its expression could preempt attention and at the same time the cognitive resources needed for

Table 8.4. *Percentage of time in positive expression for earlier word learners (N = 6) (Pearson* r*)*

	9 months	13 months	17 months
13 months	.904	—	—
17 months	.853	.808	—
21 months	.689	.599	.618

$p < .05$.

Table 8.5. *Percentage of time in positive expression for later word learners (N = 6) (Pearson* r*)*

	9 months	13 months	17 months
13 months	(.438)	—	—
17 months	(.056)	(.138)	—
21 months	(.085)	(.564)	.629

$p < .05$ except for values in parentheses.

word learning. For the child who is temperamentally predisposed to more frequent expression of emotion, word learning would come somewhat later.

Most studies of temperament (using questionnaires and controlled observations of behavior) have in fact failed to find stability in this same age range: the last quarter of the first year and the first half of the second year. Such instability has typically been attributed to the enormous developmental strides made in this period.[45] The assumption is that instability that occurs with development in one domain is associated with instability as a consequence of development in other domains. However, the opposite was true in our studies: Aspects of language development in the second year were associated with stability in emotional expression. Stability in emotionality was found, first, between the ages of the language achievements FW and VS for the group of 12 infants as a whole (Chapter 7). When the infants were equated for age, differences among them were stable over a longer period of time but only when they were grouped according to differences in age of language achievement. The two groups of earlier and later word learners were not different at 9 months of age, before words began to appear. Earlier word learners were subsequently stable throughout the ensuing year, and later word learners showed stability only toward the end of the period, when their word learning began in earnest.

Thus, learning to say words may have a stabilizing influence on expression of affect. Given that affective communication is in place from early infancy, learning language entails a shift in attentional resources. Change in one domain (in this case, language) may require stability in another (such as emotionality) and thereby influence an infant's temperament profile. Clearly, further research will be needed to decide between these alternative explanations and to explore covariation of developments in other domains as well in the second year.[46] One such additional factor that could have influenced the children's profiles of emotional expression was how their mothers responded to them when they expressed emotion.

THE SOCIAL CONTEXT OF EMOTIONAL EXPRESSION

The importance of caregivers' responding to an infant's emotional signals has been stressed repeatedly – here and in the infancy literature more generally – for the development of emotion in general and for the social understanding of emotion in particular. Because our infants were different in their development in affect expression in the second year, we looked at how their mothers responded to their expressions of emotion at 9, 13, 17, and 21 months to determine how responses to emotional expressions might have influenced their development.[47]

The children displayed many emotional expressions, and their mothers responded to the great majority of them. They either expressed emotionally toned affect themselves, or they did or said something that was directed at the causes, consequences, or circumstances of the child's emotional experience and expression. However, the frequency with which mothers responded to emotional expression was not the primary way in which they influenced a child's emotion profile. The frequency of mothers' contingent responding at 9, 13, and 17 months did not predict subsequent frequency of children's emotional expressions or the relative frequency of positive and negative expressions. The developmental changes and individual differences among the children were not, therefore, directly attributable to how often their mothers responded to their positive and negative emotional expressions.[48] In fact, the frequency with which mothers responded to their children's emotional displays did not change; the mothers responded to emotional expressions as readily after the children learned to talk as they did before. This was true both for subgroups of earlier and later word learners and for boys as well as girls.

The mothers contributed to their children's understanding of emotional experience and expression in other ways. An emotional expression is a public display to which we can attribute a private representation, which is its meaning or what it is about (as we saw in Chapter 7). And indeed, in responding to a child's emotional expressions, the mothers were attributing mental meanings to them. At a minimum, they acknowledged the child's expression by saying things like "What?" or "Okay" to indicate that they appreciated the child's effort at expression even if they might not have understood the child's intent. And in responding the mothers conveyed meaningful messages to their children. A caregiver's own affect, action, or speech is an expression and, in the context of a child's emotional display, communicates a message to the child about the feelings and expression of those feelings in the display. Regularities over time in the meanings a child attributes to a mother's behaviors when she responds to emotional expressions contribute to understanding and learning about the experience and expression of emotion.

The mothers provided their children with a rich array of such meaningful behaviors. In addition to expressing affect themselves and talking about emotion or its expression (which are the forms of socialization most often studied in the past), mothers responded with actions and action-directed speech. Either they acted themselves or encouraged their children to act in ways to achieve their goals, or they talked about those goals and/or the situations for them. These goals and situations were typically the circumstances that surrounded a child's emotional expressions and gave rise to them.

The children's positive and negative emotional expressions were responded to differently. In responding to positive emotions, the mothers most often expressed positive affect themselves. They were also very likely to do or say something directed at maintaining a child's goal and to talk about the situational context. In response to negative expressions, mothers were least likely to express affect themselves in response. Instead, they were most likely to act in a way or say something directed at helping the child achieve a goal or change the goal, either by abandoning it or substituting a new goal. They also attended to their children's physical needs in response to negative emotions.

Thus, the mothers were most likely to respond affectively and share a child's positive expressions and least likely to respond affectively to a negative expression. A mother's talk in response to a child's emotional expression was relatively more likely to focus on the situation if the expression was a positive one and relatively more likely to focus on the child's goal when the child's expression was negative.

In sum, in their own actions and talk mothers provided information about the causes or circumstances of an emotion or provided information about how actions contribute to coping for the regulation of feelings.[49] Mothers' actions and talk about actions were their dominant form of responding to a child's emotional expression, and the rate of action-related behaviors by the mothers remained a constant in their interactions, showing no change from 9 to 21 months.

However, as the children acquired language, their mothers were increasingly likely to talk to them about the emotional experience and correspondingly less likely to express emotionally toned affect themselves. But they rarely labeled the child's emotion or talked about a child's feelings directly (see Chapter 9). This was surprising given the emphasis on talk about emotion in theoretical discussions of the processes of emotion socialization.[50] Instead, these mothers talked about a child's goal or the situation or how to achieve their goals in one or another situation – the causes and occasions for their feelings and what to do about them – rather than about the feelings themselves.[51] As with object play (Chapter 10), the mothers' propensity to act and to talk about action anticipated a developmental increase in their children's own tendency to talk about action events themselves (Chapter 9).

CONCLUSIONS

The development of expressive behaviors in the second year entails mutual and complementary adjustments between words and affect expression for the construction of mental meanings and their expression. And as we shall see in the next chapter, mental meanings attributed to the children's words showed increasing discrepancy and elaboration in this period of word learning. One essential point of this chapter has been to show how the thinking required for learning and saying words influences affect expression in particular. Neutral affect emerged as important for both learning and saying words, but it may have been more effect than cause. The expression of emotion – positively and negatively toned affect – entails appraisal of something in the situation in relation to an individual's goals and plans. This cognition for the expression of emotion was, in effect, preempted by the thinking required for learning and saying words. We saw this in the moment-to-moment contingencies between actually saying a word and expressing emotion in real time at FW. And it was also apparent in the children's development over time. Historically, the emotions were thought to interfere with thinking – the so-called disruptive effects of passion on reason. But we have seen that affect and language cooperate in conserving the essentially limited cognitive resources of the young language-learning child.

Developments in emotional expression consist of the infant's gaining control over the mechanisms of expression and modulating the forms of expression to conform to social and cultural expectations and practices.[52] Language is the most important context in which this learning occurs. Indeed, we saw the integration of speech and emotional expression, particularly positive expression, by the time the children reached VS. By learning language, children come to be able to talk about the causes, the circumstances, and the objects of their emotional experience. Caregivers – the mothers in our study – provided just these sorts of experiences with language in their own actions and talk about a child's goals and the situations for them. Moreover, they fashioned these experiences with language differently for positive and negative emotion. As a consequence, already in the single-word period infants are learning the words that can express the objects of their emotions as they continue to express *how* and *what* they feel through facial and vocal affect displays. But the words they learn in the second year are not the labels for the emotions themselves; instead, the "language of emotion" describes what emotional experiences are about. We turn next to some of these developments in word learning.

9

Developments in Word Learning

Infants start out with certain broad capacities for speech, and learning to say words depends on maturation of these capacities: both maturation of the anatomy for speech and maturation of the sensorimotor connections between audition and production systems. Learning to say words also depends on hearing other persons say words; a child has to hear their sounds and appreciate how the sounds that are heard relate to sounds the child can say. Infants begin to take account of the speech they hear and to bend their own capacities for soundmaking to accommodate the sounds of speech in the first half year of life.[1] Before the first words appear, the influence of hearing such different languages as French, English, Japanese, and Swedish is already evident in differences in the sounds of babbling.[2] But maturation and phonetic input determine which words are learned and how they are learned only in a social and informational context. It is the personal and interpersonal context that determines which words are learned in the second year.

EARLY VOCABULARIES

A critically important question for studies of the emergence of language is *What is a word?*[3] Deciding that what a child says qualifies as a word depends on judgments about the sounds emitted in the effort and their relevance to what is going on in the context. The criteria we used to judge that a word was a word were intuitive and similar to those used in other studies: relatively consistent phonetic shape and meaningfulness. This meant that we considered *ma* and *mama* to be a word for Mom when the child looked at her or at the toy family figure or gave her a cookie to eat or a toy to fix, but not when the child sang "mamamama" while cruising around the room. In addition, we required that the child's mother had to have responded at the time as though the vocalization was a word and/or at least two of the assistants in the project identified the vocalization as a conventional word at the time of transcription. We were fairly liberal in the words we allowed; we counted as words, for example, interjections like *uhoh* and *wheeee,* and idiosyncratic child forms like Robert's word *rara* (for cracker) when they met the criteria for phonetic consistency and meaningfulness.

The children's vocabularies will be described first with summaries of the numbers of words they learned from month to month and then by the kinds of words they were learning. Following these word counts, we will present results from a further analysis of development in the mental meanings their words expressed. The chapter concludes with a description of the words children learn for the "language of emotion."

Vocabulary Growth Curves

All the words each child said in the playroom sessions – from First Words until and including the month after the Vocabulary Spurt – were assembled in individual cumulative vocabularies.[4] Both word types (the different words) and tokens (frequencies of each word) were counted. All the children together said a total of 11,404 words (tokens), and these tokens embraced 326 different word types: This was the dictionary of words they learned as a group in the period from FW to 1 month after VS (VS + 1). Their developments in vocabulary growth can be summarized in several ways. The first is the monthly rate at which the group as a whole acquired new words, which we saw in Chapter 7 (Fig. 7.6). The growth in the individual cumulative vocabularies (new words in relation to old words each month) is shown in Figure 9.1 for each of the children according to age in months.

The differences among the children in their ages, rates of acquisition, numbers of words, and time span from FW to VS are clear. The interval between FW and VS ranged from only 1 month for 1 child to 8 months for 2 of them. Another difference was the shape of the curves and the degree of increase at the vocabulary spurt. The sharp increase in new words traditionally described as a vocabulary spurt was clear for 7 of the children: Clark, Dana, Greta, Reggie, Robert, Shirley, and Vivian (Shirley actually met both

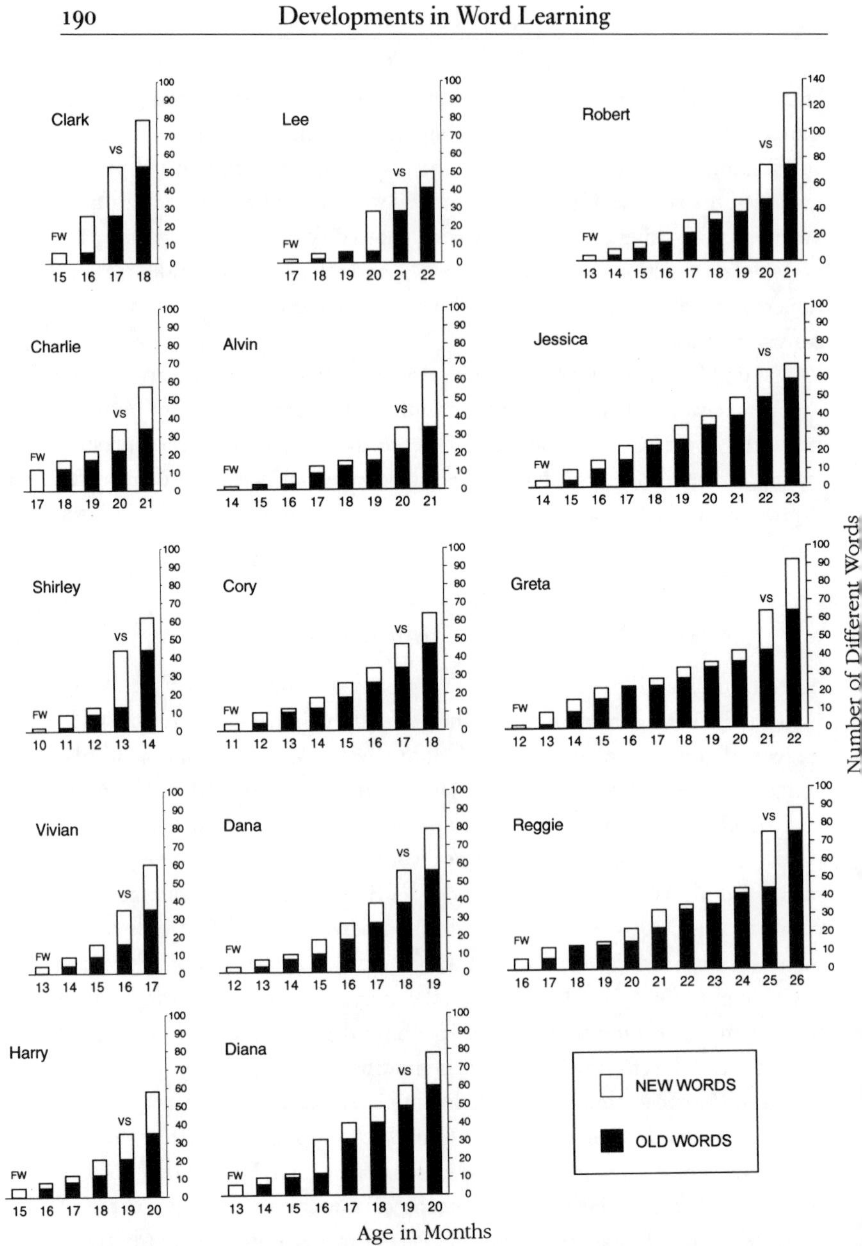

9.1 Individual cumulative vocabularies: Number of different words, new and old, each child had learned from one month to the next.

criteria in the same month, 20 words plus 12 more words). The increase was more moderate for 6 others: Alvin, Charlie, Cory, Harry, Jessica, and Lee. Diana showed the most gradual increase in new words (after a jump in new words before she had learned 20 words, at 16 months); 2 other children also learned 12 or more new words in a month before achieving a base vocabulary of 20 words (Clark and Lee). The justification for not considering such an early increase to be a vocabulary spurt – and the justification for the procedures we used as well – is that the children's ages when they reached 50 words in their vocabularies were highly correlated with age at VS for all of them: 7 reached 50 words at VS and 7 at VS + 1. All the children continued to learn new words in the month after VS, and 10 learned as many or more new words at VS + 1 as they had learned the month before, at VS.

An important feature of this study is that the playroom context was the same for all the children; they all played with the same groups of toys every month, and the toys were introduced to them on the same schedule. Because we equated the contexts and the children had the same opportunities to play with the toys, they also had the same opportunities to talk about the toys. We might have expected, then, that they would learn the same words – at least the names of the toys – and say these words with similar relative frequencies. But the children's vocabularies were quite different. The numbers of different words that they shared are shown in Figure 9.2. The numbers 1 to 14 on the *x* axis represent the number of vocabularies (one for each child); the numbers of words in each column are those said by 1, 2, 3 . . . 14 children at any time in the period of the study. Each word could theoretically have appeared in the cumulative vocabularies of all 14 children. In fact, however, most of the words (74%) were said by only 3 or fewer children, and 48% of the words appeared in only one or another vocabulary. Only 49 words (or 15% of all the words) were said by 7 or more children. Thus, the words in the cumulative vocabularies of the different children were not, by and large, the same words.[5]

One variable in the playroom context that obviously contributed to differences among the children was their mothers. In effect, the mothers symbolically represented the social and cultural experiences the children brought with them into the playroom. These experiences determined their word learning in the much larger contexts of their lives outside the playroom and contributed to the differences among them in their vocabularies.

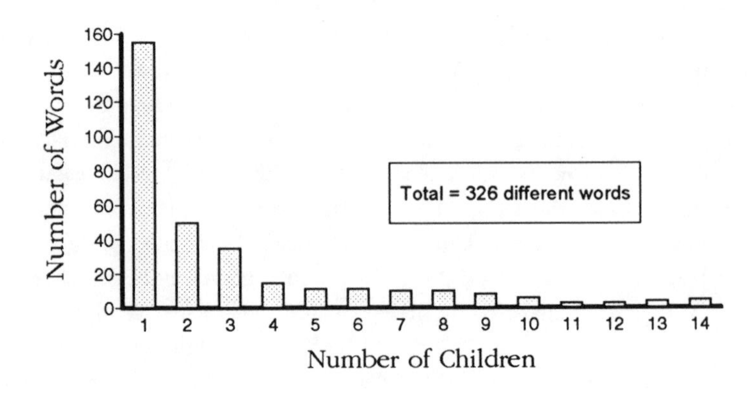

9.2 Number of words learned by 1 or more of the children

Kinds of Words in the Children's Vocabularies

The kinds of words the children learned were more important than the numbers of words. We began with the category of words that was most easily identified: names for objects. Given that the children were presented with many toys, and the same toys every month, we might have expected that names for the toys would predominate among the words they said in the playroom. Recall that we presented the infants and their mothers with different groups of toys every 8 min and with a snack midway through the hour. By the end of each session, the floor of the playroom was littered with toys. In effect, then, we provided many opportunities for the children to learn object names.

In fact, object names (including person names) accounted for only 37.4% of the 326 different word types from FW to VS + 1; the average percentage of object words and person names among all word tokens for the group of children was 42.8.[6] Only 20% of all their words were names for the toys and other objects in the playroom (*juice, door,* etc.). The different words shared by 7 or more of the individual children's vocabularies are displayed in Figure 9.3. Only 5 words appeared in the cumulative vocabularies of all 14 children; these were *baby, ball, down, juice,* and *more.* The words that were names for objects in the playroom are emphasized in Figure 9.3, and they were the only object names that were said by 7 or more of the children. The words that appeared in only 6 or fewer vocabularies are listed in the Appendix.

7	8	9	10	11	12	13	14
box	**cookie**						
choo-choo	**door**						
get	**eye**	**banana**					
girl	go	boom					
hammer	here	**bottle**	**apple**				
horse	moo	**cow**	**boy**				**baby**
in	no more	**daddy**	that			**mommy**	**ball**
out	on	**shoe**	this	**bead**	bye	no	down
sit	**truck**	**spoon**	uhoh	open	hi	oh	**juice**
two	woof	there	whee	yes	yum	up	more

Number of Children

9.3 The words learned by 7 or more of the children. Highlighting denotes words for things in the playroom.

Thus, object names did not predominate among the words these children learned. Clearly, the children brought the vocabularies they were learning in the everyday circumstances of their lives with them into our playroom each month. We were satisfied that we had indeed successfully sampled the words they were learning and that the abundance of toys did not bias them to say object names in particular. But above that, these results mean that whatever lexical principles or assumptions are at work, they need to be considerably more general than those offered so far – to explain how children learn names for objects.

Another way to look at the relative importance of object names among the words the children were learning – and therefore the extent to which lexical principles specific to learning object names can account for early word learning – is to look at the rate of learning object names over time. The percentage of new words each month that were object names did not change over time and was less than 40% for the group: in the diary data reported by 8 mothers before FW and at FW through VS+1. Individual children showed some variation in the shape of the curve, but differences among them were not systematic.[7] Thus, the children were not more likely to be learning object names when they first began saying words. We have no reason to believe, therefore, that a child will be predisposed to learn object words because of an object-specific lexical principle that would subsequently have to be overridden in order to learn other sorts of words, as has been suggested.[8]

Subsequent analyses were based on two traditional schemes from the literature for classifying early words into different kinds. The two taxonomies used to classify the words the children learned were "referential" and "expressive" words and "substantive" and "relational" words.[9] As we shall see, neither one was adequate for capturing the developments that occurred in the period. Development in the period between First Words and a Vocabulary Spurt, the two achievements we used for defining the single-word period, was not in the kinds of words the children said.

Referential and Expressive Vocabularies. The distinction, introduced by Katherine Nelson, between vocabularies consisting predominantly of "general nominal" words (referential vocabularies) and those containing primarily other sorts of words (expressive vocabularies) was applied to the children's words. Nelson's original study and most subsequent studies of this aspect of early vocabularies were based on mothers' diaries or checklist reports. Either a specific number of words was used for the analysis (for example, the first 10 and 50 words as in Nelson's study) or a particular age (for example, 20 months, as in the study by Elizabeth Bates and her colleagues).[10]

In contrast, this study was based on children's cumulative vocabularies as they were sampled in the monthly playroom sessions. Diary studies are typically thought to be more reliable in capturing a child's earliest words, and indeed, several of our mothers reported words at home (3 months earlier, on average) before we heard words in the playroom. We were surprised, therefore, when we found that the children whom we studied were not different from the children in Nelson's original study in the mean age of their first 10 and first 50 word milestones. Their mean ages were also similar to more recent findings from a much larger sample of 53 infants studied by Paula Menyuk and her colleagues.[11] The results of the three studies are compared in Table 9.1.

Parenthetically, the mean age of the children at the time of VS (19 months, 1 week) was very close to the mean age at which they also reached the 50-word landmark; the mean age at FW (13 months, 26 days) was a little more than 1 month before they reached 10 words in their vocabularies. In addition, mean age at FW fell within the age range (12 to 14 months) identified for early word

Table 9.1. *Word-count landmarks*

	Age at 10 words	Age at 50 words
This study (playroom) ($N = 14$)	15.45 (2.23)[a]	19.79 (2.72)
Nelson (1973a) ($N = 18$)	15.1 (1.76)	19.6 (2.89)
Menyuk et al. (1991) ($N = 53$)	15	19.2

[a]Mean age is shown in months; standard deviations are in parentheses.
Sources: Nelson (1973a); Menyuk, Liebergott, Schultz, Chesnick, & Ferrier (1991).

recognition in carefully controlled experimental tests of comprehension.[12] We had reason to be confident, then, that our playroom sampling of the children's vocabulary growth was successful in capturing their language achievements and rate of acquisition.

Even though the children were presented with an abundance of toys in the playroom and we created a situation for the mothers and infants to play with the toys, only 3 of the 14 children reached the criterion for a referential vocabulary: 50% or more nominals (including person names) in a child's first 50 words. For the group of 14 children together, the mean percentage of nominals was 42.14% ($SD = 11.33$) when their vocabularies reached 50 words.

This result is not consistent with the original results reported by Nelson in 1973, where referential vocabularies from mothers' diaries included personal pronouns and other nominalizing forms and were reported for 10 of the 18 children. Parents, or at least some parents, may be biased to notice object names in their children's speech and report them in diaries or in response to a checklist, perhaps because object names are more salient. This was suggested as well by Julian Pine, who found only 2 of 8 children he studied with 50% or more object names in their early vocabularies. He compared words in these children's speech with words reported in their mothers' diaries; mothers did report more nouns (10% more at 50 words and 14% more at 100 words).[13] Similarly, in the study by Bates and her colleagues, parents reported that 56%

of their children's words were common nouns at 20 months, but nouns made up only 46% of the words these same children used in a recorded sample of their speech.[14] In yet another study based on spontaneous speech, nouns made up 50% or more of a child's words at 20 months for only 10 of 45 infants studied by June Hampson; for 16 of these infants, the nouns in their vocabularies were fewer than 25%.[15]

In sum, the referential–expressive distinction did not hold up for capturing vocabulary acquisition in the children we studied. The original distinction was not a developmental one, in any event, because it characterized a child's vocabulary at only one point (either when 50 words had been learned or at 20 months, for example). We turned, then, to the scheme for classifying kinds of words in early vocabularies that I had suggested in *One Word at a Time.* This was the distinction between substantive and relational words.

Substantive Words and Relational Words. Early students of child language traditionally looked for adult parts of speech (nouns, verbs, and adjectives) among the words in early vocabularies, just as researchers also looked for the sounds of adult speech in infant prespeech vocalizing and babbling. But children do not learn "adult 'parts of speech' in the course of their development before the use of syntax . . . [and] it is only coincidental that, in the adult model, 'see' and 'stop' are 'verbs'; 'there,' 'more,' and 'away' are 'adverbs'; and 'up' is a 'preposition.'"[16] Consequently, the categories used in *One Word at a Time* for capturing differences in early words were quite general; two categories, in particular, were identified: substantive and relational words.

Each category had two subcategories. The group of substantive words consisted of names for objects and names for persons. Relational words included a group of transitive words like *more, up, all gone* and such "action" or "event" words as *dance, jump, hug.* These distinctions between classes of single words were meant to capture the different sorts of concepts underlying the words children are learning in the single-word period and possible differences in the sequence in which words with different concepts might be acquired. The main point was that children were not just learning a vocabulary of nouns, or names for things, which one might have assumed from the traditional literature.[17]

Person names were used to name single instances of "objects" like *Dada,* much like the words in a language that name such single instances as the Empire State Building and the Queen of England. Other early words recorded in diary notes also had the same "$n = 1$" quality – like words for a nursing bottle or a favorite blanket, for instance. This seemed true, in particular, for object names learned early in the period that initially named specific instances and were not readily extended to new contexts and other instances. This underextension of early words has since been observed repeatedly by others as well.[18] Eventually, however, most of the substantive words were names for classes of objects with many instances, like cookies, cars, and dogs. Thus, substantive words included names for persons, other single-instance objects, and classes of objects with many instances. The relational words were the transitive, function words like *gone,* meaning disappearance, and *more,* meaning recurrence.

In the single-subject case study in *One Word at a Time,* both the number of different word types and their relative frequency of use (tokens) were compared from about 16 to 21 months. Names for persons and objects accounted for an average of 39% of the different words in the three observations before multiword speech appeared. However, relational words (types) decreased from 46% to 32% of word types.

The second development that occurred toward the end of the single-word period was an increase in frequency of substantive words (tokens), especially the frequency of person names like *Mommy* and *Baby.* Although the number of different substantive words remained essentially the same, the frequency of substantive words increased from 30% to 51% of word tokens. Other researchers have since traced the acquisition of vocabulary in terms of the relative frequency of relational and substantive words in the development of different children in the single-word period. The results have been conflicting, with different sequences reported. Some children start out with more different substantive words and learn more relational words later in the period. Other children begin with relational words and learn increasing numbers of object words. Still other children show no difference in development of the two kinds of words, using both kinds of words equally often from the beginning.[19] Karin Lifter subsequently found precisely these three sequences with the three children she studied.[20]

We looked at the monthly cumulative vocabularies of all 14 children in this study and divided the period into two time frames: all the words said before VS and all the words said at VS and VS + 1. Each of the three possible sequences was characteristic of individual children: 4 of the children increased in the relative frequency of substantive words; 6 of the children decreased; and the 4 others showed no change in the relative distribution of the substantive and relational words in their speech.

The remaining words in the children's vocabularies were a diverse group. Certain words were clearly "social" words, like *hi, bye, yes,* and *oh man;* others were parts of routines, like *three*! (in response to "one, two . . . ?"), *ouch, good,* and the names of colors. However, and importantly, many words resisted classification, and these included the deictic forms like *this, that, here,* and certain event words like *whee, bang,* and *uhoh.* Other words, like *choochoo* and *ticktock,* were ambiguous. The point is that, except for relational words and the names for persons and objects, the categories in very young vocabularies are ill defined. Two conclusions follow from this observation. The first is that different lexical principles are not at work for learning different kinds of words before children begin to learn syntax and acquire a grammar. And the other is that children are not so much learning categories of words in the single-word period as they are learning those words in the speech they hear that are relevant to what they have in mind.

In sum, even though the children had the same opportunities to play with and talk about the same toys in our playroom, their vocabularies in the playroom differed. The relative predominance of either substantive or relational words over time captures a dimension of individual differences in the cumulative growth of early vocabularies, just as the referential–expressive distinction has revealed individual differences in children's vocabularies at a single point (such as the first 50 words or 20 months). Both taxonomies can be used to describe the vocabularies of individual children, but they do not have generality and do not explain developments in word learning from First Words to a Vocabulary Spurt in the single-word period.

However, distinguishing between relational and substantive words continues to be an important window on the cognitive developments that contribute to early word learning, since all children learn both sorts of words.[21] Alison Gopnik and others have shown specific correspondences between particular words, such as object names or the different relational words, and particular developments in cognition that give rise to learning them, leading to what she and Andrew Meltzoff termed "the specificity hypothesis."[22] The kinds of words children learn correspond to the different concepts they are acquiring at the same time, as well as to other aspects of their cognitive development in the period, as we shall see in Chapter 10.

The analyses that did reveal developments in word learning from First

Words to Vocabulary Spurt for the children in our study focused on the mental meanings their words expressed. For these analyses, we looked at two aspects of the relationship between the mental meanings attributed to words and the events in the context to which they were relevant. The two analyses reported here pertain to the principles of Elaboration and Discrepancy and, together with the results from analyses already reported in Chapter 7, fill in more of the details of word learning in this period.

DEVELOPMENT IN MENTAL MEANINGS

Attributing meaning to children's speech has been a relatively conservative enterprise so far. This is because attributions based on what children say are ordinarily restricted to the conventional linguistic meanings of words and combinations of words. The practice of attributing meaning in formal analyses of child language began with my original study of children's first word combinations and was, in effect, legitimized by Roger Brown, who coined the term "rich interpretation."[23] In the following analyses, we extended the practice of rich interpretation to make attributions of mental meanings – attributions of representations in intentional states – to the words the children said. These analyses complemented the attribution of desires and beliefs to the mental meanings of words and emotional expression described in Chapter 7. And in Chapter 11 the distinction between these personal, private, mental meanings, on the one hand, and public, conventional, linguistic meanings, on the other, is discussed more fully. Here results are presented for two analyses that provided support for the principles of Discrepancy and Elaboration; development in the single-word period of these 1-year-old children was in the expression of increasingly discrepant and elaborate mental meanings.

The first analysis had to do with the dynamic–static distinction in the mental meanings attributed to words in our coding for intentional state. According to the Principle of Elaboration, the more elements and relations between them that are represented in mental meanings, the more a child will need to know of the words and structures of language for their expression. If the Principle of Elaboration is correct, then development ought to occur in the expression of mental meanings with a focus on more than one element and relations between elements, such as one expects in dynamic meanings that include an action. Static meanings without an action, other than one of "picking out," usually have a focus on only a single object. We found that development occurred in the increasing expression of meanings with dynamic action which entailed multiple elements, roles, and relations between them, rather than static, presentational kinds of meanings.

The two categories of meaning we identified were called SEE and ACT. The category SEE consisted of the predicates of presentation in the intentional states code; these were *point, see, show, give,* and *have.* An example was Shirley's turning to her mother and, showing her a cup for her to see, saying "cup."[24] The category ACT consisted of the dynamic predicates *do* and *go* in intentional states. An example was Diana's saying "up" as she climbed onto a chair.

When the children first began to say words, at FW, attributions of SEE and ACT meanings were similar in relative frequency. However, in the interval from First Words to the Vocabulary Spurt, words that expressed ACT meanings increased more than words that expressed SEE meanings (see Fig. 9.4).[25] At the time of the Vocabulary Spurt, ACT meanings were attributed to intentional states far more frequently than SEE meanings, with a ratio of more than 2 : 1. This result was true for 13 of the 14 children. Further, all the children increased in ACT expression from FW to VS except for 2 of them: Lee, who showed no change in relative frequency, and Clark.

Mental meanings with stative SEE events were directed at a single element that the child had in mind while showing, giving, pointing, or otherwise presenting. However, dynamic meanings directed at actions have several elements with different roles and relations among them, according to the details of the action. These can include an actor or agent of the action, an object affected by the action, an instrument for the action, the place to which an object is moved, and so forth. Expressions with both sorts of meanings increased, but the development that occurred was in the greater increase in expression of dynamic, ACT meanings; these came to predominate at VS relative to presentational, SEE meanings.

Thus, one development in the single-word period was this increase in number of elements, roles, and relations attributed to mental meanings directed at actions, providing support for the Principle of Elaboration. The developmental increase in the tendency to talk about dynamic action events was complemented by the mothers' behaviors with their children. In Chapter 8 we saw that mothers were most likely to act or to talk about acting when they responded to a child's emotional expression. And in Chapter 10 we shall see

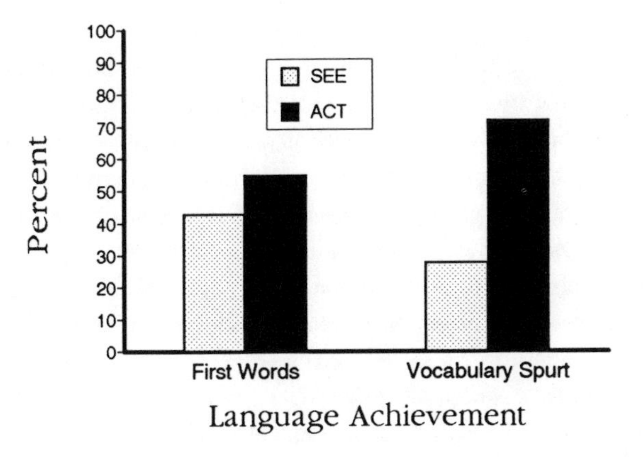

9.4 Percentage of SEE and ACT meanings attributed to words at First Words and Vocabulary Spurt.

how the mothers' actions with the toys in the playroom similarly focused on what their children could do with the toys.

The second analysis was a test of the Principle of Discrepancy. We looked at whether the elements attributed to mental meanings expressed by the children's words were already evident in the circumstances in which the words were said. According to the Principle of Discrepancy, children will acquire words and the grammar of a language as their mental meanings become increasingly discrepant from the data of perception and cannot otherwise be shared. If the Principle of Discrepancy is correct, then development in mental meanings ought to proceed in the direction of expressing what is anticipated rather than what is already evident in the context.[26] And this is what we found.

The two categories of attribution for this analysis were EVIDENT and ANTICIPATED meanings. An attributed mental meaning was considered *evident* when it was directed at something in the context that either had already taken place or was in progress. For example, Charlie looked at the toy cow and said "cow." When, in contrast, the attributed meaning was about something *anticipated*, the expression preceded the event in the context that the expression was about. One example, with the same word, was Charlie's holding up the cow for his mother to see and saying "cow"; another was his turning to her for help in putting the cow into a block and saying "cow." In the first instance, he was showing it to her in order for her to see it; in the second, he wanted her to do something with the cow. In both examples, objects and relationships in the child's mental meaning were known to Charlie; however, his mother's notice of the object or her action with it were anticipated – imminent and expected by the child but not yet evident. In anticipated events, the representations in mental meanings were constructed from knowledge in memory, being more or less cued by perceptual data.

Most of the children's words expressed meanings that were already evident, directed as they were to objects and events already present or in progress. The greater frequency of EVIDENT expression overall, at both First Words and Vocabulary Spurt, was what one might expect from the often cited here-and-now character of children's early speech. However, development occurred from FW to VS in the relative frequency of ANTICIPATED expression, with a greater increase in words expressing something about imminent objects and events (see Fig. 9.5).[27]

The developmental increase in ANTICIPATED expression was relatively greater for ACT meanings than for SEE meanings. At FW, ANTICIPATED expression was relatively more frequent with SEE, as the children said their words in presentational sorts of events (showing, giving, pointing in order that their mothers "see"). However, ANTICIPATED expression with ACT meanings increased and was relatively more frequent than for SEE meanings at the time of the Vocabulary Spurt (see Fig. 9.6). All the children except Robert increased between FW and VS in the expression of anticipative ACT meanings. These results mean that the two developments relevant to discrepancy and elaboration were coextensive. Development in the single-word period was in words with mental meanings that were both increasingly elaborated – having multiple objects, roles, and relations – and also increasingly discrepant – meanings that could not otherwise be known to a listener because they were anticipated by the child: imminent but not yet evident.

One development in word learning, then, came with the increased ability to talk about something the child had in mind that could not be shared with a listener unless it was expressed. In order to make known to others what they had in mind, the children's words had to "trigger" similar "targets" (Fauconnier's terms) in another's mental meaning to resolve the discrepancy.[28] These anticipations were still here-and-now events because they almost always concerned the objects and persons in the playroom, as when Charlie turned to his mother for help in putting the cow into a block and said "cow," and Shirley

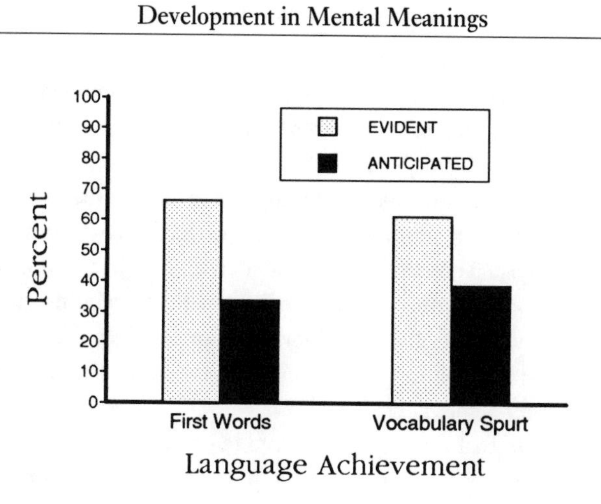

9.5 Percentage of EVIDENT and ANTICIPATED meanings attributed to words at First Words and Vocabulary Spurt.

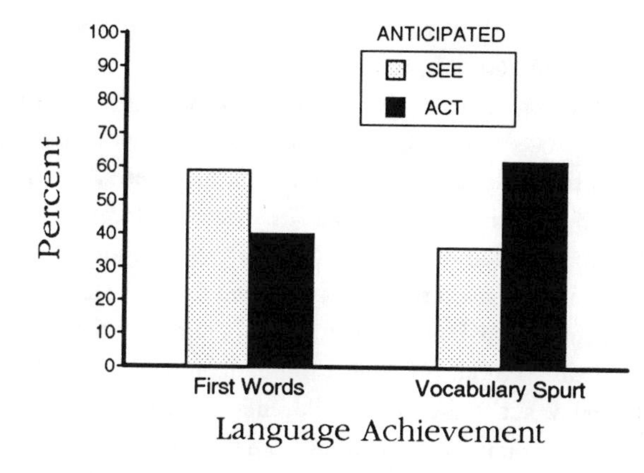

9.6 Percentage of ANTICIPATED SEE and ACT meanings attributed to words at First Words and Vocabulary Spurt.

held out a cup for her mother to see, saying "cup." Development, therefore, was in a shift from immediate to imminent here-and-now events in a child's mental meanings.

This ability to talk about what can be anticipated has its origins in very early infancy. As young as $3\frac{1}{2}$ months of age, infants have shown they can form expectations for visual events that are presented to them in a series, providing very early evidence of future-oriented behavior. By 11 months, infants can monitor successive events and attend longer to an anticipated event, particularly if the event is salient.[29] Thus, anticipation – with the discrepancy it entails – is present before language.

And it turns out that 1-year-olds are used to hearing speech from others in anticipation of the events the speech is about. In a study of early verb learning, Michael Tomasello showed that children in the single-word period (at ages 15 and 21 months) most often hear their mothers use verbs before the action named by the verb actually occurs. Mothers typically used verbs that anticipated their children's actions, presumably reading the child's mind. However, this happened primarily when a child was already focused on the object that was the goal of the anticipated action. In fact, when mothers' verbs did not typically occur during such episodes of joint attention, vocabulary growth suffered.[30] In addition, the verbs the mothers used were most often either all-purpose verbs like *do* and *go* (what we called "pro-verbs" in our studies of early syntax)[31] or were more descriptive verbs for actions that were clearly afforded by the objects the child and mother were attending to (for example, *open, throw, turn, catch, eat,* and *read*). When children were attending to an object, then, they could anticipate the most likely action with the object and learned those verbs when the mothers named them. A caregiver's words, then, can target anticipated elements in a child's mind for the child to learn those words – an example of how representations in mental meanings determine the relevance of the words children hear.

In sum, two conclusions we could draw from the results of our efforts to tap the mental meanings of our 1-year-old subjects relate to the principles of Elaboration and Discrepancy. With respect to the Principle of Elaboration, the developmental increase in expression of action meanings was evidence of the representation of multiple elements, with different roles and relations among them, in mental meanings. Whereas a word in the single-word period often names one component of action (the person doing the action or the object that is affected or some transformation with respect to persons and objects), single words do not ordinarily name the actions themselves. Thus, action expressions will require that a child learn the verbs in a language and how verbs combine with other words the child might already know or learn. In short, action meanings will provide the impetus for learning simple sentences.

According to the Principle of Discrepancy, children acquire words and linguistic structures to express something not yet evident in the context, and we saw this in the increasing expression of anticipative meanings. The importance of this development is in what it tells us about developments in the representation of mental meanings – the ability to construct a mental meaning cued by the context but not given in the context. Anticipative meanings need to be made public if other persons are to know them.

These 1-year-olds gave no indication that they consciously attended to a discrepancy between what they and others might have had in mind and purposely intended their words to resolve the discrepancy. Instead, they were motivated to sustain intersubjectivity and to influence what others might think and do in the process. The children were also not yet using the language of anticipation, and they wouldn't be for some time, at least not until after they learned the syntax of simple sentences with action verbs.[32] (The forms *will*, *wanna*, and *gonna* were rare and said only near the end of the period by 1 or 2 children.) These two developments might very well come together; 2-year-olds probably begin to learn such modal verbs of intending to do something, along with the syntax of sentences with these verbs, as they come to understand how language can resolve a discrepancy between what two people have in mind.

Expressing anticipation is tied to learning the language of emotion, because anticipated events are very often tied to feelings.[33] Anticipated mental meanings often include a plan, and planning entails goals; individuals experience and express emotion in connection with the success or failure of their plans and goals.[34] The two sorts of expression, speech and emotion, came together in this period of single-word learning as the children learned to say words to express mental meanings that had to do with their feelings – the words to express what their feelings were about.

THE LANGUAGE OF EMOTION

The children's vocabularies made clear that they were not saying words that named the emotions (see Fig. 9.3 and the Appendix). But they were learning to talk about their feelings, nonetheless. Even though they were not learning such emotion terms as *happy*, *mad*, and *sad*, they were indeed learning to talk about the things that were the objects, causes, and circumstances of such feelings. We have already seen, in Chapters 7 and 8, something of how the children expressed their emotions with positive and negative affect expression; they were quite adept at letting others know when they were pleased or distressed. Their mothers, in turn, knew easily enough when their infants were joyous, angry, frustrated, or frightened; the children did not have to tell them so with the words *happy* or *mad.* But words *were* needed to do something about the distress or to achieve and extend the joy. Accordingly, the children learned words to express *what their feelings were about* at the same time as they continued to express their feelings through displays of positive and negative affect.

In fact, acquisition of words for naming emotions and feeling states is a relatively late development, even in cultures – Samoa, for example – where talk between children and their mothers is "intensely emotional."[35] Reports in the literature of the early use of emotion words by English-speaking children have relied on mothers' reporting, through diaries and checklists, whether such words ever occur at all, and the youngest children in these studies have usually not been under 20 months old.[36] The children in our study might have said such words on occasion as well (one child, Diana, did say the words "scared" and "sorry" in the playroom), and if we had explicitly asked them, perhaps the mothers would have reported such words at home. However, they did not appear in the diaries the mothers kept, and names for the emotions were even rare in the mothers' own speech when they talked to their children in responding to their emotional expressions.

Most of the children's words were said when they were expressing neutral affect, as we saw in Chapter 8. However, what were the words the children said at the same time they were also expressing positive and negative emotion, if they were not emotion labels? Consistent with the assumption that cognition and affect collaborate for language development, we hypothesized that the words the children said at the same time they expressed emotion would be the words they knew best – the words that were easiest for them to recall and say. Given that saying words and expressing emotion both put demands on a young child's cognitive resources, integrating affect expression and speech should be easier with relatively well-known words. This was indeed the case. The words the children said with emotional expression at VS tended to be the words they also said most frequently and/or words they had learned to say at an earlier time.[37]

First, words that occurred with emotional expression tended to be among a child's most frequent words. Each child's words were rank ordered according to their overall frequency (number of tokens) at VS. These rank orders of the most frequent words were compared with the frequency ranks for those words said with emotional expression. The two rank orders were counted as matching for an individual child when at least 2 of the 3 most frequent words overall were included among the 4 most frequent words said with emotional expression. Using this criterion, the frequency rank orders matched for two thirds of the children.

We then determined whether words said with emotion were old words or new words. The words reported in the mothers' diaries, the children's words at FW, and words that were said in the interval between FW and VS were examined for the occurrence of those words said with emotionally toned affect at VS. Again, for two thirds of the children, 50% or more of the different words they said with emotional expression at VS had occurred in their vocabularies before VS. For all the children except Vivian, either frequency or previous occurrence or both predicted which words were said with emotional expression at VS.

A total of 69 different words were said with emotional valence at VS by the group of children as a whole. None of these words were names for emotions. Even in those moments, then, when the children were actually expressing emotion, they did not use words to tell others what emotion they were feeling. A small group of words were said with emotional expression by at least 3 of the children, and these are listed in Table 9.2.

There are no real surprises here. Several of the words on this list are among those one might expect would have inherent emotional connotation, in addition to their lexical meaning, for young children. These were (1) relational words frequently reported in infant vocabularies, like *no* and *more;* (2) words typically associated with well-known routines, like *hi* and *whee* (when rolling a ball, using the slide, and the like); and (3) person words (*Mama* and its variants, and *baby*), which were also said of the small rubber family figures. Of the remaining words on the list, *three* was part of the counting routine ("one, two, three!"), but the presence of *cow, spoon,* and *eye* on the list is not readily explained.

Among the words used by 4 or more children, only the highly routinized words *hi* and *whee* were said with emotionally toned affect primarily: in 90% and 79%, respectively, of total speech time (in video frames). Included as words in the speech transcription were words that have traditionally been thought of as likely to carry emotional tone: for example, such interjections as

Table 9.2. *Words said at Vocabulary Spurt with emotional expression by 3 or more children*

Word	No. of children	Total proportion of speech time
baby	8	0.41
Mama	6	0.43
hi	5	0.90
whee	5	0.79
more	4	0.19
no	3	0.50
cow	3	0.16
spoon	3	0.60
three	3	0.70
eye	3	0.67

Source: L. Bloom & Beckwith (1989).

oh and *uhoh.*[38] However, these interjections were not more likely than other words to occur with emotional expression and did not appear among the words said with emotional expression by 3 or more children.

Finally, in order to test the conclusion that words said with emotional expression at VS tended to be among the children's earliest learned and most frequent words, the lag sequential analyses reported in Chapter 8 were repeated with these words excluded from the word lists. Words were excluded for the individual children (1) if they had occurred at FW or in the mothers' diaries and/or (2) their frequency at VS was 2 standard deviations or more above the mean for the frequency of words overall. At VS, when the most frequent and earliest learned words were excluded, the profiles for 10 of the 12 children had the same shape as the original lag analysis profile but differed in amplitude: More neutral affect was expressed before words and less emotion expressed after words. Thus, the expression of emotion was particularly inhibited when these children said words that were not among their most frequent and earliest learned words and were presumably words they knew less well.

In sum, the words said at the same time the children expressed emotion tended to be words the children learned early and used most frequently, and/ or they were person words (i.e., *Mama* and *baby*) or parts of well-known play and other routines. Earlier learned and more frequent words are presumably the words a child knows best, which means they could be expected to be easier to recall and say. But more important, the words they said with emotion were words to express what their feelings were about and not names for the emotions themselves. Examples of such words are actually quite mundane: Charlie said "open" as he was opening the lock box; he smiled and said "hi" as one of the assistants came into the playroom with more toys; he said "cow" while whining and holding out the father family figure toward his mother, indicating that he wanted the father to ride the horse (which he called "cow"); and so on. But although they were ordinary examples of child language, words like these were highly relevant to Charlie in the circumstances in which he said them. This conclusion was reinforced when we looked at the mothers' speech in our playroom sessions.

Mothers' Talk about Emotion

In her dissertation, Joanne Capatides looked at what the mothers did and said in the moments surrounding their children's expression of emotionally toned affect at 9, 13, 17, and 21 months.[39] When a mother's speech before and after each affect expression by her child was examined, names of emotions were exceedingly rare and actually decreased in frequency in the period from 9 to 21 months. The mean number of emotion word tokens the mothers used in the first 30 min of the playroom sessions was 2.5, 1.17, 0.83, and 0.5 at 9, 13, 17, and 21 months, respectively. Indeed, the most frequent such word the mothers used was *like*, as in "You like that, don't you?," and *like* has only marginal status, at best, as an emotion term; other words they said were *fussy, excited, bad, all right, hurt,* and *funny*. Only three words labeled an emotion (*scared, afraid,* and *unhappy*), and each was said only once. In sum, the mothers did talk about a child's emotional experience and expression by saying things like "Why are you scared?" and, more often, "You like that, don't you?" But they did so infrequently. Most often mothers talked about what occasioned an emotional expression or the circumstances surrounding it, for example: "What's the matter? / is it stuck?"; "What do you want?"; "Is that funny?"; "Try sitting up like this"; "The truck went down the ramp."

Mothers' conversations about "feeling states" were also described by Judy Dunn and her colleagues for children in the same age range as the children we studied.[40] In the list of "feeling-state labels" that the mothers in their study used, "emotional states" was one of three categories (along with "quality of consciousness" and "sensations and physiological states"). As with the mothers in our study, the number of names of emotions in their category of "emotional states" was extremely small, and most of the words the mothers used in this category (e.g., *enjoy, mind, temper*), like *like* in our study, are not emotion terms in the sense described by Clore and Ortony.[41] In any event, the mean number of mother utterances in *any* of the three categories of feeling states in the Dunn et al. study, prorated for 30 min for the sake of comparison with our results, was 1.75 and 2.75 at 18 months and 24 months, respectively.

Thus, caregivers do not label the specific emotions per se, and they use actual labels for the emotions infrequently when talking to their 1-year-old children. Instead, the mothers in our study talked about the causes, consequences, and circumstances of their children's experience and expression of emotion (Chapter 8). They used the sorts of words that provide young children with the language for talking about why they experience one or another feeling state and what might be done about it. In turn, children's words in the single-word period are words like *Mama, baby, more, ride, ball,* and the like – words for the persons, objects, and actions in one or another of the circumstances that give rise to emotion. These vocabularies of our mothers and 1-year-olds in the context of the children's emotional experience and expression are consistent with a model in which emotions are "valenced reactions to events, agents, or objects, with their particular nature being determined by the way in which the eliciting situation is construed."[42] If emotions derive from such reactions and construals, then the fact that these are the things that early words in particular, and the language of emotion in general, are about should not be surprising.

Cognitive theories of emotion stress the importance of goals and plans and changes in the context that influence success or interfere with an individual's goals or plans. If these are the things that produce emotional experience and underlie knowledge about what emotions are,[43] then learning to talk about such items of experience is at least as important as learning the emotion terms themselves. In fact, to the extent that an infant's facial expression and postural displays of emotion are available to others, emotion terms are more redundant than informative.

In earlier research on the acquisition of the language of causality between the ages of 2 and 3 years, we showed how early expressions of causality have to do with subjective, emotion-eliciting events. Examples included "wait my mommy comes / because I will be lonely" and "I was crying because I didn't want to wake up / because it was dark, so dark."[44] Children begin to talk about the causal connections entailed in emotional experience even before they learn such linguistic terms for causality as *because, so,* and *why.* Similarly, the 1-year-olds in the present study learned the language for expressing the causes and objects of their emotion, which no doubt had to do with the success or failure of their goals and plans, before they even began to acquire a dictionary of emotion terms.

In sum, children's early words in the second year of life do not name their emotions, and so they do not *tell* us what they are feeling. Rather they continue to rely on expression of emotion through facial and postural displays of affect, and the words they are learning express what their feelings are about. Moreover, the language that 1-year-old children hear gives them the words for the sorts of experiences that are associated with different feeling states more often than it provides labels for the emotions themselves.

One of the most important aspects of emotional development is the ability to control and modulate the forms of emotional expression according to social and cultural expectations.[45] To this end, the language children hear from their caregivers helps them to regulate their own feeling states and the behaviors that give rise to and result from their feelings.[46] For example, in a study of children's negative emotional expressions, Claire Kopp showed how crying diminished with the emergence and development of language. This development was documented by Denise Kenny in a finely detailed case study, with weekly recordings of one little boy as he woke up in his crib in the morning. She showed the exquisite progression from his prespeech whimpers and crying at 11 months to his eventually calling out at 27 months with "I waking up . . . I'm waking . . . Ma . . . Ma . . . Mommy I waking up."[47]

But language does not replace affect expression, and children continue to express their feelings through affect as they learn language. Indeed, with further development they will also become aware of new and different feeling states that require increasingly more subtle and controlled forms of expression. These include the more socially and personally complex emotions (for example, jealousy, guilt, and shame). Language can express many aspects of the objects, circumstances, and feelings associated with both basic and more complex emotions but by no means all their aspects. And in fact words fail us altogether when our feelings are most intense, and we fall silent, waiting for the feelings to abate and the words to come. Terrence Brown has shown, with eloquence, how the complexity and intensity of one's feeling might be expressed in private by writing a poem before being shared when another reads the poem.[48] Poetry is a special case where personal expression transcends the interpersonal.

Our 1-year-olds were on the very threshold of language. As they learned their early words, saying only one word at a time, the words they said were small words with extensions limited to their experiences with the persons, objects, and events they were encountering in their first two years. In this same period of time they learned to crawl, to walk, to move on and out into the world. And as they learned more about themselves and more about their worlds, they learned more of the language. We know that they went on to string their words together and to acquire a grammar for simple sentences.[49] Their language learning expanded, and so too did their ability to regulate and contain emotional expressions. Infant cries and rages and shouts of joy gave way to smaller and subtler expressions of feelings as they gained control over the objects of feelings and the circumstances that cause them. This happened in large part because they learned the language to articulate these things so that other persons could know them. Thus, they acquired the power of expression: first, by saying a word, or two, and then by saying a sentence, or two, and eventually perhaps by writing a poem.

CONCLUSIONS

The children progressed at different rates in acquiring a vocabulary of words, but they all started out slowly and tentatively with only a few words and increased in rate of acquisition by the end of the period (1 month after the vocabulary spurt). Even though the context was the same for all of them, their vocabularies were different; few of the different words were said by all the children, and most were said by only 1, 2, or 3 of them. Clearly, the children brought the vocabularies they were learning in the everyday circumstances of their lives into our playroom with them each month. The words they said were varied, and fewer than 40% – both word types and tokens – were made up of object names. Thus, the principles for word learning that have received so much attention in the literature could not explain these children's word learning, since such principles are generally specific to learning the names for objects.

The words the children learned were determined by a number of things – at the least, and chief among them, the Principle of Relevance: how relevant a word happened to be for what they had in mind when they heard it originally. The kinds of words – at least insofar as kinds of words were captured by the existing taxonomies we used to describe them – appeared to be less important than the mental meanings a word can express. Certain words are specific to the concepts children acquire – words like *more* and *gone* and *up*. But those words were also probably learned in the first place because they figured in events in which the infant's thinking and feelings were engaged. One-year-old children learn to talk about the objects, causes, and circumstances of their beliefs, desires, and feelings with words that can articulate what these are – words like *Mama, uhoh,* and *no* and also words like *cow, cookie, more, gone,* and *up*. These were very often words for talking about the thematic relations between objects, and between persons and objects, in everyday events, and thematic relationships were a large part of what the children were learning in their play, as we shall see in Chapter 10. Notably absent from these children's early vocabularies were the words that name discrete emotions; emotion labels were also missing from the language the children heard when their mothers responded to their emotional expressions.

We attributed mental meanings to the children's words, and two results from these attributions were particularly revealing of development in the period. One was the increasing expression of anticipative meanings, with words that expressed something imminent but not yet evident in the context – providing evidence for the Principle of Discrepancy. The other development provided evidence for the Principle of Elaboration. This was the relative increase in expression of dynamic mental meanings involving actions – with multiple elements having different roles and relations – over meanings with a focus on a single element. These developments pointed to important changes taking place in the children's cognition for constructing mental meanings and complement the results of our analyses of how the children played with the toys we gave them in the playroom. Their play with objects provided a window on other aspects of cognitive development in relation to their language learning and is the subject of Chapter 10.

10

Developments in Cognition

We have been concerned so far with developments in affect expression and saying words. In this chapter, we turn to how the children played with the toys in the playroom as a window on developments in cognition. We will see in particular how developments in object play, saying words, and emotional expression were integrated – both in the children's development over the course of the year and a half in which we studied them and in the moment-to-moment events in the stream of spontaneous activity in which we observed them.

Karin Lifter and I used several sorts of data from the children's play for comparison with developments in language.[1] The primary data came from play in which a child did something with two objects in relation to each other. The child either took two objects apart – for example, taking a bead off the string – or constructed a thematic relation between objects – like putting a doll in the truck. The categories of play activity derived from these data, and the sequence of their emergence and achievement are the central results of the study.

Secondary data were also collected to provide a developmental context for these results and to help us understand them. One source of secondary data was the children's spontaneous finding behavior: how they located objects in the playroom to use for constructing relationships between them. In addition to the children's *spontaneous* play and finding, we also *elicited* search with the standardized graduated tasks from the Uzgiris and Hunt object permanence scale, so that we could compare the results with other studies in the literature.[2] Two measures of general maturation were age of walking and block building: We asked the infants to build a tower with 1-in. wooden cubes and compared their progress in tower building with traditional "norms" in the literature.

Finally, we looked at how the mothers provided the social context of their children's developing object knowledge in the episodes in which the mothers initiated play with the toys.

The results from analyses of these several sorts of data include (1) the categories of object play and their development, (2) corresponding developments in spontaneous search and finding, (3) progress in solving the standardized tasks on the object permanence scale, (4) progress in building a tower of 1-in. cubes, and (5) the mothers' actions with the objects when they were the ones who initiated play. Together these results tell us something about the infants' development of object knowledge in their second year, the period when they made the transition to language and acquired a vocabulary of words.

DEVELOPMENTS IN OBJECT PLAY AND KNOWLEDGE

We furnished the playroom with a variety of toys, and, as described in Chapter 6, we controlled for the amount of time toys were available for either manipulative or enactment play, although we did not use these traditional categories. We opted instead for a more descriptive categorization scheme. The group of core toys was on the playroom floor before the infant and mother arrived, and new toys were brought into the playroom every 8 min thereafter. All the children had the same opportunities to play with the same objects every month so that we could be confident of two things. Changes in the way they played with the toys could be attributed to their development and to the interaction between child and mother as a result of the child's development. And differences in their play or in their development could be attributed to differences among the children.

Constructing Thematic Relations in Play

At first an infant's actions with objects are nonspecific and limited to one object at a time. When infants play with a single object, they typically look at it attentively or put it in their mouths or bang it against a table or another suitable surface. Such early actions are applied to almost any object generally, without regard to its attributes or functions; as long as an object can be grasped and held, it may be examined, mouthed, dropped, shaken, or thrown.[3] But examining has priority; when 7- and 12-month-old infants were given an object to play with, they were relatively quick to examine it and spent more time in examining than they spent either mouthing or banging it.[4]

Examining an object provides an opportunity for the sort of "perceptual analysis" needed for early conceptual representations. Such analysis begins in the first half year of life, and although it cannot be studied directly, it can be inferred when a baby is watchful, quiet, and alert and attending to what is going on. In this perceptual analysis, infants compare what they see with something else that is also present or something that was experienced at an earlier time.[5] We can assume that during this time the baby is actively thinking about the object and what it means.

By itself, however, examining a single object does not ordinarily provide evidence of *what* the baby is thinking about the object or knows about the object, and more information is needed. Such information is available from finding behaviors and from putting objects together in play. For example, when a baby searches for and finds an object, we can attribute to the baby having that object in mind. When an infant takes two objects and constructs a configuration with them, such as putting a bead on a string or a doll in a truck, we have information for making the attribution that the infant recalled to mind, in a plan for acting, the relationship between the objects in that configuration. And when infants take objects apart and put them together again, we can attribute to them an appreciation of the reversibility of actions. These were the sorts of evidence we used in our study of developments in object play. We looked at all the events in the playroom in which the infants searched for and found an object or did something with two or more objects in relation to each other. Such actions provided evidence of what an infant called to mind about the objects and therefore knew about them at different points in time.

We have reported the results from our study of object play more fully elsewhere.[6] Here I will recount the findings that are relevant to the central thesis pursued throughout this book: Just as with emotional expression and language, developments in play depend upon a child's intentionality and the representations a child is able to set up and hold in mind. The developments in language, as we have seen, included acquiring a vocabulary of different words for more explicit expression. Developments occurred in play as the children learned to construct increasingly specific relations between objects. These developments – a vocabulary spurt in word learning and constructing specific thematic relations – occurred close together in time for all the children but at a different age for each of them. We assume they were two manifestations of developments in underlying cognition. The relevant developments in cognition consisted of knowledge about objects and about relations between objects in general, and concepts of particular objects and of the specific thematic relationships afforded between them.

This study of object play capitalized on the well-known tendency young children have to appreciate that things go together to form the ordinary themes of everyday events. Inhelder and Piaget had described children's earliest groupings of things as "graphic," based as they were on either "geometric shape" or "a relation of belonging drawn from the subject's past experience."[7] The list of such thematic relations in a young life is virtually endless. Milk is poured into and out of bottles; hats go on heads; shoes go on feet; telephones are held to ears; and so on. As a consequence, a variety of themes could be played out with the toys we presented to the children. Certain of these relationships between objects were afforded by their physical characteristics primarily, such as when one object served only as a container or a surface to support another object – similar to the first kind of grouping Inhelder and Piaget described based on geometric shape. Others, however, were also influenced by social and cultural experience in everyday events.

Categories of Play. The kinds of object play we identified are displayed in Figure 10.1. Each branching in the figure represents a coding decision, and successive branchings represent increasingly finer distinctions. The coding scheme was theoretically motivated in two ways. The first was Piaget's original description of the construction of object knowledge and the part played by *reversibility* of operations for "creating relationships among objects." The earliest understanding of means–end relations, object permanence, and the logic of groups, in the first year of life, depends on appreciating the reversibility of actions.[8] The first cut in the data, therefore, distinguished between taking objects in a configuration apart (separating) and putting objects together to form a relationship between them (constructing).

The second motivation was to preserve behaviors in coding at the level of *description* before imposing an interpretation on them – so that all the relationships constructed between objects could be accounted for. The category *constructions* was the most general and encompassed all the different relationships created with the toys. The subcategories represented increasingly finer descriptions of the different kinds of relationships that were possible in these constructions. All constructions were, in turn, either given or imposed; all imposed relations were either general or specific; and so on. The most differentiated category, at the end of the tree, are the imposed specific animate–surrogate constructions in which a child used one or more of the animate–surrogate objects (the dolls, farm animals, rubber family figures, stuffed lamb, wooden peg people, and the like).

In order to separate two objects, all an infant needed to do was take hold of one part of the configuration and pull at it for it to come apart. For example, the wooden peg persons could be separated from the seesaw in this way, or a bead could be pulled off the string, or two nested cups could be pulled apart. Alternatively, the child could knock a block from the top of a tower or dump the beads from a block or out of the truck. These separating actions did not necessarily require an understanding that the objects were related thematically, or even an understanding that the objects in the original configuration were separate objects.

In contrast, when a child deliberately brought objects together to construct a configuration with them, we could infer that the child had the thematic relation between the objects in mind. The toys in the playroom afforded many possibilities for showing how objects go together in everyday events. Certain of these thematic relations were already evident in the ways the toys were originally presented to the children in the playroom. For example, the peg persons were already seated in the seesaw, and the large wooden blocks were nested together. When the children recreated the same relationship as the one in which the objects were originally introduced into the playroom, the construction was categorized as *given*. In contrast, when the children created a relationship that was different from the way the objects were originally introduced, the result was an *imposed* construction. These were the first two categories of constructions: given and imposed relationships.

Imposed relations were either *general* or *specific*. General constructions made use of those physical properties of objects that afforded containment or support: for example, putting silverware, family figures, or beads *into* a box or *on* a surface. Specific constructions, in contrast, made use of more particular properties of the objects in relation to each other, as when the child used a toy spoon to feed the baby doll or put beads on the string. In certain specific constructions, the children used a replica of a person or an animal – for example, feeding the doll with a spoon or putting the figure of a boy on the horse. These were *animate surrogate* constructions, as opposed to other specific relations constructed with inanimate objects, such as stringing the beads or rolling the truck on the wooden roadway.

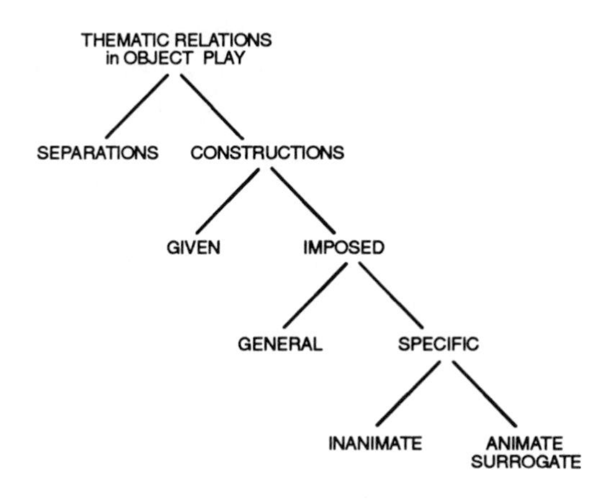

10.1 Categories of thematic relations in object play. (Adapted from Lifter & Bloom, 1989)

Thus, the analyses of object play did not begin with the categories of manipulative (so-called relational) play and enactment ("symbolic" or "pretend") play that have been used in other studies. Instead, coding actions with objects was guided by the descriptive information provided by the toys and a child's actions with them. This kind of information allowed us to (1) attribute representation of objects and relations between objects in intentional states and (2) infer developments in reversibility and the symbolic capacity that such representations required. Such actions theoretically both derive from a child's knowledge and lead to further developments in knowledge.

The diagram in Figure 10.1 is a right-branching tree to show that the categorization scheme has logical validity; the subcategories descending on the right form a hierarchy of increasingly differentiated constructions. And, as we shall see, the hierarchy was empirically valid as well, because it formed a developmental sequence. The first distinction was based on the direction of movement, either moving objects apart (separating) or moving objects together (constructing). This first distinction in the hierarchy was the first coding decision and also the first development in the children's object play; they learned to construct relations between objects after learning to take them apart. For example, the children took peg persons out of a bus, knocked down a tower of blocks, spilled the beads out of a box, took apart the two pieces that formed a slide, and so forth. Or they put objects together: for example, stacking the blocks, rolling a disk down the slide, or giving a doll a ride in the truck. Animate surrogate constructions, the last category in the hierarchy, were also the last to develop.

Two other features of the children's play with objects are captured by the schema in Figure 10.1. One was a difference of form in reversible actions: moving objects apart (separating) or moving objects together (constructing). The second was differences in content, such as between general and specific relationships and between specific relationships with inanimate or animate surrogate objects. With each coding decision, the left-branching categories were not further subcategorized. This means that separations were not analyzed after they were identified, and the remaining analyses were based on subcategories of constructions. The given relations were not analyzed further and the remaining analyses were based on subcategories of imposed relations. And so on.

These activities with the objects (separations and constructions) were frequent in the stream of the children's actions and increased over time, from an average of 59 instances at 9 months to an average of 131 actions at First Words (FW) and 179 in the month after the Vocabulary Spurt (VS + 1). Given how frequently they occurred (an average of 1 a min at 9 months and once every 20 sec at VS + 1), we could assume that these actions represented what the infants did in their everyday activities and therefore what they knew about objects and thematic relationships in everyday events. In addition, the frequency of these activities in the playroom provided an empirical justification for the categorization scheme we used to describe their object play.

Windows on Development. The ages at which we studied the children's play were theoretically motivated and based upon the children's individual rates of language development. Just as with the study of emotional expression, the strategy was to focus on those observations we already knew marked transitional change in their language development.[9] This time, however, we studied the children's play in three developmental "windows," with three monthly observations in each window. The reason for this was that other studies led us to expect variation in just how precise the correspondences between developments in language and play might be.[10] The first window was the PreSpeech Period at 9, 10, and 11 months of age, which we used as a baseline. During this time, few of the children were saying any words at all. The second window centered on First Words and included the month in which FW was identified, along with the months immediately preceding (FW − 1) and following (FW + 1). The third window centered on the Vocabulary Spurt and included the VS month, along with the months immediately before and after (VS − 1 and VS + 1).

Criteria for Development. We considered First Words and Vocabulary Spurt, the two transitions in language, as an *emergence* and an *achievement*, respectively. FW marked the beginning of word learning, a time when words were few in number, infrequent, tentative, and imprecise. VS, in contrast, marked a consolidation in word learning, a time when a sizable number of words had made their appearance and word learning began in earnest. Correspondingly, we identified two similar reference points for emergence and achievements in object play as well. Emergence of a category of play was evidence of new capacities from which we could infer qualitative changes in underlying thought. Achievement suggested a shift to mastery in play and a consolidation of the knowledge that the activities required.

We considered that a particular kind of play had emerged when 5 actions of that kind occurred and at least 2 of the 5 were different actions. For example, the two major categories that represented the first cut in the data were separations (taking a configuration apart) and constructions (creating a thematic relation). Constructions were considered to have emerged when a child produced at least 5 such actions and at least 2 were different actions, such as putting the peg person into the seesaw and putting the truck on the freeway. Achievement, a more stringent measure of developmental change than emergence, required a doubling of frequency and diversity of actions – a minimum of 10 actions of a kind, with at least 4 different actions.

These criteria for emergence and achievement were essentially arbitrary. However, we added a third, post hoc, criterion for achievement that was not arbitrary, because it was based on the relative frequency of the children's actions. Once the data were coded, we saw that constructions increased, and for all the children the relative frequencies of actions in the subcategories eventually showed an increase of at least 40% (except animate surrogate relations). Although some children might have shown an increase of 60% or 80% in one or another subcategory, all of them eventually showed increases of at least 40% in the individual subcategories. Consequently, we considered that achievement had occurred in one or another of the two subcategories of play at each branching of the play hierarchy (Fig. 10.1) when relative frequency reached 40% (in addition to the occurrence of at least 10 actions, 4 of which were different actions). For example, the development of constructions was considered an achievement when at least 40% of a child's play with two objects was constructing, as opposed to separating, and there were at least 10 such actions, 4 of which were different actions.

Developments in Constructing Thematic Relations. Using the two sets of criteria, one for emergence and one for achievement, we identified a developmental sequence in the children's play, and this can be seen in Figure 10.2. The sequence was the same for all the children, despite the extremely wide range in their ages. They all met the criteria for emergence and achievement first with constructions generally (any kind of given or imposed constructions, as opposed to separations) and then in the order imposed before inanimate specific before animate surrogate specific constructions. They progressed in their play by learning to construct thematic relations that increasingly took the more specific properties of objects into account (inanimate and then animate surrogate specific relations).

Most of the children's early actions in the PreSpeech window were separations in which they moved two objects in a configuration apart; only 20% of what the children did with the objects was constructing at 9 months. The major development from PreSpeech to First Words was in learning to construct thematic relations between the objects. Constructions increased in frequency until, at the time of the Vocabulary Spurt, they represented about half the children's activities with the toys. Thus, the children progressed from moving objects apart to moving objects together as often as they moved them apart. This development was not simply an increase in skill, for any attempt to bring two objects together was credited as a construction, whether or not it was successful.

Before the emergence of words, then, the children were far more likely to take objects apart than to put them together in a configuration. Once the objects were taken apart (by the child or the mother), they were again available for constructing, but the children did not, in general, construct relations between objects. Most often their mothers proceeded to reconstruct a configuration so that the infants could take it apart again. Thus, the earliest activities with the toys were in the unidirectional action pattern of separating. Through this early schema of separating objects, an infant can begin to learn,

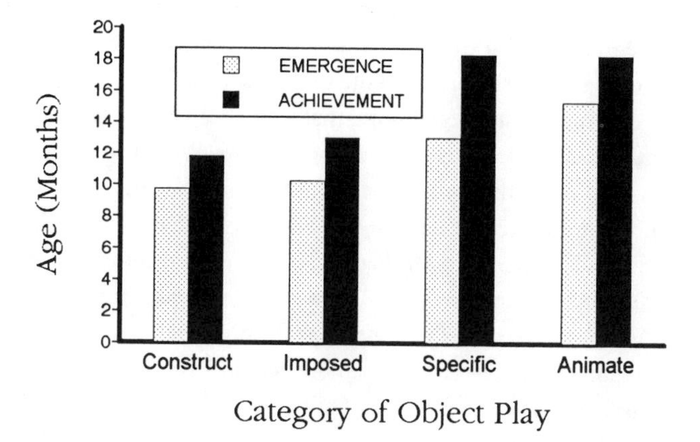

10.2 Mean age of emergence and achievement in categories of thematic relations in play. (Lifter & Bloom, 1989)

first, that objects are separate entities and, second, that they can be related to each other. Learning how to construct a thematic relation evidently begins with learning how to take it apart.

Constructing a configuration entailed a different direction of movement, from moving things apart to moving them together. This entailed an appreciation of the reversibility of action patterns, which Piaget described as a reorganization of how an infant thinks about objects.[11] The emergence of constructions indicated that an infant could think about the objects as separate entities and appreciated the reversibility of actions with them. Learning to construct thematic relations between objects is evidence, therefore, that a fundamental development in object knowledge is taking place. This kind of knowledge is of a *general* kind, because many different actions with objects enter into thematic relationships and are reversible, regardless of their particular function or perceptual characteristics. Such general object knowledge, and reversibility in particular, is central to the development of object permanence as conceptualized by Piaget. And correspondingly, at the same time that constructions emerged, the infants whom we studied began to solve the tasks considered to mark the beginning of Stage 6 on the sensorimotor scales we presented to them. This general development in object knowledge is required for learning about more particular characteristics of objects and the more specific thematic relations they afford: the kind of object knowledge required for the development of object concepts.

The beginning of constructions in the PreSpeech window corresponded to data from experimental studies showing that infants can appreciate a thematic relationship between objects by 10 months of age; however, at about 6 months, they focus only on individual objects.[12] Other developments have been reported in the literature as evidence of major cognitive change in this same period, at the end of the first year. Particular examples include the ability to group similar objects together spontaneously and the dissociation of means from ends.[13] And, indeed, the development from separating to constructing thematic relations we observed in our infants could have been related to age, since it occurred at the same time for all of them.

Although we could not know for certain whether the onset of constructions was age related, we could test whether the rate of subsequent development in the categories of constructions was related to age. To do this, we compared the two subgroups of infants who differed according to whether they reached First Words relatively earlier or later. Half the infants were below the mean age of FW, and half were above the mean, forming the two groups of earlier and later word learners, respectively. The frequency of constructions increased over time for both groups of infants, but infants who were older at the time of developments in language also did more constructing than infants who were younger at the time of the same achievements in language.[14] Constructions tended to increase, therefore, as the children grew older. This was not just because they were more skillful in accomplishing a construction. Although separations were easier – since all a child had to do was push or pull at one of the objects or dump a container, for example – any attempt at a construction was counted, whether or not the child succeeded at creating the configuration. The question remained, however, whether age also predicted developments in the kinds of thematic relations the children constructed.

The relative frequencies of given and imposed constructions did not change: About half the constructions were given and about half were imposed in all three periods. This meant that the children were as likely to recreate the configuration in which they first saw the toys together as they were to construct a new relation between them. However, development did occur within the category of imposed constructions as specific thematic relations increased and general relations decreased. This can be seen in the relative

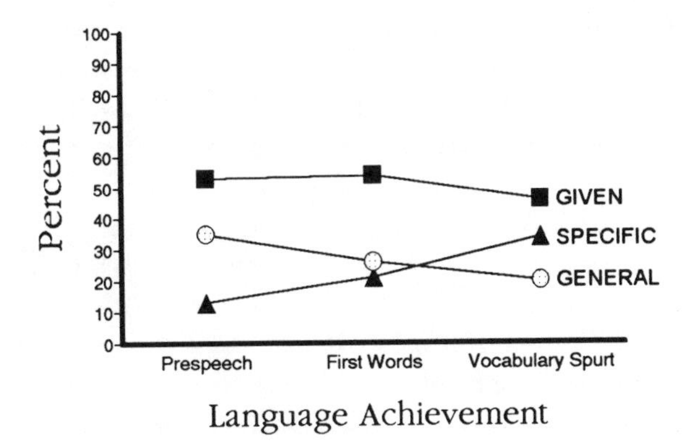

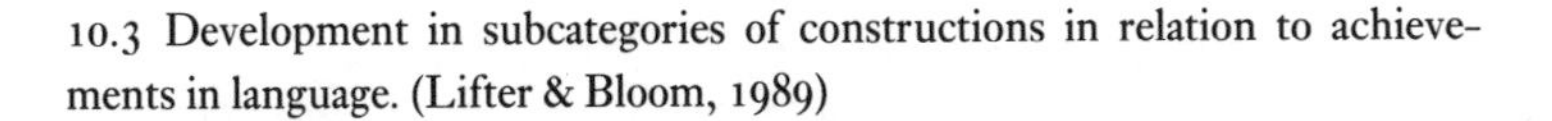
10.3 Development in subcategories of constructions in relation to achievements in language. (Lifter & Bloom, 1989)

frequencies of given relations and the two subcategories of imposed constructions in Figure 10.3.

Again, to determine if the increase in specific imposed constructions was a function only of increasing age, the results were compared for the subgroups of earlier and later word learners. Specific constructions increased over time for both groups, but the two groups did not differ in the relative frequency with which they constructed specific thematic relations. This means that the children who were younger at the time of their achievements in language were as likely to construct specific relations as the children who were older at the time of their language achievements. The increase in specific constructions was not simply a function of age but was associated with achievement in language.

Object Play and Language

The association of specific thematic relations with VS was confirmed when we looked at the intersection of developments in play and language. The children were ranked according to their ages when they reached the milestones in both play and language: FW and VS in language, and emergence and achievement of constructions, imposed constructions, and inanimate specific constructions (the animate surrogate category was not included in the ranking, because some children did not reach criteria). The rank orders, one for emergence and one for achievement, of developments in language and play were the same for all the infants, even though they differed in age. But which developments were different from one another and therefore responsible for determining the rank order?

Looking at every possible pair of developments in language and play, we determined that certain pairs did not differ statistically in their ranks whereas others did (using Scheffe contrasts for the comparisons). Two clusters of developments in play and language were identified; certain developments in play were more closely related to FW, and others were more strongly related to VS. These relationships between developments in language and play were consistent among the children despite the differences in their ages and even though the children who were older did more constructions.

The first cluster centered on First Words. The emergence of constructions (including any kind of thematic relations constructed between two objects) occurred in the PreSpeech window *before* FW (their ranks were significantly different). Achievement in constructions and both emergence and achievement of imposed thematic constructions were closely associated with FW, because they did not differ in their ranks. This result means that the children began to construct thematic relations between two objects in their play before their First Words. And this ability to construct thematic relations was consolidated as they began to say words and the different subcategories of constructing emerged.

The second cluster centered on the Vocabulary Spurt. With one exception, every development in constructing thematic relations, both emergences and achievements, occurred before VS. The exception was achievement in constructing specific thematic relations, which was closely associated with the Vocabulary Spurt. And, complementing this, every development except for VS occurred before achievement in specific constructions. These results mean that the Vocabulary Spurt toward the end of the second year was closely associated with constructing specific thematic relations that took account of differences in the particular properties of objects.

The developmental changes in language and play complemented each other, and we have attributed the correspondences between them to developments in underlying cognition.[15] The relevant cognitive developments had to do with what the infants were learning about objects, events, and relations in the world and how they were able to access that knowledge for their actions with both objects and words. The results of this study stand together with results from many other studies that have now confirmed the suggestion in *One Word at a Time* that the vocabulary spurt in language is associated with substantive changes in cognition. In addition to studies of such Piagetian constructs as object permanence, the vocabulary spurt has been associated as well with categorization abilities and concept development.[16]

Thematic Relations, Concepts, and Object Knowledge

Appreciation that things "naturally" go together to form connections in everyday events makes it possible to get along in the world. It comes as no surprise, therefore, that such thematic relations participate in children's language learning. They were identified in *One Word at a Time* in the successive single words that a 1-year-old child said; examples included "blanket . . . cover . . . head . . ." (wanting to wrap a doll's head with a piece of blanket) and "up . . . neck . . . zip . . ." (wanting to have her jacket zipped all the way). Similarly, the development of specific thematic relations between objects corresponded to the developments in language described in Chapter 9 – in particular, the increased expression of mental meanings with an action component at the time of the vocabulary spurt. And thematic relations provide the meanings for which older 1- to 2-year-olds begin to learn grammar.[17] Katherine Nelson has provided an extensive account of the importance of "event representations" for cognitive and semantic development,[18] and Ellen Markman used children's tendencies to make thematic and taxonomic associations in her studies of children's early categories and word learning.[19]

As the children in our study learned to put two objects together, they constructed increasingly specific thematic relations. They progressed from constructions with a general relationship between objects (such as containment or support) to constructing specific relations between objects that took more information about the objects into account (like the hole in a bead for a string and the function of a spoon for feeding a doll). These constructing activities, and the thematic relations they produced, provide insight into the cognitive developments taking place in this period of early word learning. These included, at least, the development of concepts – both relational concepts and object concepts – along with other and more general aspects of object knowledge. The increase in number of different words that the vocabulary spurt represents has long been attributed to developments in object concepts.[20] Once a child uses the name for an object with some regularity, one can presume something about the concept for the object. Other one-to-one mappings between word and concept can be assumed as well with the relational words that children learn (like *more, gone,* and *up*).[21]

However, arguing that concepts exist on the basis of a child's use of words is, as several people have pointed out, essentially a post hoc argument. We need evidence of concepts existing before words to show how they are important for learning words. But evidence of preword concepts has been hard to come by. In a noteworthy effort in which 1-year-olds were taught concepts and their corresponding words, children who were already advanced in word learning, with larger vocabularies at the start of the study, learned more concepts and more words than beginning word learners.[22] Thus, the children who were able to take the most advantage of opportunities to learn new words through learning relevant concepts were already cognitively prepared to do so. The intervention was less helpful to the beginning word learners, who were evidently not so cognitively prepared.

Using the evidence from our children's play, we could attribute four relational concepts in particular to the children's object knowledge. These were concepts of movement, location, containment, and support. Movement is primary, and appreciation of the movement of objects in relation to their static contexts begins in the first few months of life to guide the acquisition of knowledge, as we saw in Chapter 3. One effect of movement is change in the location of objects relative to each other: A concept or theory of location is one result of a theory of movement and its effects. And two perspectives on location that were evident from the general thematic relations the children constructed were containment and support – two locative concepts that depend on appreciating the "graphic," or physical, properties of those things that afford containment or support for other things.

These relational concepts were prelinguistic; for example, the general thematic relations of containment and support appeared before the words *in* and *on.* Shirley, for example, reached achievement in general thematic relations at 11 months, but *in* did not appear in her vocabulary until her VS, at 13 months, at which time it was said 37 times. But *on* had still not appeared at VS + 1; acquiring the concept does not mean that the word for the concept will necessarily follow. Similarly, with respect to object words, 7- to 11-month-olds have some idea of global concepts, like animals or vehicles, before basic-level concepts.[23] But we can expect that the words they will learn will be basic level *(dog* before *animal*).

However, relational concepts like containment, support, movement, and location have importance far beyond the literal word-to-concept mappings for particular words like *in* and *on.* Relational concepts provide the cognitive underpinnings for much of the semantic structure of language. The single words children learn name the objects and persons that are the participants in relationships – words like *Mama, truck, juice, neck* – and the actions or states that define relationships – words like *up, zip,* and *eat.* Eventually, children learn a grammar to express relationships among persons, places, and things. Relational concepts have been very little studied, and object concepts have received the lion's share of attention so far in acquisition research. However, relational concepts are at least as important for language as are object concepts.

So far we have been concerned in this chapter with developments in object play and the conclusions we have been able to draw for developments in cognition that are relevant to both play and language. We have related developments in play to conceptual development, both relational concepts and object concepts. The developments around FW could be attributed to development in object knowledge that is best described as *general* knowledge because it has to do with many different objects. The developments around VS could be attributed to the more specific knowledge of objects that is entailed in objects concepts. And critical for understanding both general and specific object knowledge is the assumption of object permanence.

Object permanence, like several other parts of Piaget's theory, is no longer taken as seriously in many quarters as it once was. Demonstrations that infants are considerably more competent than was formerly believed is one reason (as discussed in Chapter 4). However, a more important reason is that the fundamental constructivism of Piaget's theory is often ignored. An infant's appreciation of the permanence of objects, independent of movement and location, was never presented by Piaget as a sudden insight – an all-or-nothing, now-you-have-it achievement – in the second year. It has its beginnings in the first few months of life and develops gradually. Clearly, what a 6-month-old knows about objects is limited by both biology and experience; the brain is still extremely immature, and the infant is not yet moving out into the world. But just as clearly, the processes of perceptual analysis and integration are well under way, and the 6-month-old has begun to "know" about persons, objects, and events.[24] The precise nature of what an infant knows is far from clear, but it most probably includes knowledge of particular instances that allow the recognition of salient individuals and a global, general kind of knowledge about objects in general. This general object knowledge pertains to movable objects and the background objects that afford the context against which objects move.

The infants playing with objects in our playroom likewise showed us something of what they knew about objects in general by the end of the first year. When they constructed a configuration between objects, after first learning to take it apart, they showed an ability to consider objects as separate entities and an appreciation of reversibility. This kind of knowledge was displayed in their actions between 9 and 11 months of age and has been demonstrated in 10-month-old infants in experimental studies.[25] Although this general object knowledge does not equal object permanence, it nonetheless figures in the process whereby object permanence develops.

Constructions emerged in the infants' play before First Words, the fragile and tentative beginning of language. The emergence of new behaviors, such as beginning to say words or to construct thematic relations in play, indicates a time of change and transition. Achievement, in contrast, suggests a shift to mastery and stabilization of the knowledge that the behaviors require. The relatively long period between FW and VS (4.4 months, on average), and between emergence and achievement of specific relations (5 months, on average), suggests the developments in cognition needed to support mastery and stabilization of words and this kind of knowledge about objects.

The developmental achievements we identified with the vocabulary spurt and specific constructions toward the end of the second year depended upon particular object knowledge that was both physical and conventional. Inanimate specific relations required knowledge of the characteristics inherent in the physical properties of objects (for example, the hole in the wooden beads and the flexible string). Both words and animate surrogate relations required additional *conventional* knowledge about objects that was not afforded by their physical characteristics. For example, the thematic relation between the spoon and the doll or between the person figures and the horse or truck was not given by the physical characteristics of the objects. Like words, it had to be learned from social and cultural convention. In both examples, the child had to recall a particular relation from memory, one that was more discrepant from the data of perception than the earlier given and general constructions, and hold that relation in mind for the act of constructing. Clearly, such representation required development of the symbolic capacity, and we assume that the children acquired full object permanence in the interval in which this development took place.

Three additional sorts of data support these conclusions. One is the children's performance with the tasks that elicit search on the Uzgiris and Hunt object permanence scales, and another is their spontaneous search and finding in the playroom. The third is the findings from two aspects of their physical development that we took to be evidence of maturational change – as compared with the cognitive developmental changes we have described in play, language, and emotional expression. They were learning to walk (gross motor development) and increasing in their skill with block building (finer motor development).

Elicited Search (Scale Performance)

Most studies that compare developments in language and thought have used ordinal scales to measure sensorimotor development. The instrument developed by Uzgiris and Hunt is the most comprehensive attempt to operationalize the behaviors reported by Piaget in his "infant" books and consists of six scales, one of which tests for object permanence.[26] Most researchers who have used the scales have inferred stage-level scores from comparison with Piaget's original descriptions, although Uzgiris and Hunt themselves did not equate the tasks with stage level.

Elsewhere we have pointed out several problems in the way the scales have been used.[27] One problem is that correlations between developments in different domains are inconclusive with respect to the direction of influence between them. Another is that language is *spontaneous* in everyday activities, and spontaneous language has been correlated with behaviors *elicited* by the tasks on the scales. Another problem is that only one kind of action is elicited on the tasks (uncovering an object hidden by a cloth), but children learn about objects from a wide range of actions.

Most troubling, however, is that the scales themselves are typically identified with the construct they purport to measure. The particular way in which a measurement instrument is interpreted determines its usefulness, and in this case what is being measured – object permanence – is often confused with the index of measurement.[28] Thus, performance on individual items of the object permanence scale is equated with progress toward achieving object permanence, and passing or not passing the items on the scale is interpreted to mean that the child has or has not acquired object permanence. And most often a rigid expectation of precise correspondence between performance on the scales and progress in language is brought to interpreting the results. Such an expectation, then, compounds all the other problems mentioned.

In a widely cited study by Roberta Corrigan that purported to show no relation between object permanence and the vocabulary spurt, the actual result was that full object permanence (using standardized scale performance) and a vocabulary spurt occurred close in time (within a few weeks of one another).[29] In commenting on this result, Moshe Anisfeld pointed out that

> the synchrony between achievement of full object permanence and rise in vocabulary is impressive, especially when one considers that the number of words uttered at any one short period of time, such as a 30-minute testing session, is a function not only of cognitive capacity but also of need and interest. Corrigan . . . herself reached a less positive conclusion about the relation between cognitive and linguistic development, but this is because she expected a narrow and rigid relation and did not make allowances for the complex vicissitudes of development. One should not expect two related capacities to appear exactly within the same narrow time span. . . . Although both object permanence and the symbolic use of words depend on internal representation, they need not become manifest at the same moment in time. . . . I am impressed by her finding that the vocabulary growth-spurt and the attainment of full object permanence appeared within weeks of one another and not discouraged by her finding that they did not appear in exactly the same testing sessions.[30]

Recent theory in infant cognition has turned away from the Piagetian notion of "stage" and brought the whole notion of sensorimotor thought into question.[31] However, many studies have used the scales to compare developments in thought and language in the second year. For this reason, we did so as well, so that we might have a basis for comparing our results with those other results in the literature.[32] We compared developments in the children's language and spontaneous play with two tasks on the scales in particular. These were the tasks that marked the beginning and end of the transitional period between sensorimotor and preoperational thought in Piaget's theory – the long period of development often characterized in global terms as Stage 6. Criteria for solving these tasks came from Piaget's own descriptions of object permanence development and attributions made by other researchers. The first task, at the beginning of the transitional period, was finding an object hidden by a cloth in a single invisible hiding (where the child does not see the object disappear under the cloth). The task that marked the end of the transitional period was finding the object after a succession of invisible hidings.

The children were in the transitional Stage 6 period for most of the time we studied them, as has been the case in other studies of the single-word period.[33] All of them had solved the first task – the single invisible hiding – before First Words. Several of them took as long as 10 months before they finally solved the last task, and 3 children never did solve it. For the 11 children who did solve the last task, marking the end of the transitional period, 1 did so by FW, 7 by VS, and 3 sometime after VS. Thus, the beginning and end of the transitional period between sensorimotor and preoperational thought in Piaget's theory, at least as measured by these two tasks on the object permanence scales, coincided roughly with the two language achievements (except for the 1 child who had solved the task by FW).

The relationships between solving the tasks and developments in object play can be seen in Table 10.1. The earliest developments in play occurred before the beginning of the transition, and the later developments tended to occur after it. Except for achievement in specific constructions and the animate surrogate constructions, all the developments occurred before the end of the transition. Thus, the developments in language and play were essentially bracketed by the tasks that marked the beginning and end of the long period of development known as Stage 6, and to that extent, the scales were diagnostic of developments in the single-word period. In contrast, the children's spontaneous play provided details of the developments occurring within the period and gave evidence that the single-word period is not a developmental plateau, as had been suggested.[34]

Developments in language and play occurred together and were integrated because of the developments in cognition they shared. Object permanence was only one part of that development and by itself cannot be explanatory. The critical cognitive developments in infancy are in acquiring knowledge and in procedures for accessing and representing aspects of knowledge in relation to the data of perception.[35] The children learned to construct thematic relations when seeing two objects served as a cue for recalling a relationship between them. Further evidence of developments in recall and

Table 10.1. *Number of children reaching developments in play before, during, and after the beginning and end of the transitional (Stage 6) period (as measured by object permanence tasks)*

	Beginning			End		
	Before	During[a]	After	Before	During[a]	After
Construction						
(EMERGE)	(14)	—	—	(11)	—	—
ACHIEVE	5	6	3	11	—	—
Imposed						
(EMERGE)	(12)	(1)	(1)	(11)	—	—
ACHIEVE	5	3	6	11	—	—
Specific						
(EMERGE)	(2)	(4)	(8)	(11)	—	—
ACHIEVE	—	—	14	4	5	2
Animate surrogate						
(EMERGE)	(1)	—	(10)	(7)	(1)	(1)
ACHIEVE	—	—	9	2	2	3

[a]Developments in play and solving the task occurred in the same monthly observation.
Source: Lifter & Bloom (1989).

representation in intentional states came when the children located objects in the playroom and, eventually, searched for and found objects in the playroom to use for constructing thematic relations.

Spontaneous Search and Finding

As early as age 9 months, the children showed us by their actions that they knew the objects in the playroom were available even though they were not in fact looking at them. For example, at 9 months Cory cast one of the nesting blocks aside and slightly behind her, reached for another one in front of her, and then turned back to pick up the first one, obviously expecting to find it. These earliest search behaviors consisted of *relocating* an object that had previously been put aside *by the child,* who then looked back at it and perhaps touched it or picked it up. The interval between putting the object aside and turning back to it was very brief, only a few seconds.[36] Piaget had described similar success by infants, beginning at 6 months, in finding objects when it was the infant who happened to drop the object or cast it aside, in contrast to an object he had hidden from the infant's view by covering it with a cloth. He described these instances as "the beginnings of permanence attributed to images perceived . . . from the child's action in movements of accommodation."[37] However, recent experimental studies using preferential looking by Baillargeon, Spelke, and their colleagues have shown that infants as young as 6 months can appreciate the continued existence of a hidden object when it is tied to movement other than their own (Chapter 3).

The study of how children search for and find objects is important for a number of reasons.[38] First, we have just seen that systematic changes in finding objects that are purposely hidden for the child (scale performance) can be diagnostic of developments in cognition that contribute to play and language. Looking for an object that is outside the perceptual field with intent to find it is evidence that the child has the object in mind and appreciates at least its temporary, or what Piaget called "practical," permanence. And finding behaviors are evidence of the ability to hold an absent object in mind for what Judy DeLoache called "natural memory."[39] We have, in fact, several sources of memory-related behavior in the first year. Infant searching – both spontaneous finding and finding elicited in response to the demands of object permanence tasks – complement experimental preferential looking data from very young infants.[40]

In this study, we defined *finding* as any action in which the children looked for objects outside their perceptual field – defined as a 180° arc to the right and left. These included objects close to hand and objects across the room for which they had to look up and away from what they were already attending to or doing. The analysis of spontaneous search and finding centered on two things. The first was whether search was purposive in the context of constructing activities with the objects: Did a child then use the found object to construct a thematic relation? This first distinction was between finding-to-construct and simple finding. The second was whether the new construction with a found object continued a prior constructing activity: Did the search have the support of a prior construction in mind? This was the distinction between finding with and without support. Finding-with-support took the form of a preceding equivalent construction; for example, a child stacked two boxes and turned around to find another box to add to the tower. Finding-without-support happened without an immediately preceding equivalent construction; for example, a child pulled the pillowcase from the cardboard box, looked for and found the doll, and then covered her.

Simple finding was observed for most of the children during the PreSpeech period, at about the same time as they began to construct thematic relations between objects. And all the children were able to find an object that had been out of sight – whether to touch it, pick it up, or simply look back at it – by the time of First Words.[41] At first, what they did with an object after finding it was centered on only the single object itself; they typically mouthed it, examined it, showed it to someone else, and the like.

Approximately 4 months later on average (mean age about 15 months), the children began to use the found objects in order to construct thematic relations with other objects, but only in the context of having done a similar construction just before. This means that when the children began to find objects in order to use them in constructing, a prior constructing activity served as a cue for recalling the location of a related object to use in continuing the activity. Finding-without-support was a much later development, and only 4 of the children presented three or more different instances (mean age about 20 months); one or two instances were observed in the play of 3 other children. And, as with other developments in play as well as language, the children differed widely in age at the time of these developments in finding. But for those children who did show spontaneous finding, their ages coincided with the ages at which they reached the other developmental milestones in play and language.

Finding behaviors became progressively more independent of the children's immediately preceding activities with the objects, providing evidence that they knew the objects were about even though they were not looking at them or acting on them. At first, they constructed relations between objects already at hand and only gradually began to look for objects that had been out of sight. When the children looked for an object that was out of sight in order to use it to construct a relation with another object, their locating behavior was at first limited to finding objects for the same or similar constructions; thus, they already had in mind a potential thematic relation between the objects (finding-with-support). This development in spontaneous searching and finding – from simple finding to finding-with-support to construct a relation-

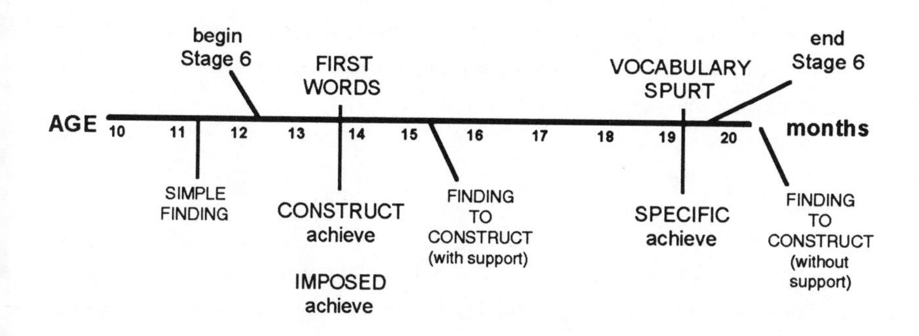

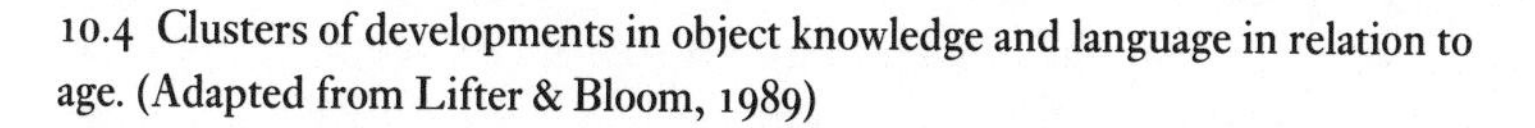

10.4 Clusters of developments in object knowledge and language in relation to age. (Adapted from Lifter & Bloom, 1989)

ship in play – had its corollary in developments in their language. Just as they came to locate objects that were out of sight in order to construct a thematic relation, their words increasingly expressed mental meanings with anticipated content that was not yet evident in the context, as described in Chapter 9.

Developments in the several kinds of object knowledge we tapped into – in relation to each other and in relation to the children' language achievement – are summarized in Figure 10.4 along a time line, from the prespeech period beginning at 10 months to 1 month after the Vocabulary Spurt. The cluster of achievements in constructions, imposed thematic relations in particular, and First Words occurred after simple finding and before the children began to find objects to use for constructing with support. Achievement in constructing specific thematic relations clustered together with the Vocabulary Spurt and beginning to find objects for constructing without prior support. The emergence of constructing thematic relations (the shift from separating to constructing) happened sometime in the interval before First Words; emergence of specific thematic relations happened some time between First Words and the Vocabulary Spurt. Performance on the elicited search tasks bracketed these developments: Entry into Stage 6 on the scales occurred after simple finding and before the First Words cluster, and the end of Stage 6 occurred close in time to the Vocabulary Spurt cluster.

We assume that these developments were systematically related because they depended on similar developments in underlying cognition that were independent of age, as opposed to simple maturation. A test of this last assumption was the progress the children showed in learning to walk and in block building, both of which were more closely related to age than to the other developments we observed.

Two Measures of Maturation

Learning to Walk. We also tracked the children's progress in learning to walk and used as our criterion of walking the ability to take two independent steps without support or assistance. The mean age of walking for the group as a whole was 12.7 months, 1 month before the mean age for First Words. However, even though the children differed in age at First Words, the groups of earlier and later word learners did not differ in average age of walking (mean age = 12.7 for both). All the later word learners took their first steps before First Words; only 2 of the earlier word learners walked before First Words. Learning to walk, as a measure of gross motor maturation, was not systematically related to age at First Words, as were the infants' early constructions in object play and their profiles of emotional expression.

Block Building. The second measure was maturation of finer motor movements, as inferred from the block building task, which was administered to all but the 3 infants who were our pilot subjects. We gave the children a pile of 1-in. wooden cubes and encouraged them to "build a high tower." We coaxed them and encouraged their mothers to coax them by helping them at first, or showing them how to stack the cubes by building a tower alongside them. We used as our criterion for passing the task, a tower of six cubes, constructed by the child without the mother's or anyone else's contributing to it (although the child could copy one of them in building a tower). None of the children succeeded in building a tower of six blocks without direct help at 18 months, but 7 children succeeded at 21 months, and the 4 others succeeded subsequently.[42]

Progress in block building was not systematically related to any of the other developments in play or language. Regardless of how old they were at the time of achievements in play, language, and solving the object permanence tasks – all related to each other – the children were similar in age when they passed the block building task. For example, Shirley, who reached First Words and

Vocabulary Spurt at 10 and 13 months, respectively, and Jessica, who reached these same developments at 14 months and 22 months, were both able to build a tower of six blocks at 21 months but not at 18 months. We concluded from this that block building is a motor skill that is age related and determined by maturation. In contrast, developments in play and language were systematically related despite the considerable variation among the children in age. This means that these developments were not simply a function of age and general maturation but rather were related to each other through the relationship of each to developments in cognition.

THE SOCIAL CONTEXT OF OBJECT PLAY

How the mothers interacted with their children as they played with the toys was explored with 8 of the children by Lorraine Harner and Tricia Gronell.[43] We anticipated that a mother's actions with and on behalf of her infant would be sensitive to the child's developing abilities in language and play. For this reason, we looked at mother–child interactions when the infants were equated for language development rather than for age: at a PreSpeech baseline, at 10 months, and three language achievements, First Words, Vocabulary Spurt, and Multiword Speech. (Only results that reached significant levels of statistical reliability are mentioned here.)

We purposely looked at mothers' *initiations* of object play with their infants in an effort to evaluate their naive "teaching" activities. We found that the mothers in our study were clearly tuned into their infants and, as good teachers might be expected to do, took into account the focus of a child's attention for maximizing understanding. The basic findings were these: The frequency with which the mothers *initiated* play with the objects decreased as the infants themselves became more competent with the toys and more independent in moving about the playroom. And the mothers were more likely to talk about the toys when the children had developed language, at VS and MW, than they had been at PreSpeech and FW. Thus, mothers were less likely to initiate play as the children increased in overall competence, but they talked more to the children when initiating play as the children increased in language ability. The mothers were aware of and sensitive to the developing abilities of their children in play and language, and they acted with them accordingly. In these respects, the social context they provided when playing with their children showed the same sensitivities caregivers have shown in the ways they talk to young children.[44]

Mothers were also sensitive to the need to minimize any discrepancy between what they and their children had in mind in these interactions. When a mother initiated play at PreSpeech and FW, she was most likely to choose the same toy her child had been playing with, or one equivalent to it. And she chose either a toy the child had been playing with or looking at more often than a toy the child was only touching. In these earlier sessions, then, a mother tended to select toys for play that her child was most engaged with, evidently appreciating the need to minimize discrepancy. This difference diminished, and by VS and MW they were more likely to use toys the children were only touching (so that differences in choosing toys the children acted on, looked at, or only touched were no longer significant).

The content of their actions and talk about the toys also changed. At PreSpeech and FW, they were more likely than they were later on, at VS and MW, to show their children what to do with the toys, and they also talked more about the *function* of the toys than named them. Thus, early in development, when infants were relatively less experienced and competent with the toys, a mother was more likely to show her child what to do and to talk about what could be done with the toys. In this regard, the mothers anticipated the children's development by demonstrating action possibilities with the toys. In turn, the major development in the children's play was the construction of increasingly specific thematic relations with the toys. And, correspondingly, the children themselves talked increasingly about action events, with multiple elements and relations between elements, implying more elaborated mental meanings (Chapter 9).

Although these findings characterized the mothers and their interactions with their children, in other respects the mothers were different. For example, Harry's mother always insisted on talking with the members of the research team (one behind the camera and the other who brought in the toys); the other mothers talked primarily to their children. Diana's mother was usually reluctant to get down on the floor, as the other mothers did, to play with her and sat at some distance in one of the chairs. Shirley's mother frequently prompted her to talk about one thing or another; Jessica's and Clark's mothers were more laid back, preferring to follow their children's lead in interacting with them. And so forth. Nevertheless, when they did initiate play with the toys, all the mothers showed the sensitivities described above.

CONCLUSIONS

The knowledge very young infants have about objects and events is impressive, as we saw in Chapter 4. The cognition that brought the infants in our study to the threshold of language at the end of the first year continued to develop in the second year as they acquired a vocabulary of words. Cognitive developments in the second year of life manifest themselves in a variety of ways and include, at least, the ability to form categories and concepts.[45] The developments described in this chapter complement these findings from other studies. First, the infants we studied showed development in symbolic capacity, which enabled the representations they expressed in their actions with objects in the first place. Development in categories of constructions provided evidence for the Principle of Discrepancy – with achievement in imposed relations – and for the Principle of Elaboration – with the achievement of specific relations. Development from separations to constructions, and in imposed and increasingly specific thematic relations, were evidence of underlying representations that were both more elaborated and more discrepant from the way the infants saw the toys as they were brought into the playroom.

And, second, the infants showed us developments in object knowledge that were both general and specific. They learned at least these three things about objects in general: the continuity or permanence of objects in time and space for their actions on them; the reversibility of actions with objects; and the general relational concepts of movement, location, containment, and support. And the specific thematic relations they learned to construct with inanimate and animate surrogate objects were evidence of particular knowledge in the form of object concepts and more specific relational concepts.

The words they learned were very much related to these developments in cognition. We saw in Chapters 7 and 9 that language learning in the second year was more than just the gradual accumulation of words; developments occurred in the sorts of mental meanings the children came to express with the vocabulary spurt. And the words they learned were not predominantly names of objects, even though objects were abundant in the playroom; rather they included names for transitive relations that were possible between objects and other kinds of words as well. So, for example, the few words said by all the children included the object names *baby, ball,* and *juice* and also the relational words *more* and *down*. Other relational words – *up, in, on, open, go, that, there,* and the like – were frequent in the children's vocabularies. We now see why this was so; these are just the kinds of words that can express the sorts of relationships the children were learning to construct in play. The words they were learning included names for relations between things as well as names of things. This basic insight has certainly been captured before;[46] the results in this chapter further document some of the reasons to explain it. The children's actions gave relevance to the words they were saying and, we can assume, to words they heard and learned in similarly relevant contexts.

The final chapter brings these findings together with the other developments we have seen in affect expression, word learning, and social connectedness with other persons for an integrated model of word learning and development in the second year of life.

11

Meaning and Expression

> Meanings are in persons' minds, not in words, and when we say that a word has or possesses such and such meanings,we are really saying that it has evoked, or caused, those meanings. Until it gets into a mind, a word is only puffs of air or streaks of ink.
>
> (Edward Lee Thorndike)[1]

This book has been about how words get into minds. Acquiring the power of expression comes with learning the public, conventional meanings of a language for expressing and articulating the private, personal meanings in a mind. One-year-olds have been hearing words for some time, but words come to have meaning only when infants can appreciate the connections between what they hear (or the gestures they see) and what they are thinking and feeling. And because words express what a child's beliefs, desires, and feelings are about, they are only part of what happens in early language development. We tapped into some of what happens with early word learning when we looked at how the children played with objects and expressed emotion as they and their mothers spent an hour together each month in our playroom.

Let's go back to the simple example from an earlier chapter:

> A child picks up a small block, says "more," puts it on top of another block, smiles, and looks at her mother. Her mother smiles back.

Clearly, "more" was not just a puff of air. Just as the word had meaning, each of the child's other actions had meaning as well, by themselves and in relation to each other. Picking up another block, saying "more," putting the two blocks together, looking at mother, smiling – these were dynamic events, and the developments that contributed to them were systematically related. For the young child, the process of learning language comes together with processes of development in other domains.

The first purpose of this concluding chapter is to integrate the developments we observed in language, affect expression, and object play for a model of early development in the second year. The second purpose is to show how the public, shared, and conventionally constructed meanings in language are learned by children to express the personal, private, and mentally constructed meanings they have in mind.

AN INTEGRATIVE MODEL

To learn a language is to learn the *conventional* forms and procedures for combining them in *relevant* utterances for *coherent* discourse. The forms and procedures of a language are *conventional* because the persons who contrived the language in the first place had to agree on them. A child's words and sentences are *relevant* because they make sense and are pertinent to what the child and others have in mind. And the discourse the child constructs with words and sentences in collaboration with other persons is *coherent* because it is connected in more or less appropriate ways. At least this much about early child language – its conventionality, relevance, and coherence – is noncontroversial.

What is controversial is the theoretical stance we take in efforts to explain language acquisition in the first few years. One such effort takes its lead from adult theory, as when, for example, research in syntax acquisition begins with a theory of *adult* grammar and asks whether and how that theory is learnable.[2] The principles and procedures of the grammar to be acquired are nowhere accessible; children hear sentences but learn a grammar. The questions for the child are: What is the grammar? and How do I learn it? The analogy is the adult linguist, whose job it is to discover the grammar of a language. The questions for the linguist are: What is the grammar? and How do I figure out what it is? The assumption is that if linguists can answer these questions they will not only have learned what the grammar is but will also have discovered how the child learns it. However, linguists have great difficulty answering these questions. Because the task has proved so difficult for linguists, and because the principles and procedures for grammar that the child needs to learn are not themselves given in the environment, the assumption is that children must have a head start. This head start takes the form of innate, specifically *linguistic* constraints that guide the child in discovering a grammar.[3]

The acquisition of word meanings has similarly been approached as a logic problem. The analogy used for a child's acquiring words is the dilemma of "radical translation" posed by Quine: How does the linguist–philosopher know the intensional meaning of a word in an unknown language from its extensional use in an ambiguous context?[4] The questions for the child are: How do I know what a word refers to? and How do I learn its meaning? The linguist–philosopher's dilemma has prompted those who study lexical acquisition to assume that children would be unable to learn word meanings without a head start. This head start includes certain linguistic constraints, or "lexical principles," that guide a child's word learning, as was discussed in Chapter 5.[5]

If one begins with an attempt to explain how the child learns what the adult knows about language, then the task for the child is indeed a formidable one. But, such a research enterprise is theoretically driven entirely from the perspective of *adult* theory and ignores as irrelevant the first-person perspective of the child. It may ultimately be that something specifically linguistic contributes to how a grammar is acquired in the third and fourth years. In fact, learning one aspect of the language has to help in learning its other aspects. As language is acquired, it is used for learning a great deal about the world, including more about the language itself, and this knowledge is, by definition, specifically linguistic. For this reason, linguistic assumptions acquired early in language learning can be expected to "bootstrap" subsequent language learning. But they are assumptions the child comes to as a consequence of learning language.

Another theoretical stance, a *developmental* one, begins with the *child,* what the child *knows,* and how what the child knows *changes* over time. From a child's naive perspective, the task is a more tractable one because, in fact, the child does indeed have a head start. But that head start does not depend on language or on specifically linguistic constraints on learning. The head start with which infants begin their language learning careers comes from *who they are* as the products of their development in the first two years of life.

The core of development that brings an infant to the threshold of language in the second year is in the integration of affect, cognition, and social connectedness to other persons. Children learn language in the first place because they strive to maintain intersubjectivity with other persons – to *share* what they and other persons are feeling and thinking. Affect expression has been in place as the vehicle of intersubjectivity since birth and is well established by the end of the first year.[6] One-year-olds have also had a year or more of learning about the world. The result of their early cognitive development is the representation of mental meanings that are potentially expressible in language. In fact, personal, private mental meanings *require* expression and need to be articulated if they are to be shared with other persons. Language does this in a way that the forms of affect expression cannot.

We studied how cognition, affect, and social connectedness come together for the transition from infancy to language in the second year by exploring developments in the three domains of ordinary activity: words, affect expression, and object play. We expected the children to grow smarter as they grew older and to increase in their competencies all around. And they did. In the period from 9 months to 2 years, they all learned to say words; they all built a substantial vocabulary of words; and eventually they were saying sentences. They all increased in the number of thematic relations they constructed with the toys. They also learned to walk in this period of time. Just looking at the children equated for age, then, they all got better at everything they did in the playroom. However, the more important findings had to do with the contingencies *among* developments in their language, play, and affect expression, independent of their chronological age.

The *knowledge* we set out to explain was language – more specifically, the acquisition of a vocabulary of words in the second year – with the basic assumption that language is learned in the context of other developments in a child's life. The *behaviors* we observed were saying words, putting objects together in play, and expressing affect. We looked at the details of these behaviors as they developed over time from late infancy through the second year.

The integrative model proposed here for the process of language development in the second year came out of our efforts to reenact the transition from infancy to language. The explicit focus in this reenactment was on the representations in intentional states underlying the acts of expression and interpretation for which language is learned.[7] The result of this intentionality perspective is a model with three basic components and three explanatory principles. The three *components* are, not surprisingly, cognition, affect, and the social connectedness between infants and other persons. The three *principles* invoked for explaining the emergence and development of language in the second year are the principles of Relevance, Discrepancy, and Elaboration.

These principles are basic, elementary generalizations about development in a child's mind and about the interaction between the developing mind of the child and a socially mediated, perceptible context. The Principle of Relevance means that words a child hears from others will be learned if they connect with what the child is thinking and feeling. A word could theoretically mean any number of things, but in enough situations in which the child hears it, the range of options for sharing meaning with the author of the word are already greatly diminished. The Principle of Discrepancy means that a child's contents of mind go beyond what can be seen and heard by other persons, so that a shared context cannot be exploited for understanding, and expression will be required. The Principle of Elaboration is about the enrichment of the representations a child can construct in mind for going beyond the information given and building possible worlds. These principles are neither a child's operating procedures for processing language nor things the child might already know about language – as are lexical (and grammatical) principles. Instead, they are generalizations about how the developing mind and its connections to a social and physical world determine that language will be learned.

The intentional states in children's actions and feelings make the words a child hears interesting and determine their *relevance* for learning in the first place. *Discrepancy* between what a child has in mind and what someone else has in mind happens when contents of mind differ from what can be perceived and need to be shared between the two of them. *Elaboration* of mental meanings occurs as a child's knowledge in memory and capacities for retrieval and recall expand the representations that are possible for mental meanings. The increasing elaboration of mental meanings – with more elements, roles, and relations between elements having different roles – requires that the child learn more of the language for their expression. These three principles explain the developments observed in the children's behaviors and contribute to understanding how social connectedness, affect, and cognition come together for developments in language.

Support for the Principle of Relevance in word learning is abundant in the literature, particularly in studies of joint attention and shared understanding in social interactions.[8] These studies have, by and large, emphasized the contributions of a "good enough" language tutor – one who takes a child's focus of attention into account in the interaction and thereby enhances language learning.

However, the research project in this book built on yet another basic assumption of the Principle of Relevance from the child's point of view: Intentional states in a child's actions and feelings determine the words a child will *say*, just as they determine the words the child will learn. We could never be certain of an exact moment of word learning – if word learning can happen in a moment. But we could feel confident in assuming that the circumstances in which children say words are correlated with the circumstances in which they are learning those words. And, indeed, the children showed us they were saying words that had to do with what their play and their expressions of emotion were about. Moreover, their words were not predicted by the relative frequencies of word classes in adult English. Only about one third of all the different words the 14 children said in the playroom were names of objects, even though they were presented with an abundance of toys and with the same toys every month. Nouns account for about one half of the entries in a dictionary of English.[9] The distribution of words in the children's vocabularies was based on what was relevant to them in the stream of activity in the playroom more than it reflected the distribution of kinds of words in the language.

We have evidence of the Principle of Discrepancy from the mental meanings we attributed to the children's words (in Chapter 9) and developments in their play (Chapter 10). When they first began to say words, they were most likely to be talking about things that were already evident in the situation. For example, Charlie looked at the toy cow in our playroom and said "cow." However, by the time of the vocabulary spurt, the children were talking more about *anticipated* action events that were imminent but not yet evident to someone else. An example with the same word was Charlie's turning to his mother for help in putting the cow into a block and saying "cow." The single word "cow" expressed the evident meaning; Charlie and his mother both knew what he was saying. But the same word was insufficient by itself for expressing the anticipative meaning. In order to express such discrepant meanings, Charlie would need to learn other words, notably verbs and the structures for simple sentences, to articulate the thematic relations between the cow, his mother as the agent of an action, and the block as its destination. The development from evident to anticipative meanings in the period from First Words to Vocabulary Spurt supported the Principle of Discrepancy: that children will be pressed to learn language in order to express meanings that cannot be known by someone else unless they are made manifest in an expression.

Other support for the Principle of Discrepancy was in developments in play. When the children put objects together early on, they were most likely to construct given relations, which were not different from the configurations in which the toys were presented originally, or general relations, which were afforded by the graphic, physical properties of the objects as containers or surfaces for support. Thus, early constructions with the toys were not discrepant from the original experiences with the toys, or they were afforded by the shapes of the toys as either containers or surfaces. The chidren's later constructions with the toys were more specific to the different perceptual properties of the objects as well as to social and conventional themes in everyday events. Similarly, they progressed from finding objects to use in play with the support of having already constructed a similar thematic relation, to finding objects without such support. Developments in play, therefore, complemented developments in word learning that showed less reliance on things given in the world and more reliance on representations in mental meanings that went beyond things given in the world.

The Principle of Elaboration was supported by additional findings in language and play. The children were also increasingly likely to express *action meanings* that entailed a movement, often with a change in location. An example was Greta's saying "up" as she climbed onto a chair. When the children first began to say words, they were as likely to express dynamic, action meanings as to express what we called presentational meanings that entailed showing, seeing, pointing – for example, when a child turned to her mother and showed her a cup for her to see. Presentational meanings were similar to the "proto-declaratives" in prelinguistic gestures and early words described by Bates and her colleagues.[10] They have a focus on a single element that the child has in mind while showing, giving, pointing, or otherwise presenting. However, action meanings have several elements, with different roles and relations between elements, according to the dynamics of the action. In the interval in which they progressed from their first words to a vocabulary spurt, words that expressed action meaning increased relative to the frequency of the more stative, presentational kinds of meanings. And, correspondingly, the children's thematic constructions in play included more different kinds of specific relationships with both inanimate and animate surrogate objects.

Thus, another development in the single-word period was this increase in mental meanings having more elements, with different roles and relations between them – for both words and object play – consistent with the Principle of Elaboration. The increase in expression of action meanings in the single-word period was coextensive with increasing expression of anticipative meanings and constructing imposed specific thematic relations in play. The more words the children learned, the more they talked about anticipated actions: in particular, what they themselves were about to do.[11] These developments would provide the impetus to learn verbs of movement and location for simple sentences, which in fact the children subsequently proceeded to do.[12]

These are cognitive principles – drawing as they do on developments in mental representation in particular – and they are also quite general; we might expect they would apply to other developments as well. In fact, one goal of the research in this book has been to show how learning language fits in with other developments also going on in the same period of time, and for this very reason we expect the same principles to apply in other domains. This is the essence of the "organismic" developmental point of view: "Every behavioral act, whether outward bodily movement or internalized cognitive operation, gains its significance and status in terms of its role in the overall functioning of the organism."[13] We have been concerned in particular with how word learning "gains its significance and status" in the context of the young child's social connectedness and developments in affect and cognition.

Social Connectedness

We assumed that everything that happened in the playroom and in our home visits happened *because* the children were, in Dan Stern's words, "profoundly social creatures." The children were always in a social context; their mothers were immediately accessible while they played with the toys, and mothers treated their expressions – affect and speech – as communicative events and responded accordingly. Experiences with other persons in the context of a child's everyday activities are a critical component in any model of development. For this reason, in addition to our studies of the children's behaviors, we also looked at how the mothers contributed to their children's learning experiences in the playroom. One of these analyses focused on how the mothers responded to their children's emotional expressions (Chapter 8) and the other on the mothers' contributions to their children's object play (Chapter 10) in this period of early word learning.

In these interactions, the mothers were clearly responsive to the principles of Relevance, Discrepancy, and Elaboration. They showed they were sensitive to their infants' thoughts and feelings and sensitive as well to the need infants might have for resolving discrepancy between what they had in mind at any one point in time and what others might have had in mind at the same time. Mothers strove to enhance the relevance of their own speech and action and to avoid discrepancy, in the first place, by tuning into a child's focus of attention. When the toy a mother chose for play was one her child had already been playing with or looking at, or when she responded to a child's expression of emotion with a focus on the child's goal or something in the situation relevant to the goal, she minimized discrepancy to create a shared understanding. And by showing or telling a child what to do in the situation surrounding an emotional experience, or what to do with the toys in playing with them, her own affect and action contributed to the relevance of her speech. And she was showing her child how discrepancy can be resolved through expression in speech and other actions. At the same time, she was elaborating a child's mental meanings by actions and talk directed at what to do with the toys in play or about the causes or circumstances of an emotional experience.

Socialization is a mutual process: It is influenced by a child's development as much as it influences that development. The form and content of social interactions change as caregivers come to attribute increasingly more to a child's mental meanings with the child's development. Socialization, then, is in the relationship between the child and the context and reflects the impact children have on their own development. At the same time, changes in the form and content of social interaction contribute to development by helping a child to interpret perceptions and feelings, to elaborate mental meanings, and to increase understanding. Just as children learn the forms of language from the patterns and regularities they infer in the speech they hear, they learn about emotion and acting in the world by inferring patterns and regularities in the expressions and other actions their caregivers use in responding to them.[14] In sum, caregivers are sensitive to the abilities and needs of children and adjust their responses to what they perceive those to be – whether in language, play, or emotional expression. Such parent sensitivities have been described in the development of children from different cultures and different subgroups as well as children with Down's Syndrome, preterm infants, and unresponsive or hyperactive children.[15]

The dynamic events that make up a child's social context afford information for guiding social perceptions, just as the structure of the physical world affords object perception in the sense proposed by J. J. Gibson. This is so, however, only when the information in social events is compatible to the perceiver, or "perceiver referenced," that is, so long as the information is *relevant.*[16] Thus, how children tune in to information in the social context depends on what they have in mind – their own goals, expectations, and actions. Caregivers seem to know this intuitively and use the information they in turn take from the child about the child to provide structured, useful information in their interactions.[17] The mutuality in the mothers' socialization practices when they played with their children and responded to their emotional expressions echoed the bidirectionality inherent in the relationship between developments in language and socialization.[18]

We do not have evidence that the mothers literally "scaffolded" their children's learning, in ways related to those Vygotsky described, by actively providing them with the experiences they were ready to incorporate into their own thinking. But the evidence is clear that mothers provided information that was highly relevant for what their children were learning; they were hardly passive. If the children were Piaget's children by virtue of the active part they took in their own learning and development,[19] their mothers were Vygotsky's mothers by virtue of their own active part in that development. They did more than provide comfort and companionship in the social context. By tuning in to both a child's level of development and what the child was feeling and thinking about at the moment, they provided the kind of relevant "guided participation" Barbara Rogoff described as the social context for development.[20] This mutual understanding and social connectedness between the children and their mothers was one component in the process of transition from infancy to language and was intimately bound up with the other two: affect and cognition.

Affect

The affective life of a child is generally considered crucial to all aspects of development, whether one's perspective is traditional psychodynamic theory, attachment theory, or the more recent emotions theory.[21] In contrast, affect has virtually been ignored in accounts of language acquisition. And though Piaget acknowledged that affect is the fuel that drives the engine of cognitive development, he had relatively little explicit to say about it.[22] However, the evidence from the children we studied made clear that affect was a major component in the processes that contribute to their development in the second year. But this contribution was not a straightforward one, because emotionally toned and neutral affect expression differed in their effects.

The children differed in their profiles of emotionality just as they differed in onset and rate of word learning. Two vignettes are presented here to highlight the differences among them.

When Shirley was 10 months old, she looked up at the clock on the playroom wall, stared at it, and said, very softly, "ticktock"; her mother literally cheered. She had reported that Shirley began saying "ticktock" at home when she was 8 months old, and here was the evidence to show us just how precocious her baby was. Shirley was also one of our most serious children; she watched her mother and others in the playroom and handled the toys with the calm, sustained attention we see in the Figure 7.1 photos of her at 11 and 22 months (examples of neutral affect). In fact, Shirley spent 95% of the time at FW (10 months) and 93% of the time at VS (3 months later) in neutral affect expression.

Jessica was one of our most emotionally expressive children. Her photo is the example we used of +3 positive affect in Figure 7.4; she spent 78% and 68% of her time at FW and VS, respectively, in neutral affect expression. She was also our most talkative child who often chattered long strings of unintelligible sounds, unintelligible to her mother and to us, with words and phrases thrown in as she grew older. She said her first intelligible words in the playroom when she was 14 months, 3 days, and her vocabulary spurt was identified 8 months later, at 22 months.

Shirley and Jessica were both developing "normally" and "happily." They were similar to each other in many respects but different from one another in others, and both their similarities and differences were characteristic of the other children as well. One may well ask why they were different, but that was not the goal of our study. We were more concerned with what the similarities and the differences among the children might mean than we were with the source of their differences.

In the interval between First Words and a Vocabulary Spurt, with the children equated for language achievement rather than chronological age, the numbers of words in the children's vocabularies increased, but frequency of emotional expression neither increased nor decreased. We drew two conclusions from this result. First, development in the single-word period in the second year of life is more than just an increase in overall expressivity. The children learned to say more words, and their linguistic expression increased, but they did not also express emotion more frequently than they had before they started saying words. And, second, the fact that emotional expression did not decrease from FW to VS meant that expression through speech did not *replace* emotional expression. Given the importance of emotional expression in social and communicative exchanges in infancy, we might have expected a decrease as 1-year-olds learned to use words instead. But these children did not say words instead of expressing affect. They continued to express their feelings through displays of affect as they learned language for articulating what their feelings were about.

We boldly made attributions of the mental meanings expressed by the children's words and emotional expressions independent of one another (Chapter 7). One of our procedural assumptions was that an expression, whether in affect, speech, or other action, is a license to attribute the intentional state of the expresser. These mental meanings were coded, on the most general level, as beliefs and desires. Desires were more frequent than beliefs; the children were expressing how they wanted to change the world more often than they expressed something about what they believed the world to be. Desires were expressed twice as often as beliefs by both speech and emotional expression and primarily concerned the children *themselves* rather than their mothers as actors for changing the world. The children expressed desires concerning their own actions in regard to their own purposes and goals; their words and emotional expressions were not used primarily as tools for getting other persons to do things.

However, most of the *beliefs* they expressed had something to do with other persons, primarily their mothers, who were playing with them in our playroom. In addition, when mental meanings were beliefs about the mother – something she did or had done – they were expressed primarily by displays of emotion. Thus, the *social* importance of emotional expression, and the part it played in infancy for maintaining intersubjectivity, continued into the period of word learning in the second year.

In addition, saying words and expressing emotion were closely associated with one another in real time (Chapter 8). A peak in emotional expression occurred immediately after words. We interpreted the heightened probability that emotion would occur after a word to mean that these children were talking about things that were occasions for the experience and expression of emotion. However, the words the children were learning were not the names of the emotions. Even in those moments when the children were actually expressing emotion, they did not use words to tell others what it was they were feeling. They didn't have to. Children's feelings can be attributed to the affect display itself, which is just what their mothers had been doing, virtually since birth. The children's words – words like *Mama, cookie, more, no, up* – named the persons, objects, and other circumstances that were the causes and consequences of their feelings rather than the feelings themselves. Thus, affect and language provide two different forms, one biologically determined and the other socially contrived, for expressing different aspects of mental meanings.

In fact, the children's mothers themselves rarely used the names of emotions when talking to a child in response to the child's expressing emotion (Chapter 8). They talked to the children instead about their goals and about the outcomes of their efforts to achieve their goals in the larger situation in which a child's emotion was experienced and expressed. They directed their children's attention to the circumstances around an emotion and encouraged them to think about and act on the physical and social context in order to change it. In this way, the children learned something about their emotional experiences and ways to regulate their emotions through *action* and through *talk about* action that was directed at the causes and objects of an emotional experience.

Moreover, the information the children received in the context of their emotional expressions was different for positive and negative affect expression. Mothers were more likely to express emotion themselves and to share the affect when their children expressed positive emotion than when they expressed negative emotion; affect expression was the mothers' most frequent response to a child's positive expressions. In contrast, mothers were most likely to act or to talk about action around the situation when a child expressed negative emotion. Thus, the mothers were socializing their children's experience and expressions of emotion differently according to the valence of the expression – providing a shared affective experience when the expression was positive and talking about or modeling coping strategies when the expression was negative. They were not socializing the discrete categories of emotion, since they rarely named the different emotions or talked about emotions themselves directly.[23]

The contribution from affect to development has been emphasized in a number of different theoretical perspectives. Clearly, lack of affect is a state of pathology in which development is seriously delayed and compromised; in normally developing children, affect is always present. In psychodynamic developmental theories – beginning with Freud and continuing through Klein, Mahler, Winnicot, and most recently Stern – "affects are privileged as attributes of experience."[24] The "organizing function" of affect has received a good deal of attention as well in more behaviorally oriented theories of infant emotion and development, particularly those that emphasize the functions of emotions for the motivation and organization of actions.[25] At the most basic level, actions are performed in order to promote or maintain positive affect and avoid or discourage negative affect, consistent with the classic "pleasure principle" of Freud. And long before infants themselves can control their own actions or the actions of others, their caregivers work at managing things so as to relieve their distress and promote states of satisfaction and pleasure.[26] The finding that emotional expression clustered in real time with words was consistent with these functionalist accounts of emotion and emotional development. The children were indeed learning words to talk about things they found interesting and that gave rise to their emotions.

The functional role of affect in behavior and development has figured prominently in theories that are tied to the discrete emotions – the so-called basic, or "Darwinian," categories of emotion like joy, anger, disgust, sadness, and the like.[27] Because we did not code for them, we cannot speak to the motivational role that the different categories of emotions might have played in the children's actions and in their expressive development. However, the discrete emotions could not have accounted for most of the children's actions, because the discrete emotions were relatively infrequent – judging by the fact that nonneutral expression accounted for only 16% of coded time, on average – just as they have been in studies where they were explicitly coded.[28] The children we studied were expressing neutral affect most of the time, and, as reported earlier, this high percentage of neutral affect is consistent with other reports in the literature from infants and children of different ages and in different settings. When they weren't expressing neutral affect, they expressed positive emotion primarily. Achieving and maintaining neutral affect along with positive feelings could well have motivated all the children's actions, which would be consistent with almost any theoretical account.

The part played by neutral affect in the children's actions and development was an important result in the data. In differential emotions theory, neutral affect is ordinarily assigned to the emotions category *interest.* The question of whether interest is or is not a true category of emotion was raised in Chapter 7; it is not typically included in the list of the so-called basic, or "Darwinian," emotions. If one holds interest to be an emotion, then the answer to the question of whether emotion motivates action, including acts of expression, is yes. But this is not illuminating, because it adds nothing to the widely accepted fact that learning and acting typically depend on states of active awareness and attention – that is, interest. The importance of neutral affect is in fact in the link it affords between affect and cognition.

Cognition

Developments in play and word learning were attributed to underlying developments in cognition and in particular to the symbolic capacity for representation in intentional states. Development also occurred in the collaboration required between cognition and affect for words, emotions, and object play, and the evidence for this came from the infants' expression of neutral affect. The children were expressing primarily neutral affect in moments before saying words at the time of First Words. The cognitive activity for constructing a mental meaning and for recalling and saying words preempted the cognitive resources needed for the experience and expression of emotion. By the time of the Vocabulary Spurt, the children had gotten it together and were able to say words and express emotion at the same time. However, saying words with emotion occurred with these constraints: The emotion expressed was primarily positive emotion, at low levels of intensity, and the words that were said were among the children's earliest learned and most frequent words, the words they knew best.

Collaboration between cognition and affect for learning language was also evident in the interaction of both kinds of expression – speech and emotion – with object play. In our most recent research, we have looked at the moment-to-moment contingencies among expressive behaviors and the episodes of object play in which the children constructed thematic relations with the toys.

Expressive behaviors tended to be inhibited when the children were engaged with objects and, in certain kinds of object play, were more inhibited *before* the target behavior. These results meant that, in those moments, the children were expressing neutral affect and were not talking – in order to conserve the cognitive resources needed for planning and executing actions. Other studies have also shown that children tend not to talk or express emotion during object play.[29] The cognitive abilities of the young language-learning child are still essentially quite immature, and development is the result of "limitations and coordinations interacting with a dynamically changing environment."[30] Expressing emotion, manipulating objects, and saying words exploit a child's limited resources and require collaboration between cognition and affect.

The immediate effects we observed in real time complemented the developmental effects we saw across time from 9 months to 2 years. First, developments in word learning (First Words and then the Vocabulary Spurt) were closely associated with developments in object play (beginning to construct thematic relations and the achievement in constructing specific thematic relations, respectively). Children who learned words earlier also learned to construct specific relations earlier; they also expressed proportionally more neutral affect. Thus, earlier age of language achievement was associated with both earlier achievement of specific relations and expression of neutral affect. Neutral affect expression is a continuation of the quiet alert states of early infancy and is, presumably, an optimal state for the sort of attention that learning requires. Attending to words in order to learn them and building increasingly specific imposed relations in play required the cognitive resources that a child might otherwise have spent on the cognition required for the experience and expression of emotion. Thus, one kind of evidence of the influence from cognition on the integration of language, emotional expression, and object play was inferred from the expression of neutral affect.

Other evidence from object play also informed us of developments in cognition in this same period for the representations in intentional states. This was evident when we looked at what the children did when they put two or more of the toys together to create a thematic relationship between them. The thematic relations they constructed in play provided evidence of developments in the ability to set up mental meanings that were increasingly discrepant and elaborated. Very young children begin to appreciate that things go together thematically very early on. Objects, and persons and objects, form meaningful relationships with one another because of the functions each can serve in relation to the other, and these go beyond simple associations. Knowing the functional connections between objects is part of knowing about the individual objects themselves. Certain things are related because of the perceptions they afford: for example, things that can serve as containers or surfaces for other things. Other things are thematically related because of social convention: for example, putting shoes on feet, eating with a spoon, and riding a horse. In addition, thematic relations depend on how things are proportionally related topographically; their contours and relative sizes have to fit one another (as the children showed us they appreciated when they diligently worked at fitting the nesting boxes together, for example).

The children we studied spent much of their time in the playroom taking things apart and putting things together to construct thematic relations between them. The development that occurred in this period of early word learning was in constructing increasingly *specific* thematic relations. The frequency of general relations of containment or support decreased as the construction of specific relations between objects increased (Chapter 10). Even though they differed in age, reaching achievement in constructing specific relations occurred close in time to the Vocabulary Spurt for all the children. Specific thematic relations embraced a wider variety of kinds of constructions between objects than just containment and support and were evidence that a child could hold in mind more elaborated mental meanings for enactment in play. The increase in learning new words was coextensive with learning to construct more specific thematic relations in play because of the similar developments in cognition they both required. In addition, a key result of the developments in constructing relationships between objects in play was that the children were acquiring the basis for the semantic meaning relations of early sentences.

FROM MENTAL MEANINGS TO LANGUAGE

The study of meaning in child language is ordinarily the study of the linguistic meanings invested in the words and grammatical forms of language. Knowing what a child's messages are about, one can infer something of what the child assumes the words in the message mean. This assumption has been carried forward seriously in child language research since the early 1970s, when it was first introduced for the study of early syntax. The suggestion then was that children use the meanings of words and the relational meanings between words to discover categories and rules for syntax. Meaning, therefore, could not be ignored in the effort to understand syntax acquisition.[31] Children learn the syntax of simple sentences to express a core of basic meanings. Later they learn the syntax of complex sentences to express other meanings that connect the basic meanings of two or more simple sentences. The importance of semantics for syntax acquisition was extended and formalized in contemporary learnability research as "semantic bootstrapping."[32] The idea is now virtually taken for granted – not only for child grammar but also in research on thematic roles and relations in the adult sentences that provide the input children receive for learning a grammar.

The meanings in children's simple sentences are of two kinds. Certain meanings come from the particular words that children use often in their early phrases, words like *more* and *no.* For example, "more juice" *means* recurrence because "more" means recurrence; the meanings of negation in little sentences like "no fit" and "no dirty soap" (nonexistence, rejection, denial) come from the meaning of *no.* More important, however, are the grammatical meanings in sentences with two or more constituents of verbs (whether the verb itself is actually said or not): the little sentences children say like "Mommy pigtail," "read book," "Baby do it," "this go there." The meanings in the majority of these early sentences come from categories of verbs that name actions and the thematic roles that nouns and pronouns have as agents, places, or themes in relation to those actions.[33]

The point is that the meanings of words and sentences belong to the language. To learn the forms of the language is to learn their meanings: the conventional, shared, and public meanings the linguistic forms have for the persons who use them. The semantics of simple sentences is in the thematic meaning relations between verbs and nouns (or pronouns); the syntax of simple sentences is the formal configurations in which these meaning relations can appear.

It has not been difficult to see the connection between meanings in early sentences and the cognitive developmental history of the young language-learning child. In particular, the semantic roles in early sentences build on what the child already knows about MOVEMENT and LOCATION. Two critical features that help define thematic relations are how things move in relation to one another and how things are located relative to one another. The importance of the two conceptual notions of movement and location has long-standing precedence in developmental psychology and has since assumed credibility in theoretical linguistics as well. Piaget in his several infant books stressed again and again that children learn about objects in the world by acting on them and perceiving them in different places.[34] Infants move objects themselves and watch as other persons move objects from place to place, and they discover the objects anew in different places. Through these perceptions and actions in the first two years of life, children come to appreciate the effects of movement and location for constructing a theory of objects and space. The semantics of their early sentences builds on the conceptual knowledge acquired in infancy through these appreciations.[35]

A child's theories of movement and location participate in a crucial way in language learning, because they define the thematic relations that determine the semantics of sentences. This is so not only for children's early sentences,[36] but for sentences in the adult language as well. In adult linguistics, "the semantics of motion and location provide the key to a wide range of further semantic fields."[37] The grammatical "theme" of a sentence in adult grammar is the object that is affected by the movement named by the verb, or "that argument which undergoes the motion or change in state denoted in the predicate."[38] The other parts, or arguments, of a sentence name the participants in the movement, who does the action, where things are located, and the like. The thematic relations in early sentences most often include inanimate objects that are affected by an action (the grammatical theme, or what we called "affected object" in our studies in the 1970s), animate nouns as actors or agents, and the places to which actors or objects move. Clearly, discovering how things go together in everyday events – knowledge evident in the children's play with objects in their period of early word learning – contributes to the meanings of early sentences.

Such knowledge contributes as well to the meanings of the words children learn in the second year before they acquire procedures for sentences. The children learned names for objects, but they also learned names for the kinds of relationships that were possible between persons and objects and between objects: words like *more, in, down,* and the like. They said these words, and also presumably learned these words, because they were relevant to what they had in mind: representations directed at actions and interactions with their mothers and objects in their play.

Establishing the connections between mental meanings and the conventional meanings of a language requires at least these developments. To begin with, developments in symbolic capacity are required for the representations in a child's mental meanings. The construction of a mental meaning begins when an object, an event, another word or words, or even a prior mental meaning evokes something from memory – early on, it might be a prior episode that is evoked; later on, something abstracted from a schema or concept. Second, cognitive developments are required for forming the concepts of objects, events, and relations that are abstracted from episodes and become a child's knowledge base, out of which representations in mental meanings are constructed. And third, to construct increasingly discrepant and elaborated mental meanings requires development in memory processes of recognition, retrieval, and recall for accessing what is in the knowledge base in relation to the data of perception.

Once a child learns something about objects and events and something about words as reproducible units of sound (or gesture), word learning consists of good old-fashioned associative learning. In the beginning, the data for learning the meanings of language are in the circumstances of use in which children hear words and sentences. The meanings of early words like *cookie, gone, more,* and *Mama,* or little sentences like "eat meat" or "throw ball," can be gotten from the connections between the words and their corresponding events. Eventually, meaning in language becomes increasingly arbitrary and is no longer transparent in circumstances of use. Words like *citizen, honor,* and *trust* are learned indirectly through the other words a child already knows. Associative learning has been revised in contemporary theory as "connectionism" and has come a long way since the days of E. L. Thorndike (who was the original connectionist; see the 1949 anthology of his papers, *Selected Writings from a Connectionist's Psychology*). Connectionism may be debated in the realm of syntax for some time to come, but so far it promises a more parsimonious account of lexical learning than a theory based on a priori lexical principles.[39]

A different perspective is offered by those who suggest that children would be unable to begin to learn words in the first place unless they were equipped with certain language-specific principles that provide the foundation for word learning.[40] The claim is that a child could not begin to learn words without them, because such principles make word learning possible. However, this perspective and the research enterprise it inspires have ignored everything else going on in a young child's life that contributes to the relevance of words for learning them – in particular, those things that contribute to developments in cognition and a child's affective life.

In fact, Quine's thesis of the indeterminacy of translation – which motivates research on lexical principles – was presented by him in clearly behaviorist and avowedly anti-intentionality terms: There are "no propositional attitudes but only the physical constitution and behavior of organisms." The only admissible evidence for translating *gavagai* to *rabbit* would be the "stimulations" available to both speakers: The translation "turns solely on correlations with non-verbal stimulation."[41] Quine's philosophical argument for the indeterminacy of translation is a logical one; our task in explaining word learning is a psychological one. By focusing on intentionality for a theory of language development, we have emphasized the mind of the child and its development in a social context. The emphasis is on how the development of cognitive capacities and the affective life of the child determine the mental meanings a child can construct, which in turn determine what the child expresses and interprets of what others say.

CONCLUSIONS

An important part of the mental plans we construct when saying words and sentences is the representation we have in mind for the word or sentence to express. These representations are the mental meanings that underlie acts of expression and result from acts of interpretation. They are private, personal meanings in contrast to the conventional meanings in language, which are public and shared. The capacities for constructing these mental meanings change in the first several years of language learning, and the use of language can be diagnostic of such change. For example, 1-year-olds progress from representations with a focus on a single element to representing more than one element with a relationship between them. A child's words make these underlying representations manifest and so can reveal their development. But we still need to understand the processes by which this development occurs; such understanding has been the goal of this book. In particular, we have invoked the three principles of Relevance, Discrepancy, and Elaboration for explaining the developments we observed in word learning, affect expression, and object play.

Children come through the single-word period and arrive at the threshold of acquiring a grammar with a set of fairly well-defined capacities. First, they know a sizable number of words, and words are integrated into a child's affective life – both emotionally toned affect and neutral affect – in several ways. Word learning is intimately connected to a child's emotional life because infants learn language to talk about, and thereby to share, the things their feelings are about: the persons, objects, and events that are the causes and circumstances of emotion. But expressing emotion and learning words require collaboration between cognition and affect, and the result of this collaboration is to recruit states of neutral affect. Neutral affect promotes the states of attention needed for constructing mental meanings in a plan for *saying* words in acts of expression, and for *learning* words in acts of interpretation. This collaboration for the conservation of resources is one of the developments in cognition required for language learning.

Another is a child's conceptual development. Infants acquire *concepts* of persons, objects, and relations in the first two years and come to appreciate *thematic relationships* among things that go together in everyday events. The appreciation of thematic relations, together with early concepts, yields theories of objects, movement, and location. These developments are, in turn, coextensive with acquiring a vocabulary of words, as we found in the developmental relationship between object play and word learning. Concepts and theories have their beginnings in the first year and develop through the second year as children acquire words. In turn, the concepts associated with the single words of the 1-year-old form the basis for the semantic–syntactic learning of the 2-year-old.

If language is to keep up with developments in cognition, affect, and social connectedness, the 2-year-old will need to acquire the procedures for sentences. Acquiring a grammar means learning to translate conceptual categories into linguistic categories for describing thematic relations in sentences. Just as the affect displays of infancy could not express the mental meanings of the 1-year-old, the single words that served the 1-year-old can neither express nor articulate the more elaborated and discrepant mental meanings in the desires, beliefs, and feelings of the 2-year-old. Children achieve the power of expression by learning the public, conventional meanings of a language for expressing and articulating the private, personal meanings they have in mind. This happens because of a child's social connectedness with other persons who need or want to know what the child has in mind, and developments in cognition and affect are integrated with one another in the endeavor.

APPENDIX

Dictionary of Words in the Playroom

Words listed here were said by 1–6 of the children; the words learned by 7 or more children were reported in Figure 9.3.

Said by 1 Child (N = *156*)

agua (water)
all
all fall down
apple juice
around
ashes
baba (food)
bag
bagel
baseball
bear
be back
bicycle
bleed
block
bobby pins
book
boomboom
bounce
buckle
burp
Burt
bus
button
camera
candy
castle
cat
chain
chew
chip
clock
cocoa
coffee
come on
cube
daisy
dance
ding
dirt
dish
don't
doo (rooster)
doo (Yankee Doodle)
dot
easy
egg
fall off
fine
fit
five
fix
flower
four
garbage
get down
get it
giddyup
gobble
gonna
go sleep
Grover
guitar
hair
hand
hello
help me
hide
hold it
hole
hoo
hop
how
how! (greeting)
hug
inside
I see
I wanna go
keep
knee
knock
lap
leg
let
little
make
man!
Marjory Daw
me eat
move
muffin
need
neigh
night
oh dear
oink
one two three four five six
orange
other
over
peach
peel

picture
pie
pillow
pinky
plane
plum
pool
pop
pour
pretty
pull
push
put
quiet
raisin
read
roll
scared
school
see this
sheet
silver
sorry
stand
star
stay
string
stroller
tada
tap
tea
throw
tickle
tie
tired
to
towel
train
tummy
turn
TV
wait
wee wee (3 pigs)
wee wee (train sound)
whack
what's
what's that
where are you
whew
will
won't
wow
yo
zipper

Note. In addition, 11 different person names (family members, friends, and the like) were each said by one child and are not included here.

*Said by 2 Children (*N = *49)*

a
again
alright
bang
big
blanket
boo
booboo
boot
broke
cheese
clean
cover
cry
dirty
(all) done
doodoo (feces)
ear
eeayeeayo
good
grandmother (meema, nanny)
high
key
kiss
light
meat
mine
Mother (person name)
mouth
not
oh boy
okay
one two three
pee pee
people
play
ready
sh
(oh) shit
stop
the
tick tock
toes
top
unh unh
walk
wanna
who
zoom

*Said by 3 Children (*N = *35)*

all gone
are
beep
bite
blue
bump
come
cracker
doll
Ernie
fell
foot
green
hat
hot
I want
look
me
meow
milk
nose
oh no
oops
red
right
see
sheep
sleep

slide
some
thank you
three
uh huh
where
yay

Said by 4 Children (N = *15*)

and
away
back
close
grapes
hey
nice
ouch
pig
please
ride
want
what
yellow
you

Said by 5 Children (N = *11*)

baa
chair
do
dog
investigator (person name)
huh
is
man
my
seesaw
self (person name)

Said by 6 Children (N = *11*)

car
cup
eat
fork
I
it
knife
off
one
pear
toy

Notes

1. THE POWER OF EXPRESSION

1 Taylor (1985, p. 238).
2 Danto (1973); Taylor (1979, 1985).
3 L. Bloom & Beckwith (1986).
4 E.g., Danto (1973); Fodor (1979); Searle 4(1983); Taylor (1985).
5 E.g., the "mental models" of Johnson-Laird (1983); the "mental spaces" of Fauconnier (1985); the "complex mental attitudes" of Pollack (1990); and the products in consciousness of the "computational mind" of Jackendoff (1987).
6 E.g., Bretherton (1988), Reddy (1991), Trevarthen (1979), and Vedeler (1987).
7 Searle (1983).
8 Emde (1984); Newson (1977); Papoušek, Papoušek, & Koester (1986); Rogoff (1990); D. Stern (1985); Trevarthen (1977, 1979); Trevarthen & Hubley (1978); Werner & Kaplan (1963).
9 In the sense described in the papers in Astington, Harris, & Olson (1988); Wellman (1990); and others.
10 Freyd (1983).
11 E.g., Bates, Benigni, Bretherton, Camaioni, & Volterra (1979); Bruner (1983); Dore (1975); Shatz & O'Reilly (1990).
12 Vygotsky (1978, pp. 24–26) (*Mind and Society,* originally published in 1930 as *Tool and Symbol*).
13 De Laguna (1927/1963, pp. 19, 21).
14 Ogden and Richards (1923/1946, p. 24).
15 Wittgenstein (1934–35/1958, pp. 172–173).
16 Malinowski (1923) and (1935, Vol. 1, pp. 8–9).
17 Sampson (1980, p. 224).
18 Bates et al. (1979).
19 Nelson (1988, p. 224).

20 Shatz & O'Reilly (1990, p. 145).
21 Bruner (1983, p. 17).
22 L. Bloom (1974a); Fauconnier (1985); Fodor (1979).
23 Fauconnier (1985, p. 2).
24 As summarized, for example, in Taylor (1985).
25 Quoted in de Laguna (1927/1963, p. 17).
26 Augustinius (397/1945, p. 9).
27 C. Stern & Stern (1907), translated and quoted in Blumenthal (1970, p. 91).
28 Malinowski (1923, p. 310).
29 Taylor (1979, p. 79).
30 With respect to development, see in particular McCarthy (1954).
31 R. Brown (1965, p. 328).
32 Taylor (1979).
33 Sperber & Wilson (1986, p. 63).
34 Heider (1958).
35 L. Bloom (1973); Bretherton (1988); Golinkoff (1983a, 1983b).
36 Astington & Gopnik (1988); L. Ferguson & Gopnik (1988); Wellman (1985a, 1990).
37 Burke (1935); Piaget (1972/1973).
38 Taylor (1985).
39 L. Bloom (1970, 1976, 1991a); L. Bloom & Lahey (1978); L. Bloom, Miller, & Hood (1975).
40 E.g., Arnold (1960); Campos, Barrett, Lamb, Goldsmith, & Stenberg (1983); Frijda (1986); Lazarus (1984, 1991); Oatley & Johnson-Laird (1987); Roseman (1984); Stein & Levine (1987).
41 E.g., Ochs & Schieffelin (1989).
42 Bretherton & Beeghly (1982); Bretherton, Fritz, Zahn-Wexler, & Ridgeway (1986); Clore & Ortony (1987); Ridgeway, Waters, & Kuczaj (1985).
43 Pepper (1942).
44 For example, Campos et al. (1983); Hesse & Cicchetti (1982); Sroufe (1979).
45 Fogel et al. (1992); Fogel & Thelen (1987). See L. Bloom (1992) for commentary.

2. REPRESENTATION AND EXPRESSION

1 G. Miller, Galanter, & Pribram (1960, pp. 12–13).
2 Fauconnier (1985, p. 1).
3 E.g., among many others, L. Bloom (1970, 1973); R. Brown (1956, 1958); Carey (1982); Golinkoff, Mervis, & Hirsh-Pasek (1991); Gopnik & Meltzoff (1986b); MacNamara (1982); Markman (1989); Mervis (1987); Nelson (1974, 1985).

4 E.g., Bates (1976); Bates et al. (1979); L. Bloom (1973); L. Bloom, Lifter, & Broughton (1985); R. Brown (1973); Gopnik & Meltzoff (1984); J. Mandler (1988); McCune-Nicolich (1981); Tomasello & M. Farrar (1984).
5 See Perner (1991) for discussion of problems in defining *represent,* in particular with respect to distinguishing between *representing* as the process and *representation* as the product that is its result.
6 E.g., M. Barrett (1985); Bates, Bretherton, & Snyder (1988); Dromi (1987); Kuczaj & Barrett (1986); MacNamara (1982); McShane (1980); Nelson (1985); Schlesinger (1982); Sinha (1988); and M. Smith & Locke (1988).
7 In the sense of Brentano (1966), Danto (1973), Fodor (1979), and Searle (1983), among others.
8 Danto (1983, pp. 251–252).
9 Taylor (1985).
10 For exceptions, see L. Bloom (1974a); Campbell (1979, 1986); Golinkoff (1986); Gopnik (1982); Greenfield (1980); Hamburger & Crain (1987).
11 Campbell's distinction between "phenic" and "cryptic" domains of thought (1979, p. 420).
12 L. Ferguson & Gopnik (1988, p. 229). These authors described a "minimalist concept of mental representation," which is required for a "commonsense view of the world" (pp. 226–228). See L. Bloom (1974a) for an account of the part played by representations in consciousness for mediating between knowledge in memory and different kinds of contexts, especially linguistic contexts, for early language. See also G. Miller (1962).
13 Fauconnier (1985).
14 E.g., Ekman & Friesen (1978); Izard (1971).
15 E.g., Campos et al. (1983); Frijda (1986); G. Mandler (1990); Oatley (1992); Oatley & Johnson-Laird (1987); Roseman (1984); Stein & Jewett (1987); Stein & Levine (1987).
16 E.g., J. Mandler (1983); Moscovitch (1984); Piaget (1937/1954); Werner & Kaplan (1963).
17 E.g., J. Brown (1964); Olson & Sherman (1983).
18 E.g., McCall & McGhee (1977).
19 J. Mandler (1988).
20 E.g., Wellman & Somerville (1982).
21 Searle (1984, p. 60).
22 Anglin (1977); M. Barrett (1986); Bates et al. (1979); L. Bloom (1973); Dore, Franklin, Miller, & Ramer (1976); Dromi (1987); Nelson (1985).
23 Fauconnier (1985, pp. 1–2).
24 G. Miller (1979).
25 L. Bloom (1973); Dore et al. (1976); Ewing (1984); Scollon (1976).

26 L. Bloom, Lahey, Hood, Lifter, & Fiess (1980).
27 Freeman-Moir (1982), citing J. Baldwin, *Mental development in the child and the race: Methods and processes* (New York, 1895); Piaget (1947/1960, p. 101).
28 E.g., Cohen (1976); Fantz (1964); McCall & McGhee (1977); Ruff (1978), and many others.
29 Rovee-Collier, Sullivan, Enright, Lucas, & Fagen (1980); Vander Linde, Morrongiello, & Rovee-Collier (1985).
30 E.g., M. Barrett, Harris, & Chasin (1991); Bates et al. (1979); L. Bloom (1973); L. Bloom et al. (1985); Corrigan (1983); J. Mandler (1984); Nelson (1982, 1985); Piaget (1937/1954).
31 Oviatt (1980) and Golinkoff & Hirsh-Pasek (1987).
32 See, for example, Baddely (1986) and Case (1978, 1985), in particular, regarding information processing, and Bjorklund and Demetriou (1988) regarding resource models.
33 Exceptions include L. Bloom (1970, 1974a); L. Bloom & Beckwith (1989); L. Bloom, Miller, & Hood (1975); Lahey & Bloom (in press); Shatz (1977a); and Turkewitz, Ecklund-Flores, & Devenny (1990).
34 Johnson-Laird (1983). See N. Benson (1990) and Pascual-Leone (1987) for discussion of developmental changes in processing capacity.
35 E.g., Pylyshyn & Demopoulos (1986).
36 As reviewed by Lahey & Bloom (in press). See in particular work by Baddely (1986) and Case (1978, 1985).
37 G. Miller et al. (1960, pp. 213–214).

3. THE EMERGENT INFANT

1 E. Gibson (1969, p. 13).
2 J. Gibson (1966, p. 285).
3 I thank Lila Braine for pointing this out to me with the analogy to animals reared in the dark, who do not adapt to light even when it can be determined that they perceive light.
4 G. Miller (1962).
5 See, for example, the papers in S. Gelman & Byrnes (1991) and Neisser (1987).
6 For example, J. Mandler (1988, 1992) and papers in Carey & Gelman (1991) and Weiskrantz (1988).
7 L. Bloom (1981, 1991a) regarding children; Jackendoff (1983, 1991) regarding conceptual structure in adult linguistic theory. See Chapter 11 for discussion of both.
8 The section that follows was adapted from an original version that appeared in L. Bloom & Lahey (1978).

9 E.g., Bower (1974); Halford (1989); Ruff (1980); and Tronick (1972).
10 L. Bloom (1973); Huttenlocher (1974); Leopold (1939); Nelson (1973a); and many others since.
11 The traditional Piagetian account that follows here is from Piaget's three infant books; *The Construction of Reality in the Child* (1937/1954), *The Psychology of Intelligence* (1947/1960), and *The Origins of Intelligence in Children* (1936/1952).
12 Bower (1974).
13 Ruff (1980).
14 See Wellman, Cross, & Bartsch (1986) for further discussion.
15 Piaget (1947/1960, p. 112).
16 DeLoache (1984).
17 Piaget (1947/1960, p. 116).
18 Gopnik (1988a).
19 See also Fischer (1980).
20 Baillargeon, Spelke, & Wasserman (1985). For summaries of these studies, see Baillargeon (1992) and Spelke (1988, 1991).
21 Kellman & Spelke (1983).
22 Spelke (1988, p. 168).
23 Spelke (1991, p. 139).
24 Ibid.
25 E.g., Bower (1974).
26 Piaget (1937/1954).
27 Spelke (1988, pp. 168 and 181).
28 Piaget (1947/1960, p. 66).
29 Halford (1989, p. 329).
30 L. Bloom et al. (1985, p. 158).
31 I thank Herbert Ginsburg for pointing this out.
32 E.g., Hampshire (1967).
33 Piaget (1937/1954).
34 Parts of this section appeared originally in L. Bloom & Lahey (1978).
35 E. Gibson (1969, pp. 151–152). Gibson quoted J. Attneave (Transfer of experience with a class-schema to identification-learning of patterns and shapes, *Journal of Experimental Psychology, 54* [1957], 81–88) who conceived of a schema of an object as a "prototype" or "representation of the central tendency or commonality" of the objects in a class.
36 Piaget (1937/1954); Sapir (1921).
37 Rosch & Mervis (1975); Rosch, Mervis, Gray, Johnson, & Boyes-Braem (1976).
38 J. Mandler & Bauer (1988); J. Mandler, Fivush, & Reznick (1987).
39 J. Mandler & Bauer (1988, p. 262).
40 R. Brown (1956).

41 Mervis (1987); Mervis & Mervis (1982).
42 E.g., Medin & Wattenmaker (1987); Murphy & Medin (1985).
43 Keil (1989; 1991, p. 219), Wannemacher & Seiler (1983).
44 Freyd (1983).
45 Corter & Gluck (1992).
46 J. Gibson (1979).
47 L. Bloom (1973).
48 Leslie (1988, pp. 185–186).
49 See the experiments and discussion in Golinkoff, Harding, Carlson, & Sexton (1984).
50 Oakes & Cohen (1990).
51 Piaget (1954/1981).
52 L. Bloom (1970, 1973); Gopnik (1988b); Gopnik & Meltzoff (1986a); McCune-Nicolich (1981).
53 L. Bloom (1991a); L. Bloom & Capatides (1987b); L. Bloom & Lahey (1978).

4. THE EXPRESSIVE INFANT

1 DeCasper & Fifer (1980).
2 Eimas, Siqueland, Jusczyk, & Vigorito (1971).
3 The material in this chapter on the development of expression in infancy is far from exhaustive. I have chosen to present certain relevant themes in detail rather than review more of the field in less detail. Fortunately, several authors have reviewed the extensive literature on research and theory in infant expression. For a thorough review and balanced critique of emotional development, see Campos et al. (1983); also Izard & Malatesta (1987); Sroufe (1979, 1984); and Thompson (1990). For a thorough review of prespeech vocalizing in infancy, see Locke (1983).
4 Maurer & Maurer (1988, p. 209).
5 Darwin (1892/1913, pp. 347–348).
6 I owe this felicitous phrase to Richard Beckwith.
7 Darwin (1892/1913, pp. 178–179, 350).
8 Izard (1971, 1977).
9 Izard (1979a).
10 This account of differential emotions theory and development is from Izard & Malatesta (1987).
11 K. Barrett & Campos (1987); Campos & Barrett (1984, p. 235).
12 Campos et al. (1983); Oatley (1988); Stein & Levine (1987).
13 Campos & Barrett (1984); Kopp (1987, 1989). See Thompson (1990) for an extensive review.
14 Mahler, Pine, & Bergman (1975); Sroufe (1984); Thompson (1990). See also Tomkins (1970) regarding the role of affect for motivation in general.

15 Piaget (1954/1981, p. 5).
16 Kopp (1987, 1989); Thompson (1990, p. 3).
17 L. Bloom & Beckwith (1989); Dunn (1986); Fischer, Shaver, & Carnochan (1990).
18 For a history of this low point in infancy research, see the review by Mary Cover Jones (1933).
19 Bridges (1932, p. 325).
20 In 1927, Charlotte Bühler published a study of 69 infants in the first year and described their positive and negative "reactions" (1927/1930).
21 Johnson, Emde, Pannabecker, Stenberg, & Davis (1982); Klinnert, Sorce, Emde, Stenberg, & Gaensbauer (1984).
22 For example, Gaensbauer (1982); Malatesta, Culver, Tesman, & Shepard (1989).
23 Malatesta et al. (1989), extrapolated from Table *A*1. These authors also coded affect expression during a 1-min reunion episode after a separation, but these data are not included here. The MAX facial coding scheme developed by Izard and used by him and by Malatesta in their developmental studies distinguishes among expressions of eight basic emotions: interest, joy, surprise, sadness, anger, disgust, contempt, and fear.
24 Ekman & Friesen (1976, 1978); Oster & Ekman, 1978; Oster, Hegley, & Nagel (1992).
25 Oster (1978, pp. 61, 70).
26 As suggested to me by Kathleen Bloom.
27 Izard (1986); Wozniak (1986).
28 E.g., M. Lewis & Brooks (1978); M. Lewis, Brooks, & Haviland (1978).
29 K. Barrett & Campos (1987); Campos & Barrett (1984).
30 For example, M. Lewis, Sullivan, & Michalson (1984). Nevertheless, overt signs of expression may have an inverse relationship to individuals' internalized autonomic responses (Buck, 1984; H. Jones, 1930, 1935).
31 Cruttenden (1982). For discussion of this point, see L. Bloom & Lahey (1978, p. 89).
32 Bullock & Russell (1986); Ortony & Turner (1990).
33 Adamson & Bakeman (1982, 1985); Bullock & Russell (1986); Demos (1986); Emde (1984); Papoušek et al. (1986); Ricciuti & Poresky (1972); Stechler & Carpenter (1967); D. Stern, Barnett, & Spieker (1983); Thompson (1990); G. Young & Decarie (1977).
34 Beebe (1973); Rothbart (1973); Sroufe and Waters (1976); R. Washburn, a study of the smiling and laughing of infants in the first years of life, *Genetic Psychology Monographs, 6* (1929), 398–537, cited in Malatesta (1981).
35 Hilke (1988).
36 Bühler (1927/1930, p. 63); S. Jones, Collins, & Hong (1991). The form of 17-month-olds' smiles (e.g., mouth shape) also differs according to whether infants

are smiling at their mothers or at the toys they are playing with (S. Jones, Raag, & Collins, 1990).

37 Jersild (1954, p. 834).

38 As pointed out by Fogel & Reimers (1989).

39 See Papoušek et al. (1986) and Cole, Barrett, & Zahn-Wexler (1992) regarding neutral affect expression by infants and preschool children, respectively. In addition, extrapolating from the data presented by Adamson & Bakeman (1985) and Malatesta et al. (1989) yielded a very similar result.

40 E.g., Brazelton (1979); Lamb & Campos (1982); G. Olson & Sherman (1983); Wolfe (1965).

41 Scherer (1986).

42 E.g., Malatesta (1981); G. Young & Decarie (1977). See this paper by Malatesta, in particular, for a thorough review of the relevant ontogenetic and phylogenetic literature.

43 Walker-Andrews & Lennon (1991).

44 M. M. Lewis (1936, p. 42).

45 Fernald (1990); Guillaume (1927); Kaplan (1970); Kaplan & Kaplan (1971); Leopold (1939); M. M. Lewis (1936); Morse (1972).

46 Fernald et al. (1989).

47 M. M. Lewis (1936, pp. 46–47), citing C. Bühler & H. Hetzer, Das erste Verstandnis für Ausdruck in ersten Lebensjahr, *Zeitschrift für Psychologie* (1928).

48 M. M. Lewis (1959).

49 Roe (1975).

50 Kent (1981).

51 For a critical review of the evidence for this functional view of crying, see Malatesta (1981).

52 Bateson (1975); Hilke (1988); Rothbart (1973); Sroufe & Waters (1976); Stark (1980, 1986). In recent research by Kathleen Bloom, 3-month-olds were typically not smiling at the same time they vocalized; instead they seemed to be "concentrating," and if they smiled, it was after their vocalizing was responded to (personal communication).

53 Rothbart (1973); Sroufe & Waters (1976).

54 Fogel & Thelen (1987); van Beek (1991).

55 L. Bloom & Lahey (1978).

56 Stark (1986, p. 171).

57 Kent (1981); Netsell (1981); Studdert-Kennedy (1979).

58 K. Bloom (1988); K. Bloom, Russell, & Wassenberg (1987).

59 Oller (1980); Oller & Eilers (1988); Stark (1980, 1986).

60 Mitchell & Kent (1990); B. Smith, Brown-Sweeney, & Stoel-Gammon (1989).

61 Petitto & Marentette (1991, p. 1495).

62 Fogel (1981); Papoušek & Papoušek (1977).
63 Jakobson (1941/1968).
64 Oller & Eilers (1988); Oller, Wieman, Doyle, & Ross (1976, p. 1).
65 E.g., Locke (1988); Schwartz (1988); B. Smith (1988); Vihman, Macken, Miller, Simmons, & Miller (1985); Vihman & Miller (1988). See also the historical note by Ingram (1991) calling attention to this basic observation of the relationship between the forms of first words and infants' vocalizations in the early cross-linguistic work of I. Gheorghov (Le développement du langage chez l'enfant, in *Premier Congrès International de Pédologie* [Vol. 2, pp. 201–218], Brussels: Librairie Misch & Thron, 1911).
66 E.g., C. Ferguson & Farwell (1975); MacKain (1988).
67 Eimas et al. (1971).
68 Clarkson & Berg (1983).
69 For reviews of this research, see Aslin, Pisoni, & Jusczyk (1983); Eimas & Miller (1981); Kuhl (1987); and Yeni-Komshian, Kavanagh, & Strange (1980).
70 Kuhl & Miller (1975).
71 Aslin & Pisoni (1980).
72 J. Miller & Eimas (1983, p. 162).
73 Marler (1976).
74 Kuhl (1987).
75 These results have come largely from the research of Kuhl and her colleagues, summarized in Kuhl (1987).
76 Kuhl & Meltzoff (1984, 1988).
77 MacKain (1988).
78 Talk of the Town (1987).
79 K. Bloom (1974, 1990).
80 Fraiberg (1977).
81 Bateson (1975).
82 Beebe & Jaffe (1992).
83 Jaffe, Stern, & Peery (1973).
84 D. Stern, Jaffe, Beebe, & Bennett (1975); see also Jasnow et al. (1988).
85 Rheingold, Gewirtz, & Ross (1959).
86 Weisberg (1963).
87 K. Bloom (1977, 1990); K. Bloom & Esposito (1975).
88 Legerstee (1991); Legerstee, Pomerleau, Malcuit, & Feider (1987).
89 M. Lewis & Freedle (1973).
90 Delack (1976); Delack & Fowlow (1978).
91 See also D'Odorico & Franco (1991).
92 Ochs & Schieffelin (1983).
93 Schieffelin (1990).

94 See, for example, the papers in Bullowa (1979); Feagans, Garvey, & Golinkoff (1983); Golinkoff (1983c); M. Lewis & Rosenblum (1978); Lock (1978); Schaffer (1977); and Tronick (1982).
95 E.g., Bretherton (1988); Emde (1984); Newson (1977); Papoušek et al. (1986); Rogoff (1990); D. Stern (1985); Trevarthen (1977, 1979); Trevarthen & Hubley (1978); Werner & Kaplan (1963).
96 See, for example, Bruner (1977); Kaye (1977); Schaffer, Collis, & Parsons (1977).
97 Bruner (1975); Bullowa (1979); Ryan (1974).
98 Bakeman & Adamson (1984); Bates (1976); de Laguna (1927/1963); Newson (1979); D. Stern (1977); Sugarman (1978); Trevarthen & Hubley (1978).
99 Collis (1979); D. Edwards (1978); D. Stern (1985).
100 Bruner (1975); Richards (1978); Ryan (1974).
101 R. Clark (1978); Newson (1978).
102 Lock (1978a); Shotter (1978); Trevarthen & Hubley (1978).
103 D. Stern (1985).
104 Mahler et al. (1975).
105 D. Stern (1985, p. 19).
106 M. Lewis & Brooks (1978).
107 By Golinkoff (1983b) and Kagan (1981), respectively.
108 Emde (1983, p. 165).
109 D. Stern (1985, p. 28).
110 See, for example, M. Lewis & Michalson (1983) and Izard & Malatesta (1987) for two very different perspectives – social and biological, respectively – for explaining emotional development.
111 L. Bloom & Lahey (1978).

5. THE TRANSITION TO LANGUAGE

1 The first published infant biography was by Tiedemann in 1787; for a survey of the early biographical studies, see Dennis (1949). Excerpts from several early diaries of language development are reprinted in Bar-Adon & Leopold (1971).
2 L. Bloom (1973); E. Clark (1973); Nelson (1973a).
3 M. Barrett (1985); Bates et al. (1988); Dromi (1987); Kuczaj & Barrett (1986); MacNamara (1982); McShane (1980); Nelson (1985); Schlesinger (1982); Sinha (1988); and M. Smith & Locke (1988).
4 Dewey (1935, p. 251). This summary by Dewey was based largely on a survey in French by O. Decroly, (*Comment l'enfant arrive à parle chez l'enfant*, Vols. 1–2, Cahiers de la Centrale, 1934) and is quoted as well in McCarthy (1946, 1954).
5 E.g., Oller (1980); Oller et al. (1976); Stark (1980, 1986).
6 E.g., Bateson (1975); Bullowa (1979); Fogel & Thelen (1987); Harding & Golinkoff (1979). See K. Bloom (1990) for a review.

7 For an exception to this general consensus, see Dromi (1987).
8 See in particular Dore (1983); Dore et al. (1976); Halliday (1975); Leopold (1939); Vihman & McCune (1992).
9 Leopold (1939, p. 164).
10 In particular by Bonvillian, Orlansky, & Novack (1983); Orlansky & Bonvillian (1988). See Newport & Meier (1985) for discussion.
11 Goodwyn & Acredolo (1993); Petitto (1991).
12 Meier & Newport (1985).
13 Bates et al. (1979, p. 51). See also Whitehurst, Kedesdy, & White (1982).
14 E.g., Anglin (1977); M. Barrett (1985); M. Barrett et al. (1991); Bates et al. (1979); L. Bloom (1979); Dore (1983); Dromi (1987); Nelson (1985); Nelson & Lucariello (1985); Schlesinger (1982); Werner & Kaplan (1963).
15 L. Bloom (1973); Schlesinger (1982).
16 Augustinius (397/1945, pp. 8–9). Children also depend on what they *overhear* in the nonostensive conversations of other persons. Daphne Fox pointed out to me how much deaf children miss in this regard.
17 Beckwith (1991).
18 Sperber & Wilson (1986, p. 63).
19 Quine (1960, pp. 28–29).
20 There have been many treatments and discussions of Quine's "Gavagai"; I refer the reader in particular to the cogent and engaging analysis by David Premack (1986).
21 E.g., E. Clark (1987); Hirsh-Pasek, Golinkoff, & Reeves (in press); Landau, Smith, & Jones (1988); Markman (1989, 1992); Markman & Hutchinson (1984); Waxman & Kosowski (1990); Waxman & Senghas (1992).
22 In particular the reviews by Golinkoff et al. (1991) and Nelson (1988); Markman's (1989) extensive review of the literature relevant to her own contributions; and papers in Gelman & Byrnes (1991).
23 Chomsky (1965). See, for example, Carey (1982); E. Clark (1987); Gathercole (1987); Markman (1989, 1992); Nelson (1988); Newport (1981); Soja, Carey, & Spelke (in press); papers in S. Gelman & Byrnes (1991).
24 Nelson (1988, pp. 240–241).
25 Sperber & Wilson (1986, p. 46).
26 Fauconnier (1985, pp. 168–169).
27 Golinkoff et al. (1991).
28 E.g., Freyd (1983); Markman (1992); Newport (1981).
29 E.g., Golinkoff, Hirsh-Pasek, Bailey, & Wenger (1992); Golinkoff et al. (1991); Landau et al. (1988); Markman (1989, 1992). See also R. Brown (1958) an MacNamara (1982).
30 E.g., Bates et al. (1988); L. Bloom (1973); Gopnik (1982); Hampson & Nelson (in press); Nelson (1973a); Nelson, Hampson, & Shaw (1993); Pine (1992).

31 E.g., Tomasello & Kruger (1992) and several contributors to S. Gelman & Byrnes (1991).
32 Markman (1989).
33 Summarized in ibid.
34 See in particular J. Mandler (1983, 1984); Nelson (1985).
35 Lifter & Bloom (1989); see Chapter 10.
36 Markman (1989, pp. 28, 36).
37 See citations in Markman (1989), and see Nelson (1988) and Golinkoff et al. (1991, 1992).
38 Markman (1989, p. 37).
39 Bates et al. (1988); L. Bloom (1973); Gopnik (1982, 1988b); Hampson & Nelson (in press); McCune-Nicolich (1981); Nelson (1973a); Pine (1992); and the results in Chapter 9.
40 Markman (1992).
41 M. Barrett (1978); Dromi (1987).
42 Markman (1989) and E. Clark (1987, 1991), respectively.
43 Markman (1989, p. 190). Parenthetically, the mutual exclusivity hypothesis is inconsistent with the results in Markman & Hutchinson (1984): When shown a dog and some dog food and asked to "find another *sud*," children typically chose another dog, presumably having little difficulty accepting a new name for a category for which they already knew a name. See also Golinkoff et al. (1991); Merriman & Bowman (1989); Nelson (1988).
44 Carey & Bartlett (1978).
45 E. Clark (1991, p. 31).
46 Golinkoff et al. (1991, pp. 6, 55). See also the results of experiments with adults and 2-year-olds in Golinkoff et al. (1992). Markman has also more recently suggested that "multiple mechanisms are to be expected for solving important problems" (1992, p. 94).

Golinkoff et al.'s (1992) "novel name for a nameless category" principle is consistent with the "bias to fill lexical gaps" that leads a child to assume that a new word names an object for which the child does not already have a word (E. Clark, 1987; Merriman & Bowman, 1989).
47 Quine (1960, p. 28).
48 Braunwald (1978).
49 An exception to this common observation is the study by Huttenlocher & Smiley (1987); they claimed that the children in their study applied object names "taxonomically," using object words only with the correct (adult) range of referents. See, however, the critique of their study by Nelson (1988), who pointed out that the older ages of their subjects and the methods they used could have been

responsible for the results Huttenlocher & Smiley reported and hence their conclusions.

50 Werner (1948).

51 E.g., Anglin (1977); Bowerman (1978); E. Clark (1973); Dromi (1987); Greenfield (1973); Rescorla (1980).

52 L. Bloom (1973, p. 72).

53 See Anglin (1977); M. Barrett (1986); M. Barrett et al. (1991); Bates et al. (1979); Braunwald (1978); Dromi (1987); Gruendel (1977); McShane (1980); Reich (1976); Schlesinger (1982).

54 M. Barrett et al. (1991).

55 E.g., Mervis & Mervis (1982).

56 L. Bloom (1973, pp. 72–73).

57 Bowerman (1978, p. 273).

58 E.g., Rescorla (1980). A possible third category of idiosyncratic extension was reported by Dromi (1987) as "unclassified extension," or the ambiguous use of words. Examples occurred in her data most often with the earliest words her daughter used. However, it is not clear whether they constitute a real category for the child or have more to do with the possibility that the data available for interpretation were incomplete.

59 Reproduced in Bar-Adon & Leopold (1971, p. 37).

60 L. Bloom (1973, p. 79); see also Kuczaj (1986); Nelson (1985). Since this example in *One Word at a Time* I have had the experience of standing at a fence next to a young family with a small child and actually seeing the mother point to a horse in the field and hearing her say, "Look at that big *dog*." Carolyn Mervis has since documented the tendency most parents have to use words they believe their child is most likely to understand (Mervis & Mervis 1982).

61 M. Barrett (1986); Bates et al. (1979); L. Bloom (1973); L. Bloom & Hafitz (1985); Dore (1983); Greenfield, Reilly, Leaper, & Baker (1985); Nelson (1985); Nelson & Lucariello (1985); Werner & Kaplan (1963).

62 E.g., Piaget (1947/1960).

63 See in particular M. Barrett (1985); Bates et al. (1979); L. Bloom (1973); Dockrell & Campbell (1986); Dromi (1987); Greenberg & Kuczaj (1982); Nelson (1985); Schlesinger (1982) for different versions of something like this chain of events.

64 E.g., L. Bloom (1973); Gopnik & Choi (1990); Gopnik & Meltzoff (1986b); Schlesinger (1982). This observation is ordinarily assumed by most researchers but is sometimes not clearly understood.

65 Greenberg & Kuczaj (1982); Kuczaj (1986); Nelson 1985; Schlesinger (1982).

66 Bates et al. (1979), citing the phenomenon of "word realism," make the point that even older preschool children can continue to believe that a word is a part of the object that it names (p. 60).

67 In R. Brown (1965, pp. 311–312).

68 See *One Word at a Time* (L. Bloom, 1973) for an account of how saying a word can cue a chaining of thematically related successive words.

69 Oviatt (1982); Woodward, Markman, & Fitzsimmons (1991).

70 Carey & Bartlett (1978); Dollaghan (1985).

71 Leaving aside the obvious production requirements for saying the word.

72 Chapman, Bird, & Schwartz (1990); Dollaghan (1985).

73 E.g., Nelson (1985).

74 L. Bloom & Beckwith (1986); L. Bloom, Beckwith, Capatides, & Hafitz (1988).

75 Campbell (1979, p. 424).

76 Dockrell & Campbell (1986, p. 151).

77 C. Stern & Stern (1907). See Also L. Bloom (1973); Corrigan (1978); Dromi (1987); Goldfield & Reznick (1990); Gopnik & Meltzoff (1987); Nelson (1973a).

78 Fischer, Pipp, & Bullock (1984).

79 Nelson (1985, pp. 97, 85).

80 See L. Bloom et al. (1985) and Lifter & Bloom (1989).

81 Fischer et al. (1984); Kagan (1981); Langer (1980).

82 Gopnik & Meltzoff (1987).

83 Lucariello (1987).

84 E.g., Gentner (1982); Goldin-Meadow, Seligman, & Gelman (1976); Schwartz & Leonard (1984); Tomasello & Kruger (1992).

85 Gopnik & Choi (1990).

86 The title of a book by Joseph Jaffe and Stanley Feldstein (1970) that subsequently proved to be prophetic for vocal exchanges with infants. See D. Stern et al. (1975) and, more recently, Beebe & Jaffe (1992); Jasnow et al. (1988).

87 Bruner (1975, p. 18); see Bruner's later work, especially *Child's Talk* (1983).

88 Dore (1975, p. 37).

89 Dore (1983, 1985).

90 Griffiths (1985, p. 89); the taxonomy he used is attributed to J. Searle, A taxonomy of illocutionary acts, in K. Gunderson (Ed.), *Minnesota studies in the philosophy of science* (Vol. 7, pp. 344–369), Minneapolis: University of Minnesota Press, 1975.

91 The original C. Stern & Stern (1907) study has not been translated from the German. This passage is a citation of the 1907 study that appeared in W. Stern (1924, p. 162) and was reprinted in Bar-Adon & Leopold (1971, p. 46).

92 These words are used by both Helen Keller (p. 22) and Anne Sullivan (pp. 312, 315) in *The Story of My Life* (Keller 1902/1905).

93 A "supplementary account of Helen Keller's life and education" was published along with the autobiography (1902/1905), edited by John Albert Macy and based upon contemporary reports and letters from Anne Mansfield Sullivan. These

letters during the first year of her work with Helen were addressed to Sophia C. Hopkins at the Perkins Institution.

94 Sullivan (1905, p. 312).

95 Ibid., p. 316.

96 Beginning with the Sterns (1907). See, for example, Dore (1978); Dromi (1987); Gillis (1986); Gopnik & Meltzoff (1987); McShane (1980).

97 Bates et al. (1979).

98 E.g., Rescorla (1980).

99 Gershkoff-Stowe & Smith (1991).

100 As far as I know, connectionist models have not been extended to children's early word learning, which would seem to be a natural venue. For a connectionist account at the level of lexical items (the polysemous word *over*), see Harris (1990).

101 Schwartz (1988); see also MacKain (1988).

102 See also Dockrell & Campbell (1986).

103 Carey (1978) and G. Miller (1986, p. 9; Miller's is a conservative estimate based on the average high school graduate's knowing about 80,000 words, according to dictionary sampling).

104 Dromi (1987); the numbers given here were read from the tick marks on the figure.

105 Goldfield & Reznick (1990).

106 Bates et al. (1988).

107 Dale (1991); Dale, Bates, Reznick, & Morisset (1989).

108 E.g., Bruner (1975, 1983); Lock (1978a); Sugarman (1978); Tomasello (1988).

109 Bates et al. (1979); Franco & Butterworth (1991); Lempert & Kinsbourne (1985); Werner (1948).

110 Akhtar, Dunham, & Dunham (1991); Masur (1982); Roth (1987); Tomasello & Farrar (1986).

111 Bretherton (1988); Golinkoff (1986).

112 Mervis & Mervis (1982).

113 Gopnik (1982); Gopnik & Meltzoff (1986b).

114 Hamburger & Crain (1987).

115 Beckwith (1988).

6. TRANSLATION FROM THEORY TO METHOD

1 See, for example, L. Bloom (1974b); L. Bloom & Lahey (1978).

2 Uzgiris & Hunt (1975).

3 Braine (1963); R. Brown & Bellugi (1964); R. Brown & Fraser (1963); W. Miller & Ervin (1964).

4 The first published report from this study of early syntax appeared in L. Bloom (1970), and subsequent reports were published as a collection in L. Bloom (1991a); the rationale for the criteria for selecting the subjects in this study is discussed in L. Bloom (1991a, ch. 1).
5 Slobin (1985).
6 Blake (1984); P. Miller (1982); Stockman & Vaughn-Cook (1989).
7 Feagans & Haskins (1986).
8 Hart (1982); Tough (1982).
9 Herbers (1982).
10 We tried to recruit children of Asian-American parents but were unsuccessful, most likely because, unfortunately, we had no Asian-Americans on our research team.
11 I thank Robert T. Carter for pointing this out to me.
12 Schieffelin (1991).
13 According to the norms provided by Gesell & Amatruda (1941). Because we were administering the Uzgiris & Hunt (1975) object permanence scales for theoretically motivated reasons (see Chapter 10), we were reluctant also to use other standardized assessments that might have added stress to the sessions, such as the Bayley Scale of Infant Development (Bayley, 1969) or the Strange Situation (Ainsworth & Wittig, 1969).
14 The three children who were not presented with the task were the three who had been the original subjects of Karin Lifter's dissertation (1982) and the pilot subjects for the larger study.
15 Following a tradition begun by Peggy Miller in her study of the language development of three girls from a white working-class community in South Baltimore (1982) and Ira Blake in her study of the language development of three working-class black children in New York City (1984). The children whose portraits are presented here were chosen simply because they were drawn at the time the data were being collected; several other portraits were begun at that time but not finished.
16 Caldera, Huston, & O'Brien (1989).
17 O'Brien & Nagle (1987).
18 Furrow, Nelson, & Benedict (1979); Newport, Gleitman, & Gleitman (1977).
19 Scheer, Beckwith, & Bloom (1990). The analyses were performed twice, first at the end of the single-word period when the children had begun to use a great many different words (the Vocabulary Spurt) and again when they began to combine words to form their first simple sentences (Multi-word Speech). The results were essentially the same at both times.
20 Capatides (1990); Capatides & Bloom (1993).
21 Beckwith, Bloom, Albury, Raqib, & Booth (1985).

22 See McCarthy (1954) for a thorough review of this literature, and Templin (1957) for what was no doubt the best and probably the last effort in this era of research.
23 E.g., R. Brown (1957).
24 Chomsky (1957).
25 E.g., Braine (1963); R. Brown & Fraser (1963); W. Miller & Ervin (1964).
26 Sapir (1921, p. 10).
27 L. Bloom (1970).
28 R. Brown (1973).
29 Bates (1976); Ervin-Tripp (1964).
30 Schieffelin (1979, 1990).
31 Lévi-Strauss (1963, p. 272). The material in this section appeared originally in L. Bloom (1974b).
32 Beer (1973, pp. 49, 54).
33 Ochs (1979, p. 44).
34 Ochs (1979).
35 L. Bloom & Lahey (1978); J. Edwards (1992).
36 E.g., L. Bloom (1973); L. Bloom & Lahey (1978).
37 Gesell (1935, p. 6), quoted in Beckwith et al. (1985).
38 This section contains material presented originally in Beckwith et al. (1985).
39 Beckwith, Tinker, & Bloom (1993).
40 Beckwith, et al. (1985); L. Bloom (1974b); L. Bloom & Lahey (1978); J. Edwards (1992); MacWhinney & Snow (1992); Ochs (1979).

7. DEVELOPMENTS IN EXPRESSION

1 The results in this chapter were reported originally in L. Bloom, Beckwith, Capatides, & Hafitz (1988).
2 See Schlosberg (1952, 1954); Woodworth (1938); and, more recently, Bullock & Russell (1986). See Schlosberg (1954) and P. Young (1959), for accounts of the "pleasantness-unpleasantness" and intensity dimensions of emotion; D. Stern et al. (1983) for discussion of gradient and categorical information in the emotional signal.
3 See Adamson & Bakeman (1982), Ricciuti & Poresky (1972), and Stechler & Carpenter (1967) for examples of studies that used gradient information in the study of affect expression and emotional development.
4 Ekman & Friesen (1978).
5 The procedures we used for coding, with reliability measures and results, have been reported in a number of publications from this study: for example, L. Bloom & Beckwith (1989); L. Bloom, Beckwith, & Capatides (1988); L. Bloom, Beckwith, Capatides, & Hafitz (1988); L. Bloom & Capatides (1987a); Capatides & Bloom (1993).

6 Indeed, the children tended not to express emotion during certain kinds of object play (Beckwith, Tinker, & L. Bloom, 1993); other research has shown that children playing with toys alone in the presence of their mothers are most apt to be expressing the emotions category of interest (presumably neutral affect) (Phillips & Sellitto, 1990).
7 Cole et al. (1992); Papoušek et al. (1986); Malatesta et al. (1989).
8 As Michael Lewis reminded me.
9 See Connell & Furman (1984) and Emde & Harmon (1984) for justification of a focus on times of known transition for analyses in longitudinal studies.
10 The mothers' diaries were not used as a source of their children's new words from month to month, because mothers were inconsistent in their reporting. Some were highly motivated to keep a diary and faithful to the task; others were more casual and less persistent; and some simply weren't interested or motivated (despite our encouragement).
11 L. Bloom (1970, 1991a); R. Brown (1973); Cazden (1968).
12 See Beckwith (1988), Rispoli (1987), and Rispoli & Bloom (1987) for aspects of the children's development around MW.
13 Danto (1973); de Sousa (1987).
14 E.g., Campos et al. (1983); Stein & Levine (1987).
15 See, for example, the sorts of rules that have been proposed for determining whether we are licensed to attribute to children an intention to act or to communicate, or some sort of planning, suggested by Bates (1976), Bretherton (1988), Greenfield (1980), and Harding & Golinkoff (1979).
16 E.g., Dennett (1978, 1983).
17 These attributions for emotional expressions and words were not independent, because of the instances in which a word was said at the same time a child also expressed emotion. For this reason, the data were treated only descriptively.
18 Adamson & Bakeman (1982); S. Jones et al. (1991); M. Lewis & Michalson (1983).
19 E.g., Campos & Stenberg (1981); Feinman & Lewis (1983); Klinnert, Campos, Sorce, Emde, & Svejda (1983).
20 Bullowa (1979) and Adamson & Bakeman (1985), respectively.

8. DEVELOPMENTS IN AFFECT EXPRESSION

1 Arnold (1960).
2 E.g., Lazarus (1991); G. Mandler (1984, 1990); Oatley & Johnson-Laird (1987); Roseman (1984); Schachter & Singer (1962); Stein & Levine (1987, 1990).
3 E.g., Isen (1984, 1990).
4 E.g., Campos et al. (1983); Frijda (1986); Scherer (1984); Sroufe, Schork, Motti, Lawroski, & LaFreniere (1984); Wozniak (1986).

5 E.g., Izard (1977); M. Lewis & Michalson (1985).

6 This issue has a history in the literature, which I will sidestep here and instead cite the well-known "debate" between Zajonc (1980, 1984) and Lazarus (1982, 1984) and the research and discussion that have fallen out from these two efforts to explain the relative primacy of emotion and cognition.

7 E.g., Darwin (1892/1913); Izard, Huebner, Risser, McGinnes, & Dougherty (1980).

8 E.g., Dore (1983); Emde, Gaensbauer, & Harmon (1976); Lock (1978b); Stechler & Carpenter (1967); D. Stern (1977).

9 Cited in Aarsleff (1976, p. 10).

10 E.g., Dore (1983); Hilke (1988); Trevarthen (1979).

11 Halliday (1975); D. Stern (1985).

12 Camras (1985); Davitz (1964, 1969); Scherer (1986).

13 The original report of this research is in L. Bloom & Beckwith (1989); see also Beckwith, Tinker, & Bloom (1993) for subsequent related findings.

14 Among others, Kinsbourne (1988); Rothbart (1973); Stein & Jewett (1987).

15 Bakeman (1978); Sackett (1974, 1979).

16 This result was reported originally in L. Bloom & Beckwith (1989). We are currently extending the analysis to the children's object play (Beckwith, Tinker, & Bloom, 1993). Several changes were made in the context of this second study. All the children's transcripts were verified once again by independent coders, which resulted in some changes to the data base. More important, the lag analysis program for determining the occurrence of behaviors around target events was substantially revised, as were the procedures for obtaining the baseline rate of a behavior and computing z-scores. Another adjustment was made in determining the occurrence of a lagged variable (such as emotional expression) during the target event (such as words or object play) in order to correct for the two sources of possible error in onset times when two events were coded instead of one. This adjustment corrected for what in the original report had been an overestimation of overlapping emotional expression with words as the targets. The corrected result (presented in Fig. 8.4) retained the essential features of the original result.

17 Dore (1983, p. 168).

18 E.g., Hilke (1988).

19 E.g., Malatesta (1981, p. 15).

20 Kinsbourne (1975, p. 81).

21 See Best & Queen (1989), Kinsbourne & Bemporad (1984), and Tucker & Frederick (1989) for reviews of the relevant literature.

22 E.g., Berndt, Caramazza, & Zurif (1983); Blumstein & Cooper (1974); Kent (1984); Levy (1969); V. Molfese, Molfese, & Parsons (1983); Ross (1985).

23 Best (1988).
24 E.g., Kirk (1985); Levy (1985); D. Molfese, Freeman, & Palermo (1975); Witelson (1987).
25 Tucker (1986, p. 273); see also Turkewitz, Ecklund-Flores, & Devenny (1990).
26 The original report of this analysis is in L. Bloom & Capatides (1987a).
27 E.g., L. Bloom & Lahey (1978); R. Brown (1973).
28 This finding dates from the classic study of Edith Davis in 1937. More recently, however, research has shown that the language development of first- and second-born children does not really differ qualitatively (e.g., Toledano, 1991).
29 Tests for independent samples, $t = -3.085$, $p = .012$ at FW; but $p = .328$ and .843 at VS and MW, respectively. Confidence levels for these comparisons are given here because they have not been reported elsewhere.
30 Reported originally in L. Bloom & Capatides (1987a).
31 Epport (1987) and Nachman (1986). A related finding is that mothers' reports of how often their infants smile and laugh at 8 and 12 months of age were correlated with lower scores on the Bayley Scales of Infant Development, a measure that includes a number of language-relevant items (Fagen, Singer, Ohr, & Fleckenstein, 1987).
32 Hart (1982); Tough (1982).
33 I thank Robert T. Carter for suggesting that we do this.
34 E.g., McCall (1979, 1986).
35 The original report of this analysis is in L. Bloom, Beckwith, & Capatides (1988).
36 I thank Kathleen Bloom for suggesting the two subgroups.
37 Adamson & Bakeman (1985).
38 E.g., J. Brown (1964); Kopp & Vaughn (1982); Olson & Sherman (1983).
39 Kagan (1979, p. 175).
40 Carol Malatesta was kind enough to review several of our videotapes on February 19, 1987 and code them according to the Affex coding scheme.
41 Izard (1986).
42 E.g., Allport (1937); Goldsmith (1983); Goldsmith & Campos (1982); Rothbart (1981).
43 Allert, Scholom, & Koller (1984); Campos et al. (1983); Goldsmith & Campos (1982); McCall (1986); Plomin & Dunn (1986).
44 Reported originally in Wikstrom & Bloom (1987).
45 E.g., Allert et al. (1984); McCall (1986); Thomas & Chess (1977).
46 Connell & Furman (1984); Dunn (1986); Fogel & Thelen (1987).
47 This analysis was Joanne Capatides' doctoral dissertation; see Capatides (1990) and Capatides & Bloom (1993).
48 Such effects have been found with much younger infants (Bell & Ainsworth, 1972; Malatesta, Grigoryev, Lamb, Albin, & Culver 1986).

49 L. Bloom & Capatides (1987a); Capatides & Bloom (1993); Kopp (1987, 1989); Thompson (1990).
50 E.g., Hochschild (1979); M. Lewis & Michalson (1983); M. Lewis & Saarni (1985).
51 As has been reported also by Dunn, Bretherton, & Munn (1987) and P. Miller & Sperry (1987).
52 Izard & Malatesta (1987); Ochs & Schieffelin (1989).

9. DEVELOPMENTS IN WORD LEARNING

1 See, for example, K. Bloom (1990); Kuhl & Meltzoff (1984); Studdert-Kennedy (1979). Speech, however, is not a privileged modality for language, as we know from studies of the acquisition of signed words (e.g., Goodwyn & Acredolo, 1993; Newport & Meier, 1985; and Petitto & Marentette, 1991).
2 De Boysson-Bardies & Vihman (1991).
3 See, for example, Dore (1983); Dore et al. (1976); Vihman & McCune (1992).
4 Erin Tinker and Cheryl Margulis performed the prodigious work of confirming the accuracy of the original transcriptions, assembling the individual cumulative vocabularies, and summarizing them for the 14 children in the analyses reported here; see L. Bloom, Tinker, & Margulis (1993).
5 For these analyses, we counted all the forms in which a particular word appeared as only a single different word: for example, *Ma, Mama, Mommy,* and *Ema* (Hebrew) were counted as the single word type *Mama*. Person names were rare and were included only if all the children had the opportunity to say the same words (e.g., *Bert* and *Ernie*). The children's own names, names of the investigators, and grandmothers' names were counted as the generic names *self, investigator, grandmother* only once (see the appendix); other person names ($n = 11$) were not counted.
6 These results are presented more fully in L. Bloom et al. (in press).
7 L. Bloom et al. (in press).
8 Markman (1992); see Chapter 5.
9 From Nelson (1973a) and L. Bloom (1973), respectively.
10 Nelson (1973a); Bates et al. (1988).
11 Menyuk, Liebergott, Schultz, Chesnick, & Ferrier (1991). Their population included 27 full-term babies and 26 infants born prematurely, but the two groups did not differ (using chronological age for the prematures). The data they reported were obtained from both home-visit recordings and mother diaries.
12 Golinkoff & Hirsh-Pasek (1987); Oviatt (1980).
13 Pine (1992).
14 Bates et al. (1988).
15 Personal communication, November 3, 1992; Hampson & Nelson (in press).
16 L. Bloom (1973, p. 112); see also L. Bloom & Lahey (1978).

17 See in particular Dorothea McCarthy's reviews (1946, 1954).
18 E.g., Anglin (1977); M. Barrett (1986); M. Barrett et al. (1991); Reich (1976). When the observation of underextension has been disputed, it is usually because the data are simply too sparse. For example, Huttenlocher and Smiley (1987) claimed that such instances of word use did not occur, but a careful reading of their procedures and the data they report reveal that their sampling procedures most probably missed their subjects' earliest word use (see Nelson, 1988).
19 E.g., Corrigan (1978); McCune-Nicolich (1981); Menn & Hazelkorn (1977).
20 Lifter (1982).
21 L. Bloom (1973). Lorraine McCune, Alison Gopnik, and Michael Tomasello (among others) have since examined the concepts underlying relational words more thoroughly in relation to other developments in cognition (Gopnik, 1982, 1988b; Gopnik & Choi, 1990; Gopnik & Meltzoff, 1984, 1987; McCune-Nicolich, 1981; Tomasello & M. Farrar, 1984).
22 Gopnik & Meltzoff (1986a).
23 L. Bloom (1970); R. Brown (1973).
24 These were similar to the pre-linguistic "proto-declaratives" described by Bates et al. (1979).
25 This analysis is reported more fully in L. Bloom (in press); both this and the subsequent analysis were carried out with the help of Jeremie Hafitz.
26 Previous research that has looked for evidence of "displaced speech" has typically focused on talk about past events (e.g., Sachs, 1983).
27 Chi-square $(1, N = 14) = 5.273, p = .022$.
28 Fauconnier (1985). The considerable effort this can take in the "negotiation of meaning" in children's early conversations with caregivers has been documented by Roberta Golinkoff (1983b, 1986).
29 In studies by Haith, Hazan, and Goodman (1988) and Ruff, Capozzoli, Dubiner, and Parrinello (1990), respectively.
30 Tomasello & Kruger (1992).
31 L. Bloom (1991a).
32 L. Bloom, Rispoli, Gartner, & Hafitz (1989); Gee & Savasir (1985).
33 Bratman (1987).
34 E.g., Campos et al. (1983); Oatley (1988, 1992); Oatley & Johnson-Laird (1987); Roseman (1984); Stein & Levine (1989).
35 Ochs (1986, p. 252); see also Beckwith (1991); L. Bloom & Beckwith (1989); Smiley & Huttenlocher (1989).
36 E.g., Bretherton et al. (1986); Ridgeway et al. (1985).
37 L. Bloom & Beckwith (1989).
38 Sapir (1921).
39 Capatides (1990); Capatides & Bloom (1993); see Chapter 8.

40 Dunn et al. (1987).
41 Clore & Ortony (1987).
42 Ortony, Clore, & Collins (1988, p. 13).
43 E.g., Oatley (1988, 1992); Oatley & Johnson-Laird (1987); Roseman (1984); Stein & Levine (1989).
44 Bloom & Capatides (1987b); Hood & Bloom (1979); see also Bretherton et al. (1986).
45 Izard & Malatesta (1987); Ochs & Schieffelin (1989).
46 E.g., Kopp (1989); Thompson (1990); Capatides & Bloom (1993).
47 Kenny (1985, p. 32).
48 T. Brown (1991).
49 Beckwith (1988); Rispoli (1987); Rispoli & Bloom (1987).

10. DEVELOPMENTS IN COGNITION

1 Lifter (1982) and Lifter & Bloom (1989); see also L. Bloom et al. (1985).
2 Uzgiris & Hunt (1975; "The Development of visual pursuit and the permanence of objects").
3 Kopp (1976).
4 Ruff (1986).
5 J. Mandler (1988, 1992).
6 In particular in Lifter & Bloom (1989).
7 Inhelder & Piaget (1964/1969, p. 45); see also R. Gelman & Baillargeon (1983, p. 201) for relevant discussion of such groupings or "schemas" based on a "spatiotemporal" or "part-whole organization," and Markman (1981, 1989). The terms "syntagmatic" or "complementary" associations, relations, or groupings have been used in studies of early cognitive development, particularly those concerned with children's categorizations. The term "thematic relations" has currency in linguistic theory, owing in particular to the semantic theory of Jackendoff (1972), who cited J. Gruber, *Studies in lexical relations* (Bloomington: Indiana University Linguistics Club, 1965), p. 29, for the "fundamental semantic notion . . . [of] *Theme* of a sentence."
8 Piaget (1937/1954, p. 171).
9 Connell & Furman (1984); Emde & Harmon (1984).
10 See L. Bloom et al. (1985) for a review.
11 Piaget (1937/1954).
12 Oakes & Cohen (1990).
13 Kagan (1984); Langer (1980); McCall, Eichorn, & Hogarty (1977); Nelson (1973b); Sugarman (1981, 1982); Zelazo & Kearsley (1980); Zelazo & Leonard (1983).
14 As in previous chapters, only results that reached statistically reliable levels are mentioned here; the details can be found in Lifter & Bloom (1989).

15 Bates et al. (1979); L. Bloom et al. (1985); Piaget (1937/1954); Sinclair (1970).
16 L. Bloom (1973). See, among others, Corrigan (1983); Fischer & Corrigan (1981); Gopnik & Meltzoff (1987); McCune-Nicolich (1981); Nelson & Lucariello (1985).
17 L. Bloom (1991a).
18 Nelson (1985, 1986).
19 Markman (1989).
20 L. Bloom (1973); Nelson (1985); Nelson & Lucariello (1985); Sinclair (1970).
21 L. Bloom (1973); see also Gopnik (1988b) and McCune-Nicolich (1981).
22 Lucariello (1987).
23 J. Mandler, Bauer, & McDonough (1991).
24 Baillargeon (1992); L. Cohen (1988); J. Mandler (1988, 1992); Spelke (1991).
25 Oakes & Cohen (1990).
26 Uzgiris & Hunt (1975).
27 L. Bloom et al. (1985).
28 Broughton (1981); Broughton & Zahaykevich (1980).
29 Corrigan (1978).
30 Anisfeld (1984, p. 81).
31 E.g., Brainerd (1978); L. Cohen (1988); Fischer (1980); Leslie (1988); J. Mandler (1988, 1992); Spelke (1988, 1991).
32 Lifter & Bloom (1989).
33 E.g., Bates et al. (1979); Corrigan (1978).
34 Bates et al. (1979); Nelson (1979).
35 J. Mandler (1984).
36 L. Bloom et al. (1985); see also Ashmead & Perlmutter (1980) for examples of recalling an object in a temporary location in the context of ongoing activity at 11 months of age.
37 Piaget (1937/1954, p. 18).
38 Fischer & Jennings (1981); Wellman (1985b); Wellman & Somerville (1982).
39 As opposed to "mediated" memory (DeLoache, 1984).
40 J. Mandler (1988); Sophian (1980).
41 Similar success in finding objects through self-initiated activity was reported in this same age range by Benson & Uzgiris (1985).
42 Age 21 months is a very old norm for building a tower of six blocks (in Gesell & Amatruda, 1941). I thank Lila Braine for suggesting this task to us.
43 Harner, Bloom, & Gronell (1991).
44 E.g., Broen (1972); Snow (1972); Snow & Ferguson (1977).
45 Gopnik & Meltzoff (1987); Lucariello (1987); J. Mandler (1992).
46 In particular, L. Bloom (1973); Gopnik (1982); McCune-Nicolich (1981); and Tomasello & M. Farrar (1984).

11. MEANING AND EXPRESSION

1 Thorndike (1946, p. 294).

2 My reference here is to the host of theoretical and empirical studies centered largely in the Northeast around MIT and inspired by the linguistic theories of adult grammar developed by Noam Chomsky and his followers in the last 35 years. For the relevant citations and discussion of this "learnability" perspective contrasted with a developmental perspective, see, among others, L. Bloom (1991a), Freeman (1989), and Ingram (1989).

3 L. Bloom (1991a).

4 Quine (1960).

5 E.g., E. Clark (1991); Golinkoff et al. (1991); Markman (1989, 1992); Waxman & Senghas (1992). See Chapters 5 and 9.

6 Emde (1984); Newson (1977); Papoušek & Papoušek (1986); Rogoff (1990); D. Stern (1985); Trevarthen (1977, 1979); Trevarthen & Hubley (1978); Werner & Kaplan (1963).

7 See the citation of G. Miller et al. (1960) in the conclusion to Chapter 2.

8 Akhtar et al. (1991); Bruner (1977, 1983); Masur (1982); Tomasello & J. Farrar (1986).

9 *Collins English Dictionary* (1979 ed.); Richard Beckwith, personal communication. Comparisons between the children's words in our study and word counts in dictionaries are from work in progress in collaboration with Richard Beckwith, Erin Tinker, and Cheryl Margulis. We shall also be able to report, eventually, the extent to which the relative frequency of nouns in their mothers' speech in the playroom (and in other corpora of adult speech) matched the relative frequency of object names in the children's speech.

10 Bates et al. (1979).

11 This essential finding, that very young children learning language talk primarily about their own intentions, has been in the literature at least since L. Bloom (1970) and has been reported in several studies since: for example, Huttenlocher, Smiley, & Charney (1983).

12 Beckwith (1988); Rispoli (1987).

13 Werner & Kaplan (1963, pp. 4–5).

14 Capatides (1990); Capatides & Bloom (1993).

15 E.g., respectively Scheiffelin (1979); Brooks-Gunn & Lewis (1982); Malatesta et al. (1986); Bugental (1985). Reviewed in Capatides (1990).

16 McArthur & Baron (1983, p. 218), citing J. Gibson's (1979) theory of affordances in the physical world for a complementary theory of social perception. See also Zebrowitz (1990).

17 Holzman (1984); Rogoff (1990); Tomasello & J. Farrar (1986).

18 For variations on this theme in studies of language acquisition, see, for example, Holzman (1984); Shatz (1981); Tomasello (1992a).
19 Although Piaget acknowledged the necessity of socialization processes for development, he generally ignored the part they play in development; it simply wasn't what he was interested in (Ginsburg, 1981).
20 Rogoff (1990, p. 65 and passim); see also Bruner (1977, 1983).
21 For such "functionalist" accounts of the part played by emotion in development, see, for example, K. Barrett & Campos (1987); Izard (1977); Izard & Malatesta (1987); Sroufe (1979, 1984); D. Stern (1985); and Thompson (1990) as well as the enormous literature on attachment theory and research.
22 Piaget (1954/1981).
23 Capatides & Bloom (1993).
24 D. Stern (1985, pp. 244–245).
25 Among others, Campos et al. (1983); Izard (1977, 1986); Izard & Malatesta (1987); Sroufe (1979, 1984).
26 E.g., K. Barrett & Campos (1987); Bell & Ainsworth (1972); Izard (1979b). For reviews of this literature, see Capatides & Bloom (1993); Thompson (1990); Tronick (1989).
27 See, in particular, Izard (1977, 1986); Izard & Malatesta (1987).
28 Malatesta et al. (1989); Phillips & Sellitto (1990).
29 Beckwith, Tinker, & L. Bloom (1993); Weiner-Margulies et al. (1992) and Phillips & Sellitto (1990), respectively.
30 Turkewitz et al. (1990, p. 595).
31 Bloom (1970); Brown (1973); Schlesinger (1971).
32 Grimshaw (1981); Pinker (1984).
33 See the studies in Bloom (1991a) and, in particular, Bloom et al. (1975).
34 Piaget (1936/1952; 1937/1954; 1945/1962).
35 Bloom, 1973; Brown, 1973; Bates, 1976; and many others since.
36 L. Bloom (1970, 1991a).
37 Jackendoff (1983, p. 188), citing J. Gruber (see Chapter 10, n. 7).
38 Bresnan (1983, p. 24).
39 E.g., Davis (1992); Pinker & Mehler (1988); see Harris (1990).
40 E.g., Clark (1991); Hirsh-Pacek et al. (in press); Markman (1989, 1992). See Chapter 5.
41 Quine (1960, pp. 221, 32).

References

Aarsleff, H. (1976). An outline of language-origins theory since the Renaissance. In S. Harnad, H. Steklis, & J. Lancaster (Eds.), *Origins and evolution of language and speech* (pp. 4–13). Annals of the New York Academy of Sciences (Vol. 280). New York: New York Academy of Sciences.

Adamson, L., & Bakeman, R. (1982). Affectivity and reference: Concepts, methods, and techniques in the study of 6- to 18-month-old infants. In T. Field & A. Fogel (Eds.), *Emotion and early interaction* (pp. 213–236). Hillsdale, NJ: Erlbaum.

Adamson, L., & Bakeman, R. (1985). Affect and attention: Infants observed with mothers and peers. *Child Development, 56,* 582–593.

Ainsworth, M., & Wittig, B. (1969). Attachment and the exploratory behavior of one-year-olds in a strange situation. In B. Foss (Ed.), *Determinants of infant behavior* (Vol. 4, pp. 113–136). London: Methuen.

Akhtar, N., Dunham, F., & Dunham, P. (1991). Directive interactions and early vocabulary development: The role of joint attentional focus. *Journal of Child Language, 18,* 41–49.

Allert, A., Scholom, A., & Koller, T. (1984, April). *Relationships between parent and child temperament ratings: Infant to toddler; and a temperament case study: Infant to toddler to preschooler.* Paper presented at the Fourth Biennial Conference on Infant Studies, New York.

Allport, G. (1937). *Personality: A psychological interpretation.* New York: Holt.

Anglin, J. (1977). *Word, object, and conceptual development.* New York: Norton.

Anisfeld, M. (1984). *Language development from birth to three.* Hillsdale, NJ: Erlbaum.

Arnold, M. (1960). *Emotion and personality: Psychological aspects* (Vol. 1). New York: Columbia University Press.

Ashmead, D., & Perlmutter, M. (1980). Infant memory in everyday life. In M. Perlmutter (Ed.), *Children's memory* (pp. 1–16). New Directions for Child Development, Vol. 10. San Francisco: Jossey-Bass.

Aslin, R., & Pisoni, D. (1980). Some developmental processes in speech perception. In G. Yeni-Komshian, J. Kavanagh, & C. Ferguson (Eds.), *Child phonology: Vol. 2. Perception and production* (pp. 67–96). New York: Academic Press.

Aslin, R., Pisoni, D., & Jusczyk, P. (1983). Auditory development and speech perception in infancy. In M. Haith & J. Campos (Eds.), *Handbook of child psychology: Vol. 2. Infancy and developmental psychobiology* (pp. 573–688). New York: Wiley.

Astington, J., & Gopnik, A. (1988). Knowing you've changed your mind: Children's understanding of the seeing-knowing distinction. In J. Astington, P. Harris, & D. Olson (Eds.), *Developing theories of mind* (pp. 193–206). Cambridge: Cambridge University Press.

Astington, J., Harris, P., & Olson, D. (Eds.) (1988). *Developing theories of mind.* Cambridge: Cambridge University Press.

Augustinius, Saint, Bishop of Hippo (1945). *The confessions of St. Augustine* (E. Pusey, Trans.). London: Dent; New York: Dutton. (Original work published 397)

Baddely, A. (1986). *Working memory.* Oxford: Oxford University Press.

Baillargeon, R. (1992). The object concept revisited: New directions in the investigation of infants' physical knowledge. In C. Granrud (Ed.), *Visual perception and cognition in infancy* (pp. 265–315). Carnegie-Mellon Symposium on Cognition, Vol. 23. Hillsdale, NJ: Erlbaum.

Baillargeon, R., Spelke, E., & Wasserman, S. (1985). Object permanence in 5-month-old infants. *Cognition, 20,* 191–208.

Bakeman, R. (1978). Untangling streams of behavior: Sequential analyses of observational data. In G. Sackett (Ed.), *Observing behavior: Vol. 2. Data collection and analysis methods* (pp. 63–78). Baltimore: University Park Press.

Bakeman, R., & Adamson, J. (1984). Coordinating attention to people and objects in mother-infant and peer-infant interaction. *Child Development, 55,* 1278–1289.

Bar-Adon, A., & Leopold, W. (1971). *Child language: A book of readings.* Englewood Cliffs, NJ: Prentice-Hall.

Barrett, K., & Campos, J. (1987). Perspectives on emotional development: II. A functionalist approach to emotions. In J. Osofsky (Ed.), *Handbook of infant development* (2nd ed., pp. 555–578). New York: Wiley.

Barrett, M. (1978). Lexical development and overextension in child language. *Journal of Child Language, 5,* 205–219.

Barrett, M. (Ed.) (1985). *Children's single-word speech.* New York: Wiley.

Barrett, M. (1986). Early semantic representations and early word-usage. In S. Kuczaj & M. Barrett (Eds.), *The development of word meaning* (pp. 39–67). New York: Springer.

Barrett, M., Harris, M., & Chasin, J. (1991). Early lexical development and maternal speech: A comparison of children's initial and subsequent use of words. *Journal of Child Language, 18,* 21–40.

Bates, E. (1976). *Language in context.* New York: Academic Press.

Bates, E., Benigni, L., Bretherton, I., Camaioni, L., & Volterra, V. (1979). *The emergence of symbols: Communication and cognition in infancy.* New York: Academic Press.

Bates, E., Bretherton, I., & Snyder, L. (1988). *From first words to grammar.* Cambridge: Cambridge University Press.

Bateson, C. (1975). Mother-infant exchanges: The epigenesis of conversational interaction. In D. Aaronson & R. Rieber (Eds.), *Developmental psycholinguistics and communication disorders* (pp. 101–113). Annals of the New York Academy of Sciences, Vol. 263. New York: New York Academy of Sciences.

Bayley, N. (1969). *Bayley scales of infant development.* New York: Psychological Corp.

Beckwith, R. (1988). *Learnability and psychologically constrained grammars.* Unpublished PhD dissertation, Teachers College, Columbia University.

Beckwith, R. (1991). The language of emotion, the emotions, and nominalist bootstrapping. In C. Moore & D. Frye (Eds.), *Children's theories of mind* (pp. 77–95). Hillsdale, NJ: Erlbaum.

Beckwith, R., Bloom, L., Albury, D., Raqib, A., & Booth, R. (1985). Technology and methodology. *Transcript Analysis, 2,* 72–75.

Beckwith, R., Tinker, E., & Bloom, L. (1993, March). *The integration of expressive behaviors and object play.* Poster presented at a meeting of the Society for Research in Child Development, New Orleans.

Beebe, B. (1973). Ontogeny of positive affect in the third and fourth months of the life of one infant. *Dissertation Abstracts International, 35* (2), 1014*B*.

Beebe, B., & Jaffe, J. (1992, May). *Mother-infant vocal dialogues.* Paper presented at the International Conference on Infant Studies, Miami.

Beer, C. (1973). A view of birds. In A. Pick (Ed.), *Minnesota symposia on child psychology* (Vol. 7, pp. 47–86). Minneapolis: University of Minnesota Press.

Bell, S., & Ainsworth, M. (1972). Infant crying and maternal responsiveness. *Child Development, 43,* 1171–1190.

Benson, J., & Uzgiris, I. (1985). Effect of self-initiated locomotion on infant search activity. *Developmental Psychology, 21,* 923–931.

Benson, N. (1990). *Mental capacity constraints on early symbolic processing: The origin of language from a cognitive perspective.* Unpublished doctoral dissertation, York University.

Berndt, R., Caramazza, A., & Zurif, E. (1983). Language functions: Syntax and semantics. In S. Segalowitz (Ed.), *Language functions and brain organization* (pp. 5–28). New York: Academic Press.

Best, C. (1988). The emergence of cerebral asymmetries in early human development: A literature review and a neuroembryological model. In S. Segalowitz & D. Molfese (Eds.), *Developmental implications of brain lateralization* (pp. 5–34). New York: Guilford Press.

Best, C., & Queen, H. (1989). Baby, it's in your smile: Right hemiface bias in infant emotional expressions. *Developmental Psychology, 25,* 264–276.

Bjorklund, D. (Ed.) (1990). *Children's strategies: Contemporary views of cognitive development.* Hillsdale, NJ: Erlbaum.

Blake, I. (1984). *Language development in working class black children: An examination of form, content, and use.* Unpublished PhD dissertation, Teachers College, Columbia University.

Bloom, K. (1974). Eye contact as a setting event for infant learning. *Journal of Experimental Child Psychology, 17,* 250–263.

Bloom, K. (1977). Patterning of infant vocal behavior. *Journal of Experimental Child Psychology, 23,* 367–377.

Bloom, K. (1988). Quality of adult vocalizations affects the quality of infant vocalizations. *Journal of Child Language, 15,* 469–480.

Bloom, K. (1990). Selectivity and early infant vocalization. In J. Enns (Ed.), *The development of attention: Research and theory* (pp. 121–136). New York: Elsevier North-Holland.

Bloom, K., & Esposito, A. (1975). Social conditioning and its proper control procedures. *Journal of Experimental Child Psychology, 19,* 209–222.

Bloom, K., Russell, A., & Wassenberg, K. (1987). Turn taking affects the quality of infant vocalizations. *Journal of Child Language, 14,* 211–227.

Bloom, L. (1970). *Language development: Form and function in emerging grammars.* Cambridge, MA: MIT Press.

Bloom, L. (1973). *One word at a time: The use of single-word utterances before syntax.* The Hague: Mouton.

Bloom, L. (1974a). Talking, understanding and thinking: Developmental relationship between receptive and expressive language. In R. Schiefelbusch & L. Lloyd (Eds.), *Language perspectives – Acquisition, retardation, and intervention* (pp. 285–312). Baltimore: University Park Press.

Bloom, L. (1974b). The accountability of evidence in studies of child language (pp. 82–88). [Commentary on F. Schacter, K. Kirshner, B. Klips, M. Friedricks, & K. Sanders, *Everyday preschool interpersonal speech usage* (1974)]. In *Monographs of the Society for Research in Child Development, 39* (Serial No. 156).

Bloom, L. (1976). An integrative perspective on language development: Keynote address. In *Papers and reports on child language development* (No. 12, pp. 1–22). Department of Linguistics, Stanford University.

Bloom, L. (1981). The importance of language for language development: Linguistic determinism in the 1980s. In H. Winitz (Ed.), *Native language and foreign language acquisition* (pp. 160–171). Annals of the New York Academy of Sciences, Vol. 379. New York: New York Academy of Sciences.

Bloom, L. (1990). Developments in expression: Affect and speech. In N. Stein, B. Leventhal, & T. Trabasso (Eds.), *Psychological and biological approaches to emotion* (pp. 215–245). Hillsdale, NJ: Erlbaum.

Bloom, L. (1991a). *Language development from two to three.* New York: Cambridge University Press.

Bloom, L. (1991b). Representation and expression. In N. Krasnegor, D. Rumbaugh, R. Schiefelbusch, & M. Studdert-Kennedy (Eds.), *Biological and behavioral determinants of language development* (pp. 117–140). Hillsdale, NJ: Erlbaum.

Bloom, L. (1992). Patterns are not enough. [Commentary on Fogel et al. (1992)]. *Social Development,* 1, 143–146.

Bloom, L. (in press). Meaning and expression. In W. Overton & D. Palermo (Eds.), *The ontogenesis of meaning.* Hillsdale, NJ: Erlbaum.

Bloom, L. (1993). Transcription and coding for child language research: The parts are more than the whole. In J. Edwards & M. Lampert (Eds.), *Talking data: Transcription and coding in discourse research* (pp. 149–166). Hillsdale, NJ: Erlbaum.

Bloom, L., & Beckwith, R. (1986). *Intentionality and language development.* Unpublished manuscript.

Bloom, L., & Beckwith, R. (1989). Talking with feeling: Integrating affective and linguistic expression in early language development. *Cognition and Emotion, 3,* 313–342.

Bloom, L., Beckwith, R., & Capatides, J. (1988). Developments in the expression of affect. *Infant Behavior and Development, 11,* 169–186.

Bloom, L., Beckwith, R., Capatides, J., & Hafitz, J. (1988). Expression through affect and words in the transition from infancy to language. In P. Baltes, D. Featherman, & R. Lerner (Eds.), *Life-span development and behavior* (Vol. 8, pp. 99–127). Hillsdale, NJ: Erlbaum.

Bloom, L., & Capatides, J. (1987a). Expression of affect and the emergence of language. *Child Development, 58,* 1513–1522.

Bloom, L., & Capatides, J. (1987b). Sources of meaning in complex syntax: The sample case of causality. *Journal of Experimental Child Psychology, 43,* 112–128.

Bloom, L., & Hafitz, J. (1985, April). *Developments in word learning in the single-word period.* Paper presented at a meeting of the Society for Research in Child Development, Toronto.

Bloom, L., & Lahey, M. (1978). *Language development and language disorders.* New York: Wiley.

Bloom, L., Lahey, M., Hood, L., Lifter, K., & Fiess, K. (1980). Complex sentences: Acquisition of syntactic connectives and the semantic relations they encode. *Journal of Child Language, 7*, 235–261.

Bloom, L., Lifter, K., & Broughton, J. (1985). The convergence of early cognition and language in the second year of life: Problems in conceptualization and measurement. In M. Barrett (Ed.), *Children's single word speech* (pp. 149–178). London: Wiley.

Bloom, L., Miller, P., & Hood, L. (1975). Variation and reduction as aspects of competence in language development. In A. Pick (Ed.), *Minnesota symposia on child psychology* (Vol. 9, pp. 3–55). Minneapolis: University of Minnesota Press.

Bloom, L., Rispoli, M., Gartner, B., & Hafitz, J. (1989). Acquisition of complementation. *Journal of Child Language, 16*, 101–120.

Bloom, L., Tinker, E., & Margulis, C. (in press). *The words children learn. Cognitive Development.*

Blumenthal, A. (1970). *Language and psychology: Historical aspects of psycholinguistics.* New York: Wiley.

Blumstein, S., & Cooper, W. (1974). Hemispheric processing of intonation contours. *Cortex, 10*, 146–158.

Bonvillian, J., Orlansky, M., & Novack, L. (1983). Developmental milestones: Sign language acquisition and motor development. *Child Development, 54*, 1435–1445.

Bower, T. G. R. (1974). *Development in infancy.* San Francisco: Freeman.

Bowerman, M. (1978). The acquisition of word meaning: An investigation into some current conflicts. In N. Waterson & C. Snow (Eds.), *The development of communication* (pp. 263–287). New York: Wiley.

Braine, M. (1963). The ontogeny of English phrase structure: The first phase. *Language, 39*, 1–13.

Brainerd, C. (1978). The stage question in cognitive-developmental theory. *Behavioral and Brain Sciences, 2*, 173–213.

Bratman, M. (1987). *Intention, plans, and practical reason.* Cambridge, MA: Harvard University Press.

Braunwald, S. (1978). Context, word and meaning: Towards a communicational analysis of lexical acquisition. In A. Lock (Ed.), *Action, gesture and symbol: The emergence of language* (pp. 485–527). New York: Academic Press.

Brazelton, T. (1979). Evidence of communication in neonatal behavioral assessment. In M. Bullowa (Ed.), *Before speech: The beginning of interpersonal communication* (pp. 79–88). Cambridge: Cambridge University Press.

Brentano, F. (1966). *The true and the evident.* (R. Chrisholm, Ed.; R. Chrisholm, I. Politzer, & K. Fischer, Trans.). New York: Humanities Press. (Original work published 1930).

Bresnan, J. (1982). The passive in lexical theory. In J. Bresnan (Ed.), *The mental representation of grammatical relations* (pp. 1–86). Cambridge, MA: MIT Press.

Bretherton, I. (1988). How to do things with one word: The ontogenesis of intentional message making in infancy. In M. Smith & J. Locke (Eds.), *The emergent lexicon: The child's development of a linguistic vocabulary* (pp. 225–260). San Diego: Academic Press.

Bretherton, I., & Beeghly, M. (1982). Talking about internal states: The acquisition of an explicit theory of mind. *Developmental Psychology, 18,* 906–921.

Bretherton, I., Fritz, J., Zahn-Wexler, C., & Ridgeway, C. (1986). Learning to talk about emotions: A functionalist perspective. *Child Development, 57,* 529–548.

Bridges, K. (1932). Emotional development in early infancy. *Child Development, 3,* 324–341.

Broen, P. (1972). The verbal environment of the language learning child. *ASHA Monographs, No. 17.* Washington, DC: American Speech and Hearing Association.

Brooks-Gunn, J., & Lewis, M. (1982). Affective exchanges between normal and handicapped infants and their mothers. In T. Field & A. Fogel (Eds.), *Emotion and early interaction* (pp.161–188). Hillsdale, NJ: Erlbaum.

Broughton, J. (1981). Piaget's developmental structuralism: II. Logic and psychology. *Human Development, 24,* 195–225.

Broughton, J., & Freeman-Moir, D. (1982). *The cognitive developmental psychology of James Mark Baldwin: Current theory and research in genetic epistemology.* Norwood, NJ: Ablex.

Broughton, J., & Zahaykevich, M. (1980). Personality and ideology in ego development. In J. Gabel, B. Rousset, & V. Trinh van Thao (Eds.), *Actualité de la dialectique dans les sciences sociales* (pp. 151–210). Paris: Anthropos.

Brown, J. (1964). States in newborn infants. *Merrill-Palmer Quarterly, 10,* 313–327.

Brown, R. (1956). Language and categories. Appendix to J. Bruner, J. Goodnow, & G. Austin, *A study of thinking.* New York: Wiley.

Brown, R. (1957). Linguistic determinism and the part of speech. *Journal of Abnormal and Social Psychology, 55,* 1–5.

Brown, R. (1958). *Words and things.* New York: Free Press.

Brown, R. (1965). *Social psychology.* New York: Free Press.

Brown, R. (1973). *A first language, the early stages.* Cambridge, MA: Harvard University Press.

Brown, R., & Bellugi, U. (1964). Three processes in the child's acquisition of syntax. *Harvard Educational Review, 34,* 133–151.

Brown, R., & Fraser, C. (1963). The acquisition of syntax. In C. Cofer & B. Musgrave (Eds.), *Verbal behavior and verbal learning: Problems and processes* (pp. 158–197). New York: McGraw-Hill.

Brown, T. (1991, June). *Affective dimensions of meaning.* Plenary address at the Annual Symposium of the Jean Piaget Society, Philadelphia.

Bruner, J. (1975). The ontogenesis of speech acts. *Journal of Child Language, 2,* 1–19.

Bruner, J. (1977). Early social interaction and language acquisition. In H. Schaffer (Ed.), *Studies in mother-infant interaction* (pp. 271–289). London: Academic Press.

Bruner, J. (1983). *Child's talk: Learning to use language.* New York: Norton.

Buck, R. (1984). *The communication of emotion.* New York: Guilford.

Bugental, D. (1985). Unresponsive children and powerless adults: Cocreators in affectively uncertain caregiving environments. In M. Lewis & C. Saarni (Eds.), *The socialization of emotions* (pp. 239–261). New York: Plenum.

Bühler, C. (1930). *The first year of life* (P. Greenberg & R. Ripin, Trans.). New York: John Day. (Original work published 1927)

Bullock, M., & Russell, J. (1986). Concepts of emotion in developmental psychology. In C. Izard & P. Read (Eds.), *Measuring emotions in infants and children* (Vol. 2, pp. 203–237). Cambridge: Cambridge University Press.

Bullowa, M. (Ed.) (1979). *Before speech: The beginning of interpersonal communication.* Cambridge: Cambridge University Press.

Burke, K. (1935). *Permanence and change: An anatomy of purpose.* Berkeley and Los Angeles: University of California Press.

Caldera, Y., Huston, A., & O'Brien, M. (1989). Social interactions and play patterns of parents and toddlers with feminine, masculine, and neutral toys. *Child Development, 60,* 70–76.

Campbell, R. (1979). Cognitive development and child language. In P. Fletcher & M. Garman (Eds.), *Language acquisition* (pp. 419–436). Cambridge: Cambridge University Press.

Campbell, R. (1986). Language acquisition and cognition. In P. Fletcher & M. Garman (Eds.), *Language acquisition: Studies in first language development* (2nd ed., pp. 30–48). Cambridge: Cambridge University Press.

Campos, J., & Barrett, K. (1984). Toward a new understanding of emotions and their development. In C. Izard, J. Kagan, & R. Zajonc (Eds.), *Emotions, cognition, and behavior* (pp. 229–263). New York: Cambridge University Press.

Campos, J., Barrett, K., Lamb, M., Goldsmith, H., & Stenberg, C. (1983). Socioemotional development. In M. Haith & J. Campos (Eds.), *Handbook of child psychology: Vol. 2. Infancy and developmental psychobiology* (pp. 783–915). New York: Wiley.

Campos, J., & Stenberg, C. (1981). Perception, appraisal and emotion: The onset of social referencing. In M. Lamb & L. Sherrod (Eds.), *Infant social cognition* (pp. 273–314). Hillsdale, NJ: Erlbaum.

Camras, L. (1985). Socialization of affect communication. In M. Lewis & C. Saarni (Eds.), *The socialization of emotions* (pp. 141–160). New York: Plenum.

Capatides, J. (1990). *Mothers' socialization of their children's experience and expression of emotion.* Unpublished PhD dissertation, Teachers College, Columbia University.

Capatides, J., & Bloom, L. (1993). Underlying process in the socialization of emotion. In C. Rovee-Collier & L. Lipsett (Eds.), *Advances in infancy research* (Vol. 8, pp. 99–135). Hillsdale, NJ: Erlbaum.

Carey, S. (1978). The child as word learner. In M. Halle, J. Bresnan, & G. Miller (Eds.), *Linguistic theory and psychological reality* (pp. 264–293). Cambridge, MA: MIT Press.

Carey, S. (1982). Semantic development: The state of the art. In E. Wanner & L. Gleitman (Eds.), *Language acquisition: The state of the art* (pp. 347–389). Cambridge: Cambridge University Press.

Carey, S., & Bartlett, E. (1978). Acquiring a single new word. *Papers and Reports on Child Language Development* (No. 15, pp. 17–29). Department of Linguistics, Stanford University.

Carey, S., & Gelman, R. (1991). *The epigenesis of mind: Essays on biology and cognition.* Hillsdale, NJ: Erlbaum.

Case, R. (1978). Intellectual development from birth to adulthood: A neo-Piagetian interpretation. In R. Siegler (Ed.), *Children's thinking: What develops?* (pp. 37–72). Hillsdale, NJ: Erlbaum.

Case, R. (1985). *Intellectual development: Birth to adulthood.* New York: Academic Press.

Cazden, C. (1968). The acquisition of noun and verb inflections. *Child Development, 39,* 433–438.

Chapman, R., Bird, E., & Schwartz, S. (1990). Fast mapping of words in event contexts by children with Down Syndrome. *Journal of Speech and Hearing Disorders, 55,* 761–770.

Chomsky, N. (1957). *Syntactic structures.* The Hague: Mouton.

Chomsky, N. (1965). *Aspects of the theory of syntax.* Cambridge, MA: MIT Press.

Clark, E. (1973). What's in a word? On the child's acquisition of semantics in his first language. In T. Moore (Ed.), *Cognitive development and the acquisition of language* (pp. 65–110). New York: Academic Press.

Clark, E. (1987). The principle of contrast: A constraint on language acquisition. In B. MacWhinney (Ed.), *Mechanisms of language acquisition* (pp. 1–33). Hillsdale, NJ: Erlbaum.

Clark, E. (1991). Acquisitional principles in lexical development. In S. Gelman & J. Byrnes (Eds.), *Perspectives on language and thought* (pp. 31–71). Cambridge: Cambridge University Press.

Clark, R. (1978). The transition from action to gesture. In A. Lock (Ed.), *Action, gesture and symbol: The emergence of language* (pp. 231–257). London: Academic Press.

Clarkson, M., & Berg, K. (1983). Cardiac orienting and vowel discrimination in newborns: Crucial stimulus parameters. *Child Development, 54,* 162–171.

Clore, G., & Ortony, A. (1987). The semantics of the affective lexicon. In V. Hamilton, G. Bower, & N. Frijda (Eds.), *Cognitive perspectives on emotion and motivation* (pp. 367–397). Dordrecht: Kluwer Academic.

Cohen, L. (1976). Habituation of infant attention. In T. Tighe & R. Leaton (Eds.), *Habituation: Perspectives from child development, animal behavior, and neurophysiology* (pp. 207–238). Hillsdale, NJ: Erlbaum.

Cohen, L. (1988). An information processing approach to infant cognitive development. In L. Weiskrantz (Ed.), *Thought without language* (pp. 211–288). Oxford: Oxford University Press.

Cole, P., Barrett, K., & Zahn-Wexler, C. (1992). Emotion displays in two-year-olds during mishaps. *Child Development, 63,* 314–324.

Collins, A., & Quillian, M. (1972). How to make a language user. In E. Tulving & W. Donaldson (Eds.), *Organization of Memory* (pp. 309–351). New York: Academic Press.

Collis, G. (1979). Describing the structure of social interaction in infancy. In M. Bullowa (Ed.), *Before speech: The beginning of interpersonal communication* (pp. 111–130). Cambridge: Cambridge University Press.

Connell, J., & Furman, W. (1984). The study of transitions: Conceptual and methodological issues. In R. Emde & R. Harmon (Eds.), *Continuities and discontinuities in development* (pp. 153–173). New York: Plenum.

Corrigan, R. (1978). Language development as related to Stage 6 object permanence development. *Journal of Child Language, 5,* 173–189.

Corrigan, R. (1983). Cognitive correlates of language: Different criteria yield different results. *Child Development, 50,* 617–631.

Corter, J., & Gluck, M. (1992). Explaining basic categories: Feature predictability and information. *Psychological Bulletin, 111,* 291–303.

Cruttenden, A. (1982). How long does intonation acquisition take? *Papers and Reports on Child Language Development* (Vol. 21, pp. 112–118). Department of Linguistics, Stanford University.

Dale, P. (1991). The validity of a parent report measure of vocabulary and syntax at 24 months. *Journal of Speech and Hearing Research, 34,* 565–571.

Dale, P., Bates, E., Reznick, S., & Morisset, C. (1989). The validity of a parent report instrument of child language at twenty months. *Journal of Child Language, 16,* 239–249.

Danto, A. (1973). *Analytical philosophy of action.* Cambridge: Cambridge University Press.

Danto, A. (1983). Toward a retentive materialism. In L. Cauman, I. Levi, C. Parsons, & R. Schwartz (Eds.), *How many questions? Essays in honor of Sidney Morgenbesser* (pp. 243–255). Indianapolis, IN: Hackett.

Darwin, C. (1913). *The expression of the emotions in man and animals.* New York: Appleton. (Original work published 1892)

Darwin, C. (1971). A biographical sketch of an infant [excerpt]. In A. Bar-Adon & W. Leopold (Eds.), *Child language: A book of readings* (pp. 27–28). Englewood Cliffs, NJ: Prentice-Hall. (Original work published 1877 in *Mind, 2,* 285–294)

Davis, E. (1937). The development of linguistic skill in twins, singletons with siblings, and only children from age five to ten years. *Institute of Child Welfare Monographs, 14.* Minneapolis: University of Minnesota Press.

Davis, S. (Ed.) (1992). *Connectionism: Theory and practice.* New York: Oxford University Press.

Davitz, J. (1964). *The communication of emotional meaning.* New York: McGraw-Hill.

Davitz, J. (1969). *The language of emotion.* New York: Academic Press.

De Boysson-Bardies, B., & Vihman, M. (1991). Adaptation to language: Evidence from babbling and first words in four languages. *Language, 67,* 297–319.

De Laguna, G. (1963). *Speech: Its function and development.* Bloomington: Indiana University Press. (Original work published 1927)

De Sousa, R. (1987). *The rationality of emotion.* Cambridge, MA: MIT Press.

DeCasper, A., & Fifer, W. (1980). Of human bonding: Newborns prefer their mothers' voices. *Science, 208,* 1174–1176.

Delack, J. (1976). Aspects of infant speech development in the first year of life. *Canadian Journal of Linguistics, 21,* 17–37.

Delack, J., & Fowlow, P. (1978). The ontogenesis of differential vocalizing: Development of prosodic constrastivity during the first year of life. In N. Waterson & C. Snow (Eds.), *The development of communication* (pp. 93–110). New York: Wiley.

DeLoache, J. (1984). Oh where, oh where: Memory-based searching by very young children. In C. Sophian (Ed.), *Origins of cognitive skills* (pp. 57–80). Hillsdale, NJ: Erlbaum.

Demetriou, A. (Ed.) (1988). *The neo-Piagetian theories of cognitive development: Toward an integration.* New York: Elsevier North-Holland.

Demos, V. (1986). Crying in early infancy: An illustration of the motivational function of affect. In T. Brazelton & M. Yogman (Eds.), *Affective development in infancy* (pp. 39–73). Norwood, NJ: Ablex.

Dennett, D. (1978). *Brainstorms.* Montgomery, VT: Bradford Books.

Dennett, D. (1983). Intentional systems in cognitive ethology: The "Panglossian paradigm" defended. *Behavioral and Brain Sciences, 6,* 343–390.

Dennis, W. (1949). Historical beginnings of child psychology. *Psychological Bulletin, 46*, 224–235.

Dewey, E. (1935). *Behavior development in infants: A survey of the literature on prenatal and postnatal activity 1920–1934*. New York: Columbia University Press.

Dockrell, J., & Campbell, R. (1986). Lexical acquisition strategies in the preschool child. In S. Kuczaj & M. Barrett (Eds.), *The development of word meaning* (pp. 121–154). New York: Springer-Verlag.

D'Odorico, L., & Franco, F. (1991). Selective production of vocalization types in different communicative contexts. *Journal of Child Language, 18*, 475–499.

Dollaghan, C. (1985). Child meets word: "Fast mapping" in preschool children. *Journal of Speech and Hearing Research, 28*, 449–454.

Dore, J. (1975). Holophrases, speech acts, and language universals. *Journal of Child Language, 2*, 21–40.

Dore, J. (1978). Conditions for the acquisition of speech acts. In I. Markova (Ed.), *The social context of language* (pp. 87–111). London: Wiley.

Dore, J. (1983). Feeling, form, and intention in the baby's transition to language. In R. Golinkoff (Ed.), *The transition from prelinguistic to linguistic communication* (pp. 167–190). Hillsdale, NJ: Erlbaum.

Dore, J. (1985). Holophrases revisited: Their "logical" development from dialog. In M. Barrett (Ed.), *Children's single-word speech* (pp. 23–58). London: Wiley.

Dore, J., Franklin, M., Miller, R., & Ramer, A. (1976). Transitional phenomena in early language acquisition. *Journal of Child Language, 3*, 13–28.

Dromi, E. (1987). *Early lexical development*. Cambridge: Cambridge University Press.

Dunn, J. (1986). Commentary: Issues for future research. In R. Plomin & J. Dunn (Eds.), *The study of temperament: Changes, continuities and challenges* (pp. 163–171). Hillsdale, NJ: Erlbaum.

Dunn, J., Bretherton, I., & Munn, P. (1987). Conversations about feeling states between mothers and their young children. *Developmental Psychology, 23*, 132–139.

Edwards, D. (1978). Social relations and early language. In A. Lock (Ed.), *Action, gesture and symbol: The emergence of language* (pp. 449–469). New York: Academic Press.

Edwards, J. (1992). Computer methods in child language research: Four principles for the use of archived data. *Journal of Child Language, 19*, 435–458.

Eimas, P., & Miller, J. (Eds.) (1981). *Perspectives on the study of speech*. Hillsdale, NJ: Erlbaum.

Eimas, P., Siqueland, E., Jusczyk, P., & Vigorito, J. (1971). Speech perception in infants. *Science, 171*, 303–306.

Ekman, P., & Friesen, W. (1976). *Pictures of facial affect*. Palo Alto, CA: Consulting Psychologists.

Ekman, P., & Friesen, W. (1978). *Facial Action Coding System.* Palo Alto, CA: Consulting Psychologists.

Emde, R. (1983). The prerepresentational self and its affective core. In A. Solnit, R. Eissler, & P. Neubauer (Eds.), *The psychoanalytic study of the child* (Vol. 38, pp. 165–192). New Haven, CT: Yale University Press.

Emde, R. (1984). Levels of meaning for infant emotions: A biosocial view. In K. Scherer & P. Ekman (Eds.), *Approaches to emotion* (pp. 77–107). Hillsdale, NJ: Erlbaum.

Emde, R., Gaensbauer, T., & Harmon, R. (1976). *Emotional expression in infancy.* New York: International Universities Press.

Emde, R., & Harmon, R. (1984). Entering a new era in the search for developmental continuities. In R. Emde & R. Harmon (Eds.), *Continuities and discontinuities in development* (pp. 1–11). New York: Plenum.

Epport, K. (1987). *The relationship between facial affect expressiveness and language ability in children born preterm and "at-risk."* Unpublished doctoral dissertation, University of California, Los Angeles.

Ervin-Tripp, S. (1964). An analysis of the interaction of language, topic, and listener. In J. Gumperz & D. Hymes (Eds.), The ethnography of communication. *American Anthropologist, 66* (16, Pt. 2), 86–102.

Ewing, G. (1984). *Presyntax: The development of word order in early child speech.* Unpublished doctoral dissertation, University of Toronto.

Fagen, J., Singer, J., Ohr, P., & Fleckenstein, L. (1987). Infant temperament and performance on the Bayley Scales of Infant Development at 4, 8, and 12 months of age. *Infant Behavior and Development, 10,* 505–512.

Fantz, R. (1964). Visual experience in infants: Decreased attention to familiar patterns relative to novel ones. *Science, 146,* 668–670.

Fauconnier, G. (1985). *Mental spaces: Aspects of meaning construction in natural language.* Cambridge, MA: MIT Press.

Feagans, L., Garvey, C., & Golinkoff, R. (Eds.) (1983). *The origins and growth of communication.* Norwood, NJ: Ablex.

Feagans, L., & Haskins, R. (1986). Neighborhood dialogues of black and white 5-year-olds. *Journal of Applied Developmental Psychology, 7,* 181–200.

Feinman, S., & Lewis, M. (1983). Social referencing and second order effects in ten-month-old infants. *Child Development, 54,* 878–887.

Ferguson, C., & Farwell, C. (1975). Words and sounds in early language acquisition. *Language, 51,* 419–439.

Ferguson, L., & Gopnik, A. (1988). The ontogeny of common sense. In J. Astington, P. Harris, & D. Olson (Eds.), *Developing theories of mind* (pp. 226–243). Cambridge: Cambridge University Press.

Fernald, A. (1990). Intonation and communicative intent in mothers' speech to infants: Is the melody the message? *Child Development, 60*, 1497–1510.

Fernald, A., Taeschner, T., Dunn, J., Papoušek, M., De Boysson-Bardies, B., & Ikuko, F. (1989). A cross-language study of prosodic modifications in mothers' and fathers' speech to preverbal infants. *Journal of Child Language, 16*, 477–501.

Fischer, K. (1980). A theory of cognitive development: The control and construction of hierarchies of skills. *Psychological Review, 87*, 477–531.

Fischer, K., & Corrigan, R. (1981). A skill approach to language development. In R. Stark (Ed.), *Language behavior in infancy and early childhood* (pp. 245–273). New York: Elsevier North-Holland.

Fischer, K., & Jennings, S. (1981). The emergence of representation in search: Understanding the hider as an independent agent. *Developmental Review, 1*, 18–30.

Fischer, K., Pipp, S., & Bullock, D. (1984). Detecting discontinuities in development: Method and measurement. In R. Emde & R. Harmon (Eds.), *Continuities and discontinuities in development* (pp. 95–121). New York: Plenum.

Fischer, K., Shaver, P., & Carnochan, P. (1990). How emotions develop and how they organize development. *Cognition and Emotion, 4*, 81–127.

Fodor, J. (1979). *The language of thought*. Cambridge, MA: Harvard University Press.

Fogel, A. (1981). The ontogeny of gestural communication: The first six months. In R. Stark (Ed.), *Language behavior in infancy and early childhood* (pp. 17–44). New York: Elsevier North-Holland.

Fogel, A., Nwokah, E., Dedo, J., Messinger, D., Dickson, K., Matusov, E., & Holt, S. (1992). Social process theory of emotion: A dynamic systems approach. *Social Development, 1*, 122–142.

Fogel, A., & Reimers, M. (1989). On the psychobiology of emotions and their development. [Commentary on Malatesta, Culver, Tesman, & Shepard, 1989]. *Monographs of the Society for Research in Child Development, 54* (Serial No. 219), 105–113.

Fogel, A., & Thelen, E. (1987). Development of early expressive and communicative action: Reinterpreting the evidence from a dynamic systems perspective. *Developmental Psychology, 23*, 747–761.

Fraiberg, S. (1977). *Insights from the blind*. New York: Basic.

Franco, F., & Butterworth, G. (1991, April). *Infant pointing: Prelinguistic reference and co-reference*. Paper presented at a meeting of the Society for Research in Child Development, Seattle.

Freeman, N. (1989). Review of Brian MacWhinney, *Mechanisms of language acquisition* (Hillsdale, NJ: Erlbaum, 1987). *Journal of Child Language, 16*, 470–475.

Freeman-Moir, D. (1982). The origins of intelligence. In J. Broughton & D. Freeman-Moir (Eds.), *The cognitive-developmental psychology of James Mark Baldwin:*

Current theory and research in genetic epistemology (pp. 127–168). Norwood, NJ: Ablex.

Freyd, J. (1983). Shareability: The social psychology of epistemology. *Cognitive Science, 7,* 191–210.

Frijda, N. (1986). *The emotions.* Cambridge: Cambridge University Press.

Furrow, D., Nelson, K., & Benedict, H. (1979). Mothers' speech to children and syntactic development: Some simple relationships. *Journal of Child Language, 6,* 423–442.

Gaensbauer, T. (1982). Regulation of emotional expression in infants from two contrasting environments. *Journal of the American Academy of Child Psychiatry, 21,* 163–171.

Gathercole, V. (1987). The contrastive hypothesis for the acquisition of word meaning: A reconsideration of the theory. *Journal of Child Language, 14,* 493–531.

Gee, J., & Savasir, I. (1985). On the use of WILL and GONNA: Towards a description of activity-types for child language. *Discourse Processes, 8,* 143–175.

Gelman, R., & Baillargeon, R. (1983). A review of some Piagetian concepts. In J. Flavell & E. Markman (Eds.), *Handbook of child psychology: Vol. 3. Cognitive development* (pp. 167–230). New York: Wiley.

Gelman, S., & Byrnes, J. (Eds.) (1991). *Perspectives on thought and language: Interrelations in development.* Cambridge: Cambridge University Press.

Gentner, D. (1982). Why nouns are learned before verbs: Linguistic relativity vs. natural partitioning. In S. Kuczaj (Ed.), *Language development: Vol. 2. Language, thought, and culture* (pp. 301–333). Hillsdale, NJ: Erlbaum.

Gershkoff-Stowe, L., & Smith, L. (1991, April). *Changes in pointing and naming during the naming explosion.* Poster presented at a meeting of the Society for Research in Child Development, Seattle.

Gesell, A. (1935). Cinemanalysis: A method of behavior study. *Journal of Genetic Psychology, 47,* 3–16.

Gesell, A., & Amatruda, C. (1941). *Developmental diagnosis: Normal and abnormal child development, clinical methods and practical applications.* New York: Hoeber.

Gibson, E. (1969). *Principles of perceptual learning and development.* New York: Appleton-Century-Crofts.

Gibson, J. (1966). *The senses considered as perceptual systems.* Boston, MA: Houghton Mifflin.

Gibson, J. (1979). *The ecological approach to visual perception.* Boston, MA: Houghton Mifflin.

Gillis, S. (1986). The child's "nominal insight" is actually a process: The plateau-stage and the vocabulary spurt in early lexical development. *Antwerp Papers in Linguistics, University of Antwerp.*

Ginsburg, H. (1981). Piaget and education: The contributions and limits of genetic epistemology. In I. Sigel, D. Brodzinksy, & R. Golinkoff (Eds.), *Piagetian theory and research: New directions and applications* (pp. 315–330). Hillsdale, NJ: Erlbaum.

Goldfield, B., & Reznick, J. (1990). Early lexical acquisition: Rate, content, and the vocabulary spurt. *Journal of Child Language, 17,* 171–183.

Goldin-Meadow, S., Seligman, M., & Gelman, R. (1976). Language in the two-year-old: Receptive and productive stages. *Cognition, 4,* 189–202.

Goldsmith, H. (1983). Genetic influences on personality from infancy to adulthood. *Child Development, 54,* 331–355.

Goldsmith, H., & Campos, J. (1982). Toward a theory of infant temperament. In R. Emde & R. Harmon (Eds.), *The development of attachment and affiliative systems: Psychobiological aspects* (pp. 161–189). New York: Plenum.

Golinkoff, R. (1983a). Infant social cognition: Self, people, and objects. In L. Liben (Ed.), *Piaget and the foundations of knowledge* (pp. 179–200). Hillsdale, NJ: Erlbaum.

Golinkoff, R. (1983b). The preverbal negotiation of failed messages: Insights into the transition period. In R. Golinkoff (Ed.), *The transition from prelinguistic to linguistic communication* (pp. 57–78). Hillsdale, NJ: Erlbaum.

Golinkoff, R. (Ed.) (1983c). *The transition from prelinguistic to linguistic communication.* Hillsdale, NJ: Erlbaum.

Golinkoff, R. (1986). "I beg your pardon?" The preverbal negotiation of failed messages. *Journal of Child Language, 13,* 455–476.

Golinkoff, R., Harding, C., Carlson, V., & Sexton, M. (1984). The infant's perception of causal events: The distinction between animate and inanimate objects. In L. Lipsitt & C. Rovee-Collier (Eds.), *Advances in infancy research* (Vol. 3, pp. 145–165). Norwood, NJ: Ablex.

Golinkoff, R., & Hirsh-Pasek, K. (1987, October). *A new picture of language development: Evidence from comprehension.* Paper presented at the Boston University Child Language Conference, Boston.

Golinkoff, R., Hirsh-Pasek, K., Bailey, L., & Wenger, N. (1992). Young children and adults use lexical principles to learn new nouns. *Developmental Psychology, 28,* 99–108.

Golinkoff, R., Mervis, C., & Hirsh-Pasek, K. (1991). Early object labels: The case for lexical principles. Manuscript submitted for publication.

Goodwyn, S., & Acredolo, L. (1993). Symbolic gesture vs. word: Is there a modality advantage for onset of symbol use? *Child Development, 64,* 688–701.

Gopnik, A. (1982). Words and plans: Early language and the development of intelligent action. *Journal of Child Language, 9,* 303–318.

Gopnik, A. (1988a). Conceptual and semantic development as theory changes: The case of object permanence. *Mind and Language, 3,* 197–216.

Gopnik, A. (1988b). Three types of early word: The emergence of social words, names and cognitive-relational words in the one-word stage and their relation to cognitive development. *First Language, 8,* 49–70.

Gopnik, A., & Choi, S. (1990). Do linguistic differences lead to cognitive differences? A cross-linguistic study of semantic and cognitive development. *First Language, 10,* 199–215.

Gopnik, A., & Meltzoff, A. (1984). Semantic and cognitive development in 15- to 21-month-old children. *Journal of Child Language, 11,* 495–513.

Gopnik, A., & Meltzoff, A. (1986a). Relations between semantic and cognitive developments in the one-word stage: The specificity hypothesis. *Child Development, 57,* 1040–1053.

Gopnik, A., & Meltzoff, A. (1986b). Words, plans, and things: Interactions between semantic and cognitive developments in the one-word stage. In S. Kuczaj & M. Barrett (Eds.), *The development of word meaning* (pp. 199–223). New York: Springer-Verlag.

Gopnik, A., & Meltzoff, A. (1987). The development of categorization in the second year and its relation to other cognitive and linguistic developments. *Child Development, 58,* 1523–1531.

Greenberg, J., & Kuczaj, S. (1982). Towards a theory of substantive word-meaning acquisition. In S. Kuczaj (Ed.), *Language development: Vol. 1. Syntax and semantics* (pp. 275–312). Hillsdale, NJ: Erlbaum.

Greenfield, P. (1973). Who is "Dada"? Some aspects of the semantic and phonological development of a child's first words. *Language and Speech, 16,* 34–43.

Greenfield, P. (1980). Toward an operational and logical analysis of intentionality: The use of discourse in early child language. In D. Olson (Ed.), *The social foundations of language and thought* (pp. 254–279). New York: Norton.

Greenfield, P., Reilly, J., Leaper, C., & Baker, N. (1985). The structural and functional status of single-word utterances and their relationship to early multi-word speech. In M. Barrett (Ed.), *Children's single-word speech* (pp. 233–267). New York: Wiley.

Griffiths, P. (1985). The communicative functions of children's single-word speech. In M. Barrett (Ed.), *Children's single-word speech* (pp. 87–112). New York: Wiley.

Griffiths, P. (1986). Early vocabulary. In P. Fletcher & M. Garman (Eds.), *Language acquisition: Studies in first language development* (2nd ed., pp. 279–306). Cambridge: Cambridge University Press.

Grimshaw, J. (1981). Form, function, and the language acquisition device. In C. Baker & J. McCarthy (Eds.), *The logical problem of language acquisition* (pp. 165–182). Cambridge, MA: MIT Press.

Gruendel, J. (1977). Referential extension in early language development. *Child Development, 48*, 1567–1576.

Guillaume, P. (1927). Les débuts de la phrase dans le langage de l'enfant. *Journal de Psychologie, 24*, 1–25.

Haith, M., Hazan, C., & Goodman, G. (1988). Expectation and anticipation of dynamic visual events by 3.5-month-old babies. *Child Development, 59*, 467–479.

Halford, G. (1989). Reflections on 25 years of Piagetian cognitive developmental psychology. *Human Development, 32*, 325–357.

Halliday, M. (1975). *Learning how to mean – Explorations in the development of language.* London: Arnold.

Hamburger, H., & Crain, S. (1987). Plans and semantics in human processing of language. *Cognitive Science, 11*, 101–136.

Hampshire, S. (1967). *Thought and action.* New York: Viking.

Hampson, J., & Nelson, K. (in press). The relation of maternal language to variation in rate and style of language acquisition. *Journal of Child Language.*

Harding, C., & Golinkoff, R. (1979). The origins of intentional vocalizations in prelinguistic infants. *Child Development, 50*, 33–40.

Harner, L., Bloom, L., & Gronell, T. (1991, June). *Social construction of object knowledge from preverbal through multi-word stages.* Paper presented at a meeting of the Jean Piaget Society, Philadelphia.

Harris, C. (1990). Connectionism and cognitive linguistics. *Connection Science, 2*, 7–34.

Hart, B. (1982). Process in the teaching of pragmatics. In L. Feagans & D. Farran (Eds.), *The language of children reared in poverty* (pp. 199–218). New York: Academic Press.

Heider, F. (1958). *The psychology of interpersonal relations.* New York: Wiley.

Herbers, J. (1982, July 20). Poverty rate 14%, termed highest since '67. *New York Times*, pp. A1, A18.

Hesse, P., & Cicchetti, D. (1982). Perspectives on an integrated theory of emotional development. In D. Cicchetti & P. Hesse (Eds.), *Emotional development* (pp. 3–48). New Directions for Child Development, No. 16. San Francisco: Jossey-Bass.

Hilke, D. (1988). Infant vocalizations and changes in experience. *Journal of Child Language, 15*, 1–15.

Hirsh-Pasek, K., Golinkoff, R., & Reeves, L. (in press). Constructivist explanations for language acquisition may be insufficient: The case for lexical principles. In W. Overton & D. Palermo (Eds.), *The ontogenesis of meaning.* Hillsdale, NJ: Erlbaum.

Hochschild, A. (1979). Emotion work, feeling rules, and social structure. *American Journal of Sociology, 85,* 551–575.

Holzman, M. (1984). Evidence for a reciprocal model of language development. *Journal of Psycholinguistic Research, 13,* 119–146.

Hood, L., & Bloom, L. (1979). What, when, and how about why: A longitudinal study of early expressions of causality. *Monographs of the Society for Research in Child Development, 44* (Serial No. 181).

Huttenlocher, J. (1974). The origins of language comprehension. In R. Solso (Ed.), *Theories in cognitive psychology: The Loyola Symposium* (pp. 331–368). New York: Halsted.

Huttenlocher, J., & Smiley, P. (1987). Early word meanings: The case of object names. *Cognitive Psychology, 19,* 63–89.

Huttenlocher, J., Smiley, P., & Charney, R. (1983). Emergence of action categories in the child: Evidence from verb meanings. *Psychological Review, 90,* 72–93.

Ingram, D. (1989). *First language acquisition: Method, description and explanation.* Cambridge: Cambridge University Press.

Ingram, D. (1991). An historical observation on "Why 'Mama' and 'Papa'?" *Journal of Child Language, 18,* 711–713.

Inhelder, B., & Piaget, J. (1969). *The early growth of logic in the child.* New York: Norton. (Original work published 1964)

Isen, A. (1984). Toward understanding the role of affect in cognition. In R. Wyer & T. Srull (Eds.), *Handbook of social cognition* (pp. 179–236). Hillsdale, NJ: Erlbaum.

Isen, A. (1990). The influence of positive and negative affect on cognitive organization: Some implications for development. In N. Stein, B. Leventhal, & T. Trabasso (Eds.), *Psychological and biological approaches to emotion* (pp. 75–94). Hillsdale, NJ: Erlbaum.

Izard, C. (1971). *The face of emotion.* New York: Appleton-Century-Crofts.

Izard, C. (1977). *Human emotions.* New York: Plenum.

Izard, C. (1979a). *The Maximally Discriminative Facial Movement Coding Scheme (MAX).* Newark, DE: Instructional Resources Center, University of Delaware.

Izard, C. (1979b). Emotions as motivations: An evolutionary-developmental perspective. In H. Howe (Ed.), *Evolutionary and developmental perspectives* (pp. 163–200). Nebraska Symposium on Motivation, 1978, Vol. 26. Lincoln: University of Nebraska Press.

Izard, C. (1986). Approaches to developmental research on emotion-cognition relationships. In D. Bearison & H. Zimiles (Eds.), *Thought and emotion: Developmental perspectives* (pp. 21–37). Hillsdale, NJ: Erlbaum.

Izard, C., & Dougherty, L. (1982). Two complementary systems for measuring facial expressions in infants and children. In C. Izard (Ed.), *Measuring emotions in infants and children* (pp. 97–126). Cambridge: Cambridge University Press.

Izard, C., Huebner, R., Risser, D., McGinnes, G., & Dougherty, L. (1980). The young infant's ability to produce distinct emotion expressions. *Developmental Psychology, 16,* 132–140.

Izard, C., & Malatesta, C. (1987). Perspectives on emotional development: I. Differential emotions theory of early emotional development. In J. Osofsky (Ed.), *Handbook of infant development* (pp. 494–554). New York: Wiley.

Jackendoff, R. (1972). *Semantic interpretation in generative grammar.* Cambridge, MA: MIT Press.

Jackendoff, R. (1983). *Semantics and cognition.* Cambridge, MA: MIT Press.

Jackendoff, R. (1987). *Consciousness and the computational mind.* Cambridge, MA: MIT Press.

Jackendoff, R. (1991, June). *Word meanings and what it takes to learn them.* Plenary Address at a meeting of the Jean Piaget Society, Philadelphia.

Jaffe, J., & Feldstein, S. (1970). *Rhythms of dialogue.* New York: Academic Press.

Jaffe, J., Stern, D., & Peery, J. (1973). "Conversational" coupling of gaze behavior in prelinguistic human development. *Journal of Psycholinguistic Research, 2,* 321–329.

Jakobson, R. (1968). *Child language, aphasia and phonological universals.* The Hague: Mouton. (Original work published 1941)

Jasnow, M., Crown, C., Feldstein, S., Taylor, L., Beebe, B., & Jaffe, J. (1988). Coordinated interpersonal timing of Down-Syndrome and nondelayed infants with their mothers: Evidence for a buffered mechanism of social interaction. *Biological Bulletin, 175,* 355–360.

Jersild, A. (1954). Emotional development. In L. Carmichael (Ed.), *Manual of child psychology* (2nd ed., pp. 833–917). New York: Wiley.

Johnson, W., Emde, R., Pannabecker, B., Stenberg, C., & Davis, M. (1982). Maternal perception of infant emotion from birth through 18 months. *Infant Behavior and Development, 5,* 313–322.

Johnson-Laird, P. (1983). *Mental models: Towards a cognitive science of language, inference, and consciousness.* Cambridge, MA: Harvard University Press.

Jones, H. (1930). The galvanic skin reflex in infancy. *Child Development, 1,* 106–110.

Jones, H. (1935). The galvanic skin reflex as related to overt emotional expression. *American Journal of Psychology, 47,* 241–251.

Jones, M. C. (1933). Emotional development. In C. Murchison (Ed.), *A handbook of child psychology* (2nd ed., pp. 271–302). Worcester, MA: Clark University Press.

Jones, S., Collins, K., & Hong, H. (1991). An audience effect on smile production in 10-month-old infants. *Psychological Science, 2,* 45–49.

Jones, S., Raag, T., & Collins, K. (1990). Smiling in older infants: Form and maternal response. *Infant Behavior and Development, 13,* 147–165.

Kagan, J. (1979). Structure and process in the human infant: The ontogeny of mental representation. In M. Bornstein & W. Kessen (Eds.), *Psychological development from infancy: Image to intention* (pp. 159–182). Hillsdale, NJ: Erlbaum.

Kagan, J. (1981). *The second year.* Cambridge, MA: Harvard University Press.

Kagan, J. (1984). *The nature of the child.* New York: Basic.

Kaplan, E. (1970). Intonation and language acquisition. *Papers and Reports on Child Language Development* (Vol. 1, pp. 1–21). Stanford, CA: Committee on Linguistics, Stanford University.

Kaplan, E., & Kaplan, G. (1971). The prelinguistic child. In J. Eliot (Ed.), *Human development and cognitive processes* (pp. 358–381). New York: Holt, Rinehart & Winston.

Kaye, K. (1977). Toward the origin of dialogue. In H. Schaffer (Ed.), *Studies in mother-infant interaction* (pp. 89–117). London: Academic Press.

Keil, F. (1989). *Concepts, kinds, and cognitive development.* Cambridge, MA: MIT Press.

Keil, F. (1991). Theories, concepts, and the acquisition of word meaning. In S. Gelman & J. Byrnes (Eds.), *Perspectives on thought and language: Interrelations in development* (pp. 197–221). Cambridge: Cambridge University Press.

Keller, H. (1905). *The story of my life* (J. Macy, Ed.). New York: Doubleday, Page. (Original work published 1902)

Kellman, P., & Spelke, E. (1983). Perception of partially occluded objects. *Cognitive Psychology, 15,* 483–524.

Kenny, D. (1985). *The transition from prelinguistic to linguistic vocalizations.* Unpublished doctoral dissertation, Teachers College, Columbia University.

Kent, R. (1981). Articulatory-acoustic perspectives on speech development. In R. Stark (Ed.), *Language behavior in infancy and early childhood* (pp. 105–121). New York: Elsevier North-Holland.

Kent, R. (1984). Brain mechanisms of speech and language with special reference to emotional interactions. In R. Naremore (Ed.), *Language science: Recent advances* (pp. 281–383). San Diego, CA: College-Hill Press.

Kinsbourne, M. (1975). The mechanism of hemispheric control of the lateral gradient of attention. In P. Rabbitt & S. Dornic (Eds.), *Attention and performance* (Vol. 5, pp. 81–97). New York: Academic Press.

Kinsbourne, M. (1988). A model of adaptive behavior related to cerebral participation in emotional control. In G. Gainotti (Ed.), *Emotions and the dual brain* (pp. 248–260). New York: Springer-Verlag.

Kinsbourne, M., & Bemporad, E. (1984). Lateralization of emotion: A model and the evidence. In N. Fox & R. Davidson (Eds.), *The psychobiology of affective development* (pp. 259–281). Hillsdale, NJ: Erlbaum.

Kirk, U. (1985). Hemispheric contributions to the development of graphic skill. In C. Best (Ed.), *Hemispheric function and collaboration in the child* (pp. 193–228). New York: Academic Press.

Klinnert, M., Campos, J., Sorce, J., Emde, R., & Svejda, M. (1983). Emotions as behavior regulators: Social referencing in infancy. In R. Plutchik & H. Kellerman (Eds.), *Emotion: Theory, research, and experience* (pp. 57–86). New York: Academic Press.

Klinnert, M., Sorce, J., Emde, R., Stenberg, C., & Gaensbauer, T. (1984). Continuities and change in early emotional life: Maternal perceptions of surprise, fear, and anger. In R. Emde & R. Harmon (Eds.), *Continuities and discontinuities in development* (pp. 339–354). New York: Plenum.

Kopp, C. (1976). Action schemes of 8-month-old infants. *Developmental Psychology, 12,* 361–362.

Kopp, C. (1987). The growth of self-regulation: Caregivers and children. In N. Eisenberg (Ed.), *Contemporary topics in developmental psychology* (pp. 34–55). New York: Wiley.

Kopp, C. (1989). Regulation of distress and negative emotions: A developmental view. *Developmental Psychology, 25,* 343–354.

Kopp, C., & Vaughn, B. (1982). Sustained attention during exploratory manipulation as a predictor of cognitive competence in preterm infants. *Child Development, 53,* 174–182.

Kuczaj, S. (1986). Thoughts on the intensional basis of early object word extension: Evidence from comprehension and production. In S. Kuczaj & M. Barrett (Eds.), *The development of word meaning* (pp. 99–120). New York: Springer-Verlag.

Kuczaj, S., & Barrett M. (Eds.) (1986). *The development of word meaning.* New York: Springer-Verlag.

Kuhl, P. (1987). Perception of speech and sound in early infancy. In P. Salapatek & L. Cohen (Eds.), *Handbook of infant perception: Vol. 2. From perception to cognition* (pp. 275–382). Orlando, FL: Academic Press.

Kuhl, P., & Meltzoff, A. (1984). The intermodal representation of speech in infants. *Infant Behavior and Development, 7,* 361–381.

Kuhl, P., & Meltzoff, A. (1988). Speech as an intermodal object of perception. In A. Yonas (Ed.), *Perceptual development in infancy* (pp. 235–266). Minnesota symposia on child psychology (Vol. 20). Hillsdale, NJ: Erlbaum.

Kuhl, P., & Miller, J. (1975). Speech perception by the chinchilla: Voiced-voiceless distinction in alveolar plosive consonants. *Science, 190,* 69–72.

Lahey, M., & Bloom, L. (in press). Variability and language learning disabilities: An information processing perspective. In G. Wallach & K. Butler (Eds.), *Language learning disabilities in school-age children and adolescents: Some underlying principles and applications.* Columbus, OH: Macmillan / Merrill.

Lamb, M., & Campos, J. (1982). *Development in infancy.* New York: Random House.

Landau, B., Smith, L., & Jones, S. (1988). The importance of shape in early lexical learning. *Cognitive Development, 3,* 299–321.

Langer, J. (1980). *The origins of logic: Six to twelve months.* New York: Academic Press.

Lazarus, R. (1982). Thoughts on the relations between emotion and cognition. *American Psychologist, 37,* 1019–1024.

Lazarus, R. (1984). On the primacy of cognition. *American Psychologist, 39,* 124–129.

Lazarus, R. (1991). *Emotion and adaptation.* New York: Oxford University Press.

Legerstee, M. (1991). Infant sounds. *First Language, 11,* 327–343.

Legerstee, M., Pomerleau, A., Malcuit, G., & Feider, H. (1987). The development of infants' responses to people and a doll: Implications for research in communication. *Infant Behavior and Development, 10,* 81–95.

Lempert, H., & Kinsbourne, M. (1985). Possible origin of speech in selective orienting. *Psychological Bulletin, 97,* 62–73.

Leopold, W. (1939). *Speech development of a bilingual child* (Vol. 1). Evanston, IL: Northwestern University Press.

Leslie, A. (1988). The necessity of illusion: Perception and thought in infancy. In L. Weiskrantz (Ed.), *Thought without language* (pp. 185–210). Oxford: Clarendon Press.

Lévi-Strauss, C. (1963). *Structural anthropology* (C. Jacobson & B. Schoept, Trans.). New York: Basic.

Levy, J. (1969). Possible basis for the evolution of lateral specialization of the human brain. *Nature, 224,* 614–615.

Levy, J. (1985). Interhemispheric collaboration: Single-mindedness in the asymmetric brain. In C. Best (Ed.), *Hemispheric function and collaboration in the child* (pp. 11–31). New York: Academic Press.

Lewis, M., & Brooks, J. (1978). Self-knowledge and emotional development. In M. Lewis & L. Rosenblum (Eds.), *The development of affect* (pp. 205–226). New York: Plenum.

Lewis, M., Brooks, J., & Haviland, J. (1978). Hearts and faces: A study in the measurement of emotion. In M. Lewis & L. Rosenblum (Eds.)., *The development of affect* (pp. 77–123). New York: Plenum.

Lewis, M., & Freedle, R. (1973). Mother-infant dyad: The cradle of meaning. In P. Pliner, L. Krames, & T. Alloway (Eds.), *Communication and affect: Language and thought* (pp. 127–155). New York: Academic Press.

Lewis, M., & Michalson, L. (1983). *Children's emotions and moods.* New York: Plenum.

Lewis, M., & Michalson, L. (1985). Faces as signs and symbols. In G. Zivin (Ed.), *The development of expressive behavior: Biology-environment interactions* (pp. 153–180). New York: Academic Press.

Lewis, M., & Rosenblum, L. (1978). Introduction: Issues in affect development. In M. Lewis & L. Rosenblum (Eds.), *The development of affect* (pp. 1–10). New York: Plenum.

Lewis, M., & Saarni, C. (1985). Culture and emotions. In M. Lewis & C. Saarni (Eds.), *The socialization of the emotions* (pp. 1–17). New York: Plenum.

Lewis, M., Sullivan, M., & Michalson, L. (1984). The cognitive-emotional fugue. In C. Izard, J. Kagan, & R. Zajonc (Eds.), *Emotions, cognition, and behavior* (pp. 264–288). Cambridge: Cambridge University Press.

Lewis, M. M. (1936). *Infant speech: A study of the beginnings of language.* New York: Harcourt Brace.

Lewis, M. M. (1959). *How children learn to speak.* New York: Basic.

Lifter, K. (1982). *Development of object related behavior during the transition from prelinguistic to linguistic communication.* Unpublished PhD dissertation, Teachers College, Columbia University.

Lifter, K., & Bloom, L. (1989). Object play and the emergence of language. *Infant Behavior and Development, 12,* 395–423.

Lock, A. (1978a). The emergence of language. In A. Lock (Ed.), *Action, gesture and symbol: The emergence of language* (pp. 3–18). New York: Academic Press.

Lock, A. (Ed.) (1978b). *Action, gesture and symbol: The emergence of language.* New York: Academic Press.

Locke, J. (1983). *Phonological acquisition and change.* New York: Academic Press.

Locke, J. (1988). The sound shape of early lexical representation. In M. Smith & J. Locke (Eds.), *The emergent lexicon: The child's development of a linguistic vocabulary* (pp. 3–22). San Diego: Academic Press.

Lucariello, J. (1987). Concept formation and its relation to word learning and use in the second year. *Journal of Child Language, 14,* 309–332.

MacKain, K. (1988). Filling the gap between speech and language. In M. Smith & J. Locke (Eds.), *The emergent lexicon: The child's development of a linguistic vocabulary* (pp. 51–74). San Diego: Academic Press.

MacNamara, J. (1982). *Names for things.* Cambridge, MA: MIT Press.

MacWhinney, B., & Snow, C. (1992). The wheat and the chaff: Or four confusions regarding CHILDES. *Journal of Child Language, 19,* 459–471.

Mahler, M., Pine, F., & Bergman, A. (1975). *The psychological birth of the human infant.* New York: Basic.

Malatesta, C. (1981). Infant emotion and the vocal affect lexicon. *Motivation and Emotion, 5,* 1–23.

Malatesta, C., Culver, C., Tesman, J., & Shepard, B. (1989). The development of emotion expression during the first two years of life. *Monographs of the Society for Research in Child Development, 54* (Serial No. 219).

Malatesta, C., Grigoryev, P., Lamb, C., Albin, M., & Culver, C. (1986). Emotion socialization and expressive development in preterm and full term infants. *Child Development, 57,* 316–330.

Malinowski, B. (1946). The problem of meaning in primitive languages. In C. Ogden & I. Richards, *The meaning of meaning* (pp. 296–336). New York: Harcourt Brace. (Original work published 1923)

Malinowski, B. (1935). *Coral gardens and their magic* (Vols. 1–2). London: Allen & Unwin.

Mandler, G. (1984). *Mind and body: Psychology of emotion and stress.* New York: Norton.

Mandler, G. (1990). A constructivist theory of emotion. In N. Stein, B. Leventhal, & T. Trabasso (Eds.), *Psychological and biological approaches to emotion* (pp. 21–43). Hillsdale, NJ: Erlbaum.

Mandler, J. (1983). Representation. In J. Flavell & E. Markman (Eds.), *Handbook of child psychology: Vol. 3. Cognitive development* (pp. 420–494). New York: Wiley.

Mandler, J. (1984). Representation and recall in infancy. In M. Moscovitch (Ed.), *Infant memory: Its relation to normal and pathological memory in humans and other animals* (pp. 75–101). New York: Plenum.

Mandler, J. (1988). How to build a baby: On the development of an accessible representational system. *Cognitive Development, 3,* 113–136.

Mandler, J. (1992). How to build a baby: II. Conceptual primitives. *Psychological Review, 99,* 587–604.

Mandler, J., & Bauer, P. (1988). The cradle of categorization: Is the basic level basic? *Cognitive Development, 3,* 237–264.

Mandler, J., Bauer, P., & McDonough, L. (1991). Separating the sheep from the goats: Differentiating global categories. *Cognitive Psychology, 23,* 263–298.

Mandler, J., Fivush, R., & Reznick, J. (1987). The development of contextual categories. *Cognitive Development, 2,* 339–354.

Markman, E. (1981). Two different principles of conceptual organization. In M. Lamb & A. Brown (Eds.), *Advances in developmental psychology* (Vol. 1, pp. 199–236). Hillsdale, NJ: Erlbaum.

Markman, E. (1989). *Categorization and naming in children.* Cambridge, MA: MIT Press.

Markman, E. (1992). Constraints on word learning: Speculations about their nature, origins, and domain specificity. In M. Gunnar & M. Maratsos (Eds.), *Minnesota symposia on child psychology* (Vol. 25, pp. 59–101). Hillsdale, NJ: Erlbaum.

Markman, E., & Hutchinson, J. (1984). Children's sensitivity to constraints on word meaning: Taxonomic vs. thematic relations. *Cognitive Psychology, 16,* 1–27.

Marler, P. (1976). An ethological theory of the origin of vocal learning. In S. Harnad, H. Steklis, & J. Lancaster (Eds.), *Origins and evolution of language and speech* (pp. 386–395). New York: New York Academy of Sciences.

Masur, E. (1982). Mothers' responses to infants' object-related gestures: Influences on lexical development. *Journal of Child Language, 9,* 23–30.

Maurer, D., & Maurer, C. (1988). *The world of the newborn.* New York: Basic.

McArthur, L., & Baron, R. (1983). Toward an ecological theory of social perception. *Psychological Review, 90,* 215–238.

McCall, R. (1979). Qualitative transitions in behavioral developments in the first two years of life. In M. Bornstein & W. Kessen (Eds.), *Psychological development in infancy: Image to intention* (pp. 183–224). Hillsdale, NJ: Erlbaum.

McCall, R. (1986). Issues of stability and continuity in temperament research. In R. Plomin & J. Dunn (Eds.), *The study of temperament: Changes, continuities and challenges* (pp. 13–25). Hillsdale, NJ: Erlbaum.

McCall, R., Eichorn, D., & Hogarty, P. (1977). *Transitions in early mental development.* Chicago: University of Chicago Press for the Society for Research in Child Development.

McCall, R., & McGhee, P. (1977). The discrepancy hypothesis of attention and affect in infants. In I. Uzgiris & F. Weizmann (Eds.), *The structure of experience* (pp. 179–210). New York: Plenum.

McCarthy, D. (1946). Language development in children. In L. Carmichael (Ed.), *Manual of child psychology* (pp. 476–581). New York: Wiley.

McCarthy, D. (1954). Language development in children. In L. Carmichael (Ed.), *Manual of child psychology* (2nd ed., pp. 492–630). New York: Wiley.

McCune-Nicolich, L. (1981). The cognitive basis of relational words in the single word period. *Journal of Child Language, 8,* 15–34.

McShane, J. (1980). *Learning to talk.* Cambridge: Cambridge University Press.

Medin, D., & Wattenmaker, W. (1987). Category cohesiveness, theories, and cognitive archaeology. In U. Neisser (Ed.), *Concepts and conceptual development: Ecological and intellectual factors in categorization* (pp. 25–62). Cambridge: Cambridge University Press.

Menn, L., & Hazelkorn, S. (1977). Now you see it, now you don't: Tracing the development of communicative competence. In J. Kegl (Ed.), *Proceedings of the Seventh Annual Meeting of the Linguistic Society* (pp. 249–259). Chicago.

Menyuk, P., Liebergott, J., Schultz, M., Chesnick, M., & Ferrier, L. (1991). Patterns of early lexical and cognitive development in premature and full-term infants. *Journal of Speech and Hearing Research, 34,* 88–94.

Merriman, W., & Bowman, L. (1989). The mutual exclusivity bias in children's word learning. *Monographs of the Society for Research in Child Development, 54* (Serial No. 220).

Mervis, C. (1987). Child-basic object categories and early lexical development. In U. Neisser (Ed.), *Concepts and conceptual development: Ecological and intellectual factors in categorization* (pp. 201–233). Cambridge: Cambridge University Press.

Mervis, C., & Mervis, C. (1982). Leopards are kitty-cats: Object labeling by mothers for their 13-month-olds. *Child Development, 53,* 267–273.

Miller, G. (1962). *Psychology: The science of mental life.* New York: Harper & Row.

Miller, G. (1979). Images and models, similes and metaphors. In A. Ortony (Ed.), *Metaphor and thought* (pp. 202–250). Cambridge: Cambridge University Press.

Miller, G. (1986). *How school children learn words.* Cognitive Science Laboratory Report 7, Princeton University.

Miller, G., Galanter, E., & Pribram, K. (1960). *Plans and the structure of behavior.* New York: Holt-Dryden.

Miller, J., & Eimas, P. (1983). Studies on the categorization of speech by infants. *Cognition, 13,* 135–165.

Miller, P. (1982). *Amy, Wendy, and Beth: A study of early language development in South Baltimore.* Austin: University of Texas Press.

Miller, P., & Sperry, L. (1987). The socialization of anger and aggression. *Merrill-Palmer Quarterly, 33,* 1–31.

Miller, W., & Ervin, S. (1964). The development of grammar in child language. In U. Bellugi & R. Brown (Eds.), The acquisition of language. (pp. 9–34). *Monographs of the Society for Research in Child Development, 29* (Serial No. 92).

Mitchell, P., & Kent, R. (1990). Phonetic variation in multisyllabic babbling. *Journal of Child Language, 17,* 247–265.

Molfese, D., Freeman, R., & Palermo, D. (1975). The ontogeny of brain lateralization for speech and nonspeech stimuli. *Brain and Language, 2,* 356–368.

Molfese, V., Molfese, D., & Parsons, C. (1983). Hemisphere processing of phonological information. In S. Segalowitz (Ed.), *Language functions and brain organization* (pp. 29–49). New York: Academic Press.

Morse, P. (1972). The discrimination of speech and nonspeech stimuli in early infancy. *Journal of Experimental Child Psychology, 14,* 477–492.

Moscovitch, M. (Ed.) (1984). *Infant memory: Its relation to normal and pathological memory in humans and other animals.* New York: Plenum.

Murphy, D., & Medin, D. (1985). The role of theories in conceptual coherence. *Psychological Review, 92,* 289–316.

Nachman, P. (1986, September). *A comparison of toddlers cared for by mothers and substitute caregivers at the Margaret S. Mahler Research Nursery.* Paper presented at the meetings of the San Francisco Psychoanalytic Institute, San Francisco.

Neisser, U. (Ed.) (1987). *Concepts and conceptual development: Ecological and intellectual factors in categorization.* Cambridge: Cambridge University Press.

Nelson, K. (1973a). Structure and strategy in learning to talk. *Monographs of the Society for Research in Child Development, 38* (Serial No. 149).

Nelson, K. (1973b). Some evidence for the cognitive primacy of categorization and its functional basis. *Merrill-Palmer Quarterly, 19,* 21–39.

Nelson, K. (1974). Concept, word and sentence: Interrelations in acquisition and development. *Psychological Review, 81,* 267–285.

Nelson, K. (1979). The role of language in infant development. In M. Bornstein & W. Kessen (Eds.), *Psychological development from infancy: Image to intention* (pp. 307–337). Hillsdale, NJ: Erlbaum.

Nelson, K. (1982). The syntagmatics and paradigmatics of conceptual development. In S. Kuczaj (Ed.), *Language development: Vol. 2. Language, thought, and culture* (pp. 335–364). Hillsdale, NJ: Erlbaum.

Nelson, K. (1985). *Making sense: The acquisition of shared meaning.* New York: Academic Press.

Nelson, K. (1986). *Event knowledge: Structure and function in development.* Hillsdale, NJ: Erlbaum.

Nelson, K. (1988). Constraints on word learning. *Cognitive Development, 3,* 221–246.

Nelson, K., Hampson, J., & Shaw, L. (1993). Nouns in early lexicons: Evidence, explanations, and implications. *Journal of Child Language, 20,* 61–84.

Nelson, K., & Lucariello, J. (1985). The development of meaning in first words. In M. Barrett (Ed.), *Single word speech* (pp. 59–86). London: Wiley.

Netsell, R. (1981). The acquisition of speech motor control: A perspective with directions for research. In R. Stark (Ed.), *Language behavior in infancy and early childhood* (pp. 126–156). New York: Elsevier North-Holland.

Newport, E. (1981). Constraints on structure: Evidence from American Sign Language. In W. Collins (Ed.), *Aspects of the development of competence* (pp. 93–124). Minnesota symposia on child psychology (Vol. 14). Hillsdale, NJ: Erlbaum.

Newport, E., Gleitman, L., & Gleitman, H. (1977). Mother, I'd rather do it myself: Some effects and non-effects of maternal speech style. In C. Snow & C. Ferguson (Eds.), *Talking to children: Language input and acquisition* (pp. 89–107). Cambridge: Cambridge University Press.

Newport, E., & Meier, R. (1985). The acquisition of American Sign Language. In D. Slobin (Ed.), *The crosslinguistic study of language acquisition* (Vol. 1, pp. 881–938). Hillsdale, NJ: Erlbaum.

Newson, J. (1977). An intersubjective approach to the systematic description of mother-infant interaction. In H. Schaffer (Ed.), *Studies in mother-infant interaction* (pp. 47–61). London: Academic Press.

Newson, J. (1978). Dialogue and development. In A. Lock (Ed.), *Action, gesture and symbol: The emergence of language* (pp. 31–42). London: Academic Press.

Newson, J. (1979). The growth of shared understandings between infant and caregiver. In M. Bullowa (Ed.), *Before speech: The beginning of interpersonal communication* (pp. 207–222). Cambridge: Cambridge University Press.

Oakes, L., & Cohen, L. (1990). Infant perception of a causal event. *Cognitive Development, 5,* 193–207.

Oatley, K. (1988). Plans and the communicative function of emotion. In V. Hamilton, G. Bower, & N. Frijda (Eds.), *Cognitive perspectives on emotion and motivation* (pp. 345–364). Dordrecht: Kluwer Academic.

Oatley, K. (1992). *Best laid schemes: The psychology of emotions.* Cambridge: Cambridge University Press.

Oatley, K., & Johnson-Laird, P. (1987). Towards a cognitive theory of emotions. *Cognition and Emotion, 1,* 29–50.

O'Brien, M., & Nagle, K. (1987). Parents' speech to toddlers: The effect of play context. *Journal of Child Language, 14,* 269–279.

Ochs, E. (1979). Transcription as theory. In E. Ochs & B. Schieffelin (Eds.), *Developmental pragmatics* (pp. 43–72). New York: Academic Press.

Ochs, E. (1986). From feelings to grammar: A Samoan case study. In B. Schieffelin & E. Ochs (Eds.), *Language socialization across cultures* (pp. 251–272). Cambridge: Cambridge University Press.

Ochs, E., & Schieffelin, B. (1983). *Acquiring conversational competence.* London: Routledge & Kegan Paul.

Ochs, E., & Schieffelin, B. (1989). Language has a heart. *Text, 9,* 7–25.

Ogden, C., & Richards, I. (1946). *The meaning of meaning.* New York: Harcourt Brace. (Original work published 1923)

Oller, K. (1980). The emergence of the sounds of speech in infancy. In G. Yeni-Komshian, J. Kavanagh, & C. Ferguson (Eds.), *Child phonology: Vol. 1. Production* (pp. 93–112). New York: Academic Press.

Oller, K., & Eilers, R. (1988). The role of audition in infant babbling. *Child Development, 59,* 441–449.

Oller, K., Wieman, L., Doyle, W., & Ross, C. (1976). Infant babbling and speech. *Journal of Child Language, 3,* 1–11.

Olson, G., & Sherman, T. (1983). Attention, learning, and memory in infants. In M. Haith & J. Campos (Eds.), *Handbook of child psychology: Vol. 2. Infancy and developmental psychobiology* (pp. 1001–1080). New York: Wiley.

Orlansky, M., & Bonvillian, J. (1988). Early sign language acquisition. In M. Smith & J. Locke (Eds.), *The emergent lexicon: The child's development of a linguistic vocabulary* (pp. 263–292). San Diego: Academic Press.

Ortony, A., Clore, G., & Collins, A. (1988). *The cognitive structure of emotions.* Cambridge: Cambridge University Press.

Ortony, A., & Turner, T. (1990). What's basic about basic emotions? *Psychological Review, 97,* 315–331.

Oster, H. (1978). Facial expression and affect development. In M. Lewis & L. Rosenblum (Eds.), *The development of affect* (pp. 43–75). New York: Plenum.

Oster, H., & Ekman, P. (1978). Facial behavior in child development. In A. Collins (Ed.), *Minnesota symposia on child psychology* (Vol. 11, pp. 231–276). Hillsdale, NJ: Erlbaum.

Oster, H., Hegley, D., & Nagel, L. (1992). Adult judgements and fine-grained analysis of infant facial expressions: Testing the validity of a priori coding formulas. *Developmental Psychology, 28,* 1115–1131.

Oviatt, S. (1980). The emerging ability to comprehend language: An experimental approach. *Child Development, 51,* 97–106.

Oviatt, S. (1982). Inferring what words mean: Early development in infants' comprehension of common object names. *Child Development, 53,* 274–277.

Papoušek H., & Papoušek M. (1977). Mothering and the cognitive head-start. In H. Schaffer (Ed.), *Studies in mother-infant interaction* (pp. 63–85). London: Academic Press.

Papoušek H., Papoušek, M., & Koester, L. (1986). Sharing emotionality and sharing knowledge: A microanalytic approach to parent-infant communication. In C. Izard & P. Reed (Eds.), *Measuring emotions in infants and children* (Vol. 2, pp. 93–123). Cambridge: Cambridge University Press.

Pascual-Leone, J. (1987). Organismic processes for neo-Piagetian theories: A dialectical causal account of cognitive development. *International Journal of Psychology, 22,* 531–570.

Pepper, S. (1942). *World hypotheses: A study in evidence.* Berkeley and Los Angeles: University of California Press.

Perner, J. (1991). *Understanding the representational mind.* Cambridge, MA: MIT Press.

Petitto, L. (1991, April). *Are the linguistic milestones in signed and spoken language acquisition similar or different?* Paper presented at a meeting of the Society for Research in Child Development, Seattle.

Petitto, L., & Marentette, P. (1991). Babbling in the manual mode: Evidence for the ontogeny of language. *Science, 251,* 1493–1496.

Phillips, R., & Sellitto, V. (1990). Preliminary evidence on emotions expressed by children during solitary play. *Play and Culture, 3,* 79–90.

Piaget, J. (1952). *The origins of intelligence in children.* New York: International Universities Press. (Original work published 1936)

Piaget, J. (1954). *The construction of reality in the child.* New York: Basic. (Original work published 1937; Ballantine Books ed. published 1971)

Piaget, J. (1960). *The psychology of intelligence.* Paterson, NJ: Littlefield, Adams. (Original work published 1947)

Piaget, J. (1962). *Play, dreams and imitation in childhood.* New York: Norton. (Original work published 1945)

Piaget, J. (1973). *The child in reality: Problems of genetic psychology.* New York: Penguin. (Original work published 1972)

Piaget, J. (1974). *Understanding causality.* New York: Norton. (Original work published 1971)

Piaget, J. (1981). *Intelligence and affectivity: Their relationship during child development* (T. Brown & C. Kaegi, Trans.). Palo Alto, CA: Annual Reviews, Inc. (Original work published 1954)

Pine, J. (1992). How referential are "referential" children? Relationship between maternal report and observational measures of vocal composition and usage. *Journal of Child Language, 19,* 75–86.

Pinker, S. (1984). *Language learnability and language development.* Cambridge, MA: Harvard University Press.

Pinker, S., & Mehler, J. (Eds.) (1988). *Connections and symbols.* Cambridge, MA: MIT Press.

Plomin, R., & Dunn, J. (Eds.) (1986). *The study of temperament: Changes, continuities and challenges.* Hillsdale, NJ: Erlbaum.

Pollack, M. (1990). Plans as complex mental attitudes. In P. Cohen, J. Morgan, & M. Pollack (Eds.), *Intentions in communication* (pp. 77–103). Cambridge, MA: MIT Press.

Premack, D. (1986). *"Gavagai!" or the future history of the animal language controversy.* Cambridge, MA: MIT Press.

Pylyshyn, Z., & Demopoulos, W. (Eds.) (1986). *Meaning and cognitive structure: Issues in the computational theory of mind.* Norwood, NJ: Ablex.

Quine, W. (1960). *Word and object.* Cambridge, MA: MIT Press.

Reddy, V. (1991). Playing with others' expectations: Teasing and mucking about in the first year. In A. Whiten (Ed.), *Natural theories of mind: Evolution, development and simulation of everyday mindreading* (pp. 143–158). Oxford: Blackwell Publisher.

Reich, P. (1976). The early acquisition of word meaning. *Journal of Child Language, 3,* 117–123.

Rescorla, L. (1980). Overextension in early language development. *Journal of Child Language, 7,* 321–335.

Rheingold, H., Gewirtz, J., & Ross, H. (1959). Social conditioning of vocalizations in the infant. *Journal of Comparative Physiological Psychology, 52,* 68–73.

Ricciuti, H., & Poresky, R. (1972). Emotional behavior and development in the first year of life: An analysis of arousal, approach-withdrawal, and affective responses. In A. Pick (Ed.), *Minnesota symposia on child psychology* (Vol. 6, pp. 69–96). Minneapolis: University of Minnesota Press.

Richards, M. (1978). The biological and the social. In A. Lock (Ed.), *Action, gesture and symbol: The emergence of language* (pp. 21–30). London: Academic Press.

Ridgeway, D., Waters, E., & Kuczaj, S. (1985). Acquisition of emotion-descriptive language: Receptive and productive vocabulary norms for ages 18 months to 6 years. *Developmental Psychology, 21,* 901–908.

Rispoli, M. (1987). *The development of the transitive/intransitive distinction: Conceptual and semantic origins.* Unpublished PhD dissertation, Teachers College, Columbia University.

Rispoli, M., & Bloom, L. (1987). The conceptual origins of the transitive/intransitive distinction. *Papers and Reports of the Child Language Research Forum* (Vol. 26, pp. 96–103). Department of Linguistics, Stanford University.

Roe, K. (1975). Amount of infant vocalization as a function of age: Some cognitive implications. *Cognitive Development, 46,* 936–941.

Rogoff, B. (1990). *Apprenticeship in thinking: Cognitive development in social context.* New York: Oxford University Press.

Rosch, E., & Mervis, C. (1975). Family resemblances: Studies in the internal structure of categories. *Cognitive Psychology, 7,* 573–605.

Rosch, E., Mervis, C., Gray, W., Johnson, D., & Boyes-Braem, P. (1976). Basic objects in natural categories. *Cognitive Psychology, 8,* 382–439.

Roseman, I. (1984). Cognitive determinants of emotions: A structural theory. In P. Shaver (Ed.), *Review of personality and social psychology: Emotions, relationships, and health* (Vol. 5, pp. 11–36). Beverly Hills, CA: Sage.

Ross, E. (1985). Modulation of affect and nonverbal communication by the right hemisphere. In M. Mesulam (Ed.), *Principles of behavioral neurology* (pp. 239–257). Philadelphia: F. A. Davis.

Roth, P. (1987). The temporal characteristics of maternal verbal styles. In K. Nelson & A. Van Kleeck (Eds.), *Children's language* (Vol. 6, pp. 137–158). Hillsdale, NJ: Erlbaum.

Rothbart, M. (1973). Laughter in young children. *Psychological Bulletin, 80,* 247–256.

Rothbart, M. (1981). Measurement of temperament in infancy. *Child Development, 52,* 569–578.

Rovee-Collier, C., Sullivan, M., Enright, M., Lucas, D., & Fagen, J. (1980). Reactivation of infant memory. *Science, 208,* 1159–1161.

Ruff, H. (1978). Infant recognition of the invariant form of objects. *Child Development, 49*, 293–306.

Ruff, H. (1980). The development of perception and recognition of objects. *Child Development, 51*, 981–992.

Ruff, H. (1986). Components of attention during infants' manipulative exploration. *Child Development, 57*, 105–114.

Ruff, H., Capozzoli, M., Dubiner, K., & Parrinello, R. (1990). A measure of vigilance in infancy. *Infant Behavior and Development, 13*, 1–20.

Ryan, J. (1974). Early language development: Towards a communicational analysis. In M. Richards (Ed.), *The integration of a child into the social world* (pp. 185–213). Cambridge: Cambridge University Press.

Sachs, J. (1983). Talking about the then and there: The emergence of displaced reference in adult-child discourse. In K. Nelson (Ed.), *Children's language* (Vol. 4, pp. 1–28). Hillsdale, NJ: Erlbaum.

Sackett, G. (1974). *A nonparametric lag sequential analysis for studying dependency among responses in behavioral observation scoring systems.* Unpublished paper presented at the Western Psychological Association, San Francisco.

Sackett, G. (1979). The lag sequential analysis of contingency and cyclicity in behavioral interaction research. In J. Osofsky (Ed.), *Handbook of infant development* (pp. 623–649). New York: Wiley.

Sampson, G. (1980). *Schools of linguistics.* Stanford, CA: Stanford University Press.

Sapir, E. (1921). *Language.* New York: Harcourt Brace.

Schachter, S., & Singer, J. (1962). Cognitive, social, and physiological determinants of emotional state. *Psychological Review, 69*, 379–399.

Schaffer, H. (Ed.) (1977). *Studies in mother-infant interaction.* London: Academic Press.

Schaffer, H., Collis, G., & Parsons, G. (1977). Vocal interchange and visual regard in verbal and pre-verbal children. In H. Schaffer (Ed.), *Studies in mother-infant interaction* (pp. 291–324). London: Academic Press.

Scheer, S., Beckwith, R., & Bloom, L. (1990, April). *Environmental effects on language input.* Poster presented at the International Conference on Infant Studies, Montreal.

Scherer, K. (1984). On the nature and function of emotion: A component process approach. In K. Scherer & P. Ekman (Eds.), *Approaches to emotion* (pp. 293–318). Hillsdale, NJ: Erlbaum.

Scherer, K. (1986). Vocal affect expression: A review and a model for future research. *Psychological Bulletin, 99*, 143–165.

Schieffelin, B. (1979). *How Kaluli children learn what to say, what to do, and how to feel: An ethnographic study of the development of communicative competence.* Unpublished PhD dissertation, Teachers College, Columbia University.

Schieffelin, B. (1990). *The give and take of everyday life: Language socialization of Kaluli children.* New York: Cambridge University Press.

Schieffelin, B. (1991, April). *Code-switching in Haitian Creole.* Paper presented at a meeting of the New York Child Language Group, New York.

Schlesinger, I. (1971). Production of utterances and language acquisition. In D. Slobin (Ed.), *The ontogenesis of grammar* (pp. 63–101). New York: Academic Press.

Schlesinger, I. (1982). *Steps to language: Toward a theory of native language acquistion.* Hillsdale NJ: Erlbaum.

Schlosberg, H. (1952). The description of facial expressions in terms of two dimensions. *Journal of Experimental Psychology, 44,* 229–237.

Schlosberg, H. (1954). Three dimensions of emotion. *Psychological Review, 61,* 81–88.

Schwartz, R. (1988). Phonological factors in early lexical acquisition. In M. Smith & J. Locke (Eds.), *The emergent lexicon: The child's development of a linguistic vocabulary* (pp. 185–222). San Diego: Academic Press.

Schwartz, R., & Leonard, L. (1984). Words, objects, and actions in early lexical acquisition. *Journal of Speech and Hearing Research, 27,* 119–127.

Scollon, R. (1976). *Conversations with a one year old, A case study of the developmental foundation of syntax.* Honolulu: University Press of Hawaii & Research Corporation of the University of Hawaii.

Searle, J. (1983). *Intentionality: An essay in the philosophy of mind.* Cambridge: Cambridge University Press.

Searle, J. (1984). *Minds, brains and science.* Cambridge, MA: Harvard University Press.

Shatz, M. (1977). The relationship between cognitive processes and the development of communication skills. In C. Keasey (Ed.), *Social cognitive development* (pp. 1–42). Nebraska symposium on motivation (Vol. 25). Lincoln: University of Nebraska Press.

Shatz, M. (1981). Learning the rules of the game: Four views of the relation between grammar acquisition and social interaction. In W. Deutsch (Ed.), *The child's construction of language* (pp. 17–38). London: Academic Press.

Shatz, M., & O'Reilly, A. (1990). Conversational or communicative skill? A reassessment of two-year-olds' behaviour in miscommunication episodes. *Journal of Child Language, 17,* 131–146.

Shotter, J. (1978). The cultural context of communication studies: Theoretical and methodological issues. In A. Lock (Ed.), *Action, gesture and symbol: The emergence of language* (pp. 43–78). London: Academic Press.

Sinclair, H. (1970). The transition from sensory-motor behavior to symbolic activity. *Interchange, 1,* 119–126.

Sinha, C. (1982). Representational development and the structure of action. In G. Butterworth & P. Light (Eds.), *Social cognition: Studies of the development of understanding* (pp. 137–162). Chicago: University of Chicago Press.

Sinha, C. (1988). *Language and representation: A socio-naturalistic approach to human development.* New York: New York University Press.

Slobin, D. (Ed.) (1985). *The crosslinguistic study of language acquisition.* Hillsdale, NJ: Erlbaum.

Smiley, P., & Huttenlocher, J. (1989). Young children's acquisition of emotion concepts. In C. Saarni & P. Harris (Eds.), *Children's understanding of emotion* (pp. 27–49). Cambridge: Cambridge University Press.

Smith, B. (1988). The emergent lexicon from a phonetic perspective. In M. Smith & J. Locke (Eds.), *The emergent lexicon: The child's development of a linguistic vocabulary* (pp. 75–106). San Diego: Academic Press.

Smith, B., Brown-Sweeney, S., & Stoel-Gammon, C. (1989). A quantitative analysis of reduplicated and variegated babbling. *First Language, 9,* 175–190.

Smith, M., & Locke, J. (Eds.) (1988). *The emergent lexicon: The child's development of a linguistic vocabulary.* San Diego: Academic Press.

Snow, C. (1972). Mothers' speech to children learning language. *Child Development, 43,* 549–565.

Snow, C., & Ferguson, C. (Eds.) (1977). *Talking to children: Language input and acquisition.* Cambridge: Cambridge University Press.

Soja, N., Carey, S., & Spelke, E. (1991). Ontological categories guide young children's inductions of word meaning: Object terms and substance terms. *Cognition, 38,* 179–211.

Sophian, C. (1980). Habituation is not enough: Novelty preferences, search, and memory in infancy. *Merrill-Palmer Quarterly, 26,* 239–257.

Spelke, E. (1988). The origins of physical knowledge. In L. Weiskrantz (Ed.), *Thought without language* (pp. 168–184). Oxford: Clarendon Press.

Spelke, E. (1991). Physical knowledge in infancy: Reflections on Piaget's theory. In S. Carey & R. Gelman (Eds.), *The epigenesis of mind: Essays on biology and cognition* (pp. 133–169). Hillsdale, NJ: Erlbaum.

Sperber, D., & Wilson, D. (1986). *Relevance: Communication and cognition.* Cambridge, MA: Harvard University Press.

Sroufe, A. (1979). Socioemotional development. In J. Osofsky (Ed.), *Handbook of infant development* (pp. 462–516). New York: Wiley.

Sroufe, A. (1984). The organization of emotional development. In K. Scherer & P. Ekman (Eds.), *Approaches to emotion* (pp. 109–128). Hillsdale, NJ: Erlbaum.

Sroufe, A., Schork, E., Motti, F., Lawroski, N., & LaFreniere, P. (1984). The role of affect in social competence. In C. Izard, J. Kagan, & R. Zajonc (Eds.), *Emotions, cognition, and behavior* (pp. 289–319). Cambridge: Cambridge University Press.

Sroufe, A., & Waters, E. (1976). The ontogenesis of smiling and laughter: A perspective on the organization of development in infancy. *Psychological Review, 83,* 173–189.

Stark, R. (1980). Stages of speech development in the first year of life. In G. Yeni-Komshian, J. Kavanagh, & C. Ferguson (Eds.), *Child phonology: Vol. I. Production* (pp. 73–92). New York: Academic Press.

Stark, R. (1986). Prespeech segmental feature development. In P. Fletcher & M. Garman (Eds.), *Language acquisition: Studies in first language development* (2nd ed., pp. 149–174). Cambridge: Cambridge University Press.

Stechler, G., & Carpenter, G. (1967). A viewpoint on early affective development. In J. Hellmuth (Ed.), *Exceptional infant: The normal infant* (Vol. 1, pp. 164–189). Seattle: Special Child Publications.

Stein, N., & Jewett, J. (1987). A conceptual analysis of the meaning of basic negative emotions: Implications for a theory of development. In C. Izard & P. Read (Eds.), *Measurement of emotion in infants and children* (Vol. 2, pp. 238–267). New York: Cambridge University Press.

Stein, N., & Levine, L. (1987). Thinking about feelings: The development and origins of emotional knowledge. In R. Snow & M. Farr (Eds.), *Aptitude, learning, and instruction: Vol. 3. Cognition, conation, and affect* (pp. 165–197). Hillsdale, NJ: Erlbaum.

Stein, N., & Levine, L. (1989). The causal organisation of emotional knowledge: A developmental study. *Cognition and Emotion, 3,* 343–378.

Stein, N., & Levine, L. (1990). Making sense out of emotion: The representation and use of goal-structured knowledge. In N. Stein, B. Leventhal, & T. Trabasso (Eds.), *Psychological and biological approaches to emotion* (pp. 45–73). Hillsdale, NJ: Erlbaum.

Stern, C., & Stern, W. (1907). *Die Kindersprache.* Leipzig: Barth.

Stern, D. (1977). *The first relationship.* Cambridge, MA: Harvard University Press.

Stern, D. (1985). *The interpersonal world of the infant.* New York: Basic.

Stern, D., Barnett, R., & Spieker, S. (1983). Early transmission of affect: Some research issues. In J. Call, E. Galenson, & R. Tyson (Eds.), *Frontiers of infant psychiatry* (pp. 74–84). New York: Basic.

Stern, D., Jaffe, J., Beebe, B., & Bennett, S. (1975). Vocalizing in unison and in alternation: Two modes of communication within the mother-infant dyad. In D. Aronson & R. Rieber (Eds.), *Developmental psycholinguistics and communication disorders* (pp. 89–100). Annals of the New York Academy of Sciences, Vol. 263. New York: New York Academy of Sciences.

Stern, W. (1924). *Psychology of early childhood* (Anna Berwell, Trans.). London: Allen & Unwin.

Stockman, I., & Vaughn-Cook, F. (1989). Addressing new questions about black children's language. In R. Fasold & D. Schiffrin (Eds.), *Language change and variation* (pp. 275–300). Current issues in linguistic theory (Vol. 52). Philadelphia: John Benjamins.

Studdert-Kennedy, M. (1979). *The beginnings of speech.* Status Report on Speech Research, SR-58. New Haven, CT: Haskins Laboratories.

Sugarman, S. (1978). Some organizational aspects of preverbal communication. In I. Markova (Ed.), *The social context of language* (pp. 49–66). London: Wiley.

Sugarman, S. (1981). The cognitive basis of classification in very young children: An analysis of object-ordering trends. *Child Development, 52,* 1172–1178.

Sugarman, S. (1982). Developmental change in early representational intelligence: Evidence from spatial classification strategies and related verbal expressions. *Cognitive Psychology, 14,* 410–449.

Sullivan, A. (1905). A supplementary account of Helen Keller's life and education. In H. Keller (J. Macy, Ed.), *The story of my life* (pp. 283–403). New York: Doubleday, Page. (Original work published 1902)

The talk of the town (1987, March 9). *New Yorker,* p. 26.

Taylor, C. (1979). Action as expression. In C. Diamond & J. Teichman (Eds.), *Intentions and intentionality: Essays in honor of G. E. M. Anscombe* (pp. 73–89). Ithaca, NY: Cornell University Press.

Taylor, C. (1985). *Philosophical papers: Vol. 1. Human agency and language.* Cambridge: Cambridge University Press.

Templin, M. (1957). *Certain language skills in children.* Minneapolis: University of Minnesota Press.

Thomas, A., & Chess, S. (1977). *Temperament and development.* New York: Brunner/Mazel.

Thompson, R. (1990). Emotional self-regulation. In R. Thompson (Ed.), *Socioemotional development* (pp. 367–467). Nebraska symposium on motivation (Vol. 36). Lincoln: University of Nebraska Press.

Thorndike, E. L. (1946). The psychology of semantics. *American Journal of Psychology, 59,* 613–632.

Thorndike, E. L. (1949). *Selected writings from a connectionist's psychology.* New York: Appleton-Century-Crofts.

Toledano, J. (1991). *Context and the language development of children with older siblings.* Unpublished PhD dissertation, Teachers College, Columbia University.

Tomasello, M. (1988). The role of joint attentional processes in early language development. *Language Sciences, 10,* 69–88.

Tomasello, M. (1992). The social bases of language acquisition. *Social Development, 1,* 67–87.

Tomasello, M., & Farrar, J. (1986). Joint attention and early language. *Child Development, 57,* 1454–1463.

Tomasello, M., & Farrar, M. (1984). Cognitive bases of lexical development: Object permanence and relational words. *Journal of Child Language, 11,* 477–493.

Tomasello, M., & Kruger, A. (1992). Joint attention on actions: Acquiring verbs in ostensive and non-ostensive contexts. *Journal of Child Language, 19,* 311–333.

Tomkins, S. (1970). Affect as the primary motivational system. In M. Arnold (Ed.), *Feelings and emotions: The Loyola Symposium* (pp. 101–121). New York: Academic Press.

Tough, J. (1982). Language, poverty, and disadvantage in school. In L. Feagans & D. Farran (Eds.), *The language of children reared in poverty* (pp. 3–17). New York: Academic Press.

Trevarthen, C. (1977). Descriptive analysis of infant communication behavior. In H. Schaffer (Ed.), *Studies in mother-infant interaction* (pp. 227–270). London: Academic Press.

Trevarthen, C. (1979). Communication and cooperation in early infancy: A description of primary intersubjectivity. In M. Bullowa (Ed.), *Before speech: The beginning of interpersonal communication* (pp. 321–347). Cambridge: Cambridge University Press.

Trevarthen, C., & Hubley, P. (1978). Secondary intersubjectivity: Confidence, confiding and acts of meaning in the second year. In A. Lock (Ed.), *Action, gesture and symbol: The emergence of language,* (pp. 183–229). London: Academic Press.

Tronick, E. (1972). Stimulus control and the growth of the infant's effective visual field. *Perception and Psychophysics, 11,* 373–375.

Tronick, E. (Ed.) (1982). *Social interchange in infancy: Affect, cognition, and communication.* Baltimore: University Park Press.

Tronick, E. (1989). Emotions and emotional communication in infants. *American Psychologist, 44,* 112–119.

Tucker, D. (1986). Neural control of emotional communication. In P. Blanck, R. Buck, & R. Rosenthal (Eds.), *Nonverbal communication in the clinical context* (pp. 258–307). University Park: Pennsylvania State University Press.

Tucker, D., & Frederick, S. (1989). Emotion and brain lateralization. In H. Wagner & T. Manstead (Eds.), *Handbook of psychophysiology: Emotion and social behavior* (pp. 27–70). New York: Wiley.

Turkewitz, G., Ecklund-Flores, L., & Devenny, D. (1990). Development of sensorimotor capacities relevant to speech and concurrent task performance. In G. Hammond (Ed.), *Cerebral control of speech and limb movements* (pp. 595–610). New York: Elsevier North-Holland.

Uzgiris, I., & Hunt, J. (1975). *Assessment in infancy.* Urbana: University of Illinois Press.

van Beek, Y. (1991, May). *Preterms, posture and the development of early communication.* Paper presented at a meeting of the International Society for Infant Studies, Miami.

Vander Linde, E., Morrongiello, B., & Rovee-Collier, C. (1985). Determinants of retention in 8-week-old infants. *Developmental Psychology, 21,* 601–613.

Vedeler, D. (1987). Infant intentionality and the attribution of intentions to infants. *Human Development, 30,* 1–17.

Vihman, M., Macken, M., Miller, R., Simmons, H., & Miller, J. (1985). From babbling to speech: A reassessment of the continuity issue. *Language, 61,* 397–446.

Vihman, M., & McCune, L. (1992). *When is a word a word?* Manuscript submitted for publication.

Vihman, M., & Miller, R. (1988). Words and babble at the threshold of language acquisition. In M. Smith & J. Locke (Eds.), *The emergent lexicon: The child's development of a linguistic vocabulary* (pp. 151–183). San Diego: Academic Press.

Vygotsky, L. (1978). *Mind in society: The development of higher psychological processes* (M. Cole, V. John-Steiner, S. Scribner, & E. Souberman, Eds.). Cambridge, MA: Harvard University Press. (Original work published 1930).

Walker-Andrews, A., & Lennon, E. (1991). Infants' discrimination of vocal expressions: Contributions of auditory and visual information. *Infant Behavior and Development, 14,* 131–142.

Wannemacher, W., & Seiler, T. (1983). Introduction: Historical trends of research in concept development and the development of word meaning. In T. Seiler & W. Wannemacher (Eds.), *Concept development and the development of word meaning* (pp. 1–14). Berlin: Springer-Verlag.

Waxman, S., & Kosowski, T. (1990). Nouns mark category relations: Toddlers' and preschoolers' word-learning biases. *Cognitive Development, 61,* 1461–1473.

Waxman, S., & Senghas, A. (1992). Relations among word meanings in early lexical development. *Developmental Psychology, 28,* 862–873.

Weiner-Margulies, M., Rey-Barboza, R., Cabrera, E., & Anisfeld, M. (1992). *During play toddlers speak less when they exert more effort.* Manuscript submitted for publication.

Weisberg, P. (1963). Social and nonsocial conditioning of infant vocalization. *Child Development, 34,* 377–388.

Weiskrantz, L. (Ed.) (1988). *Thought without language.* Oxford: Clarendon Press.

Wellman, H. (1985a). The child's theory of mind: The development of conceptions of cognition. In S. Yussen (Ed.), *The growth of reflection in children* (pp. 169–206). San Diego: Academic Press.

Wellman, H. (1985b). Introduction. In H. Wellman (Ed.), *Children's searching* (pp. ix-xiii). Hillsdale, NJ: Erlbaum.

Wellman, H. (1990). *The child's theory of mind.* Cambridge, MA: MIT Press.

Wellman, H., Cross, D., & Bartsch, K. (1986). Infant search and object permanence: A meta-analysis of the A-not-B error. *Monographs of the Society for Research in Child Development, 51* (Serial No. 214).

Wellman, H., & Somerville, S. (1982). The development of human search ability. In M. Lamb & A. Brown (Eds.), *Advances in developmental psychology* (Vol. 2, pp. 41–84). Hillsdale, NJ: Erlbaum.

Werner, H. (1948). *Comparative psychology of mental development.* New York: Science Editions.

Werner, H., & Kaplan, B. (1963). *Symbol formation.* New York: Wiley.

Whitehurst, G., Kedesdy, J., & White, T. (1982). A functional analysis of word meaning. In S. Kuczaj (Ed.), *Language development: Vol. 1. Syntax and semantics* (pp. 397–427). Hillsdale, NJ: Erlbaum.

Wikstrom, P., & Bloom, L. (1987, July). *The role of temperament in the emergence of language.* Paper presented at the Fourth International Congress for the Study of Child Language, Lund.

Winnicott, D. (1971). *Playing and reality.* London: Tavistock.

Witelson, S. (1987). Neurobiological aspects of language in children. *Child Development, 58,* 653–688.

Wittgenstein, L. (1958). *The blue and brown books.* Oxford: Blackwell Publisher. (Original work published 1934–35)

Wolfe, P. (1965). The development of attention in young infants. *Annals of the New York Academy of Sciences, 118,* 815–830.

Woodward, A., Markman, E., & Fitzsimmons, C. (1991, April). *Children's rate of learning new words: Is the naming explosion a "Learning Explosion"?* Paper presented at a meeting of the Society for Research in Child Development, Seattle.

Woodworth, R. (1938). *Experimental psychology.* New York: Holt.

Wozniak, R. (1986). Notes toward a co-constructive theory of the emotion-cognition relationship. In D. Bearison & H. Zimiles (Eds.), *Thought and emotion: Developmental perspectives* (pp. 39–64). Hillsdale, NJ: Erlbaum.

Yeni-Komshian, G., Kavanagh, J., & Strange, W. (Eds.) (1980). *Child phonology: Vol. 2. Perception.* New York: Academic Press.

Young, G., & Decarie, T. (1977). An ethology-based catalogue of facial/vocal behaviour in infancy. *Animal Behaviour, 25,* 95–107.

Young, P. (1959). The role of affective processes in learning and motivation. *Psychological Review, 66,* 104–125.

Zajonc, R. (1980). Feeling and thinking: Preferences need no inferences. *American Psychologist, 35,* 151–175.

Zajonc, R. (1984). On primacy of affect. In K. Scherer & P. Ekman (Eds.), *Approaches to emotion* (pp. 259–270). Hillsdale, NJ: Erlbaum.

Zebrowitz, L. (1990). *Social perception.* Buckingham, Bucks., England: Open University Press.

Zelazo, P., and Kearsley, R. (1980). The emergence of functional play in infants: Evidence for a major cognitive transition. *Journal of Applied Developmental Psychology, 1,* 95–117.

Zelazo, P., & Leonard, E. (1983). The dawn of active thought. In K. Fischer (Ed.), *Levels and transitions in children's development* (pp. 37–50). New directions for child development (No. 21). San Francisco: Jossey-Bass.

Name Index

Subject Index